D1784172

GLOBAL TERRORISM ISSUES AND DEVELOPMENTS

GLOBAL TERRORISM ISSUES AND DEVELOPMENTS

RENE A. LARCHE
Editor

Nova Science Publishers, Inc.
New York

For permission to use material from this book please contact us:
Telephone 631-231-7269; Fax 631-231-8175
Web Site: http://www.novapublishers.com

NOTICE TO THE READER

The Publisher has taken reasonable care in the preparation of this book, but makes no expressed or implied warranty of any kind and assumes no responsibility for any errors or omissions. No liability is assumed for incidental or consequential damages in connection with or arising out of information contained in this book. The Publisher shall not be liable for any special, consequential, or exemplary damages resulting, in whole or in part, from the readers' use of, or reliance upon, this material.

Independent verification should be sought for any data, advice or recommendations contained in this book. In addition, no responsibility is assumed by the publisher for any injury and/or damage to persons or property arising from any methods, products, instructions, ideas or otherwise contained in this publication.

This publication is designed to provide accurate and authoritative information with regard to the subject matter covered herein. It is sold with the clear understanding that the Publisher is not engaged in rendering legal or any other professional services. If legal or any other expert assistance is required, the services of a competent person should be sought. FROM A DECLARATION OF PARTICIPANTS JOINTLY ADOPTED BY A COMMITTEE OF THE AMERICAN BAR ASSOCIATION AND A COMMITTEE OF PUBLISHERS.

Library of Congress Cataloging-in-Publication Data

Global terrorism issues and developments / Rene A. Larche (editor).
     p. cm.
   Includes index.
   ISBN-13: 978-1-60021-930-6 (hardcover)
   ISBN-10: 1-60021-930-6 (hardcover)
   1. Terrorism. 2. Victims of terrorism. 3. Terrorism--Prevention. I. Larche, Rene A.
HV6431.G564 2008
363.325--dc22
                          2007030869

Published by Nova Science Publishers, Inc. ✤ *New York*

CONTENTS

PREFACE

Terrorism is usually described as violence or the perception or threat of imminent violence. Terrorism has been used by a broad array of political organizations in furthering their objectives; both right-wing and left-wing political parties, nationalistic, and religious groups, revolutionaries and ruling governments. Those labeled "terrorists" rarely identify themselves as such, and typically use other generic terms or terms specific to their situation, such as: separatist, freedom fighter, liberator, revolutionary, vigilante, militant, paramilitary, guerrilla, rebel, jihadi or mujaheddin, or fedayeen, or any similar-meaning word in other languages. Sadly is has become a global profession which has come to color all aspects of life from travel, to office locations to pervasive fear. This new book presents important issues and ideas dealing with terrorism.

Chapter 1 - Despite many publications about terrorism it remains ill-defined and under-theorized. Domination of the discourse by antiterrorist legislation and political rhetoric has impeded social scientific research as political and legal terms remain overly dependent on reifications. Starting with an everyday conceptual definition of terrorism, the concept is broken down into dimensions, forms, and a typology. Possible theoretical approaches are discussed with attention to different frames of reference and levels of abstraction. This chapter tries to establish a clearer ground for theory building.

Chapter 2 - In most radiation scenarios, injury to the bone marrow and gastrointestinal tract are the main determinants of survival because of their rapidly proliferating stem/progenitor cell compartments. While significant progress has been made in the medical management of radiation-induced bone marrow injury, the management of gastrointestinal radiation toxicity remains symptomatic and underdeveloped. Moreover, combined injury (radiation injury combined with other types of trauma or sepsis) may exacerbate intestinal injury compared to what is seen after radiation exposure alone. For these reasons, the importance of gastrointestinal injury as a critical determinant of survival in a radiation terrorism scenario has increased significantly.

This chapter provides an overview of the significance of intestinal toxicity in the non-therapeutic radiation exposure setting and discusses how radiation, when combined with other types of trauma or sepsis, may be associated with increased mortality and morbidity. Novel concepts pertinent to the mechanisms of intestinal damage are also reviewed, with special emphasis on the importance of endothelial cell dysfunction in radiation injury, sepsis, and ischemia-reperfusion injury. Finally, various strategies to prevent or mitigate intestinal toxicity after radiation exposure and after traumatic injuries are discussed.

Chapter 3 - The authors conduct a need-based method of allocation of United States Department of Homeland Security (DHS) funds to states and local governments based on the distribution of sources of electric power generation and compare the results of using this method with the distribution of population and per capita income. The authors also examine the impact of weighting the spatial distribution of the electric power sources by geographical area, which is a surrogate for vulnerability to terrorist attack. Results show strong correlations between DHS grants, population distribution, energy consumption and energy generation, although the last two are less correlated with the distribution of funds than is population. When area is used as surrogate for vulnerability, then the correlations decline. There is a weak relationship with per capita income. Each approach produces slightly different winners and losers with regard to anti-terrorism funding. Efforts to develop the science required to make risk and vulnerability based allocations is discussed.

Chapter 4 - A well known assumption in all human conflicts is the capacity of every human being to inflict destructiveness on our fellow man. In war, these murderous impulses are justified through political authority. However, for the individual terrorist, a complex set of emotional processes are triggered which are often based in a feeling of injustice, real or imagined, against the enemy which is usually a national or international government. This paper uses concepts from Kleinian psychoanalysis to illustrate how the mind can powerfully be convinced that revenge and retaliation are the only ways to correct a perceived wrong. An appraisal of this specific threat in any society could help contain the destructive consequences of terrorism and also provide major clues as to the prevention of such actions. As in the consulting room, such acting out can only be prevented by those in authority taking seriously the grievances of the terrorist state of mind and act to repair real or imagined psychic injures which pose a threat to society today.

Chapter 5 - In the present chapter the authors build upon their previous research (Zywiak et al., 2003a) by adding results from the control group to the previously examined case monitored group. The authors also examine healthcare utilization following 9-11, types of relapse, and 12 months of post 9-11 Timeline Followback data. The authors earlier results suggested a relapse rate of 42% for clients recently completing an inpatient detoxification. In the present chapter with a larger sample size the authors now estimate that 40% relapsed. These results suggest an increased burden on the regional healthcare system. Predictor analyses suggest that relapses were more likely for older clients, and for clients not cohabiting nor married. Twelve-month outcome data suggest that drinking following 9-11 was related to drinking a year later. Follow-up calls from formal treatment programs following disasters, and publicity for cost-effective mutual-help meetings following disasters are recommended. Further, prospective studies with larger samples, with repeated assessments across a number of domains are recommended to advance knowledge regarding general reactions and individual differences in reactions to man-made and natural disasters.

Chapter 6 - The authors consider the risk to major hazard plant from terrorists deliberately causing catastrophic industrial accidents: here the authors focus on loss-of-containment events of toxic or flammable substances such as chlorine or LPG.

The local population is clearly at risk from such catastrophic events and fatalities may number in the hundreds or thousands: this represents a significant ``weapon'' in the hands of terrorist groups.

Risk assessment of major hazard plant typically neglects the possibility of terrorist attack; the authors discuss possible reasons for this. The authors argue that terrorism may usefully be treated as a rational behaviour and in doing so it becomes possible to assess the risks it causes. The authors outline a basic risk assessment methodology for terrorism and analyse the vulnerability of major hazard plant to terrorist attack: They identify eight factors (access, security, opacity, secondary hazard, robustness, law enforcement response, victim profile, and political value) that might be used as a starting point for more formal risk assessment and management.

Chapter 7 - Background: The identification of facial emotional expressions is a crucial component of social and emotional development. Although recent studies indicate that terrorism induced trauma has a negative impact on child psychological functioning, no previous studies have ever investigated the effects of terrorism on children's face emotion processing. This study reports pilot information on free labeling of facial expressions of emotions in a group of severely traumatized children surviving the terrorist attack in Beslan 3 months after their school siege. These children were compared with a group of non exposed children matched by age and gender.

Method: Participants were 66 children with a mean age of 9.85 years (SD=1.33) who were either exposed or not exposed to the terrorist attack in Beslan, Russia. Children were tested on free labeling of 10 facial expression stimuli representing happiness, sadness, anger, disgust, fear and surprise. All responses were judged by two raters on valence and specific emotion category.

Results: Children of both groups equally recognized the correct specific category of happiness. However, significant differences were found in responses to negative emotions stimuli. Terrorism exposed children more frequently attributed a negative valence to anger and correctly recognize it whereas non exposed children more frequently attributed a negative valence to fear and identified it correctly. On the contrary, exposed children did not recognize fear. The qualitative analysis of the "non responses" category revealed the presence of other labels that significantly differed between the two groups. For example, terrorism exposed children frequently mentioned suspect and offence, whereas not exposed children often described face stimuli as thoughtful or concentrated.

Conclusions: These results suggest that terrorism may impact on children's perception of facial expression of negative emotions. Findings are discussed in terms of their implications for child development; clinical suggestions are given for working with children surviving terrorism.

Chapter 8 - In this paper, the authors focus on the impact that trauma from terror can have on parents and parenting and the vicarious effects that can be passed on to children. Central to the paper is a discussion of a "transmission model" that casts trauma-related disturbances in the home and care giving environment as primary transmitters of transgenerational effects. Primary tenets of the model are that (1) Parents' trauma from terror affects parenting and the home-environment, (2) Adverse home environments and compromised parenting stress children, and (3) Chronic stress disturbs child development. The authors also discuss environmental and biological/genetic factors that may moderate the impact of terror-exposure on parents and the risk that can be transmitted to the young. Finally, the authors suggest alternative models of transmission and directions and challenges of future research.

Chapter 9 - Chemical warfare agents have been employed previously as a weapon of war on several occasions, from World War I to the Gulf War. Among chemical warfare agents, nerve gas "sarin" was used for the first time as a weapon of terrorism in the 1990s. The 1994 Matsumoto sarin attack in Japan was the first chemical terrorism attack against the general public by a religious cult. In the 1995 Tokyo subway sarin attack, the same religious cult released sarin gas into crowded subway commuter trains during the morning rush hour. Twelve passengers died, and about 5500 people were harmed. Sarin is a highly toxic nerve gas that can cause death within minutes or a few hours. The biochemical mechanism of nerve gas involves cholinergic hyperstimulation by inhibition of the crucial enzyme "acetylcholinesterase". Therapy for nerve agent toxicity is divided into three major categories, including decontamination, respiratory support, and antidotes. All of these therapies should be provided simultaneously as soon as possible after the exposure. In this chapter, the author will review toxicology, assessment, management, and prevention for chemical terrorism of sarin nerve gas as well as other toxic nerve agents. To minimize the possible catastrophic impact on the public, the author will provide recommendations based on detailed analysis of the Tokyo subway sarin attack and a systematic review of the current scientific literature.

Chapter 10 - Recently the authors carried out a quasi-experimental study on the effects of the terrorist attacks against the railways in Madrid and found that these attacks provoked a generalized prejudice directed not only against groups regarded as the responsible of the attacks but also against other non-related group (Jews). A generalized displacement toward more conservative values and political options was also found. Here the authors present two follow-up experimental studies designed to analyse the socio-psychological processes that might underlie these changes. The first study manipulated, through pictures, the salience of death- related thoughts without involving any personal or group based threat. The generalized increment of prejudices and group bias are reproduced but only at an implicit level. The second study proved that mortality salience affects how social dilemmas are approached. Participants assigned to the mortality salient condition approached a health related dilemma in terms of losses, independently of how it was experimentally framed. In contrast, control participants shifted their choices in function of the experimental manipulation. The authors discuss the implications of these results in terms of understanding the effects of terrorism from the Terror Management Theory.

EXPERT COMMENTARIES

In: Global Terrorism Issues and Developments
Editor: Rene A. Larche, pp. 3-11

ISBN: 978-1-60021-930-6
© 2008 Nova Science Publishers, Inc.

Commentary A

TERRORISM: THE THREAT OF NEW TECHNOLOGY

Alessia Ceresa
University of Treno, Italy

Abstract

The intent of this article is to evidence the progressive changes that National and International Terrorism has developed in the light of a brand new instrument, such as New Technology, largely spread on the 'global market' through the second half of the years '90s.

In fact, the doctrine defines New Technology as a set of goods and services which has a double context of application:

- New Technology as 'modern weapons': CBRNE armaments (Chemical weapons, Biological/bacteriological weapons, Radiological weapons, Nuclear weapons and Enhance highly explosive material)
- New Technology as 'mass-media': new channel of communication (for ex. Internet and Intranet)

In particular, International Terrorism exploits both opportunities offered by New Technology; while National Terrorism concentrates the attention on the strong capability of New Technology to be utilised as effective vehicle of information-exchange.

The modality of collecting *data* on this topic is an in-depth analysis of doctrine, journal articles, participant observation on Internet and interview of privileged witnesses. The result from a methodological research perspective is a qualitative study of 'how', 'why', 'where', 'when' National and International Terrorism requires the New Technology intervention on the three aspects which characterise any terrorist organisation life:

- Organisational aspect
- Operational aspect
- Logistic aspect

Besides, the result of the present study is a clear picture of the capability of any terrorist organisation to be extremely dynamic and flexible through the decades (chronological assessment), to adequate its structure and strategic components to the progressive cultural changes of any society of reference.

The conclusion demonstrates that there is a defined and concrete menace by New Technology set of goods and services, as it gives an alternative to the 'traditional' criminal instruments exploited by Terrorism (for ex. hijacking, murders, bomb-outrages and so on), developing also a new form of Terrorism: Cyberterrorism.

Moreover New Technology, as a brand new channel of information-exchange is a valid facilitator factor for any terrorist organisation to express itself, both in the internal/external communication tactic choice.

Finally, it is also possible to foresee a basic program of terrorism prevention/repression action, developing the existent instruments/methods and creating new strategies to contrast this ever-changing *phenomenon*.

Introduction

The second half of the years '90s has been characterised for the progressive and rapid spread on a large scale of a brand new *phenomenon*: 'New Technology'. This event has modified the way of living and connecting people, developing a 'global communication network', introducing new channels of information-exchange and strengthen the already existent ones.

The 'physiological' transformation of the 'modern societies' into a 'global technological society' has the effect to increase the communication vehicles, since New Technology is able to overcome any geographical frontier.

In concrete, the positive effect in introducing New Technology and a system capable to create a global data-base accessible to anybody beyond the spatial/temporal barriers, has also 'pathological' aspects.

The negative consequences are demonstrated by a misuse of the technological components:

- The introduction of the s.c. mass-destruction armaments or CBRNE weapons: Chemical weapons, Biological/bacteriological weapons, Radiological weapons, Nuclear weapons and Enhance highly explosive material [1];
- The diffusion of new forms of crime, where computers are the targets or the instruments to reach the subversive aim: the s.c. 'computer crimes' [2];
- The exploitation of the technological channels of communication for criminal purposes or illegal activities: the s.c. '(dis)information warfare' [3];
- The spread of a new form of Terrorism: the s.c. 'Cyberterrorism' or technological terrorism [4].

In particular 'Terrorism' has found a great ally in 'New Technology', since it has a significant criminological historical background.

In fact, it is possible to identify two main aspects related to the New Technology concept, adopted by Terrorism to express its violent and criminal component:

a) New Technology as (para)military instruments: the new forms of electronic warfare and a new typology of armaments (CBRNE weapons and mass-destruction weapons)
b) New Technology as a new mass-media: brand new set of tools and services which creates effective channels of communication [5].

At this point it is also important to define 'Terrorism' as intended in this research.

From an historical and sociological perspective the modern doctrine distinguish two forms of 'Terrorism' [6]:

A) National Terrorism
B) International Terrorism

The two forms of 'Terrorism' exploit in a different way the 'New Technology' variable, since National and International Terrorisms have different contexts of action, as well as a wide *spectrum* of ideological and operational intents.

Basically weather National Terrorism concentrates the attention on New Technology as an effective and powerful channel of communication/information-exchange; International Terrorism utilises New Technology both as brand new technological 'mass-destruction armaments' or CBRNE weapons and as a new 'mass-media'.

National Terrorism

'National Terrorism': any organisation characterised by an ideological reason based on political motivations (BR-PCC – Italy, Anarchic Inspired Groups – Italy), separatist movements (ETA – Spain, Corsican terrorism), extreme religious belief (IRA – Ireland) or social reasons (Black-Bloc, No-Global, Pacifist, Social Centres, Ecoterrorism). The adjective 'National' means that terrorism is geographically/culturally/politically/sociologically located in a specific context of reference.

The wide *spectrum* of National Terrorism typologies as mentioned, can be classified within three aspects:

1) Organisational aspect
2) Operational aspect
3) Logistic aspect

1) *Organisational Aspect:* The 'Structure' of Any Subversive Movement

New Technology has a great influence on this component, as it facilitates the communication/information streams.

There are two forms of communication/information-exchange:

a) '*External communication*': the contact of the terrorist movement with the social and institutional 'world'.

New Technology and in particular Internet are exploited for a 'proselytism and recruitment campaign'.

In fact the most important nationalist subversive movements have official web-sites[1] and often a related e-mail system.

In particular, the 'e-mail system' can send any text, vocal message and/or image in few minutes in any part of the world. It can be also protected through special cryptographic programs: for ex. the s.c. PGP program (Pretty Good Privacy) [7].

The 'chat-group' can connect several people in real-time, anywhere located, discussing on a common topic.

It represents the first-touch within a complex selection and recruitment procedure of potential adepts: it tests the ideological motivations (Italian BR-PCC).

b) *Internal communication*': the contact among the subjects formally and substantially belonging to the criminal organisation.

New Technology has different advantages: the anonymity factor and connections at a long distance. It is used for ex. for the drafting of underground journals articles: 'La Voce' journal by BR-PCC, printed in Italy and the authors are Brigatisti hidden in France.

2) *Operational Aspect:* **The Wide Typology of Violent Activities, Expression of the Ideological Background**

There are two series of activities:

a) *'Traditional operational activities'*. The criminal common methods to express the social and political tensions across Europe from years '70s: hijackings, bomb-outrages, murders, kidnappings, urban *guerrilla* [8].

Some of these forms of threat survive till the present years, because of the powerful impact on mass-media and the 'civil world'.

b) *'New operational activities'* related to the technological instruments. For ex. a mobile used as a bomb detonator (Anarchic Inspired Groups) [9], e-mail for sending the s.c. 'claim documents' after a murder (BR-PCC), Internet for the illegal weapons-trade (IRA, ETA).

Although the use of technology for terrorist actions is circumscribed, the national terrorism is experimenting new and alternative forms of violent expression.

3) *Logistic Aspect:* **The Network of Internal/external Connections with a Terrorist Organisation**

There are two forms of logistic connections:

a) *'Ideological logistic support'*: the sustain to the ideas that justify the terrorist movement violent activities.

---

[1] www.brigaterosse.it; www.batasuna.org; www.leoncavallo.it; www.disinformazione.org; www.noglobal.org; www.kontrokultura.org; www.ecn.org and so forth

It uses the same technological instruments of the operational aspect to support the terrorist *credo*: chat-groups, subversive web-sites, e-mails, mobiles. It creates multilevel networks of connections: other terrorist and/or subversive movements sharing similar ideologies (Black-Block, No-Global and so forth), extremist Political Parties, Trade-Unions (BR-CCP, IRA, ETA).

b) *'Empirical logistic support'*: the concrete sustain to the operational violent activity from the external/internal members or from other subversive movements. Mobiles for communications during terrorist actions, Internet for weapons-trades, to publicise the terrorist criminal activity, to press similar organisations to fallow the same violent example and to collect funds.

International Terrorism

'International Terrorism': any organisation with an ideological background, expressing its criminal program beyond the geographical/social/political/religious/cultural origins.

The most important form of transnational terrorism, after the terrorist attack on September 11, 2001 in New York, is the s.c. Middle-East or Islamic terrorism, based on a wide *spectrum* of religious extreme interpretations of the *Qur'an* holy text.

Other forms of international terrorism: the Colombian 'paramilitary forces' FARC[2], characterised for an international illegal trade of weapons and drugs for funds-raising and connections with organised crime; other similar South American paramilitary groups (*Sendero Lumioso* – Peru, ELN – Colombia, AUC – Colombia, *Tupamaros* – Bolivia); Tamil Tigers (Sri Lanka)[3], as well as subversive movements related to the illegal trade of toxic material for CBRNE weapons: *plutonium* or *uranium* trade from the *ex*-USSR by separatist organisations (for ex. Chechen movement) to collect funds for their internal subversive activity.

A parallel form of terrorism, which operates on a 'virtual space' beyond the geographical frontiers is the brand new s.c. Cyberterrorism (hacking and cracking). It exploits computer programs to manipulate the information streams spread through Internet. Sometimes it is an autonomous form of crime, some other cyberterrorism is exploited by terrorist organisations for strategic reasons.

The present research uses the scheme of 'National Terrorism' to analyse the technological impact on the 'International Terrorism':

1) Organisational aspect
2) Operational aspect
3) Logistic aspect

---

[2] www.farcep.org
[3] www.eelamweb.com

1) *Organisational Aspect.* International Terrorism Utilises New Technology for Two Reasons

a) *'External communication'*: it is used for a 'proselytism and recruitment campaign', as the National Terrorism. The typology of technological instruments are also the same of the national subversive organisations, with the fundamental difference that at an international level the skilfulness in using technology and the modality is certainly more complex.

   In particular the Islamic terrorism is characterised for a galaxy of different movements, also in contrast each other, where the internal members are often extremely independent: for ex. *Jihād, al-Qā'ida, al-Aqsa* Martyrs Brigade, *Hamās, Gama'at al-Islamya, Hizbullāh* and so forth. The internal fragmentation is in contrast with an external common front against the capitalistic societies (Western Countries) and the international organisations, claiming their cultural and religious roots.

   In details Islamic terrorism exploits traditional mass-media vehicles of information: propagandistic television channels and programs, newspapers and as religious terrorism, the Mosques and religious cultural centres. Besides recently it has discovered the great power of technological instruments: extremist web-sites[4], the e-mailing system to keep contacts with the potential adepts in an anonymous form [10].

b) *'Internal communication'*: for ex. the Islamic terrorism, composed of several extremist groups spread around the Western Countries, uses technological instruments to facilitate closer contacts with the 'brain' of the organisation often located in the Middle-East Countries.

2) *Operational Aspect:* Characterised for Two Series of Activities

a) *'Traditional operational activities'*: similar to the National Terrorism strategic choice.

   It goes from the paramilitary *guerrilla* typical of the South America (Bolivia, Peru, Colombia) to the s.c. *Intifada*, the typical *guerrilla* of the Palestinian population against the Israelite soldiers, fought with stones in the streets. Other methods are: bomb-outrages (Middle-East, Europe, USA and South America), political murders (Middle-East, South America and USA) or religious murders (Middle-East), hijackings (Middle-East, Europe, USA, and South America), kidnappings and extortions (Middle-East and South America).

b) *'New operational activities'*: technological components. The strict context of new armaments and the related illegal trade of nuclear and toxic materials (the Chechen separatist movement, some Middle-East States).

   The illegal trade of weapons and drugs with the intent to raise funds for the terrorist ideological cause (Colombia, Bolivia, Peru).

---

[4]www.palestine-info.info/ar/default.aspx; www.jihadwatch.org; www.youngmuslims.ca and so forth

There is a limited use of technology for single terrorist actions, as demonstrated by latest facts: hijacking in New York and bomb-outrages in London and Madrid. They exploited 'traditional' methods of action because a bomb-outrage impact on the international society is certainly stronger that a computer sabotage.

3) *Logistic Aspect:* **Analysed within Two Contexts**

a) *'Ideological logistic support'*: technological components exploited as new communication-exchange channels.

It has different levels of connections: from the strict contact of the single terrorist organisation internal members, to the creation of a logistic ideological support network from other terrorist movements geographically far from the original subversive group, through the terrorist operation publicity.

The Middle-East terrorism then uses an advanced form of Internet communication: the s.c. 'steganography' [11]. It exploits the e-mailing system: the aim is to hide an e-mail (with or without a related 'attachment') containing secret and sensitive documents, images and/or sounds/voices behind an other 'false' e-mail (the principle of the 'Chinese boxes').

b) *'Empirical logistic support'*. It uses technology for pragmatic reasons: connecting people more rapidly at a large distance from a specific operational location (for ex. Islamic terrorist attacks in Western Countries).

The South American terrorist groups act in the opposite way: the subversive actions are located in South America, but funds are raised also in other countries (Europe and USA) through illegal trades. The same situation happens for the Chechen separatist movement from *ex*-USSR.

Conclusion

The qualitative and quantitative impact of New Technology on Terrorism is proportional to the typology of terrorist organisations. National and International Terrorism uses New Technology according to their different 'targets' and strategies.

It is important to evidence differences and common aspects between the two forms of terrorism.

Differences between National and International Terrorism:

1. New Technology as 'mass-destruction' armaments
    a) International Terrorism exploits this aspect of New Technology: s.c. CBRNE weapons (toxic materials and the related illegal international trade).
    b) National Terrorism totally excludes the possibility of using or trading the new mass-destruction armaments.

2. New Technology as new communication channel
   a) International Terrorism has an higher level and skilfulness in exploiting more complex forms of technological instruments (the s.c. 'steganography').
   b) National Terrorism instead selects a more simple and common technological instruments typology and related applications.

3. New Technology as part of a complex 'cost/benefit strategy'
   a) International Terrorism wants to renew and replace in a more substantial form the traditional instruments with new technological ones.
   b) National Terrorism has not the financial power in constantly modernizing its technological instruments.

Common aspects between National and International Terrorism:

1. The New Technology impact is focused on the organisational aspect, as an effective form of 'proselitysm and recruitment strategy'.
   The logistic aspect is also substantially influenced from technological components, both for ideological logistic support and the empirical logistic one.
2. The New Technology component is practically absent within the strict context of the operational aspect. In fact, there are nor relevant events of terrorist technological actions, neither cyberterrorism.
3. National and International Terrorist organisations are in a phase of experimenting and testing the subversive potentiality of New Technology in its several applications.

The analysis of a certain crime necessary requires the complementary study of the prevention/repression strategy both at national/international level.
The existent program is based on the following aspects:

1) Bank-accounts control: financial terrorism sources
2) Interpol/Europol data-base: information-exchange
3) Political/Diplomatic agreement
4) National Law Enforcement
5) Internet monitoring activity

A basic program to control, prevent and repress national/international terrorism should focus the attention on two points:

A) International Internet Code
B) Improvement of the s.c. 'Indirect strategy' (Intelligence) [12]

A)The drafting of an '*Internet International Code*': a form of prevention/repression against any concrete and possible misuse of this technological form of information-exchange through powerful channels of communication. In fact, nowadays a large part of the doctrine defines a new form of war: the s.c. (dis)information warfare[13], since New Technology has improved the quantitative communication aspect, but a different valuation requires the qualitative perception: there is deep discrepancy between the qualitative and quantitative information stream.

B)The '*Intelligence*' information-exchange among the States member of the International Society should improve the coordination efficiency: sending rapidly *ad hoc* task-forces in sensitive *areas*, strictly specialised in Terrorism and New Technology, able also to valuate future possible dangerous evolutions (feedback analysis).

In conclusion, the different strategies in terrorism prevention/repression must be dynamic and flexible, since National/International Terrorism has been demonstrating through the decades of being capable in rapidly modernizing its structures and operational abilities, although in deeply different geopolitical-cultural contexts of reference.

References

[1]   De Luca R. (2002). *Il Terrorismo in casa nostra*. Milano: Ed. FrancoAngeli

[2]   Strano M. (2000). *Computer Crime*. Milano: Ed. Apogeo

[3]   Berkowitz B. D. (1995). Warfare in the Information Age. *Issue in Science and Technology, Fall, Vol.12, n. 1*

[4]   Pomante G. (2000). *Hacker e Computer Crimes*. Napoli: Ed. Simone

[5]   Bassiouni M. C. (1981). Terrorism, Law enforcement and the Mass Media: Perspectives, Problems, Proposals. *Journal of Criminal Law and Criminology*, n.72

[6]   Laqueur W. (2002). *Il nuovo terrorismo*. Milano: Ed. Corbaccio

[7]   Giustozzi C, Monti A. & Zimuel E. (1999). *Segreti Spie Codi(ci)frati*. Milano: Ed. Apogeo

[8]   Laqueur W. (1987). *The Age of Terrorism*. London: Weidenfeld & Nicolson

[9]   CNN (April 10, 2001). *Roma, l'ombra delle Brigate Rosse. Bomba detonata dal telefonino*. [www.cnnitalia.it/2001/italia/04/10/rivendicazione]

[10]   Olimpio G. (2002). *La rete del terrore*. Milano: Ed. Sperling & Kupfer

[11]   Giustozzi C., Monti A. & Zimuel E. (1999). *Segreti Spie Codi(ci)frati*. Milano: Ed. Apogeo

[12]   Sun Tzu & Cleary T. (2000). *The Art of War*. Boston & London: Shambhala Publications Inc.

[13]   Berkowitz B. D. (1995). Warfare in the Information Age. *Issue in Science and Technology, Fall, Vol. 12, n. 1*

In: Global Terrorism Issues and Developments
Editor: Rene A. Larche, pp. 13-16
ISBN: 978-1-60021-930-6
© 2008 Nova Science Publishers, Inc.

Commentary B

ETHNICITY AND TERRORISM

Atin Basuchoudhary[1] and William F. Shughart II[2]
[1]Deparatment of Economics and Business, Virginia Military Institute, USA
[2]Department of Economics, University of Mississippi, USA

The study of ethnic conflict has gained a fresh currency in a post 9/11 world. The idea of terrorism as a symptom of the clash of ethnicity/race/religion based civilizations seems to have taken hold in the cultural imagination of the general public. More dangerously, it seems to be driving both public debate as well as national policy on the issue of terrorism. I will make a case here that this approach is wrong because it frames the problem incorrectly. In other words, the theoretical construct is flawed not because there is contrarian anecdotal evidence (Huntington, 1993), but because there are serious logical flaws in the argument. A correct framing of the problem elicits certain practical policy options for reducing the level of conflict generally as well as the threat of terrorism in particular.

The notion that certain ethnic groups are predisposed to violence with other ethnic groups is superficial abstraction of reality that has very little explanatory or predictive power. It is a fact that ethnic clashes are common. But that should lead us to ask more questions. Why are groups formed along ethnic lines? Why should some such groups engage in conflict and not others? Is it correct to use ethnic or civilizational categories as the unit for analyzing ethnic conflict? What is the evidence for or against an ethnicity based "explanation" of conflict? Answering these questions will allow us to understand the motivation for conflict along ethnic lines and should provide the framework for analyses that have explanatory and predictive power.

It is possible to argue that understanding the roots of ethnic clashes ought to focus on attributes of ethnicity rather than individuals because individuals have no choice in being a member of an ethnic group or civilization. But as Sen (2006) points out that this assertion is not true. One may not have much choice over racial type but one does have a choice of the level of ethnic identity to emphasize relative to other possible identities. Moreover, it is each individual's sense of identity that motivates behavior. For example, a person living in the U.S. but born in India of Hindu parents (like me) could choose whether to eat beef or not. Eating beef deemphasizes a Hindu/Indian identity relative to an American identity. In other words ethnicity or an accident of birth does not necessarily predetermine the choice of identity and therefore the choice of behavior. And in analyzing the nature of conflict it is behavior that we are concerned with. If ethnic or civilizational identity is not predetermined then why do certain people choose to emphasize that particular identity? An answer to this question may help explain why emphasizing an ethnic identity may lead to violence among ethnic groups. Moreover, note that if people have a choice of identity then the individual should be the unit of analysis in any investigation into the role of behavior associated with ethnicity. Of course, this argument rules out superficial theoretical generalizations about groups of people i.e. "civilizations."

In the preceding paragraph I made the case that the individual is the appropriate unit of analysis and that individuals may choose to emphasize or deemphasize their ethnic or civilizational roots. What factors motivate this decision? Jonathan Haidt (2006) notes that people are very good at making instinctive decisions that benefit them. Thus, whether conscious or not, emphasizing an ethnic identity must provide a benefit to an individual. The public choice literature lays out a well documented benefit to individuals from joining groups (see for example, Buchanan, 1980). The availability of rents motivates individuals to join special interest groups. These rents are then divided among members of a group. Hardin (1995) points out that other groups who miss out on this capture are rarely compensated. This grievance over rents therefore generates conflict. Landa (1994) suggests that ethnicity forms a low cost basis for group formation. Members of an ethnic group may be easily identifiable to each other thus lowering transactions costs. Moreover, repeated interaction within and between families in an ethnic group increase cooperation and trust between members of the group. Note that using ethnicity as the basis for a group reduces the cost of choosing an ethnic identity relative to other identities. Strong ethnic stereotypes that increase the cost of choosing other non ethnic identities may further reduce the cost of an ethnic emphasis in identity.[1] Thus individuals may find it in their interests to join ethnic groups in order to share rents. This brings them into conflict with other groups.

My argument in the preceding paragraph suggests that when rents are available individuals benefit from joining ethnic groups. Capturing rents at the expense of other ethnic groups may therefore generate conflict. Terrorism may be one expression of this conflict. This line of reasoning suggests two reasons for conflict. First of all, rents are available. Second, there are no peaceful mechanisms for distributing these rents among different ethnic groups. Both these ideas suggest that conflict arises out of institutional failure rather than anything inherent in ethnicity. This of course, is a testable hypothesis. A recent emphasis on the role of institutions in generating economic growth has motivated the creation and collection of a wealth of data on institutional factors. There is also some data on measuring ethnic differences and polarization in a country. We can use this information to ask if institutions matter in generating conflict and whether certain types of institutions might be better at reducing ethnic conflict – particularly terrorism. But before I do that I must flesh out how institutions affect the availability and distribution of rents.

The extent to which rents are available and how they are distributed are driven by institutions. Rent seeking is rampant in representative democracies where the interests of a

---

[1] For example if there is a strong stereotype that a certain ethnic group is "lazy" then hard working individuals in that group may not be hired by employers from other ethnic groups thus at one stroke making it harder to work and disprove the stereotype and easier to fall back on ones own ethnic kind for support.

few (localized in the representative's district and voting for her) trump the interest of the many (dispersed across the nation and not voting for the representative). The power of government can be utilized by special interest groups to both create and then redistribute rents. This argument is also valid in societies where government is not transparent and therefore creating new rules to help certain groups at the expense of others may be easy. Note that there is little theoretical support for the idea that political freedom alone can reduce rent-seeking.

Thus irrespective of the state of political freedom, groups that are cut out of the rent seeking trough may be willing to resort to violence given the right institutional incentives. An institutional framework that encourages rent seeking can therefore facilitate violence arising out of problems from redistributing rents. Thus ethnic clashes can be interpreted as attempts by individuals to appropriate resources that cannot be obtained in any other way. Ethnic groups are merely a convenient means to an end – the appropriation of wealth by individuals. It follows that a change in the institutional structure could possibly reduce rent seeking and the conflict that could be associated with it.

So far I have tried to make the case that individuals have an incentive to join an ethnic group to share rents without regard to the state of political freedom. Since rent seeking is by definition a transfer of wealth from one group to another it is prone to generate conflict along ethnic lines. Institutions determine both the level of rents and their redistribution – thus getting the "right" institutions might be one way to reduce ethnic conflict. Ethnic clashes are not inherently based in differences in ethnicity. Rather, ethnic conflict has an institutional basis.

What might be the right set of institutions? Institutions that take away the incentive to join groups – ethnic or otherwise – in order to appropriate rents would seem to be indicated. Thus, institutions that allow individuals to retain the fruits of their labor would militate against the need of individuals to join groups to get a share of some fixed pie. In the process wealth is created because now people have an incentive to create wealth (they can keep it). Moreover, if people can create their own wealth the relative benefit of joining a group to get someone else's wealth falls when the cost of potential conflict with other groups is accounted for. Thus institutions that promote economic opportunity, i.e. those that protect private property, lead to both economic growth and less conflict.

That institutions – both political and economic – mitigate conflict and promote economic growth is generally accepted (see for example Easterly, Ritzen, and Woolcock 2006). There is, however, some evidence that institutions that support private property rights (preventing expropriation of wealth by governments and enforcement of contracts) reduce conflict where mere political rights (the right to vote and civil liberties) do not. A recent paper by Basuchoudhary and Shughart (2007) provide evidence that protecting property rights reduces the terrorism generating potential of ethnic tensions while mere political rights do not. A similar effect is noted on economic growth (Basuchoudhary, Reksulak and Parker, 2007). These papers offer a somewhat nuanced view of the generally accepted role of institutions in mitigating conflict and promoting economic growth.

If ethnic conflict can be explained by the lack of economic institutions then the solution to ethnic conflict must lie in promoting economic institutions rather than on broad inter civilizational initiatives. Enforceable laws that protect private property in Arab countries would be more effective in reducing terrorism than a dialogue about the relative merits of Christianity and Islam. In fact this is precisely what is missing in the international conversation regarding terrorism. This conversation has been hijacked by the purveyors of civilizational snake-oil and any attempt to reduce ethnic conflict seems to be grounded in broad attempts at dialogue or outright warfare between civilizations. Both approaches are wrong. Protecting private property and institutionalizing economic freedom is the right way to end ethnic conflict and uproot terrorism.

References

Basuchoudhary, A., Reksulak, M. & Parker, G. (2007). "Reducing the Impact of Ethnic Tensions on Economic Growth – Economic or Political Institutions?" Unpublished Manuscript.

Basuchoudhary, A. and W.F. Shughart. (2007). "On the Ethnic Origins of Terrorism." Unpublished Manuscript.

Buchanan, J.M. (1980). Rent Seeking and Profit Seeking. In Buchanan, J.M., Tollison,. R D. & Tullock, G. (Eds.), *Toward a Theory of the Rent Seeking Society*, 3–15. College Station: Texas A&M University Press.

Easterly, W., J. Ritzen, and M. Woolcock. 2006. "Social Cohesion, Institutions, And Growth." *Economics and Politics* v18:2 pp 103-120.

Haidt, J. (2006). *The happiness hypothesis: Finding modern truth in ancient wisdom*. New York: Basic Books.

Hardin, R. (1995). *One for All: The Logic of Group Conflict*. Princeton: Princeton University Press.

Huntington, S.P. (1993). "If Not Civilizations, What? Samuel Huntington Responds to His Critics." *Foreign Affairs*, November/December.

Landa, Janet T. (1994). *Trust, Ethnicity, and Identity: Beyond the New Institutional Economics of Trading Networks*. Ann Arbor: University of Michigan Press.

Sen, A. (2006). *Identity and Violence*. New York: Norton.

RESEARCH AND REVIEW STUDIES

In: Global Terrorism Issues and Developments
Editor: Rene A. Larche, pp. 19-60
ISBN: 978-1-60021-930-6
© 2008 Nova Science Publishers, Inc.

Chapter 1

TOWARD A THEORY OF TERRORISM: A MULTIDIMENSIONAL ANALYSIS

Geoffrey R. Skoll[*]

Criminal Justice Department, Buffalo State College, 1300 Elmwood Avenue
Buffalo NY 14222, USA

Abstract

Despite many publications about terrorism it remains ill-defined and under-theorized. Domination of the discourse by antiterrorist legislation and political rhetoric has impeded social scientific research as political and legal terms remain overly dependent on reifications. Starting with an everyday conceptual definition of terrorism, the concept is broken down into dimensions, forms, and a typology. Possible theoretical approaches are discussed with attention to different frames of reference and levels of abstraction. This chapter tries to establish a clearer ground for theory building.

Introduction

For America's national security state, terrorism replaced communism as the chief villain sometime in the 1990s. For a while, transnational organized crime looked like it might take first place, but terrorism won out after September 11, 2001 [Kerry 1997, Naylor 2002:1-11, Woodiwiss: 381-394]. An advantage to terrorism is that can be fused into such locutions as narco-terrorism, which combines the two nemeses. As of the year 2007, the United States pursues a global military policy predicated on a "global war on terror," or GWOT in military-speak. "Concisely, the US has abandoned hegemonic governance, based on the institutionalization of collective economic and security regimes, in favor of militarism, or the pursuit of American global dominance through force"[Golub 2004:19].

Domestically, the United States runs the biggest counter terror apparatus in the world. After September 11, 2001, the federal government undertook the largest single reorganization in forty years by, *inter alia*, creating the Department of Homeland Security. The FBI alone conducts over 10,000 terror investigations a year [TRAC 2003]. As of May 2006, federal agencies maintain surveillance and ongoing investigations of 6,472 individuals as terror suspects [TRAC 2006]. Theses state apparatuses enunciate and promote what has become the dominant discourse about terrorism—namely that it is a political crime against the state. Social science, in the objective Weberian sense of independence from state influence [Weber 1919/1958], has had a small voice in defining or explaining terrorism outside the hegemonic discourse. Part of the reason is that social science has produced few comprehensive theories of terrorism.

Likely, scholars from different perspectives and disciplines can formulate useful theories, but theories need a framework, therefore I offer the following framework to facilitate theory building. The framework has three purposes: polemical, typological, and operational. Its polemical purpose challenges the dominance of discourse by the state. The typological defines patterns of phenomena associated with terrorism to organize and categorize them. To this end, the framework includes types and forms of terrorism. Next, it offers a dimensional analysis to provide points of departure for theoretical and empirical research. The penultimate section contains a discussion of theories as explanations. The discussion reviews different kinds of explanations useful in the social sciences. The last part of the paper briefly reviews several possible approaches or frameworks for constructing theories of terrorism.

In that respect, I argue that a broad, quotidian definition of terrorism serves theory building best. Nonetheless, various authorities contest that approach [e.g., Jenkins 1999, Laqueur 1987:72]. Moreover, terrorism definitions have a history. The first section of the articles reviews the controversy and history of the term. The next section sets up a typology, followed by a section devoted to forms of terrorism. a section on dimensions outlines the main variables as dimensions of terrorist phenomena. The last section discusses theories, what they should explain, their appropriate levels of abstraction, and the kinds of explanations they might proffer. The order follows F. S. C. Northrop's [Northrop 1947:35-39] stages of inquiry where the first stage is identification of the problem or question, the second is gathering, ordering, and describing data, and the third stage explanation.

Definitions of Terrorism

Much as the word 'communism' was both politically weightier and more restricted in the popular discourse of the time than its denotation in the 1950s so 'terrorism' has gained weight and shrunk in range of meaning since the World Trade Center and Pentagon attacks of September 11, 2001. In the case of terrorism, a broad and ordinary understanding encourages more comprehensive and precise analyses. Unlike other treatments of the subject [e.g., Coombs and Slann 2002, Griset and Mahan 2003, and White 2003], I offer no special pleading about difficulties of defining the term.

More than thirty years ago, the US Task Force on Disorders and Terrorism proposed a serviceable definition as follows. "Terrorism is a tactic or technique by means of which a violent act or threat thereof is used for the purpose of creating overwhelming fear for coercive purposes" [Task Force 1976:3].Shortening it does no harm so a more concise version is

* E-mail: skollgr@buffalostate.edu Tel: 786-878-4512

Terrorism (n.): A coercive tactic using fear through violence or its threat. The background for the national Task Force was social turmoil accompanied by an increase in civil disorders during the early 1970s. The Task Force noted numerous airplane hijackings, bombings, and riots in cities in the United States.

Just before the September 11 attacks, the former staff director of the Task Force weighed in on the definitional controversy. H. H. A. Cooper [2001:881] begins by quoting Raymond Cohen [1990: 41-42]. "A living language has no existence independent of culture. It is not the loom of culture but its data bank. As such, it serves the needs, past and present, of a given community. As those needs change, language evolves to accommodate them." Cooper goes on to offer an elegant definition: "... [T]errorism is the intentional generation of massive fear by human beings for the purpose of securing or maintaining control over other human beings" [Cooper 2001: 883]. Cooper's 2001 definition does not require violence, but stresses control more than mere coercion. These changes improve the 1976 version as they open the possibility that terrorism is a condition, not merely an event.

A short hand version allows researchers to recognize terrorism when they see it. According to that criterion, terrorism occurs when someone makes people fearful in order to control them. The three elements are intent, fear, and control [cf. Crenshaw 1983, 1995].

History of Definitions

According to the Oxford English Dictionary, 'terrorism' first entered the English lexicon with Edmund Burke's Whiggish fears of the French Revolution. Burke [1790, 1791] characterized the Jacobin ascendancy as a reign of terror. The origin of the word reveals its affinity with a fear of popular uprisings and revolutionary governments. Historical and contemporary surveys of terrorism emphasize its political character.

People understood the meaning of the word 'terrorism' *avant la lettre*. Representations of terrorism predate the word, as attested by certain artifacts located about fifty miles south of Mosul in Iraq. The conqueror and king of Assyria Assurnasirpal (884-860 BCE) imposed his rule over conquered territories by erecting stone monuments.[1] The following inscription appears in the ruins of the temple at the foot of the pyramid at Nimrud (Calach) about fifty miles south of Mosul on the Tigris River.

[Col. 1 ll. 33-35]I am great and I am glorious, Assur-nasir-pal, a mighty King of Assyria, proclaimer of the Moon-god, worshipper of Anu, exalter of Yav, suppliant of the gods am I, servant unyielding, subduing the land of his foeman, a King mighty in battle, destroyer of cities and forests, Chief over opponents, Prince of a lands of all Kings. ...

[Col. 1 ll. 59-69]The cities of Khatu, Khalaru, Nistun, Irbidi, Mitkie, Arzanie, Zila, Khalue, cities of Gihili situated in the environs of Uzie and Arue and Arardi powerful lands, I occupied: their soldiers in numbers I slew; their spoil, their riches I carried off; their soldiers were discouraged ... my soldiers like birds (of prey) rushed upon them; of their warriors by the sword I smote down; their heads cut off in heaps I arranged ... impost tribute and a Viceroy I set over them. Bubu, son of Bubua son of the Prefect of Nistun in the city of Arbela I flayed; his skin I stretched in contempt upon the wall. At that time an image of my person I made; a

---

[1] One art historian argues that the cuneiform script not only represented its subject matter, but that contemporaries treated the inscriptions as being a part of what they represented. Therefore, the inscription of Assurnasirpal mutilating bodies was to be experienced as if he were actually there [Bahrani 2003].

history of my supremacy upon it I wrote, and (on) a mountain of the land of Ikin(?) in the city of Assur-nasir-pal at the foot I erected (it). In my own eponym in the month of July and the 24th day (probably 882 BCE).

Assurnasirpal built a cohesive Assyrian state from the "Tigris to Lebanon" [Butterfield 1996: 165-166]. The campaigns commemorated by these inscriptions took place in the mountains of Armenia. He defeated Nabu-bal-iddin, king of Babylon penetrating as far as Tyre and Sidon. He initiated the practice of mass executions. Such a fate was not limited to opposing soldiers and rulers but also applied to prisoners and civilians, including men, women, and children [Roux 1966: 263, quoting D. J. Wiseman 1952]. His inscriptions continue.

> I built a pillar over against his city gate and I flayed all the chiefs who had revolted, and I covered the pillar with their skin. Some I walled up within the pillar, some I impaled upon the pillar on stakes. ...
> Many captives from among them I burned with fire, and many I took as living captives. From some I cut off their noses, their ears and their fingers, of many I put out the eyes. I made one pillar of the living and another of heads ... [Roux 1966:263].

Thus were states built in ancient Mesopotamia [Olmstead 1918]. Shift forward in time more than four centuries to the birthplace of democracy, Athens

According to Thucydides, the Athenians used terrorism to secure Melos. In the summer of the sixteenth year of the Peloponnesian War (416 BCE) the Athenians sent an expedition to the small city of Melos, which although founded by Sparta, had remained neutral in the war between the two Greek superpowers. Melos would not submit to Athens. The Athenians plundered their territory, and then held a conference with the Melian leaders, the so-called Melian Dialogue. The Athenians pointed out to the Melians that neutrality meant nothing, nor did it profit to say that the Melians had not wronged the Athenians, " ... since you know as well as we do that right, as the world goes, is only in question between equals in power, while the strong do what they can and the weak suffer what they must" [Thucydides 5.89: 352]. The Athenians rejected friendly neutrality as that would be a sign of their own weakness. The Athenians made them an offer they could not refuse: Melos must either submit or be destroyed. But refuse they did. Athens besieged the city, and with treachery from inside the walls, Melos surrendered. At which, the Athenians killed all the men and sold the women and children into slavery. Subsequently, they sent five hundred Athenian colonists to resettle Melos [Thucydides 5.116: 357]. Despite current fantasies, democratic states such as Athens bear no small resemblance to monarchies when it comes to statecraft.

Christian good will alters the course in no great degree. Seeking to instill the blessings of that belief, the medieval Roman Catholic Church mounted crusades against evil, though not necessarily called "empires." Heresy was a constant threat. One crusade serves to illustrate.

Albi in Languedoc, southern France, was an important center in the twelfth century of the current era. A sect arose there stressing ideas deemed evil and dangerous by Rome. When a famous preacher of the time, St. Bernard of Clairvaux, traveled the area in 1147, he found the churches deserted as so-called Cathari or Puritains and followers of Peter Waldo, the Waldensians, had lured the people and local princes away from the Catholic establishment. Twenty years later, in 1167, the head of the sect went to Albi, and consecrated five new bishops. Pope Innocent III, urged on by Domingo de Guzman, Saint Dominic and founder of the inquisitorial Dominicans, decided to stamp out the Albigensians. His Holiness raised an army with the promise of unlimited looting in the Albigeois district, which had become one of the most prosperous in Europe. In 1207 the Pope accused one of the Albigensian lords, Raymond, Count of Toulouse, of murdering the papal legate, Pierre de Castlenau. Innocent sent out a call to arms with dire threats to those princes who did not join the campaign.

After two years of campaigning by the Pope's army, the Albigensians were still so strong as to require a renewal of the crusade in 1214. Upon burning five hundred towns, generally butchering all inhabitants, the head of the army, the Abbot of Citeaux, gave his famous instructions for distinguishing heretics from true believers: "Kill them all. God will know His own" [Hill 1997, McCabe 1929].

Leaving behind the religious extremism of the middle ages, the Enlightenment of the eighteenth century had a different rationale for imposing just punishments in the name of righteousness. Michel Foucault presented it most strikingly at the beginning of his *Discipline and Punish*.

> On 2 March 1757 Damiens the regecide was condemned 'to make the *amende honorable* before the main door of the Church of Paris' where he was to be 'taken and conveyed in a cart, wearing nothing but a shirt, holding a torch of burning wax weighing two pounds'; then, 'in the said cart, to the Place de Grève, where, on a scaffold that will be erected there, the flesh will be torn from his breasts, arms, thighs and calves with red-hot pincers, his right hand, holding the knife with which he committed the said parricide, burnt with sulphur, and, on those places where the flesh will be torn away, poured molten lead, boiling oil, burning resin, wax and sulphur melted together and then his body drawn and quartered by four horses and his limbs and body consumed by fire, reduced to ashes and his ashes thrown to the winds' (*Pièces originales ... ,* 372-4) [Foucault 1979: 3].

Terrorism has been part of human history from the beginning of its record and continually to the present. Elites desiring to control the masses have committed the bulk of it. They typically try to shift blame elsewhere, calling chosen enemies, "terrorists." So it should come as no surprise that the study of terrorism first stumbles against a definition of the term.

Since the coining of the word 'terrorism' by Edmund Burke the word has metamorphosed several times, as reflected in the 1936 *Encyclopedia of the Social Sciences*. J. B. S. Hardman models terrorism on nineteenth and early twentieth century political struggles. Hardman reviews the "Sinn Feiners" in Ireland between 1919 and 1921. He treats assassinations of political leaders and other luminaries as the paradigm, specifically citing the assassination of US President William McKinley and the shooting of Henry Clay Frick, an industrialist. Much of the article covers terrorism in Russia, inspired, Hardman says, by the writings of Mikhail Bakunin (1814-1876) and developed by Peter Kropotkin (1842-1921). The Russian Narodnaya Volya is a model terrorist organization for Hardman. After the assassination of Tsar Alexander II in 1881, Russian terrorism declined, but revived in 1901 with the Socialist Revolutionary Party. Hardman concludes with a brief discussion of terrorist methods in the civil war following the Bolshevist Revolution in which the Socialist Revolutionaries assassinated the German ambassador to the USSR, and made an attempt on the life of V. I. Lenin to disrupt the new Soviet regime. He notes that terrorist methods practiced by a government appear as law enforcement, and he excludes various other forms of violence such as individual or organized criminality, industrial clashes, and mob violence. Hardman takes terrorism as defiance of law.

During the Second World War the occupying armies called attacks by resistance fighters, terrorism. Beginning in the 1960s, terrorism meant airplane hijacking, kidnapping, isolated and relatively small bomb blasts, and assassinations of prominent figures. An enlightening exception is the assassination of John F. Kennedy, which was not generally considered terrorism, then or now. At the time, terrorism was associated with the Irish Republican Army and its splinters in Northern Ireland, The Red Army Faction in Germany, the ETA in Spain, and Black September and Abu Nidal in the Middle East.

From the 1960s to the 1990s airplane hijackings, assassinations and kidnappings of diplomats (loosely defined), kidnappings of civilians for ransom, and bombings prompted new national criminal laws and international conventions and treaties. International terrorism became a federal crime in the United States in 1984. Domestic terrorism followed suit in 1996. Attacks on American occupying forces in Lebanon occasioned the 1984 law, and the Oklahoma City bombing gave rise to the Antiterrorism and Effective Death Penalty Act of 1996.

This history of legislative activity is part of a complex history of changes in the meanings of terrorism. William Dyson points out that the 1998 Random House Webster's Dictionary defines terrorism as intimidation for political purposes, while earlier dictionaries—for example the 1967 Random House Dictionary of the English Language and the 1982 American Heritage Dictionary—defined terrorism in broader terms, without the special focus on terrorism as necessarily political. Common usage changed during the end of the twentieth century. The change accompanied grave and momentous political developments. Analyzing how the meaning of terrorism changed is crucial to understanding these dynamics. A working or conceptual definition gives a useful perspective on late twentieth century vicissitudes meanings of the term 'terrorism.'

Definitions under Law

US federal law did not recognize terrorism as a category of crimes until 1984. Crimes that now appear under its rubric—extortion, murder, kidnapping, and the like—had there own sections in criminal codes. Most of American law defines crimes according to objective, behavioral criteria. Two exceptions appear. The first includes political crimes. Beginning with the twentieth century, the Immigration Act of 1903 criminalized anarchist beliefs. The Immigration Act of 1917 and the Espionage and Sedition Acts of the same year also criminalized anarchism and communist beliefs. Various state syndicalism laws outlawed the Industrial Workers of the World. The Smith Act, also known as the Alien Registration Act of 1940, made political beliefs and activities conditions of immigration, and made advocacy of overthrowing the government a crime. The Internal Security Act of 1950 criminalized communism (Goldstein 1978, Preston 1963).

In 1970 the US Congress crafted another exception to the behavioral tradition in criminal prohibitions. The Organized Crime Control Act of 1970, which contains the Racketeer Influenced Corrupt Organizations Act or RICO, makes it a crime to associate with criminals. The Continuing Criminal Enterprise law, part of the Comprehensive Drug Abuse Prevention and Control Act of 1970, criminalizes those who participate in corrupt organizations, regardless of whether their own actions are illegal. This drug act includes an asset forfeiture section (§511), which confiscates property and records law enforcers think are used in corrupt organizations. In effect, the asset forfeiture clause criminalizes property.

Both the political laws and the racketeering laws criminalize association, although only the political laws criminalize beliefs and advocacy. US antiterrorism laws follow the pattern of political and racketeering legislation rather than that of the more usual criminal statutes. They use undefined terms such as 'violence,' coercion,' intimidate,' and 'influence.' They criminalize membership or participation in organizations. The Antiterrorism and Effective Death Penalty Act of 1996 (PL 104-132, 110 US stat. 1254) criminalized property in a way similar to the forfeiture provisions of the Drug Abuse Act of 1970 in the terror law's 'Financial Transactions section (18 USC 2332d). The terror law also criminalizes property in the sections 'providing material support to terrorists' (18 USC 23339a) and 'providing material support or resources to designated foreign terrorist organizations' (18 USC 2339b). The USA Patriot Act passed weeks after 9/11 (PL 107-56, 115 US Stat. 380) added 'prohibitions against the financing of terrorism' (18 USC 2339c) making it a crime to give money to an organization designated as terrorist even if the money is used for some other purpose such as charity.

The main US antiterrorist law is codified at Title 18 US Code Part I Chapter 113B. It defines terrorism in section 2331 as follows.

> As used in this chapter—(1) the term "international terrorism means activities that—(A) involve violent acts or acts dangerous to human life that are a violation of the criminal laws of the United States or of any State, or that would be a criminal violation if committed within the jurisdiction of the United States or of any State; (B) appear to be intended –(i) to intimidate or coerce a civilian population; (ii) to influence the policy of a government by intimidation or coercion; or (iii) to affect the conduct of a government by mass destruction, assassination or kidnapping; and (C) occur primarily outside the territorial jurisdiction of the United States, or transcend national boundaries in terms of the means by which they are accomplished the persons they appear intended to coerce, or the locale in which their perpetrators operate or seek asylum;
>
> ...
>
> (5) the term "domestic terrorism" means activities that—(A) involve acts dangerous to human life that are a violation of the criminal laws of the United States or of any State; (B) appear intended—(i) to intimidate or coerce a civilian population; (ii) to influence the policy of a government by intimidation or coercion; or (iii) to affect the conduct of a government by mass destruction, assassination or kidnapping; and (C) occur primarily within the territorial jurisdiction of the United States.

A search using LEXIS-NEXIS® discloses broader uses of the term 'terrorism' under laws by the states of the United States. Only one state, Nebraska, has none. The states commonly include terrorism in chapters of their criminal codes covering crimes against persons such as rape, murder, aggravated assault, and so on. California, Florida, and New York, to name just a few, have laws against street gangs or organized crime, which include terrorism in the code. Other states include terrorism as part of older laws against varieties of labor organizing and political agitation.

New York State provided a rationale for its 'Anti-terrorism Act of 2001.' New York's legislators cited the September 11 attacks along with bombings of American embassies in Kenya and Tanzania in 1998, the Oklahoma City bombing of 1994, Pan Am Flight 103 in Lockerbie, Scotland in 1988, the 1997 shooting atop the Empire State Building, the murder of

Ari Halberstam on the Brooklyn Bridge in 1994, and the 1993 bombing of the World Trade Center (New York Penal §490.00).

Ohio modeled its anti-terrorism law (Ohio Rev. Code 2909.21-25) on that of New York and the federal law. As with many states, Ohio incorporated terrorism in ordinary criminal laws as an enhancement. For instance, if a kidnapper also terrorizes, the court can add years to the sentence. Also, Ohio passed criminal syndicalism laws (Ohio Rev. Code 13421-23) after World War I to curtail labor organizing and leftist political agitation. In his illuminating review of Ohio's courts application of these laws, Nathaniel Stewart summarizes their approach.

> These cases should inform any modern discussion of terrorism. ... Taken together they demonstrate that courts have viewed crimes as disparate as theft, child abuse, and firearms possession to be crimes of "terror." Likewise, "terror" at common law so closely aligned with fear, apprehension, and attempts to intimidate "peaceful people," helps make sense of recent legislative efforts like Ohio's that have enacted statutes targeting such purposeful intimidation and called it "terrorism." Insofar as terrorism is conceptually understood and statutorily defined as a crime committed with intent to influence populations and policies, its meaning proves remarkably consistent with its semantic common law relative, "terror." [Stewart 2005:126].

Stewart is correct about the confluence of ordinary meanings of words such as terror, terrorize, and terrorism. Nonetheless, he goes astray in believing that ordinary understandings produce legislation [Stewart 2005:128], at least when it comes to terrorism laws. In this case, the legislation changed the ordinary meanings, and the impetus for legislative change came from political attempts to expand state power at the national level. Federal antiterrorist legislation gave verbal form and the force of law to ideology.

Consider the state of antiterrorism laws and the general understanding of terrorism before 1984. First, there was no federal law criminalizing terrorism, nor did international law criminalize terrorism. Federal and international laws, treaties, and conventions prohibited acts such as airplane hijacking, kidnapping, extortion, murder, and so on. They expressed the norm that criminal law should outlaw behavior, not intentions, goals, or communicative influence. In this they agree with the American jurist, Oliver Wendell Holmes Jr.

> Public Policy, that is to say, legislative considerations, are at the bottom of the matter; the considerations being, in this case, the nearness of the danger, the greatness of the harm, and the degree of apprehension felt. When a man buys matches to fire a haystack, or starts on a journey meaning to murder at the end of it, there is still considerable chance that he will change his mind before he comes to the point. But when he has struck the match, or cocked and aimed the pistol, there is very little chance that he will not persist to the end, and the danger becomes so great that the law steps in [Holmes 1881].

There is still no international law against terrorism, because there is no international consensus on its meaning. Instead, treaties and conventions cite certain acts as international crimes [Bassiouni 2001]. For the United States, on the other hand, terrorism is a violent act against the government or to influence the government. This differs from what most Americans meant by terrorism in, say, 1980, judging by standard dictionaries of the time. Changes in meaning and US divergence from the international community flow directly from national politics.

Ronald Reagan probably became president of the United States because of events both he and his political opponents called terrorism. The Iranian hostage crisis soon became a political catastrophe for the administration of President Jimmy Carter. Once Iranians overthrew the Shah and seized the US embassy in Tehran, Ronald Reagan used the hostage crisis to get elected. Even before his election, Reagan announced a "war on terrorism" [Wills 2003:195 citing Evans and Novak 1981]. Once in office, the Reagan administration formulated a policy in keeping with a book by the journalist Claire Sterling. Sterling argued that the USSR had promulgated a web of terrorist operations throughout the world [Sterling 1981]. Reagan predicated his foreign policy on the defeat of the USSR so with a simple logic, every bit of terrorism expressed Soviet interests, and therefore the US should strive to eliminate it. In 1983 events intervened.

In the midst of a civil war in Lebanon, Israel invaded the country June 6, 1982. The US sent troops. April 18, 1983 a truck bomb damaged the US embassy in Beirut, killing 63 people, of whom 17 were Americans. October 23, 1983 another truck bomb demolished a US Marine barracks. Two hundred twenty Marines and 21 Navy medical personnel were killed. These events led to the enactment of the 1984 *Act to Combat International Terrorism*, which made international terrorism a federal crime.

April 19, 1995 a truck bomb blew up part of the Alfred P. Murrah federal office building in Oklahoma City. The blast engulfed a child care center. The bombing killed 168 people. Two years earlier, February 26, 1993, there had been a blast in the World Trade Center. It killed six and injured 1,042 with some structural damage to the building. At the time, in 1993, the US Justice Department advocated federal legislation against domestic terrorism, but Congress did not pass it. The Oklahoma City bombing spurred passage of the *Antiterrorism and Effective Death Penalty Act of 1996*, criminalizing domestic terrorism.

The attacks against the World Trade Center and Pentagon September 11, 2001 prompted enactment of the *USA Patriot Act* on October 26, 2001(PL 107-56, 115 Stat. 272-403). These three laws—the *1984 Act to Combat International Terrorism, Antiterrorism and Effective Death Penalty Act of 1996,* and the *USA Patriot Act*—are the main laws criminalizing terrorism. Their main codification is 18 USC 2331 *et seq.* Each law directed a change in the meaning of terrorism. The 1984 law defined international terrorism. The 1996 and 2001 laws added domestic terrorism and expanded criminal liability. These legal definitions changed the definition in common usage as reflected in dictionaries. In other words, law changed custom. This contradicts the notion that law is derived from custom. It is no small difference.

The consequences of the legislative enactments have culminated in massive growth of a US national security state. The Department of Homeland Security represents that growth domestically. Assertions of US extraterritoriality for its criminal laws represent it on a global scale. The laws articulate the ideology supporting these security apparatuses.

Scholarly Definitions

Alex Schmid identified 109 definitions of political terrorism in a survey published in 1983. Five years later he and co-author Albert Jongman reported further proliferation of definitions. Susan Tiefenbrun [2003] compares legal and administrative definitions in the United States with legal definitions for Britain, France, the European Union, and Canada.

There are others. Definitions before 1984 show lack of consensus. Schmid and Jongman observe that "The search for an adequate definition of terrorism is still on." Nevertheless, Schmid sees progress by 1988 toward a more adequate social science definition. Note that Schmid and Jongman limit their concerns to political terrorism, and many of the disagreements and complications they report arise from the political part of the definition, not the terrorism part. The same applies to Tiefenbun's essay: the problems reside in the legal aspects.

Social scientists judge definitions largely according to pragmatic, utilitarian standards. Is a definition useful for going about the business of science, much of which centers on measurement? A definition must meet two requirements. First, does it allow the scientist to identify the object—to know it when s/he sees it? Second, does the definition identify the boundaries of the object so the scientist knows when to stop measuring? While these criteria seem basic enough, even they carry burdensome assumptions. They arise from the problematic of social science.

C. Wright Mills did not like the term, preferring social studies for fear of too closely following the positivistic science model. Even social has possibly unwanted implications, as if individuals thereby ought to be neglected. Therefore, for present purposes, the social sciences encompass the study of people and what they do and have done. Further, since the present purpose is a framework for theoretical work, a theoretical definition is in order.

Irwin Copi suggested that a theoretical definition attaches "... to the term, as intension, that property which in the context of a given theory is most useful for understanding or predicting the behaviour of those entities which comprise the (usual) extension of that term" [Copi 1956:19]. This formalized version fits with the idea of defining terrorism such that one knows what to look for to start measuring, and knows when to stop measuring.

Peter Caws [1959] sets out three approaches to definitions, or orders, as he calls them. The first is historical in which something is defined in terms of what is already known—a sort of history of a concept. The second is a logically ordered definition. In its ultimate form the logical ... [definition] can be exhibited as an axiomatized calculus in which from a small number of primitive terms (undefined within the calculus) ... all the propositions of the science may be derived" [Caws 1959:204, cf. Popper 1961:74-167-8]. The logically ordered approach aims at description and prediction via covering laws [Hempel 1965]. The third approach is heuristic, which he denotes as psychological as it aims at creating constructs in the mind. Caws' orders use a subjectivist perspective where the scientist is the subject and nature the scientific object. An objectivist perspective could use the same three categories—historical, logical, and heuristic—but in different ways. Consider the definition of 'oak tree.' One can approach it historically, for instance tracing the tree from an acorn. The logical approach would focus on such aspects as the tree's structure—trunk, bark, branches, leaves, roots, and so on—possibly in conjunction with functional or physiological dynamics. The heuristic approach would include questions of how to distinguish oak trees from other kinds of trees and other kinds of flora, the place of oak trees in ecological relations, the social uses of oak trees and their products. The most useful scientific definitions admit of all three orders from both a subjectivist and objectivist perspective.

Beyond the three approaches, Caws identifies five kinds of scientific definitions, but, in the end, sorts them into two—internal and external. The internal is a dictionary-like definition, whereas the external is encyclopedic. Dictionary-like, or lexical, definitions link words by setting up semantic fields populated by synonyms and antonyms. These internal, lexical definitions are finite and bounded. They rely on the principle of substitution where the term to be defined can be replaced in a sentence by other, presumably known terms. The problem with lexical definitions arises when one tries to analyze anything external to the lexicon: the order melts away.

> The tree of genera and species, the tree of substances, blows up in a dust of differentiae, in a turmoil of infinite accidents, in a non-hierarchical network of *qualia.* The dictionary dissolves into a potentially unordered and unrestricted galaxy of pieces of world knowledge. The dictionary thus becomes and encyclopedia, because it was in fact *a disguised encyclopedia* [Eco 1986:68].

Lexical definitions assume a particular heuristic. In the case of our oak tree, the heuristics of botany, ecology, or sociology impose models on the definition. External or encyclopedic definitions recognize a potentially infinite number of heuristics for defining a particular phenomenon. Consider Michel Foucault's example from Jorge Luis Borges about a Chinese encyclopedia.

This passage quotes a "certain Chinese encyclopaedia" in which it is written that "animals are divided into: (a) belonging to the Emperor, (b) embalmed, (c) tame, (d) sucking pigs, (e) sirens, (f) fabulous, (g) stray dogs, (h) included in the present classification, (i) frenzied, (j) innumerable, (k) drawn with a very fine camel hair brush, (l) *etc cetera,* (m) having just broken the water pitcher, (n) that from a long way off look like flies" [Foucault 1973:xv citing Borges 1964:103].

The observer always defines the object of observation before observing. In physics, the problem takes the form of Schrödinger's cat [Einstein, Podolsky, and Rosen 1935]. The social sciences face even greater complexities of observer effects. As Max Weber noted, "It is not the 'actual' interconnections of 'things' but the conceptual interconnections of problems which define the scope of the various sciences. A new 'science' emerges where new problems are pursued by new methods, and truths are thereby discovered which open up new points of view" [Weber 1949].

Therefore social scientific definitions must take into consideration the limitations imposed by particular heuristics, and allow for the possibilities of new methods and especially new problems. For example, terrorism might be an object of study by criminologists, but they have been slow, if not reluctant to take up the subject. Richard Rosenfeld offers several explanations. First, he points to the belief that terrorist violence is qualitatively different from common violence. Second, he notes that terrorism is political violence, and criminological theories only explain non-political violence [Rosenfeld 2002].

Generally, with a few exemplary exceptions, the terrorist discourse has been dominated by a counterterrorist industry. The industry has various state agencies at its center—the Department of Homeland Security, the FBI, the Pentagon, and so forth.— with quasi-private organizations such as the Center for Strategic and International Studies (e.g. Anthony Cordesman and Walter Laqueur), the Rand Corporation (e.g. Bruce Hoffman and Brian Jenkins), and the like in a symbiotic relation with them [Herman and O'Sullivan 1989,]. Scholars and researchers who strive toward a scientific understanding cannot avoid political influences entirely. Still, it is worth a try. In keeping with that effort, the definition of terrorism ought not to exclude possible manifestations of the phenomena by a restrictive ontology of the subject. Michael Scriven said such an approach should apply to all scientific definitions.

The essential point to be made is that 'definitions' are usually mnemonic devices, rough approximations which serve usefully as a first analysis of a term's meaning but require—in any important case—almost unending supplementation via examination of paradigmatic examples of the term's use [Scriven 1958: 166].

In other words, the definition should be broad. It needs to contain crucial elements, of which there seem to be three. First, terrorism involves terrifying others. Second, those who terrify, do it on purpose, not accidentally. Third, their objective is control, not for entertainment as in horror books and films. In the end, H. H. A. Cooper's definition appears to fit best. That is, "terrorism is the generation of massive fear by human beings for the purpose of securing or maintaining control over other human beings" [2001:883]. Therefore, that is the conceptual, working definition used here.

Types of Terrorism

Typologies organize phenomena. Organization makes analysis easier. Ideally, typologies are exhaustive and exclusive. That is, the categories should cover all cases of the phenomenon in question, and a case should fit into only one category. Granted, the decision of where to put a particular case may be problematic, but the ideal reduces ambiguity. All typologies have engines to sort phenomena into categories. Making the sorting mechanism transparent and explicit minimizes the danger that categorization predetermines the analytic outcome. A scientific analysis of terrorism requires an objective typology with transparent rules for sorting terror phenomena.

In his book on terrorism, William E. Dyson, a former FBI agent, identifies the following specific types of terrorism: 1. left-wing extremism, 2. right-wing extremism, 3. single-issue or special interest terrorism, 4. religious terrorism, 5. national or ethnic terrorism, 6. race-based or hate terrorism, narco-terrorism, computer or cyber-terrorism [Dyson 2005:25-32]. It is easy to see the influence of the FBI's mission in his categories. Other government agencies such as the Department of Defense, Department of State, et al., and quasi-agencies like the Rand Corporation or the United States Institute of Peace, Center for International and Strategic Studies, etc. They all bear the mark of US strategic interests so I prefer to concentrate on several illustrative academic typologies.

Paul Wilkinson—currently chair of the Centre for the Study of Terrorism and Political Violence at St. Andrews University, Scotland—constructed an exemplary typology of political terrorism. Many other typologies are derived from it or at least resemble it in their basic concept. Wilkinson proposes a terrorism typology based on several definitional distinctions. First, Wilkinson distinguishes between terror and terrorism, and he also distinguishes political terrorism from other kinds of terrorism. Within terror, Wilkinson says there are two kinds: epiphenomenal or incidental and systematic. Epiphenomenal or incidental terrorism comes from disasters either of nature or human design but which lack the intention to cause mass fear. Earthquakes and the like often cause mass fear, but human agency does not generate them Wilkinson [1977:48]. Still, one thinks of the mass fear that attended the Hurricane Katrina disaster in New Orleans. In that case fear and suffering arguably arose from human agency in the form of gross negligence to prevent the breaking of levees that brought subsequent flooding, especially to the more impoverished and Black sections of the city. Of course, failure to provide disaster relief while at the same time investing the city with armed force presumably to prevent looting raises questions about the epiphenomenal nature of the terror.

Wilkinson puts mass fear accompanying wars and revolutions into the incidental category. As he puts it, "... outbreaks of cataclysmic mass violence such as wars and revolutions inevitably bring a vast amount of epiphenomenal terror in their wake" [1977:48]. The term 'collateral damage' seems closely related where armies destroy civilians incidentally to their tactical aim of destroying opposing soldiers.

Terrorism, according to Wilkinson, entails systematic "psychological warfare [which is] explicitly intended and planned" [Ibid.]. I suppose one can make a similar distinction between the terror generated by a robber sticking up a convenience store clerk and an extortionist. The stick-up artist causes fear incidental to his aim of armed robbery, while the extortionist uses fear systematically to gain his plunder.

Wilkinson's typology of strictly political terrorism has four categories: sub-revolutionary, revolutionary, repressive, and epiphenomenal 1977:56-57, Table 3]. The first two, eponymous categories, sub-revolutionary and revolutionary, have a problem with sorting. Distinguishing political aims as total revolution from aims just short of it seems more problematic than clarifying. Wilkinson himself says that sub-revolutionary terrorism may overlap with psychopathological and criminal violence, but he does not see a similar problem with revolutionary terrorism. His third category, repressive terrorism, presumes terrorism by the state, although state terrorism is not part of his categorical criteria. Epiphenomenal terrorism seems different from his epiphenomenal terror. Wilkinson describes epiphenomenal terrorism as that carried out without specific aim, random, and occurring in larger, violent struggles which may include systematic terrorism, although systematic terrorism is not one of his categories. These categories do not come with sorting rules, at least none explicitly stated.

Another approach relies on the communicative aspect of terrorism. Martha Crenshaw uses the categories put forth by Thomas P. Thornton: 1. morale-building, 2. advertising, 3. disorientation, 4. elimination of opposition, and 5. provocative of countermeasures. Crenshaw distinguishes the categories according to their respective target audiences, the desired response, and their degree of discrimination among the assumed revolutionary goals [Schmid and Jongman 1988:50-52].

Building on the work of Ronald D. Crelinston, Alex Schmid and Albert Jongman offer a typology with a communicative orientation couched in a continuum of politics. The continuum ranges from a state of peace to a state of war. The state of peace has conventional politics with routinized rule of law legitimizing governance and opposition. The next stage on the continuum they call unconventional politics with an oppressive state apparatus using electoral manipulation, censorship, surveillance, and so on. An opposition uses nonviolent social protest, civil disobedience, non-cooperation, and the like. Violent politics is penultimate to a state of war. The state uses political imprisonment, assassination, torture, death squads, massacres, and ethnocide. The opposition uses many of the same methods along with material destruction, guerrilla warfare, and general insurgency. Among the tools of the opposition is terrorism, which they describe as "de-individuated political murder" [Schmid and Jongman 1988:58-59].

Jonathan R. White also used the continuum approach to typology, but he has since modified it. Both his efforts follow. The first puts terrorism on a spectrum of conflict. White conceives of terrorism as a form of violent civil disobedience. One end of the continuum envisions a society governed by, as White puts it, "norms, mores, and taboos" [White 2003:13], which probably assumes a non-state level of political organization. Civil law and then criminal law appear next on the continuum. A seemingly qualitative break occurs next, because he lists crime, organized crime, then disorders and riots. Terrorism is in the middle of the continuum. It is followed by guerrilla war, low-level war, and limited conventional war. The last three steps on the continuum move from unlimited conventional warfare, to selective mass destruction, and finally mass destruction. More concretely, the last stage is the nuclear holocaust so long anticipated as the outcome of the confrontation between the US and USSR in the latter part of the twentieth century.

At first blush, White's categorical continuum appears as a continuum of force. At the end of simple societies, coercion takes the form of social disapproval without mechanisms for physical control. Somewhere in the civil law to criminal law transition, force and violence appear in society's armamentarium. Then, forceful resistance to social control appears in the form of crime. One wonders how criminal law and crime can be separated, but that is another analysis. Disorders and riots seem out of place. They involve mass violence, but of a relatively unorganized kind. Unfortunately, they cannot go anywhere else on the continuum. The problem lies in a shift of categorical criteria, apparently, from degrees of force or violence to degrees of organization. The same problem crops up one step back in the movement from crime to organized crime, but there it is the reverse. As crime becomes more organized, it assumes a lower level of obedience. When it comes to mass action, less organization means more violence. The level of organization once again reverses in the movement from terrorism to increasingly complex kinds of warfare. Global nuclear war requires a high level of organization, at least until the warheads hit their mark. Then, as White observes, it is a war of "oblivion" [White 2003:13].

Problems with shifting criteria aside, White's continuum of terrorism categories holds out the possibility of fruitful development. First, it implies different kinds of human conflict at different levels of social organization and differential complexity of relationships. These should be distinguished to a degree. All societies exhibit ranges of complexity in relationships, but some kinds of relationships—for instance; those found in bureaucracies— require relatively complex societies to sustain them. Later in this paper I argue that terrorism is possible in every social relation at every level of social organization.

The second fruitful aspect of White's typology comes from its basis in kinds of coercion. Terrorism has three essential elements: intent, fear, and control. White's typology reflects the last.

Finally, White's typology offers a continuum. Other typologies have structures more like boxes; White's implies dynamism. Nonetheless, the continuum is misplaced. A main purpose, possibly the only justification, for typologies is sorting. Continua have indistinct boundaries. Typologies should have boundaries as sharp as possible. Instead of using continua for categorization, they should apply to dimensions, facets, or major variables of phenomena. I will use continua in my dimensional analysis below.

In a more recent revision, White regresses in typology formation. In the fifth edition of his book, he treats his "spectrum of conflict," as he calls his continuum, separately from his typology [White 2006:232-233]. His more recent typology consists of four categories: cyberterrorism, suicide terrorism, biological weapons of mass destruction, and chemical and nuclear weapons of mass destruction [White 2006 82-96]. He converts a potentially fruitful approach to a dead end by classifying terrorism according to techniques. Since terrorism is itself a technique of managing human relations, he has merely subdivided the phenomenon in a way that admits of potentially endless additions.

Proposed Typology

People often create fear in others, from mild to intense, and they often frighten others inadvertently. One who walks into a room where someone else expects to be alone startles the other person. While hardly qualifying as terror, startling another person lies at one end of a continuum of intensity of fear. A near miss auto accident produces a greater response, and so on along a continuum that because of its idiosyncratic, intrapsychic nature does not easily permit objective measure outside psychological laboratories. Terrorists frighten others purposefully and repeatedly. That is terrorism, the repeated resort to inducing fear to control others in some way.

I propose four types of terrorism.

- Anomic
- Disruptive
- Entrepreneurial
- Repressive

The sorting rule is social relational and situational. Anomic terrorism occurs in anomic social situations where fear governs many social interactions, a kind of Hobbesian state of nature. Disruptive terrorism appears in settled social conditions, and the terrorism disrupts institutions. Terror for profit characterizes entrepreneurial terrorism, with extortion rackets as the paradigm. Repressive terrorism commonly takes the form of state repression, although it is not limited to states as the terrorist, as people in other kinds of social organizations seek control through repressive terror.

Conditions of anomie or normlessness, following Emile Durkheim [1966:241-276], or crises of deligitimation according to Max Weber [1964:124-132] often generate terrorism. Civil wars, especially protracted ones, generate anomic terrorism such as that found in Iraq since the US invasion, Somalia, the Sudan, Colombia, and so on.

Those who object to a social order sometimes resort to terrorism to upset that order, hence disruptive terrorism. Usually, but not always, rebels turn to terrorism after trying various other methods for social change.

There might seem to be a political bias in these first two types of terrorism—the first reflecting a failed or collapsing state and the second implying revolutionary or insurgent conditions. While such politics might generate the most publicity, these types of terrorism need not assume political situations. Any level of social order can fall into relative anomie from families or households to giant corporations or ethnic or nationality groups. The same applies to disruptive terrorism. The typology does not assume a political order.

The old Sicilian Black Hand presents the paradigm of entrepreneurial terrorism. In the United States the Black Hand operated in Little Italies such as the lower east side of Manhattan where extortion racketeers threatened recent immigrants unless they paid [Nelli 1976]. Even so, traditional gangsters are not the only ones who practice entrepreneurial terrorism. Consider sweat shop factories in the Third and Fourth World. They rely on terror to discipline workers and ensure they do not unionize. Armed guards and razor wire mark these factories where workers are terrorized in ways not dissimilar from the Nazi work camps. Discrete factories are not necessary, as Nancy Scheper-Hughes [1992] describes sugar-producing, Northeast Brazil as a vast concentration camp for thirty million people. International neoliberalism through the agencies such as the International Monetary Fund and World Bank has generated much entrepreneurial terrorism.

Granted, distinguishing repressive from entrepreneurial terrorism can present difficulties as the examples mentioned above imply [e.g., van der Pilj et al. 2004]. What differentiates controlling people through fear for profit and using fear simply for the sake of ensuring they do not dissent or resist? The analyst has to gauge the overall situation. It is more a matter of emphasis than a sharp distinction. Entrepreneurial terrorism has a mainly economic motive, while politics motivates repressive terrorism. Given the dominance of capitalism as the pervasive world system [Wallerstein 1974, 1976, 2004], differentiating politics from economy depends on the judgment of the analyst. Moreover, the same terrorist phenomenon can fit into either category depending on the perspective of the study. The Andean cocaine business merges with governmental and elite struggles against insurgents. When, for instance, the Peruvian army terrorizes peasants in the Huallaga Valley [Margallanes 2003], they may do it at one time mainly for profit, and later to maintain political control. Not all situations are so difficult. The patriarch of a family who terrorizes his wife and children practices repressive terrorism, although he may have some economic motives.

Terroristic phenomena take different forms, and these admit of categorization. They do not sort into different kinds or types of terrorism, and therefore they do not strictly speaking constitute a typology. Nonetheless, forms of terrorism offer another perspective to help bring order to the field.

Forms of Terrorism

A difficulty in defining terrorism reappears when it comes to discussing its forms. Some analysts prefer to make violence definitive, but not all forms of terrorism take violent form, unless one uses a very broad definition of violence. Using violence broadly can conflate it with aggression and other phenomena better kept distinct. A special problem with terrorism concerns acts designed to damage things while not harming or threatening to harm people. For example, insurgents may blow up statues. If done with care, the attack does not threaten persons directly. Attacks on things that do threaten harm to people differ in important ways. For instance, a bombing attack on a water supply, electrical equipment, or similar essential infrastructure can pose immediate threats to health and life. But statues are not life sustaining. Statue bombing and similar acts are better understood as symbolic terrorism. The forms are as follows.

- Assassinations
- Blackmail
- Economic
- Indiscriminate weapons
- Jailing

- Symbolic
- Torture

Assassinations are murders of individuals who are usually prominent. Occasionally assassins target people who are not prominent but who hold essential roles. Terrorists using blackmail rely on the fear of exposure, targeting individuals, groups, or organizations. Economic terrorism puts stress on targets through economic means. Indiscriminate weapons include bombs and other devices of mass violence. Jailing includes all forms of deprivation of liberty through the use of physical restraint, including kidnapping. Symbolic terrorism uses attacks on or through symbols. Torture can be physical or psychological.

Assassinations gained prominence in the late nineteenth and early twentieth century. In Russia the Zemlya i Volya (Land and Freedom), succeeded by the Narodnaya Volya (People's Will), began an assassination campaign in the late 1870s. It culminated in the 1881 assassination of Tsar Alexander II. They explained their action in their program of 1879.

> Terroristic activity, consisting in destroying the most harmful person in the government, in defending the party against espionage, in punishing the perpetrators of the notable cases of violence and arbitrariness on the part of the government and the administration, aims to undermine the prestige of the government's power, to demonstrate steadily the possibility of struggle against the government, to arouse in this manner the revolutionary spirit of the people and their confidence in the success of the cause, and finally, to give shape and direction to the forces fit and trained to carry on the fight [Hardman 1936 vol. 14:578].

The stated aim of undermining the prestige of government power makes assassinations like that of Alexander II into terrorism. If governmental prestige depends, at least in part, on the power to control the populace it governs, then demonstrations of failures of control terrify government officials and their supporters. So Narodnaya Volya appears to reason. On the other hand, assassinations need not necessarily aim at terrifying. They can have more pragmatic ends. By removing a crucial person a government or other organization might collapse. US attempts to assassinate Fidel Castro could fit into this more pragmatic assassination. The issue of pragmatism versus communicative effects varies within terrorist phenomena, and it is taken up later in this article. Terrorists use assassination in all types of terrorism—anomic, disruptive, entrepreneurial, and repressive. Narodnaya Volya used terrorist assassination for disruption, but the form occurs in all types.

Blackmail is a form of terrorism occurring in a wide variety of social situations and all types of terrorism. Economic terrorism ranges from sabotage to trade embargoes, and it too can be part of any type of terrorism. Jailing refers to deprivation of liberty. Liberty of movement is crucial to human freedom. Its deprivation, therefore, threatens a human essential, and so terrifies. State imprisonment and kidnapping both fit into this form of terrorism.

Using indiscriminate weapons such as bombs may be the most stereotypical form of terrorism. Indiscriminate weapons make anyone a victim. They make death, injury, and illness unpredictable, and therefore more frightening.

Torture presents something of a special case of terrorism. Torture serves several purposes. Christopher Tindale [1996] identifies a torture typology. Interrogational torture aims to extract information. Deterrent torture discourages (or encourages) a population regarding certain activities. Dehumanizing torture changes the victim's self-conception. For this last type, dehumanizing torture, Tindale adverts to Bruno Bettleheim [1979] and Primo Levi [1988], and their descriptions of the Nazi camps during the Second World War. Tindale explains that the purpose of dehumanizing torture is to "break people as individuals and change them into docile masses" [Tindale 1996:351]. His conception brings to mind the torture described in George Orwell's *1984*. Elaine Scarry notes that torture's goal is betrayal as the torturer has "... a covert disdain for confession." Therefore, confession is not the goal, as "The nature of confession is falsified ... one betrays oneself and all those aspects of the world—friend, family, country, cause—that the self is made up of" [Scarry 1985:29].

Perhaps a fourth type, or possibly a combinatory category is what Daniel Rothenberg calls "public presentational torture," which he says is a form of state terrorism [Rothenberg, 2003]. His illustrative case is Guatemala, where a thirty-six year history of internal armed conflict is called *La Violencia*. He couches the history in the Cold War and severe domestic inequity. Guatemala is one of the better known targets of CIA intervention beginning with the regime change of President Arbenz in 1954.[2] A tactic of state forces was to leave mutilated corpses in public places.

> Counter-insurgency strategies, including the "the appearance of corpses bearing signs of torture" defined a situation of brutal intimidation and overwhelming violence: "the horror was so massive and so flagrant that it defied the imagination." The Guatemalan state's reliance on institutionalized human rights violations became the central mechanism of daily rule... .
>   . . .
> [T]orture defines the most primary component of an individual—his or her body—as a site for state action. This is done against the will of the individual and in a manner that deprives him/her of the most basic respect for autonomy, freedom, and self-protection ... torture turns responsible government on its head. . .the state is transformed from being the key guarantor of social stability to an agent of intimate brutality [p. 482].

These displays left ambiguous whether the person had been tortured or the body mutilated after death to suggest torture. In cases of actual torture, the torturers might have sought information from the victim, but not necessarily. As Elizabeth Stanley [2004:13] says regarding another regime supported by the United States, Chile under Pinochet,

> Despite the common idea that torture is used solely as a means to extract information, Chilean torturers often knew all about their victims' lives and used torture as a way to demonstrate the 'all-seeing-eye' and the power of the state. Officials engaged in torture to demonstrate to the victim and associates that *they* are watching, that *they* are in charge and can act at will.

Torture, as a form of terrorism, controls through fear. Terrorists who use torture achieve mass effects when the torture is publicized, even when the publicity appears accidental or against the interests of the torturer. Torture, as is true of all the other forms of terrorism, can appear in any type terrorism. Its communicative value does not lie in the size of the audience, as the victim may be the sole recipient of the message. Torturers sometimes torture before a small audience. It may include the torturers' superiors where the torturer is a low level functionary. Another kind of audience includes the victim's intimates—spouses, lovers,

---

[2] Jacobo Arbenz Guzman (1913-1971) served as president 1951-1954 through Guatemala's first ever universal suffrage election. United Fruit enlisted the assistance of the CIA, which initiated Operation PBFORTUNE. Later, the US supported a line of dictators by, *inter alia*, training police in counter insurgency and torture techniques at the School of the Americas.

parents, children, and the like. Mass audiences usually learn of the torture indirectly. Torture highlights an important fact of terrorism. Communication is essential to the phenomenon.

Symbolic Terrorism

Symbolic terrorism emphasizes this characteristic even more fully, and symbolic terrorism presents a more complex challenge for analysis. Only humans terrorize, and only humans can be terrorized. That is because, whatever form terrorism takes, and whatever type of terrorism it is, terrorism depends on and is filled with meaning. Other creatures can be terrified, but not terrorized. Terrorism is an exclusively human project.

Symbolic terrorism involves social myth. The myth acts as immunization through which "... a small inoculation of acknowledged evil ... [protects] it against generalized subversion [Barthes 1972:150]. Inoculations of evil become part of social knowledge that enter public discourse and inflect consensus around categories of dissidence and the state's control of them" [Nagengast 1994:120].

Take graffiti. Once a minor form of vandalism, various moral entrepreneurs made graffiti into a national criminal issue in the 1980s. Graffiti became fearsome by its association with urban street gangs. Ostensibly graffiti signified the presence of dangerous gangs, and the graffiti itself became a signal for fear, resulting in policies of eradication and severe criminalization of the unfortunate graffiteristas whom police apprehended [Ferrell 1996]. What made so-called gang graffiti so terrifying was that its symbolism was indecipherable to the uninitiated. The presumed writers of the graffiti could appear anywhere at any time. The graffiti signified a secret cabal of 'others' who could strike without warning [Clymer 2003:189-90]. The kind of moral panic illustrated by the graffiti example points to the fact that the propagators of the terroristic message need not create the symbol of terrorism. Here, the moral entrepreneurs created the terrorism based on the work of graffiti writers who, even when they were gangsters, doubtless had in mind a different audience than ordinary denizens of urban neighborhoods. Gang graffiti communicates with other gangsters, not the general public.

Witchcraft and sorcery offer another variation on symbolic terrorism. They depend for their effectiveness on shared meanings and generalized belief in their efficacy. A number of scholars focused on the phenomenon of so-called 'voodoo death' [Cannon, 1942, Lester, 1972, Lex 1974]. In voodoo death, enactment of rituals using various symbols results in the death or sometimes lesser affliction of the victim. The foregoing scholars addressed the fact that such symbolic manipulation in fact appears to cause death or disease. The phenomenon generated a minor industry because it seems to fly in the face of materialistic science. Incidents of such practices present a form of terrorism with attendant violence, apparently depending entirely on symbols. Other forms include the Ifaluk belief that ghosts are responsible for all immoral behavior among the living [Spiro 1953] and the Hehe use of magic to ensure legitimate devolution of land tenure [Winans and Edgerton 1964].

As E. E. Evans-Pritchard describes it among the Azande [1935], witchcraft causes misfortune—a buffalo gores a man, termites cause a granary to fall on someone's head, or spinal meningitis infects someone. These disasters emanate from persons. The witchcraft makes the misfortunes socially relevant. Identification of bewitchment comes from oracles, which the chiefs control. Witchcraft plays an essential role in the Azande social order. It helps preserve morality, kinship, and political authority [p.422]. Witchcraft functions as social control, and so does punishment for practicing it [Kluckhohn 1944, Nadel 1952]. Recently in the West radical feminist versions represent the witch as "a benevolent 'wise-woman,' a victim of phallogocentric hegemonies," based on mythic reconstructions of the medieval and post-medieval witch-craze in Europe [Sempruch 2004:113].

While all terrorism depends on meaningful symbolic transactions, what makes symbolic terrorism as a form of terrorism distinct from other forms is that it relies on nothing but symbols. Terrorism discourses define those acts that count as terrorism, and therefore the discourses prefigure what counts as appropriate responses. Joseba Zulaika and William A. Douglas explain how the discourses operate.

> Terrorism discourse is characterized by the confusion of sign and context provoked by the deadly atrocity of apparently random acts, the impossibility of discriminating reality from make-believe, and text from reader.
>
> . . .
>
> The discourse's victory, then, derives from imposing a literal frame of "this *is* real war," this *is* global threat," "this *is* total terror."
>
> . . .
>
> Terrorism discourse stems from such play with sign and context, actors and audiences. While it refers to violent events and seeks to interpret them, the text itself is more about threat, ritual bluff, deception, and stratagem. In semiotic terms, the sign of terror may not necessarily refer to something signified, but all the distance between the act and its meaning gets erased in the bombastic context [Zulaika and Williams 1996:29].

Terrorism takes symbolic form when there is no referent for the terrorism discourses, or the discourse and referent do not match. Where the referent is lacking, the phenomenon is Baudrillard's simulacrum [Baudrillard 1994]. In the case of mismatch, mystification and reification obtain. Nowhere is this more apparent than in laws and legal discourses. In those, violent force remains umbral, but as Robert Cover observed, "Legal interpretation takes place in a field of pain and death" [1983:1601]. In the cases of laws and regulations about terrorism, one finds it hard to avoid confusion between discourse and fact, signified and signifier [Saussure 1966/1915], sense and referent.[3]

Terrorists and the laws and security procedures purporting to nab them are but the symbolic forms of state structures of symbolic violence. State symbolic violence uses the forms of law and regulation to inscribe its demands on the bodies of citizens, much as "the apparatus" inscribed the crimes committed by miscreants in Kafka's "Penal Colony" (1961/1919).

Laws and regulations articulate procedures to inscribe forms of obedience on and in bodies. Air travelers and other citizens of the English speaking hegemonic states do not *decide* to comply with the current absurdities. They do not evaluate and judge through some public or even private discourse. Their submission comes from lifetimes of training. In day cares, nursery schools, and kindergartens, children's bodies get used to queuing in lines. Put Americans, Britishers, Canadians, or Australians in front of a gate, and they will form a line without a word said. Compliance is a physical act, all the rest is later rationalization. Drivers, attending to their cell phones or switching CDs, catch a traffic signal turn red out of the corner of their eyes. They slam on the brakes, *without thinking*. When we learn another language or play a musical instrument we strive for fluency or accomplishment by training our bodies to perform automatically. We strive to respond to signs of language or musical notation without thinking, automatically, or as Freud would have it, preconsciously. So the state strives to train the populace.

The intellectualization of bodily conformity finds cognitive schema ready to be filled. Socialization consists first of training, but also mental categories molded by a succession of state apparatuses—families, schools, factories, offices, etc. Moreover, these mental appurtenances reflect the prevailing social structures. Pierre Bourdieu (2000:178) puts it thus.

> For the problem is that, for the most part, the established order is not a problem; outside crisis situations, the question of the legitimacy of the State does not arise. The State does not necessarily need to give orders and to exert physical coercion, or disciplinary constraint, to produce an ordered social world, so long as it is able to produce incorporated cognitive structures attuned to the objective [social] structures and so secure doxic submission to the established order.

Terror laws are the explicit linguistic signs of implicit obedience. Written laws are part of a dialectical process including agents of the state and the apparatuses where they work which inscribe obedience. The red traffic signal that causes inattentive drivers to brake suddenly has volumes of traffic rules behind it. Modern legal codes legitimize state apparatuses and depend on them to enforce the laws, and both rely on habits of obedience from a populace who rationalize their submission by an invented logic of the law. It is a process of *Aufhebung* in which each element depends on the other to continually construct the edifice of the state. Today's terror laws reveal an expansion of state authority, a whole new wing of state control, ostensibly in response to terrorist threats and a crisis of state legitimacy. The laws and legal discourses themselves terrify. There may be potential airplane hijackers, but the more pervasive terrorism is wrought by the state through its discourses. That is what makes the symbolic form of terrorism.

Types and forms of terrorism together yield an overall typology. Types and forms are independent. A given type of terrorism may exhibit any one or even several different forms. For example, one could argue that the terrorism found in Iraq, especially Baghdad in 2007 is of the anomic type, as a multiparty, extensive civil war rages. Examining the many incidents of terrorism there, it would be unsurprising to find assassinations, blackmail, economic terrorism, the use of indiscriminate weapons, jailing both by authorities and kidnapping, symbolic terrorism, and torture. Indeed, the occurrence of many different forms of terrorism may define anomic terrorism. At the same time, any particular form of terrorism does not appear bound to a type. Economic terrorism may be the form entrepreneurial terrorists use, but it can just as easily occur in situations of repressive terrorism such as that found in sweatshop factories in Third and Fourth World countries, and so on with respect to other terrorism types.

---

[3] The distinction between sense and referent relies on Gottlob Frege's discussion using the morning star/evening star versus the planet Venus. Venus is the referent, but morning and evening stars have different senses [Frege 1960].

Typologies help analysts and scholars sort phenomena into categories where they can manipulate them more easily. Another important part of theory building includes the identification of dimensions or major variables associated with the phenomenon under study. Therefore, what follows presents ten main variables or dimensions of terrorism.

Dimensions of Terrorism

In *The Sociological Imagination*, C. Wright Mills [1959] warned of two opposing dangers in conceptualizing. First noting that "A concept is an idea with empirical content" [p.124], Mills went on to say that concepts can be too large for the content or too small. If too large, there is not enough information to support the idea. The danger is excessively abstract theorizing. If too small, the data overwhelm the concept, and obsessive attention to methodological detail results. He called the latter abstracted empiricism. The common problem to both dangers is that of indices, according to Mills. Abstracted empiricists solve it by limiting the scope and meanings of the concept. The law and organs of the state have done it in regard to terrorism. They define terrorism as illegal attacks on the state, and not just any state, but the law making state itself and other states allied with it. The United States as the hegemonic law maker in the world solves the problem of indices in that way.

On the other hand, grand theorizers simply do not confront the problem of indices; they just keep on elaborating the concept in relation to other, equally abstract ideas. Albert Camus expressed his objections. Writing in 1946 in an editorial entitled "The Century of Fear" in the once underground newspaper, *Combat,* Camus explained.

> Our twentieth century is the century of fear.
> . . .
> My view, however, is that rather than blame our fear, we should regard it as a basic element of the situation and try to remedy it.
> . . .
> In order to come to terms with fear, we need to understand what it signifies and what it rejects. It signifies and rejects the same fact: a world in which murder is legitimate and human life is considered futile. … Before we can build anything, we need to ask two questions: "Yes or no, directly or indirectly, do you want to be killed or assaulted? Yes or no, directly or indirectly, do you want to kill or assault? [Camus 2006/1946:257-259].

Camus later elaborated in his 1951 book *The Rebel*, that the grand theories swallowing up the discourses of the time were Communism and Capitalism, capitalized here to emphasize their hegemonic pretensions. These two grand theories offered explanations for the human condition and what should be done about it.

Mills and Camus were contemporaries. They acted within, and reacted to similar vicissitudes in the world. They criticized the same evasions of the main problems of the day. Grand theorists do not address the real lives of real human beings. Abstracted empiricists hide the lives of people in mounds of minutiae, and obsess about methodology. Indices help avoid these twin dangers which spring from modern fears of the twentieth, now turned to the twenty-first century. Ten indices of terrorism may help lay the groundwork for effective theories of terrorism, and ultimately help answer Camus' two questions.

Ten Dimensions of Terrorism

Each of the following is a dimension or main variable in the multifaceted phenomenon of terrorism. They operate independently, and they yield measures for every type and form of terrorism. They have greater or lesser relevance depending on the context of the terroristic phenomena and the goals of study. They are as follows.

1. State
2. Organization
3. Ideology
4. Network
5. Objects
6. Size
7. Proximity
8. Rationality
9. Source
10. Purpose

The state dimension indexes the extent to which terrorism is a function of the state. Terrorism against the state is at one end of this continuum, and terrorism directed by the state is at the other. Often reasonably clear, paramilitary organizations can make measuring this variable a problem. The United Self-Defense Forces (AUC) in Colombia or the loyalist, unionist, Protestant organizations in Northern Ireland like the Ulster Volunteer Force (UDF) and the Ulster Defense Association (UDA) have murky entanglement with their respective governments.

Organization measures the degree or level of organization of terrorists. It ranges from isolated individuals to nation states or even multi-state alliances such as NATO. This dimension addresses organizational complexity and its social structure.

Ideology concerns the degree to which terrorist acts come from ideological motivation. On one end there are completely pragmatic terrorists—for example, neighborhood street gangs that shake down local businesses. At the other extreme one finds terrorists fanatically devoted to some belief system. Aum Shinirikyo, notorious for the gas attack on the Tokyo subway March 20, 1995, illustrates this latter extreme.

Networks refer to the how much terrorists are connected with other terrorists. This runs the gamut from neighborhoods to global networks. The CIA operates globally, and has connections with many other terrorist organizations. Some terrorists have no network connections, such as men who terrorize their wives and children. Of course, this example of domestic abusers may not hold true, as some, at least, may connect with similarly minded individuals through internet chat rooms.

Objects measure the degree to which victims and targets of terrorism coincide. At one end they are the same groups of people; at the other end they are entirely different. The target is the object of influence. It is whom terrorists want to get their message to. The victims are those who suffer the violence. Kidnapping government officials represents an identity of targets and victims where terrorists want to influence the state—for example Aldo Moro in Italy, 1978 [Weinberg and Eubank 1987] or Tupamaro kidnappings in Uruguay in the early

1970s [Gilio 1972, Wilson 1974]. On the other hand, death squad massacres of peasants in Nicaragua [Schroeder 2000], Guatemala [Afflito 2000, Sanford 2004, UN 2002], or El Salvador [Arnson 2000] victimize individuals who are not the main targets of the terror.

Size is that of the object. Targets and victims range from individuals to states or peoples. A mugger instills terror in a lone victim on the street. Genocidal terrorists target peoples, while some terrorists aim at nation states.

Rationality is an index of the closeness of fit between fear and threat. It does not refer to the supposed rationality of the terrorists. For example, in the Salem witch trials there was a poor fit between the threat of witchcraft and the fear it generated. Although, as noted earlier, witchcraft among the Azande constitutes a seamlessly logical system [Evans-Pritchard 1935]. Barry Glassner [1999] describes a number of irrational fears among contemporary Americans. Conversely, denizens of the Nazi concentration camps had perfectly rational fears.

The source dimension measures the distance between the source of the threat and the putative terrorist actor. Currently, the US Department of Homeland Security issues warnings about terrorist attacks, which presumably come from other, usually unknown actors. In contrast, the Irish Republican Army (IRA) often gave warnings of bombs they themselves had planted.

The purposes of terrorism occupy a continuum defined by the expressive and instrumental. Terrorists with expressive purposes seek an emotional end. For example, serial killers and rapists are reputed to be motivated by the emotional release they gain from the fear of their victims. Terrorists with instrumental goals use terrorism to gain some, usually material, advantage—wealth in the case of extortion or political control in the case of death squads.

These ten dimensions offer the kind of indices Mills said that scholars need to avoid the Scylla and Charybdis of grand theorizing and abstracted empiricism. When employed on particular terrorist phenomena they help counteract the siren song of reifications, often promulgated by authorities who have a vested interest in labeling selected individuals, groups, and interests as terrorists.

These ten dimensions are exclusive of one another. They are discrete measures of variables which may correlate for a particular terrorist phenomenon, but they do not conflate them. They also are exhaustive in that they cover all terrorist phenomena. They are not exhaustive in the sense that they are all the possible relevant variables for terrorism. Possible variables important for an instance of terrorism would comprise a potentially infinite set.

These dimensions lend themselves to descriptive theory building. While some theories aim at causal explanation, it is not a definitive requirement for scientific theories. Description and measurement constitute the early stages of theory building in a quest for establishing regularities [Hempel 1958, Northrup 1947]. Moreover, they admit of multidimensional scaling techniques so that terrorism phenomena can be comparatively quantified and mapped [e.g., Greenacre and Blasius 2006].

Another advantage of these variables lies in their application to phenomena that might otherwise be incommensurable. For example, metaphorically and dramatically, at least as found in Arthur Miller's play *The Crucible*, the witch scare in 17th century Salem, Massachusetts found resonance in the anticommunism of the 1950s [Miller 2000]. The extent to which this is a valid comparison could hinge on measuring each of these historically distant phenomena according to the ten foregoing dimensions.

An Application of Dimensional Analysis

The Salem witch trials occurred in a pre-state community. Nonetheless, the citizenry conceived of witchcraft as a threat against the community as a whole, and arguably the dominant factions within it. McCarthyism explicitly identified communism as a threat against the state. In both cases, the threats were reputedly to be organized hierarchically. Satan rules witches; Stalin ruled communists. Both were strongly identified with an express ideology, and both were widely believed to be connected through social networks. In both cases, targets and victims were different. The victims were the ostensible terrorists, witches and communists, or those accused of associating with them. That is, witches and communists were believed to be afflicted, and for both the affliction could be cured through confession first, then various other procedures, all of which depended on the willing cooperation of the formerly afflicted. In both cases, the target was the people at large, those who could be persuaded of the dangerousness of the respective threats of witchcraft and communism. These audiences or targets comprised the entire communities of the respective societies, late seventeenth century New England and mid-twentieth century America. Threats associated with both were supposedly both distant and near. The communist threat was associated with a possible third world war, but at the same time, communism was something that could enter every neighborhood, workplace, or school. The same applied to witchcraft as its ultimate danger lay in damnation, but in Salem witchcraft accusations split families and households.

The next two dimensions, rationality and source, prove the effectiveness of dimensional analysis. With witchcraft and communism, these two dimensions reveal implicit theories and biases. How rational was the fear of witchcraft or communism? After the scientific revolution, which was only just commencing at the time of the Salem witch trials, most scholars would give short shrift to the rationality claims of witchcraft. But keep in mind E. E. Evans-Pritchard's study of Azande witchcraft. He concluded that science and, at least Azande, witchcraft were mutually exclusive systems of thought about which there was no absolute point from which one could judge their truth [Evans-Pritchard 1937, 1965 Winch 1964]. In other words, the rationality of witchcraft claims depends on the analyst's world view. The same can be said of the rationality of the threat of communism. In the roughly half century since the McCarthyism era, views on the rationality of the communist threat have waxed and waned according to the political zeitgeist. Scientific theories have to include explicit disclosure of ideological frameworks, and application of dimensional analysis helps reveal such assumptions.

The dimension measuring the relationship between the source of the terrorism message and the reputed terrorist actor equally reveals much about implicit assumptions. For mid-twentieth century Americans, communists were one of several threats to an idealized way of life. Others included comic books and juvenile delinquents [Gilbert 1986, Glueck & Glueck 1950]. In all cases, it was not the actors, the reputed terrorists, who sought to scare the public. The anticommunist agitators did not claim communists used the threat of communism to produce social change. The threat was supposed to be the social change that communism represented. Communists were presumably dangerous in and of themselves because of what they were doing, not what they wanted to frighten society into doing. So too, the danger of witches derived from what they did as witches, not because fear of them would cause people to give into Satan's demands. In both cases, witchcraft and communism, the source of terror came from accusers, not the objects of accusation.

The final dimension pertains to purpose. Witchcraft hysteria and McCarthyism had both instrumental and expressive ends. The instrumental part had to do with political control and no small measure of concomitant economic advantage. The expressive part of these two historic terrorisms played out in interpersonal relations. Accusations of witchcraft in seventeenth century New England and communism in mid-twentieth century America appeared in interpersonal conflicts as verbal weapons of last resort.

Arthur Miller's intuitive analogy and his artistic representation of it in *The Crucible* seem borne out by the foregoing analysis. A distinctive feature in both historical cases is that the promoters of terror warned against dangers that they described as terrifying. The terrorists of the McCarthyism era were the politicians, capitalists, and capitalist front organizations who created fear of communists. The terrorists in late seventeenth century New England were also moral entrepreneurs [Becker 1963] who manufactured a witch craze out of contemporary bits of cultural lore, an example of *bricolage* [Lévi-Strauss 1966]. As with the capitalists and politicians hundreds of years later, the New England terror promoters stood to gain materially, or at least retain their preeminent position, from the terrorism.

Typology and dimensional framework in hand, students of terrorism can approach building theories about it. So far, terrorism studies have operated with implicit theories or theories about something else masquerading as theories of terrorism. Examples include theories of human psychology, such as frustration-aggression, or theories of political science using the same terms applied to social groups. Theories of terrorism will have to use theories about humankind and its works from other disciplines, but ought not to confuse them with the subject act hand, terrorism.

Theories of Terrorism

Theories of terrorism will be social scientific. They will be theories about humans and what they do to, for, with, and against each other. Social scientific theories must recognize humans as social primates. So much for the social part. The scientific part has more complexity and perhaps more controversy. As one philosopher of science, Mary Hesse, observed over a quarter century ago, the scientificity of knowledge has been changing. The work of, among others, Thomas Kuhn, Paul Feyerabend, W. V. O. Quine, challenges previously held assumptions of science: naïve realism, the possibility of a universal scientific language, and the correspondence theory of truth [Hesse 1980:vii].

Science offers truth claims. Science is one of several human endeavors wherein those who work within it follow certain procedures and do so based on certain unquestionable assumptions. Social scientific theories of terrorism, therefore, must also use the general assumptions of science and rely on the scientific method. To say one uses science means s/he assumes that external reality exists regardless of anyone's awareness of it, humans gain access to that reality through their senses, and that the universe operates according to discoverable regularities. These assumptions underlie all scientific inquiries. Scientific method also displays certain characteristics. First, science relies on a combination of reason and observation working in concert. Second, scientific observers use controls. Third, scientific method aims at objective knowledge. The foregoing assumptions and characteristics distinguish science from other approaches offering truth claims such as religion or the arts.

Scientific theories explain observed phenomena. The explanations also have to use systematic and consistent logic; not haphazard, idiosyncratic, or coincidental. These requirements distinguish science from magic as the latter practices a technology relying on extraordinary logic [Bronowski 1978, Malinowski 1954/1925]. Scientific theories must use not only a consistent logic, but they also must comport with regularities or scientific laws, both those internal to the theory and other well established observational regularities. Certain important regularities for theories of terrorism concern regularities and models of humans and their works. While these regularities may not enter into explicit theoretical statements about terrorism, they constrain all that would strive for social scientific validity.

One such regularity is more in the nature of a model of human nature. Most clearly explicated by Clifford Geertz [1965], this model rejects the uniformitarian view associated with the European Enlightenment. The Enlightenment view held humans of a piece with nature such that all had some core that was the same the world over. Differences in time, place, and circumstance piled on top of this essential core in a sort of layer cake fashion. The Enlightenment model of uniformitarian nature clashes with the regularity that humans are always and everywhere enculturated, else they are not human. Geertz puts it thus.

> Whatever else modern anthropology asserts—and it seems to have asserted almost everything at one time or another—it is firm in the conviction that men unmodified by the customs of particular places do not in fact exist, have never existed, and most important, could not in the very nature of the case exist [1965:96].

Two important implications follow. First, the Cartesian mind-body dualism disappears. Second, reductive explanations of humankind and what it does into chemical, biological, or other similar explanations run afoul of having no empirical referents, as simply physical humans do not exist. "We are, in sum, incomplete or unfinished animals who complete or finish ourselves through culture ..." [Geertz 1965:112-113], particular cultures we ourselves create. "Our ideas, our values, our acts, even our emotions, are, like our nervous system itself, cultural products ... " [p.114]. The chemistry, biology, psychology, sociology, and culture of humans does not resemble a layer cake, but a multidimensional process in which all these natures interact producing not things, but dynamic and semi-open systems.

The foregoing dynamic, non-uniform model of humanity does not, however, negate the psychic unity of humankind. Just as all humans have the innate capacity for speech, but individual humans speak particular languages, so all have the capacity for thought, reason and observation, but the particulars vary as much as languages. We are not bound by that language or those languages we first learned; humans can and do learn other languages. Humans do not have an essential character, but we share a common heritage and therefore share common capacities, among which are those permitting learning foreign cultures and thereby gaining empathy. Simply stated, we can understand each other, because we are human. As Harry Stack Sullivan said, we are all more human than anything else.

Furthermore, the dynamic, open system model means that all human endeavors—beliefs, institutions, practices, and so on—share the same characteristic dynamism. Human works are recursive and reflexive. All human products operate dialectically with positive and negative feedback producing an ever changing social, cultural, and historical landscape. Therefore, objective knowledge of human products cannot assume fixity of its object. Physicists discovered the Heisenberg uncertainty principle in which the act of observation limited what they could describe about sub-atomic particles. Social scientists face a vastly more complicated problem in that the very nature of what they study constantly changes, not just by the fact of their study of it, but other ongoing forces, which they cannot control.

One consequence of the dialectics of social science severely limits certain approaches to the study of terrorism, but opens many others. The psychology of terrorists, for instance, has limited generalizability. On the other hand, studies of the communicability of terror have wide applicability.

Causal Explanations in Scientific Theories

Theories are nothing if not explanations. Much philosophizing about science assumes a necessary convergence of explanation and truth. Theories about planetary motion, for example, explain how the planets move if and only if the explanations are true—that is accurate. In this view, theories have truth value measured by the accuracy of prediction and/or postdiction. The postdiction alternative gains importance, because some sciences cannot predict, such as evolutionary biology. In this view explanations need not answer why questions, but they must answer how questions, and answer them in ways allowing for pre/post-diction.

This viewpoint hinges on a correspondence theory of truth. That is, statements about reality have to truly represent it. Alfred Tsarki's shorthand exemplar illustrates: 'snow is white' is true if and only if snow is white [1956/1933]. A problem arises when one begins to treat unobservables. In physics electrons present a problem; in the social sciences abstractions such as agriculture offer similar difficulties. Explanation in both cases has an epistemic meaning. Explanations using electrons cannot correspond to observable reality, and hence cannot be true according to the correspondence theory. Epistemic explanations require no such correspondence, because they function to order experience. Without electrons, explanations in physics languish; without agriculture, social explanations could not get very far.

The philosopher of science Carl Hempel expressed the epistemic position for explanations by setting up two categories. One he called deductive-nomological (DN), and the other inductive-statistical (IS). For the DN type, "The explanation ... may be regarded as an argument to the effect that the phenomenon to be explained ... was to be expected in virtue of certain explanatory facts. These fall into two groups: (i) particular facts and (ii) uniformities expressible by means of general laws" [Hempel 1965:336]. For IS type explanations the generalizations are statistical rather than uniform. IS explanations make scientific explanations a matter of probabilistic determinism. In both cases, explanations take the form of covering laws.

Two main problems reside in the covering law model. First, it makes no distinction between regularities and causes. Regularities often take the form of correlations. The example Hempel uses for IS explanations pertains to the therapeutic effectiveness of penicillin for treating streptococcus infections. Penicillin does not cure all patients, but it does cure a statistically significant portion to support penicillin's effectiveness [Hempel 1965:385]. Part of the difficulty in IS explanations in the social sciences pertains to control.

Control remains close to impossible in most social scientific research. First, ethical issues forbid the kind of control needed to ensure the kind of laboratory conditions physicists, chemists, and some biologists expect. Second, the objects under study, human beings, manipulate their environment almost always cooperatively so any attempt to apply controlled environment faces enormous obstacles. Finally, even when a degree of control obtains, generalizability declines. Social psychological laboratory experiments remain notorious in this regard. Social scientists have to deal with history and social dynamics, neither of which stands still.

Since the social sciences cannot use experimental methods very often, correlations come relatively early in stages of inquiry, long before explanations, causal or otherwise. Therefore, a goodly part of social scientific analysis consists of detecting spurious correlations. In sum, most correlations in the social sciences do not even approach law-like status.

The second, perhaps more serious problem, concerns the form of covering law explanations. They do not explain. They only describe. That may do for the behavior of electrons, but when it comes to more complex systems, especially human social systems, the explanatory goal goes beyond description. Social scientists want more than regularities, they seek explanatory force. Immediately, they confront the problem of levels of abstraction.

The problem of levels of abstraction operates in two seemingly opposite ways. On the one hand, different explanations can be equally valid, or invalid, at different levels of abstraction—for example, intrapsychic, interpersonal, intra-group, inter-group, within societies, or between societies. At the same time, the phenomenon to be explained, violence for instance, may share the same structure at all levels of abstraction. If social theories aim at complete explanation, they have to transcend the apparent contradiction.

To complicate matters further, there is the problem of morphogenesis. Briefly, morphogenesis refers to the replication of patterns at different levels of organization. Fractals show how morphogenesis applies to physical form. Fractals replicate the same structural pattern at any level of observation. A standard example is the coast of Maine. It looks jagged on a map. If one goes to the Maine coast, and scans the coast line, it looks jagged. If one sits down and examines, say, a foot long portion, it looks jagged, and so on. The fractal problem applies as well to social structures. International violent conflicts structurally resemble conflicts between individuals within those nations party to the conflict.

Morphogenesis admits of application in the social sciences. Marx analyzed capitalism as a system of political economy. Today it encompasses virtually all nations and societies. It is the dominant world system [Wallerstein 1976]. Patterns of capitalist relationships and transactions organize phenomena at all levels from the intrapsychic [Kovel 1981, Simmel 1950] to the transnational [Bartolovich 2002].

Given the problems of levels of abstraction and morphogenesis, what constitutes a complete explanation? Begin with causation. Hempel's covering law approach applies regularities to specific occurrences. A bullet is fired from a gun, and traces an arc until it falls to the ground. Laws of physics explain its movement and path. The laws are the necessary causes of the phenomenon. The efficient cause is the occurrence of firing the gun. This would be one of Hempel's DN explanations. His example of an IS explanation uses penicillin. Instead of his penicillin example, go back a step to patients' coming down with a streptococcus infection. How does one explain the clinical phenomenon of disease?

Freud [1974/1895] grappled with the problem with respect to neuroses, but his solution applies to human behavior more generally. He put forth a four-fold model including preconditions, specific cause, concurrent, and precipitating causes. Preconditions are equivalent to necessary causes; the specific cause is equivalent to the sufficient. Concurrent causes are those that accompany the specific cause and may condition it, but are not sufficient in and of themselves to produce the effect. Precipitating causes are those final events directly preceding the effect, but which cannot explain it. For instance, the assassination of Archduke Ferdinand precipitated the First World War, but most historians catalog far more complex, layered, and longstanding causes for the conflict. In many cases in the social sciences, there is no identifiable specific cause. There are only multiple co-occurring causes, all of which contribute to the effect, and some or all of which affect each other. In most cases multiple causation reigns in the social sciences; single, specific causes are rare. Real events among humans are over determined.

To explain why a match burst into flame, there are certain necessary conditions such as an oxidant, fuel in the match head, and heat. The oxidant is supplied by oxygen in the air. The fuel is the chemical compound in the match head, and heat is supplied by friction. These are necessary and sufficient conditions to explain the match flame in the abstract world of chemistry and physics. They are woefully inadequate to explain why Paul Henreid struck a match to light the two cigarettes in his mouth, handing one lit cigarette to Bette Davis in the famous scene in the 1942 movie *Now, Voyager*.

Another, broader example is Michael Stohl's [1976] study of war and domestic political violence. He found correlations between US foreign wars and political violence at home. As preliminaries, Stohl discussed several kinds of theories. He asks four questions [12-13]:

1.   What is the model of the political system?
2.   What are the types of conflict, conflict behavior, aggression, and violence?
3.   How and why would conflict, aggression, or violence occur?
4.   What are the parameters of the explanations offered, and to what types of systems and to what levels of analysis are they applicable?

He goes on to contrast Georg Simmel's notion of conflict with that of Franz Fanon. Simmel [1955:92-93] says conflict pulls groups together so tightly that they must either get along or fight one another. Fanon [1963:93] says native violent resistance against the settler population not only pulls particular colonized peoples together, but links them with anti-imperialist struggles so as to create a nation. Stohl then notes that Simmel and Fanon are referring to different aspects; Simmel to the situation and Fanon to the violent act [Stohl 1976:17]. He goes on to contrast both Simmel and Fanon with the frustration-aggression hypothesis put forth by various authors. Stohl criticizes frustration-aggression on two grounds. First, the hypothesis assumes that people at the bottom of a social hierarchy are the ones who use violence, when in fact leaders of the state use violence most frequently and prevalently. His second objection pertains to the level of abstraction embedded in the hypothesis—namely psychologistic. That is, the hypothesis assumes political violence erupts because of something about human psychology, frustration-aggression, and not as something arising from group relations (Simmel) or relations between social strata (Fanon).

Causation in the Social Sciences

Much of the problem with the covering law model of explanation comes from Hempel's project. It was to examine the logic of explanation in science. Physics was his model. Yet, as Bertrand Russell points out, physics gave up looking for causes, because it does not recognize causation. Rather, the laws of physics express functional relationships of events within specified time frames [Russell 1993/1913]. The logic of causation has to confront what Russell [1960/1910], along with Alfred North Whitehead, termed 'logical types' [Whitehead and Russell 1960/1913]. Logical typing, or levels of abstraction, deals with how paradoxes bedevil logic. Consider two: Zeno's paradox of Achilles and the tortoise, and Epimenides of lying Cretans. In Zeno's paradox, Achilles can never overtake the tortoise in a race where the tortoise has a head start, because he first has to traverse half the distance between them, then half that distance, and so on *ad infinitum*. The lying Cretans are problematic when a Cretan makes the assertion that all Cretans lie. A few moments thought by almost anyone results in solutions to the paradoxes, but only by transcending the formal logical system of the situation as given. In other words, people regularly shift from one logical type to another, one level of abstraction to another. The problem Hempel faced is that logic cannot model causal systems [Bateson 1979: 125].

C. Wright Mills [1959] maintained that any social study must explain biography, history, and their intersections in society. He elaborated with three questions. 1. What is the structure of a particular society? 2. Where does it stand in human history? 3. What varieties of people prevail in a particular society at a particular period? Answering these questions requires multiple levels of abstraction. With multiple levels of abstraction analysts must be punctilious about keeping track of units of analysis. Biological evolution offers a useful example.

In the mid-1930s Theodosius Dobzhansky, Ernst Mayer, and others solved a basic conundrum of Darwin's natural selection theory of speciation. The problem had been how to reconcile Darwin's natural selection with genetics, all the while recognizing that individual creatures carry, transmit, and express biological characteristics. Dobzhansky et al. solved it by identifying the correct unit of analysis. They showed that the force of natural selection operates on populations, not on genes, traits, or individuals.

Moving from living creatures as a whole to humankind, even more levels of abstraction come into play, and they interact, as Geertz points out. This means that humans not only carry, transmit, and express biological characteristics, but they do the same with cultural characteristics, which interact with those of biology [Dobzhansky 1951:308]. Therefore, social scientific inquiries aspiring to explanations must use multiple levels of abstraction while specifying the appropriate unit of analysis for the question or problem at hand. Accomplishing this feat needs four different kinds of explanation.

Gupreet Mahajan [1997] makes the argument for four kinds of explanation. The first kind is causal, but he points out that "... the notion of cause most appropriate for the social sciences is one that undermines the very ground on which causal explanations are frequently privileged and justified" [p. 25]. Quoting Michael Scriven [1964:409], Mahajan says that " ... there are virtually no known sufficient conditions [in social science], since human or accidental interference is almost inexhaustibly ... ." Furthermore social scientific explanation does not merely asked what *c* caused or will cause *e*; social scientists ask how and why things happen. Moreover, the crucial questions in social science often take the form of what happened, such as, 'What was the Industrial Revolution?' [Mahajan 1997:26 citing Dray 1970:156-169].

Social science explanations use not just covering laws but three additional kinds of explanation. In addition to causal explanations, there are reason-action, hermeneutic, and narrative.

Reason-action explanations focus on actors. They try to give objective reasons for why people act within a context of social forces. Reason-action explanations bring together objective covering laws of the social sciences with the recognition that history proceeds not by the abstract laws of social structures alone, but also by individuals taking certain courses of action. It brings human agency back into the causal equation.

Hermeneutic explanations also recognize human agency, but pay less attention to objective laws. Instead, they focus on the agents' world views. Hermeneutic explanations are those that try to discern the world the way the actors experience it. In effect, they put the researchers in the shoes of those whom they study, though not subjectively. They aim for objective pictures of historically particular world views [Bauman 1978].

The fourth kind of explanation, narrative, offers yet another method of accounting for things. Narrative explanations explain events in their specificity. For example, they can give the story of the beginning of the First World War as they recount the way events unfolded for the main actors. This helps researchers understand why the leaders of the great powers of Europe pushed their countries into war in 1914. Narrative explanations bridge the divide between *Verstehen* and *Erklärer*, between understanding and explanation in the narrower, causal sense. Narrative adds a dimension to deterministic explanations that underscores alternatives. Researchers use narrative to understand why actors chose particular paths when other paths were possible.

Theorists of terrorism should avail themselves of all four explanatory approaches. They might combine more than one, or perhaps all four in a single theory. Mainly, they should use those most appropriate to the kind of theory they want to construct. What follows are some promising approaches to theory-building.

Approaches to Theories of Terrorism

One promising approach combines chaos/catastrophe theory with world system analysis. Using these frameworks, terrorism functions as an attractor. As an attractor, it can destabilize stable systems and stabilize chaotic systems. Chaos theory is a shorthand, popularized term for non-linear dynamical systems. Derived from general systems theory [Bertalanffy 1968], it describes open systems. Open systems are those systems that are not completely deterministic—i.e., every state of the system cannot be derived from a fixed set of initial conditions, which is typical of nature. A kind of open system are autopoetic, which generally prevail in living creatures [Miller 1978], and they are especially characteristic of social systems. Autopoiesis literally means "self-reproduction," and expresses a fundamental complementarity between structure and function. More precisely, the term refers to the dynamics of non-equilibrium structures of organized systems such as dissipative structures, typical of natural, physical systems. Such structures remain stable for long periods of time despite matter and energy continually flowing through them. Mammals, for example, show especially complex kinds of autopoetic systems commonly referred to as homoeostasis.

Attractors affect the long-term behavior of such dynamical systems. Steady state, or equilibrium, behavior corresponds to fixed-point attractors, in which all trajectories starting from the appropriate basin-of-attraction eventually converge onto a single point. For linear dissipative dynamical systems, fixed point attractors are the only possible type of attractor. Nonlinear systems, on the other hand, harbor a spectrum of attractor types. In addition to fixed-points, periodic attractors limit cycles. There is also a class of attractors called chaotic or Lorenz [1963] attractors that have a complicated geometric structure as displayed by fractals.

Treating terrorism as a kind of attractor in the system of world capitalism yields certain insights about both terrorism and the historical developments of the capitalist system, which has been developing since about 1500. For example, the terror of the French Revolution marked a transition in the world system from one equilibrium to another. The same applies to terrorism surrounding the Russian Revolution of the first decades of the twentieth century. One should keep in mind that neither French nor Russian terrorism confined itself to Burke's so-called 'reign of terror," nor in the Russian case, the acts by the Bolshevik Cheka[4] [Mayer 2000]. In general this approach to theorizing yields the following pattern. Where terrorism becomes a focus of public attention, a change in equilibrium state is in process. As should be readily apparent, the predicted pattern applies to the terrorism of the turn of the twenty-first century.

Immanuel Wallerstein [2003] argues that major revolutions such as the French and Russian may have marked transitions in the history of world political economy, but they did not revolutionize it. These revolutions were not as revolutionary as they portended, because the dominant world system of capitalism remained vibrant. In terms of chaos theory, the revolutions were chaotic, but not explosively so, where explosive bifurcations of stable trends begin a new system [Abraham and Shaw 1992]. Wallerstein further suggests that the system currently approaches senescence. Therefore, terrorism will not only remain significant, but it will grow in significance in the coming decade. Accordingly, the world is entering a state of chaos in which chaotic attractors can mold the nature of the next world system. Of particular importance is that such chaotic attractors may appear as minor perturbations. An oft used example is that of the butterfly in Argentina whose flapping wings produce a hurricane in the south Pacific.

Added to Wallerstein's prediction, I propose that another transition in systems has been underway since about the middle of the twentieth century, which has involved signification. Eric Havelock [1983] has argued that the ancient Greeks transformed the form of signification from Mythos to Logos between the seventh and fifth centuries B.C.E. Mythos assumed a mainly oral culture, and Logos a written one. The oral culture of the ancient Greeks and other ancient peoples relied on presence and performance as the main communicative milieu. Zainab Bahrani [2003] offers a confirming viewpoint, although she does not refer to Havelock, in her discussion of representation in Assyro-Babylonian culture. Although these near eastern societies used writing long before the Greeks developed their

---

[4] Soon after the Bolsheviks formed a government on 7 November 1917, they set up Cheka (later GPU), or the Extraordinary Commission to Combat Counter-Revolution. This evolved into the secret police of the USSR, and in many ways mirrored similar organizations under the Tsarist regime.

phonetic alphabet, their culture also relied on presence and performance. Bahrani asserts that the inscriptions and the monumental architecture on which they are found, especially statues of rulers, did not just represent those personages, but conveyed their actual presence. Those who gazed upon the stelai of, for example Assurnasirpal, experienced his actual presence, *supra* note1.

The Greek revolution in signification and culture made writing the dominant form of signification. More durable and far more condensed than performance, writing reigned until about the middle of the twentieth century. Since then, signification has increasingly relied on icons. Icons appear in many different contexts, but television and computers are those most familiar. Whether they are more durable than writing is debatable, but they continue the trend toward greater condensation, as in the adage that a picture is worth a thousand words. More interesting, are computer icons that can signify many megabytes of information. The chronology runs from the ancients to about 500 B.C.E. dominated by Mythos, then from 500 B. C. E. to 1950 with Logos, and since 1950, Iconos.

Semiotics as a Framework for Theory Construction

Especially in light of the revolution in signification, another interesting approach to constructing a theory of terrorism uses semiotics. Here, semiotics refers to ideas developed by Charles Sanders Peirce [1960] around the turn of the twentieth century. Semiotics should be distinguished from the contemporary semiology of Ferdinand de Saussure [1966/1915], which most recent continental thinkers use. Valentine Nikolaevič Vološinov [1973] made unwitting use of Peircean semiotics when he worked on a Marxian theory of linguistics.

Semiotics emphasizes the communicative aspect of terrorism. Of course all communication occurs within a prevailing ideology. This is Vološinov's point. Vološinov equates ideology with signs, noting both are material: "Consciousness takes shape and being in the material of signs created by an organized group in the process of its social intercourse. . .The logic of consciousness is the logic of ideological communication, of the semiotic interaction of a social group" 1973:13]. Further, he shows the confluence of ideology and individual minds, or psyche. "The ideological sign is the common territory for both the psyche and for ideology... . Therefore, *from the standpoint of content, there is no basic division between the psyche and ideology: the difference is one of degree only*"[p.33] The dialectical quality of signs is especially apropos for a discussion of the meanings of terrorism, inasmuch as a commonplace truism is that one person's terrorist is another's freedom fighter. Vološinov captures the problematic.

> In actual fact, each living ideological sign has two faces, like Janus. Any current critical word can become a word of praise, any current truth must inevitably sound to many other people as the greatest lie. This *inner dialectic quality* [sic] of the sign comes out fully in the open only in times of social crises or revolutionary changes. In the ordinary conditions of life, the contradiction embedded in every ideological sign cannot emerge fully because the ideological sign in an established, dominant ideology is always somewhat reactionary, as it were, to stabilize the preceding factoring the dialectical flux of the social generative process, so accentuating yesterday's truth as to make it appear today's. And that is what is responsible for the refracting and distorting peculiarity of the ideological sign within the dominant ideology [pp.23-24].

Murray Edelman particularizes the preceding analysis, and applies it to contemporary politics. Relying on the sociological tradition of the construction of social problems, Edelman argues that proposals to solve problems accomplish two goals. First, they can change attitudes and behavior of individuals. Second, they are "...expressions of the same power structure that created the problems itself" Edelman 1988:27].

The attack of September 11, 2001 has become a paradigm of contemporary terrorism. The semiotics of that event yield an analysis of the conjunction of terrorism and the power of the dominant world system described by Wallerstein. That power structure is rooted in a global capitalist system symbolized by the World Trade Center. The endless replays of the second airliner hitting the tower and its subsequent collapse are the very model of spectacle. Guy DeBord describes it.

> The spectacle corresponds to the historical moment at which the commodity completes its colonization of social life. It is not just that the relationship to commodities is now plain to see—commodities are now *all* [*sic*] that there is to see; the world we see is the world of the commodity [DeBord 1995/1967:29].

DeBord goes on to say that "...the spectacle in its full development is money's modern aspect ..." [Ibid. 33]. What better example than the spectacle of an airliner, symbol of globalization, colliding with the World Trade Center, symbol of global money. Woven into narratives and discourses, spectacles are the stuff of ideology: "The spectacle is the acme of ideology" [Ibid. 150]. The dominant ideology of our time remolds real life to conform to the needs of the global system.

Semiotics, then, opens a path toward analyzing terrorism as 'propaganda by the deed,' as many nineteenth century terrorists and observers put it. The approach brings to the forefront the essential communicative character of terrorism, without which it would be simple fear.

Conclusion

The preceding tried to offer some useful tools for developing social scientific theories of terrorism. Heretofore, scholars made theoretical efforts piecemeal and too often with an ad hoc quality. We need some comprehensive theories if we are to begin understanding this phenomenon that has become a cynosure of our times.

Scholars from the many different social sciences doubtless can build an array of different kinds of theories, in keeping with their disciplinary perspective. That is all to the good. We have traveled in a theoretical desert for too long. So the motto for present ought to be, the more the better.

References

Abraham, R. H. and Shaw, C. D. (1992). *Dynamics, the Geometry of Behavior*. Second edition. Reading MA: Addison-Wesley.

Afflito, F. (2000). The Homogenizing Effects of State-Sponsored Terrorism: The Case of Guatemala. In J. Sluka (Ed.), *Death Squad: The Anthropology of State Terror* (pp. 114-126). Philadelphia: University of Pennsylvania Press.

Arnson C. J. (2000). Window on the Past: A Declassified History of Death Squads in El Salvador. In B. B. Campbell and A. D. Brenner (Eds.), *Death Squads in Global Perspective: Murder with Deniability*, (pp.85-124). New York: St. Martins Press.

Bahrani, Z. (2003). *The Graven Image: Representations in Babylonia and Assyria*. Philadelphia: University of Pennsylvania Press.

Barthes, R. (1972). *Mythologies*. A. Lavers (Trans.). New York: Noonday.

Bartolovich, C. (2002). Introduction. In C. Bartolovich and N. Lazarus (Eds.), *Marxism, Modernity, and Postcolonial Studies*. New York: Cambridge University Press.

Bassiouni, M. C. (2001). *International Terrorism: Multilateral Conventions (1937-2001)*. Ardsley NY: Transnational Publishers.

Bateson, G. (1979). *Mind and Nature: A Necessary Unity*. New York: E. P. Dutton.

Baudrillard, J. (1994/1981). *Simulacra and Simulation*. S. F. Glaser (Trans.). Ann Arbor: University of Michigan Press.

Bauman, Z. (1978). *Hermeneutics and Social Science*. New York: Columbia University Press.

Becker, H. (1963). *Outsiders: Studies in the Sociology of Deviance*. New York: The Free Press.

Bertalanffy, L. von. (1968). *General systems Theory, Foundations, Development, Applications*. New York: Braziller.

Bettleheim, B. (1979). *Surviving and Other Essays*. New York: Alfred A. Knopf.

Borges, Jorge Luis. (1964). The Analytical Language of John Wilkins. In *Other Inquisitions, 1937-1952*. R. L. C. Simms (Trans.). Austin: University of Texas Press.

Bourdieu, P. (2000/1997). *Pascalian Meditations*. R. Nice (Trans.). Stanford: Stanford University Press.

Bronowski, J. (1978). *Magic, Science, and Civilization*. New York: Columbia University Press.

Burke, E. (1790/1989). *Reflections on the Revolution in France*. In P. Langford (Ed.), *The Writings and Speeches of Edmund Burke*, volume 8. London: Clarendon Press.

————. (1791/1989). A Letter to a Member of the National Assembly. In P. Langford (Ed.), *The Writings and Speeches of Edmund Burke*, volume 8. London: Clarendon Press.

Butterfield, B. J. (1996). Annals of Assur-Nasir-Pal. In *Babylonian and Assyrian Literature*. Rev. J. M. Rodwell, M.A. (Trans.). New York: P. F. Collier & Son.

Camus, A. (2006/1946). The Century of Fear. In J. Levi-Valensi (Ed.), A. Goldhammer (Trans.), *Camus at Combat*, pp.257-260. Princeton: Princeton University Press.

————. (1956/1951). *The Rebel: An Essay on Man in Revolt*. A. Bower (Trans.). New York: Vintage Books.

Cannon, W. (1942). Voodoo Death. *American Anthropology* 44: 169-181.

Caws, P. (1959). The Functions of Definition in Science. *Philosophy of Science* 26(3):201-228.

Cohen, R. (1990). *Culture and Conflict in Egyptian-Israeli Relations: A Dialogue of the Deaf.* Bloomington: Indiana University Press.

Copi, Irwin M. (1956). Further Remarks on Definition and Analysis. *Philosophical Studies* 7(1-2):19-24.

Coombs, C.C. and Slann M. (2002). *Encyclopedia of Terrorism.* New York: facts on File.

Cooper, H. H. A. (2001). Terrorism: The Problem of Definition Revisited. *American Behavioral Scientist* 44(6):881-893.

Cover, R. (1983). Violence and the Word. *Yale Law Journal* 95: 1601-1631.

Crenshaw, M. (1983) Introduction: Reflections on the Effects of Terrorism. In *Terrorism, Legitimacy, and Power* (pp.1-37). Middletown CT: Wesleyan University Press.

————— . (1995). Thoughts on Relating Terrorism to Historical Contexts. *In Terrorism in Context* (pp. 3-24). University Park PA: Pennsylvania State University Press.

DeBord, G. (1995/1967). *The Society of the Spectacle.* D. Nicholson-Smith (Trans.). New York: Zone Books.

Dobzhansky, T. (1951). *Genetics and the Origin of Species.* Third edition. New York: Columbia University Press.

Dray, W. H. (1970). *Laws and Explanation in History.* Oxford: Clarendon Press.

Durkheim, E. (1966/1896). *Suicide*, G. Simpson (Ed.), G. Simpson and J. Spaulding (Trans.). New York: The Free Press.

Dyson, W.E. (2005). *Terrorism: An Investigator's Handbook.* Second edition. Cincinnati: Anderson Publishing.

Edelman, M. (1988). *Constructing the Political Spectacle.* Chicago: University of Chicago Press.

Einstein, A., Podolsky, B, and Rosen, N. (1935). Can Quantum-Mechanical Description of Physical Reality Be Considered Complete? *Physical Review* 47(10:777-780.

Evans, R and Novak, R. (1981). *The Reagan Revolution.* New York: E. P. Dutton, 1981.

Evans-Prichard, E. E. (1935). Witchcraft. *Africa* 8(4): 417-422.

————— . (1937). *Witchcraft, Oracles, and Magic Among the Azande.* Oxford: Oxford University Press.

————— . (1965). *Theories of Primitive Religion.* Oxford: Oxford University Press.

Fanon, F. (1963/1961). *The Wretched of the Earth.* C. Farrington (Trans.). New York: Grove Press.

Ferrell, J. (1996/1993). *Crimes of Style: Urban Graffiti and the Politics of Criminality.* Boston: Northeastern University Press, reprint.

Foucault, M. (1979/1975). *Discipline and Punish.* Alan Sheridan (Trans.). New York: Vintage Books.

Frege, G. (1960/1892). On Sense and Reference. In P. Geach and M. Black (Eds.), *Translations from the Writings of Gottlob Frege.* Oxford: Basil Blackwell.

Freud, S. (1974/1895). A Reply to Criticisms of My Paper on Anxiety Neurosis. In J. Strachey (Ed. And Trans.), *The Standard Edition of the Complete Psychological Works of Sigmund Freud* (Vol. 3: 121-140). London: Hogarth Press.

Geertz, C. (1965). The Impact of the Concept of Culture on the Concept of Man. In J. R. Platt (Ed.), *New Views of the Nature of Man*, (pp. 93-118). Chicago: University of Chicago Press.

Gilbert, J. (1986). *A Cycle of Outrage: America's Reaction to the Juvenile Delinquent in the 1950s*. New York: Oxford University Press.

Gilio, E. M. (1972). *The Tupamaro Guerrillas*. A. Edmondson (Trans). New York: Saturday Review Press.

Glassner, B. (1999). *The Culture of Fear: Why Americans Are Afraid of the Wrong Things*. New York: Basic Books.

Glueck, S. and Glueck, E. (1950). *Unraveling Juvenile Delinquency*. Cambridge: Harvard University Press.

Goldstein, R. J. (1978). *Political Repression in Modern American History*. Cambridge: Schenkman Publishing.

Golub, P.S. (2004). The Imperial Turn in the Global Political Economy. In Kees van der Pijl, Libby Assassi, and Duncan Wigan (Eds.), *Global Regulation: Managing Crises After the Imperial Turn*. New York: Palgrave Macmillan.

Greenacre, M. and J. Blasius (Eds.). 2006. *Multiple Correspondence Analysis and Related Materials*. Boca Raton FL: Chapman Hall.

Griset, P.L. and Mahan S. (2003). *Terrorism in Perspective*. Thousand Oaks CA: Sage Publications.

Hardman, J. B. S. (1936). Terrorism. In *Encyclopedia of the Social Sciences*, vol. 14. Edwin R. A. Seligman (Ed.). New York: Macmillan, 14:575-579.

Havelock, E. (1983). The Linguistic Task of the Presocratics. In K. Robb (Ed.), *Language and Thought in Early Greek Philosophy* (pp. 7-82). La Salle IL: The Hegeler Institute, Monist Library of Philosophy.

Hempel, C. G. (1958). The Theoretician's Dilemma: A Study in the Logic of Theory Construction. In H. Feigel, M. Scriven, and G. Maxwell (Eds.), *Minnesota Studies in the Philosophy of Science*, vol. 2 (pp. 37-98). Minneapolis: University of Minnesota Press.

————— . (1965) Aspects of Scientific Explanation. In *Aspects of Scientific Explanation and Other Essays in the Philosophy of Science* (pp. 331-496). Free Press.

Herman E. and O'Sullivan G. *The Terrorism Industry: The Experts and Institutions That Shape Our View of Terror*. New York: Pantheon.

Hesse, M. (1980). *Revolution and Reconstructions in the Philosophy of Science*. Bloomington: Indiana University Press.

Hill, D. (1997). "Kill Them All ... . God Will Recognize His Own." *Military History Quarterly* 9 (2), 98-108.

Holmes, O. W. Jr. (1881/1991). *The Common Law*. Boston: Little, Brown and Company (reprint New York: Dover).

Jenkins, B. M. (1999). Forward. In Ian O. Lesser (Ed.), *Countering the New Terrorism*. Santa Monica CA: Rand Corporation.

Kafka, F. (1961/1919). In the Penal Colony. *The Penal Colony: Stories and Short Pieces*, W. Muir and E. Muir (Trans.) pp.191-227. New York: Schocken Books

Kerry, J. (1997). *The New War: The Web of Crime That Threatens America's Security*. NY: Simon and Schuster.

Kluckhohn, C. (1944). *Navaho Witchcraft*. Boston: Beacon Press.

Kovel, J. (1981). *The Age of Desire: Reflections of a Radical Psychoanalyst*. New York: Pantheon.

Laqueur, W. (1987). *The Age of Terrorism*. Boston: Little, Brown.

Lester, D. (1972). Voodoo Death: Some New Thoughts on an Old Phenomenon. *American Anthropologist* 74: 386-390.

Levi, P. (1988). *The Drowned and the Saved*. R. Rosenthal (Trans.). New York: Vintage Books.

Lévi-Strauss, C. (1966/1963). *The Savage Mind*. Chicago: University of Chicago Press.

Lex, B. (1974). Voodoo Death: New Thoughts on an Old Explanation. *American Anthropologist* 76: 818-823.

Lorenz, E. N. (1963). Deterministic Nonperiodic Flow. *Journal of the Atmospheric Sciences* 20: 13—141.

Mahajan, G. (1997). *Explanation and Understanding in the Human Sciences*. Delhi: Oxford University Press.

Malinowski, B. (1954/1925). *Magic, Science, and Religion and Other Essays*. Garden City NY: Anchor Doubleday.

Margallanes, J. (2003). Drug Traffickers and Terrorism in Peru. In Viano, E. C., Margallanes, J. & Bride, L. (Eds.), *Transnational Organized Crime* (pp. 73-90). Durham NC: Carolina Academic Press.

Mayer, A. (2000). *The Furies: Violence and Terror in French and Russian Revolutions*. Princeton: Princeton University Press.

McCabe, J. 1929."The Massacre of the Albigensians." In *Religious Controversy*. London: Stratford Co. Available:

http://www.infidels.org/library/historical/joseph_mccabe/religious_controversy/chapter_23.html

Miller, A. (2000). The Crucible in History. In S. R. Centola (Ed.), *Echoes Down the Corridor: Collected Essays, 1944-2000* (pp. 274-295). New York: Viking.

Miller, J. G. (1978). *Living Systems*. New York: McGraw Hill,

Mills, C. W. (1959). *The Sociological Imagination*. New York: Oxford University Press.

Nadel, S. F. (1952). Witchcraft in Four African Societies. *American Anthropologist* 54: 18-29.

Nagengast, C. (1994). Violence, Terror, and the Crisis of the State. *Annual Review of Anthropology* 23: 109-136.

Naylor, R.T. (2002). *Wages of Crime*. Ithaca: Cornell University Press.

Nelli, H. S. (1976). *The Business of Crime: Italians and Syndicate Crime in the United States*. New York: Oxford University Press.

Northrup, F. S. C. (1947). *The Logic of the Sciences and the Humanities*. New York: Macmillan.

Olmstead, A. T. (1918). "The Calculated Frightfulness of Ashur Nasir Apal." *Journal of the American Oriental Society*, 38:209-263.

Peirce, C. S. (1960). *Collected Papers of Charles Sanders Peirce*, 8 volumes. C. Hartshorne and P. Weiss Eds.). Cambridge: Harvard University Press.

Popper, K. (1961). *The Logic of Scientific Discovery*. New York: Basic Books.

Preston, W. Jr. (1963). *Aliens and Dissenters: Federal Suppression of Radicals, 1903-1933*. Cambridge: Harvard University Press.

Rosenfeld, R. (2002) Why Criminologists Should Study Terrorism. *The Criminologist* 27(6):1-4.

Rothenberg, D. (2003). Public Presentational Torture and the Communicative Logic of State Terror. *Albany Law Review* 67: 465-499.

Roux, G. (1966). *Ancient Iraq*. Harmondsworth, Middlesex: Pelican Books.

Russell, B. (1983/1910). The Theory of Logical Types. In J. G. Slater (Ed.), *Logical and Philosophical Papers, 1909-1913, vol. 6 The Collected Papers of Bertrand Russell* (pp. 3-31). New York: Routledge.

—— (1983/1913). On the Notion of Cause. In J. G. Slater (Ed.), *Logical and Philosophical Papers, 1909-1913, vol. 6 The Collected Papers of Bertrand Russell* (pp. 190-210). New York: Routledge.

Sanford, V. (2004). *Buried Secrets: Truth and Human Rights in Guatemala*. New York: Palgrave Macmillan.

Saussure, F.de. (1966/1915). *Course in General Linguistics*. C. Bally and A. Sechehaye with A. Riedlinger (Eds.), W. Baskin (Trans.). New York: McGraw-Hill.

Scarry, E. (1985). *The Body in Pain: The Making and Unmaking of the World*. New York: Oxford University Press.

Scheper-Hughes, N. (1992). *Death Without Weeping: The Violence of Everyday Life in Brazil*. Berkeley: University of California Press.

Schmid, A. (1983). *Political Terrorism: A Research Guide to Concepts, Theories, Data Bases, and Literature*. New Brunswick NJ: Transaction Books.

——— . and Jongman, A. J. (1985). *Political Terrorism: A New Guide to Actors, Authors, Concepts, Data Bases, Theories and Literature*. New York: North Holland Publishing Company.

Scriven, M. (1958). Definitions, Explanations, and Theories. In H. Feigel, M. Scriven and G. Maxwell (Eds.), *Minnesota Studies in the Philosophy of Science, Volume II: Concepts, Theories, and the Mind-Body Problem* (pp. 99-195). Minneapolis: University of Minnesota Press.

——— . (1964). Critical Study of E. Nagel's "The Structure of Science." *Review of Metaphysics* 17(67): 403-424.

Sempruch, J. (2004). Feminist Constructions of the 'Witch' as a Fantasmatic Other. *Body & Society* 10(4): 113-133.

Simmel, G. (1950). The Metropolis and Mental Life. In K. H. Wolff (Ed. And Trans.), *The Sociology of Georg Simmel* (pp. 409-424). New York: The Free Press.

——— . (1955). Conflict. In K. H. Wolf (Ed.& Trans.), *Conflict and the Web of Group Affiliations*. New York: The Free Press.

Spiro, M. (1953). Ghosts: An Anthropological Inquiry into Learning and Perception. *Journal of Abnormal and Social Psychology* 48: 376-382.

Stanley, E. (2004). Torture, Silence, and Recognition. *Current Issues in Criminal Justice* 16 (July): 5-25.

Sterling, C. (1981). *The Terror Network: The Secret War of International Terrorism*. New York: Holt, Rinehart and Winston.

Stewart, N. (2005). Ohio's Statutory and Common Law History with 'Terrorism:' A Study in Domestic Terrorism Law. *Journal of Legislation* 32:93-128.

Stohl, M. (1976). *War and Domestic Political Violence: The American Capacity for Repression and Reaction*. Beverly Hills CA: Sage Publications.

Tarski, A. (1956/1933). The Concept of Truth in Formalized Languages. In *Logic, Semantics, Mathematics: Papers from 1923 to 1938*, J. H. Woodger (Trans.), (pp. 152-278). Oxford: Clarendon.

Task Force on Disorders and Terrorism. (1976). *Disorders and Terrorism*. Washington DC: National Advisory Committee on Criminal Justice Standards.

Thucydides. (1996). *The Peloponnesian War*. In *The Landmark Thucydides*. Richard Crawley (Trans.), Robert B. Strassler (Ed.). New York: The Free Press

Tiefenbrun, S. (2003). A Semiotic Approach to a Legal Definition of Terrorism. *ILSA Journal of International and Comparative Law*. 9:357-402.

Tindale, C. W. (1996). The Logic of Torture: A Critical Examination. *Social Theory and Practice* 22 (3): 349-374.

TRAC. (2003). TRAC Report: Criminal Enforcement against Terrorists. [Online]. Available: http://trac.syr.edu/tracreports/terrorism/report011203.html.

TRAC. (2006). TRAC Report: Criminal Terrorism Enforcement in the United States During the Five Years Since the 9/11/01 Attacks. [Online]. Available: http://trac.syr.edu/tracreports/terrorism/169.

UN. (2002). *Thirteenth Report on the Human Rights of the United Nations Verification Mission in Guatemala* A/57/336. New York: UN General Assembly.

van der Pilj, K., Assassi, L, & Wigan, D. (Eds.). (2004). *Global Regulation: Managing Crises After the Imperial Turn*. New York: Palgrave Macmillan.

Vološinov, N. V. (1973). *Marxism and the Philosophy of Language*, L. Mateka and I. R. Titunik. New York: Seminar Press.

Wallerstein, I. M. (1974-1980). *The Modern World System*, 2 vols. New York: Academic Press.

———. (1976). *The Capitalist World-Economy: essays*. New York: Cambridge University Press.

———. (2003). *The Decline of American Power: The U.S. in a Chaotic World*. New York: The New Press.

———. (2004). *World-Systems Analysis: An Introduction*. Durham NC: Duke University Press.

Weber, M. (1919/1958). Science as a Vocation. In H. H. Gerth and C. W. Mills (Eds.and Trans.), *From Max Weber: Essays in Sociology* (pp. 129-156). New York: Oxford University Press.

———. (1949) 'Objectivity' in Social Science and Social Policy. In E. A. Shils and H. A. Finch (Eds.), *The Methodology of the Social Sciences* (pp. 71-78). New York: Free Press.

———. (1966) *The Theory of Social and Economic Organization*, T. Parsons (Ed.), T. Parsons and A. M. Henderson (Trans.). New York: The Free Press.

Weinberg, L. and Eubank, W. L. (1987). *The Rise and Fall of Italian Terrorism*. Boulder CO: Westview Press.

White, J.R. (2003). *Terrorism*. Fourth edition. Belmont CA: Thompson/Wadsworth.

Whitehead, A. N. and Russell, B. (1960/1913). *Principia Mathematica, vol. 1*. Second edition. Cambridge: Cambridge University Press.

Wilkinson, P. (1977). *Terrorism and the Liberal State*. New York: John Wiley & Sons.

Wills, D. C. (2003). *The First war on Terrorism: Counter-terrorism Policy During the Reagan Administration*. Lanham MD: Rowman & Littlefield.

Wilson, Maj. C. (1974). *The Tupamaros: The Unmentionables*. Boston: Branden Press.

Winans, E. V. and Edgerton, R. B. (1964). Hehe Magical Justice. *American Anthropologist* 66: 745-764.

Winch, Peter. (1964). Understanding a Primitive Society. *American Philosophical Quarterly* 1(4): 307-324.

Woodiwiss, M. (2001). *Organized Crime and American Power*. Toronto: University of Toronto Press.

Zulaika, J. and Douglas, W. A. (1996). *Terror and Taboo: The Follies, Fables, and Faces of Terrorism*. New York: Routledge.

In: Global Terrorism Issues and Developments   ISBN: 978-1-60021-930-6
Editor: Rene A. Larche, pp. 61-100   © 2008 Nova Science Publishers, Inc.

Chapter 2

INTESTINAL TOXICITY IN RADIATION- AND COMBINED INJURY: SIGNIFICANCE, MECHANISMS, AND COUNTERMEASURES

Martin Hauer-Jensen[1,2,], K. Sree Kumar[3], Junru Wang[1], Maaike Berbee[1], Qiang Fu[1] and Marjan Boerma[1]*

[1]University of Arkansas for Medical Sciences, AR, USA
[2]Central Arkansas Veterans Healthcare System, Little Rock, AR
[3]Uniformed Services University of the Health Sciences-Armed Forces Radiobiology
Research Institute, Bethesda, MD, USA

Abstract

In most radiation scenarios, injury to the bone marrow and gastrointestinal tract are the main determinants of survival because of their rapidly proliferating stem/progenitor cell compartments. While significant progress has been made in the medical management of radiation-induced bone marrow injury, the management of gastrointestinal radiation toxicity remains symptomatic and underdeveloped. Moreover, combined injury (radiation injury combined with other types of trauma or sepsis) may exacerbate intestinal injury compared to what is seen after radiation exposure alone. For these reasons, the importance of gastrointestinal injury as a critical determinant of survival in a radiation terrorism scenario has increased significantly.

This chapter provides an overview of the significance of intestinal toxicity in the non-therapeutic radiation exposure setting and discusses how radiation, when combined with other types of trauma or sepsis, may be associated with increased mortality and morbidity. Novel concepts pertinent to the mechanisms of intestinal damage are also reviewed, with special emphasis on the importance of endothelial cell dysfunction in radiation injury, sepsis, and ischemia-reperfusion injury. Finally, various strategies to prevent or mitigate intestinal toxicity after radiation exposure and after traumatic injuries are discussed.

---

[*] Martin Hauer-Jensen, MD, PhD, Arkansas Cancer Research Center, 4301 West Markham, Slot 725, Little Rock, AR 72205, USA. Phone: (501) 686-7912; Fax: (501) 421-0022; E-mail: mhjensen@life.uams.edu

Introduction

In most radiation scenarios, injury to the bone marrow and gastrointestinal (GI) tract are the primary determinants of survival because of their rapidly proliferating stem/progenitor cell compartments. Significant progress has been made in the post-exposure management of radiation-induced bone marrow injury with hematopoietic cytokines, blood transfusions, antimicrobial therapy, and stem cell reconstitution. In contrast, the management of GI radiation toxicity remains symptomatic and underdeveloped. Therefore, recognition of the importance of GI injury as a determinant of survival and the awareness of the need for medical countermeasures against radiation focused on the GI tract have increased significantly.

The GI radiation syndrome occurs after whole body radiation exposures to doses in excess of 6 Gy in humans. Survival is extremely unlikely with the full-fledged GI radiation syndrome. Destructive changes of the intestinal epithelial lining cause breakdown of the mucosal barrier that normally separates the contents of the intestinal lumen from the gastrointestinal tissue, resulting in severe secretory diarrhea, dehydration, and electrolyte imbalance. Even after lower doses of radiation, however, the GI tract plays a major role in the pathophysiology of toxicity and clinical outcome. Hence, sepsis from enteric bacteria is an important cause of lethality after radiation exposure. This is because bacterial translocation (passage of bacteria from the intestinal lumen through the defective mucosal barrier and into the blood stream) occurs during a period of severe radiation-induced immune system compromise.

In realistic nuclear or radiation exposure scenarios, the risk of intestinal complications and the severity of injury after radiation exposure may be further compounded by other concomitant injuries as the so-called combined injury syndrome. While the biological mechanisms underlying the interactions between radiation and other types of injury are largely unknown, lethality in a combined injury situation is frequently much greater than what is seen after either type of injury alone. Therefore, elucidating the mechanisms of synergy between radiation and other traumatic injuries and developing effective countermeasures for use in the combined injury situation are critically important priorities. Moreover, because the gastrointestinal tract is critically involved in the pathophysiological response to burns, trauma, sepsis, and multiple organ dysfunction syndromes (MODS), as well as in isolated radiation syndromes, the GI tract likely plays a key role in combined injury and represents a particularly promising target for countermeasure development.

This chapter provides a general overview of the concept of combined injury. Current knowledge relative to mechanisms of intestinal radiation toxicity and interventions that may reduce intestinal radiation toxicity will then be reviewed, followed by a discussion of pathophysiology of, as well as interventions to mitigate intestinal dysfunction in burns, trauma, sepsis, and MODS. Interventions directed against common pathophysiological targets in radiation and traumatic injuries, such as, endothelial cell dysfunction and neuroimmune interactions, are particularly promising as countermeasures against combined injury and are therefore emphasized and discussed in particular detail.

Combined Injury

Combined injury is defined as radiation injury that occurs in combination with burns, blast injury, blunt or penetrating trauma, exposure to toxic chemicals, and/or exposure to infectious agents. It is estimated that combined injury occurs in up to 70% of casualties in a nuclear scenario. Because radiation injury and physical trauma for the most part exert synergistic effects, combined injury adversely affects mortality and short- and long term complication rate relative to the rates associated with isolated radiation or traumatic injury. Consequently, combined injury has substantial impact on the initial triage considerations, adversely affects outcome in casualties, increases the complexity and cost of casualty care, and poses a significant burden on the afflicted individual, their families, and medical personnel. Despite the importance of combined injury, the recent activity in the area has been limited and the literature available is mostly dated. There is a clear unmet need for renewed efforts in combined injury research that take advantage of modern knowledge, tools, and experimental techniques.

It is important to recognize that combined injury is unique and unpredictable, that the interactions among injuries is exceedingly complex, and that the relative timing of injuries is important in terms of the strength of the synergy. In fact, in certain situations, mainly those where the physical trauma is separated from the radiation injury by a short period of time, physical injury may actually protect against radiation injury [1]. A similar phenomenon applies to endotoxin, where injection before or shortly after reduces lethality [2, 3] and accelerates hematopoietic recovery [4, 5], while injection of endotoxin on day 3 after total body irradiation greatly increases lethality [3]. Despite the complexity of combined injury, some useful generally applicable pathophysiological principles are well established. For example, the latency period of the radiation syndrome is shortened, with earlier presentation and more profound development of leucopenia, anemia, and thrombocytopenia. The susceptibility to infection is increased. Wound healing processes are impaired. Sepsis and MODS occur more frequently than with radiation injury alone and, in fact, the concept of a "combined injury shock" has been proposed [6].

There is a common misconception that, because of the many possible permutations of injuries in the combined injury syndromes, the optimal management of individuals who sustain combined injury is to simply use the best treatment of radiation injury together with the best treatment of the particular traumatic injury. This is clearly incorrect, both with regard to the choice of treatment algorithms for traumatic injury, as well as with regard to the choice of countermeasures against radiation. For example, in terms of management of the traumatic injury, concomitant presence of radiation injury influences the indication for surgery, the optimal timing of surgical intervention, the choice of surgical procedure, as well as the choice of surgical technique with a particular procedure, including the choice of prosthetic material. Special considerations may also apply to the use of antimicrobials for treatment and/or prophylaxis, bowel decontamination, and probiotic interventions in the setting of combined injury. Conversely, it is critical to establish a number of factors for radiation countermeasures specifically for the combined injury situation. These factors include the efficacy, toxicity, and optimal timing of administration of the specific countermeasure in the combined injury setting, as well as pharmacokinetic-pharmacodynamic (PK-PD) and absorption-distribution-metabolism-excretion (ADME) parameters. It is also important to recognize that, because of the unpredictable relationship between radiation and traumatic injury, forward modeling of dose response relationship for radiation effects is not valid in the combined injury situation.

Because of the central role of the intestine in radiation syndromes, as well as in trauma, sepsis, and MODS, the GI tract has emerged as a critical organ system in combined injury. The following sections first discuss mechanisms, pathophysiology, and therapeutic interventions applicable to intestinal radiation injury. Subsequently, the significance of and management strategies against intestinal dysfunction in burns, trauma, sepsis, and multiple organ dysfunction are reviewed.

Intestinal Radiation Injury

To effectively convey principles of radiation toxicity in a particular organ, it is useful to consider the radiation response of that organ separately. However, to properly understand acute radiation toxicities in response to total body irradiation, it is imperative that this reductionistic view be supplemented with a proper understanding of pertinent systems biology-based principles. Total body irradiation affects all tissues and organ systems in the body and there are critical interactions among many tissues and organ systems. Although intestinal irradiation is necessary and sufficient to produce what is commonly referred to as the "gastrointestinal radiation syndrome" [7] and surgical removal of the exposed bowel can prevent the syndrome from occurring [8], it is firmly established that lethality from bowel toxicity is heavily influenced by radiation injury to other organ systems, for example, the hematopoietic system [9]. It is important to recognize that reference to the "gastrointestinal radiation syndrome" and the "hematopoietic radiation syndrome" simply indicates that toxicity in those organ systems predominate clinically, but that the pathophysiological manifestations depend heavily on interactions among multiple cell types and organ systems in the body. A recent discussion of the role of gastrointestinal radiation toxicity from the perspective of the radiation-induced MODS can be found in [10].

Intestinal radiation injury (radiation enteropathy) is classified as early (acute) or delayed (chronic) depending on when it occurs relative to radiation exposure. After total body irradiation with exposure of the entire bowel, acute radiation toxicity causes lethality at doses that are lower than those required to produce significant chronic changes. Therefore, acute intestinal toxicity is the primary concern in the setting of nuclear/radiological accidents, radiation terrorism, and radiation exposure in the battlefield.

Acute radiation injury occurs primarily as a result of mitotic and apoptotic cell death in the crypt epithelium, resulting in insufficient replacement of the surface epithelium of the intestinal villi. At moderate radiation doses, there is hypoplasia of the mucosa, while higher doses cause frank ulcerations or areas of complete epithelial denudation. Even after very low radiation doses in the range of 1 Gy, there is increased permeability of the epithelial barrier with secondary mucosal inflammation (mucositis). Breakdown of the mucosal barrier facilitates penetration of antigens, bacterial products, and digestive enzymes from the intestinal lumen into the intestinal wall, thus initiating an intense inflammatory response. The major clinical manifestations of early intestinal radiation toxicity after high doses of radiation include nausea and vomiting, secretory diarrhea, fluid-electrolyte imbalance, as well as septic complications secondary to bacterial translocation.

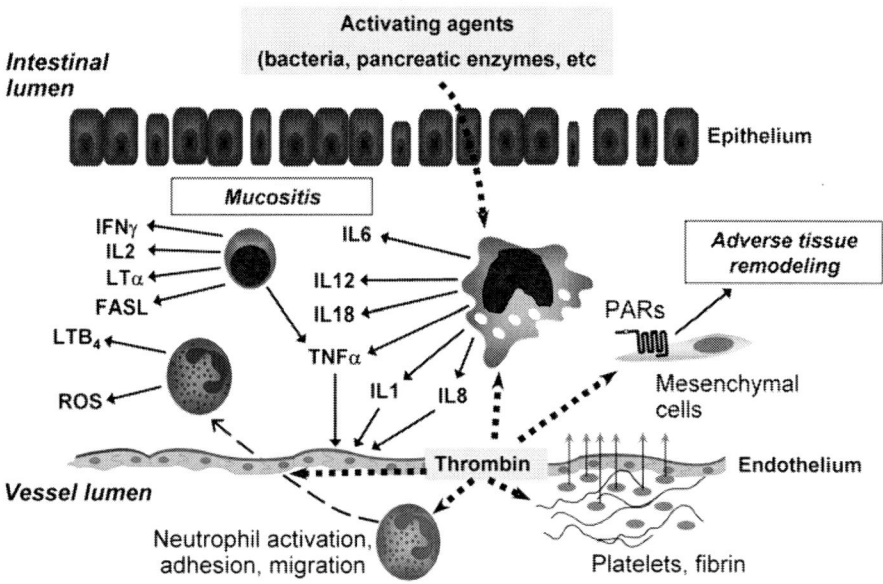

Figure 1. Schematic representation of some of the mechanisms involved in early radiation mucositis and subsequent radiation fibrosis in the intestine. Mucositis is associated with release of cytokines and other inflammatory mediators by neutrophils, macrophages, lymphocytes, and mast cells. Radiation-induced endothelial dysfunction is associated with loss of thromboresistance of the endothelial lining of blood vessels and generation of thrombin which, in addition to being an important coagulation factor, also modulates many inflammatory and fibroproliferative processes. IFNγ: interferon γ; IL2: interleukin 2; LTα: lymphotoxin α (=TNFβ); FASL: FAS ligand; LTB4: leukotriene B4; ROS: reactive oxygen species; IL6: interleukin 6; IL12: interleukin 12; IL18: interleukin 18; TNFα: tumor necrosis factor α; IL1: interleukin 1; IL8: interleukin 8; PARs: proteinase activated receptors.

Despite the dominant importance of early intestinal radiation toxicity in the total body irradiation setting, delayed intestinal radiation injury, although much less of an issue in this situation, may be relevant under certain circumstances. The pathogenesis of chronic radiation injury is more complex than that of the acute response and prominent features include vascular damage, smooth muscle degeneration, and intestinal wall fibrosis. A discussion of chronic radiation enteropathy is beyond the scope of this review and the reader is instead referred to the available texts in the published literature [11-13].

Mechanisms and Pathophysiology of Intestinal Radiation Injury

Injury from nuclear radiation occurs mainly via the generation of reactive oxygen species within tissues and cells. As a result, substantial damage occurs in cellular DNA, as well as in proteins, lipids, carbohydrates, and other complex molecules. Hence, ionizing radiation affects not only the genetic material of the cell, but also causes changes in plasma membranes, sub-cellular organelles, nuclear membranes, and various intra- and extracellular molecules. It is helpful to consider radiation responses of organs and tissues as a combination of three different injury processes that interact and together are responsible for the pathophysiological manifestations seen after radiation exposure, i.e., 1) cytocidal effects (clonogenic cell death, apoptotic cell death); 2) functional (non-cytocidal) effects; and 3) secondary (reactive) effects [14]. The schema shown in Figure 1 depicts some of the non-cytocidal and secondary effects of radiation in the intestine.

In the following discussion, we will first consider the cytocidal effects of radiation (clonogenic cell death and apoptosis) and then review some of the major changes that occur as a result of functional and secondary effects, thus contributing to the pathophysiological manifestations of intestinal radiation toxicity.

Clonogenic Cell Death and Apoptosis

Classically, cytocidal effects relate to the well known phenomenon characterized by the target-cell model. Hence, the time between irradiation and manifestation of injury depends on target-cell characteristics (radiation sensitivity, repair capacity, proliferation rate, etc.) and tissue organization. The intestinal mucosa undergoes continuous, rapid turnover, with epithelial cells proliferating in the crypts, migrating along the villi, and eventually being shed into the intestinal lumen. In rapidly renewing tissues, such as the intestinal epithelium, injury manifests itself clinically within days of the first radiation exposure when cells in the "differentiated" cellular compartment are no longer replaced by cells from the progenitor compartment. Although the crypt epithelium is considered the main target-cell compartment responsible for the acute effects of radiation, more recently other target cells, particular vascular endothelial cells, have been suggested to determine the intestinal radiation response [15, 16]. The debate on the role of vascular endothelial cell apoptosis in the GI radiation syndrome, however, is still ongoing [17].

A unique feature of the GI tract is the presence of large numbers of microbes and digestive enzymes in its lumen. These microbes are not only the cause of septic complications secondary to translocation of microbes through the damaged intestinal wall, but also seem to directly affect clonogenic cell death in several intestinal cell compartments after irradiation [18].

Inflammation

Mucosal epithelia are the primary sites for antigen entry. Although intestinal epithelium consists of only a single layer of cells, it controls the access of potential antigens and pathogens and at the same time plays a critical role in the absorption of nutrients. Moreover, the intestine is by far the largest immunological organ in the body: 50-80% of immunoglobulin-producing cells are found in the gut and 40% of T cells reside in intraepithelial lymphoid tissue. Because of the constant bombardment by antigens, some degree of intestinal "inflammation" is always present in the normal situation. In situations where the epithelial barrier is compromised, such as by radiation injury, inflammatory cell recruitment and transmigration increase by several orders of magnitude [19].

Although inflammation is clearly involved in the pathogenesis of intestinal radiation toxicity, as for example demonstrated by the use of non-selective immunomodulators, the mechanistic role of inflammation is complex. Not surprisingly, plasma levels of C-reactive protein, an acute-phase protein and marker of inflammation, and plasma levels of the inflammatory cytokine interleukin 6 (IL6), both correlate with the dose of radiation exposure in A-bomb survivors [20]. However, recent evidence indicates that inflammation cannot be looked upon as solely detrimental. Hence, activation of nuclear factor-kappa B (NFκB), a transcription factor that plays a key role in inflammation, protects against intestinal radiation injury and radiation-induced lethality [21]. It is possible that the induction of an inflammatory response before irradiation reduces radiation injury, possibly due to increased levels of tumor necrosis factor α (TNFα), a cytokine with radioprotective properties. In fact, a protective effect of NFκB activation and/or an acute phase response before radiation may help explain why wounding before radiation exposure reduces radiation lethality [1] and why even injection of non-reactive particular matter before irradiation enhances survival [22]. Similar considerations apply to the injection of endotoxin in close proximity to irradiation, as discussed in the section above on combined injury. Clearly, the timing and exact nature of the inflammatory process have a major impact on the development of radiation toxicity.

Cytokines and Growth Factors

Irradiation of normal tissues elicits prominent cellular responses, as well as changes in endogenous cytokines, growth factors, and chemokines. Some changes are epiphenomena secondary to tissue injury and inflammation, others are counteractive responses to injury, while yet others relate mechanistically to specific pathophysiologic processes.

Cytokines regulate a vast array of biological processes, including inflammation, cell proliferation, tissue remodeling, coagulation, and angiogenesis. They are critically involved in key aspects of radiation injury. Rather than an orderly cascade leading to distinct cellular responses, however, the network of biological activities of cytokines is complex and depends on cell-cell interactions within and among tissue compartments and on the local microenvironment. Cytokines have been the subject of intense study in radiation injury in many organ systems, including the GI tract [23, 24]. Studies in transgenic animal models and in models involving modulation of cytokine levels or cytokine activities support a role for many cytokines in the mechanisms of intestinal radiation injury and also demonstrate the feasibility of modulating cytokine levels or activity to influence the radiation response *in vivo* [25, 26].

Endothelial Dysfunction

Ionizing radiation has profound effects on the endothelial lining of blood vessels in normal tissues. High doses of radiation cause apoptosis [15, 27], while lower doses of radiation increase trans-endothelial permeability [28], promote inflammatory cell adhesion and infiltration [29, 30], and decrease fibrinolysis [31]. Notably, radiation causes a pronounced shift in the thrombohemorrhagic balance from the normal anti-coagulant state to a pro-coagulant state by increasing the expression of tissue factor [32] and von Willebrand factor [33] and decreasing the expression of prostacyclin [34] and thrombomodulin (TM) [35]. Collectively, these changes constitute what is commonly referred to as endothelial cell dysfunction. As shown in Figure 2, endothelial dysfunction likely plays a key role in both early and delayed radiation responses in the intestine.

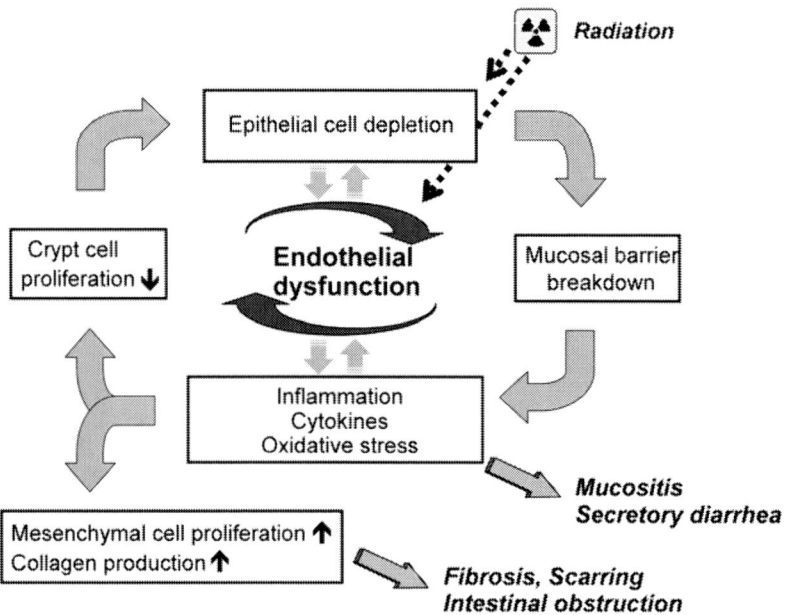

Figure 2. Model showing how interactions between epithelial and endothelial radiation injury in the intestine causes endothelial dysfunction, exacerbates acute intestinal radiation toxicity, and subsequently sustains the cycle of chronicity of intestinal radiation fibrosis. Radiation causes epithelial crypt cell death, which leads to insufficient replacement of the villus epithelium with breakdown of the epithelial barrier that normally separates intestinal tissue from the intraluminal contents of the intestine. Moreover, radiation causes endothelial dysfunction, notably a profound loss of thromboresistance and increased expression of chemokines and adhesion molecules. The combined loss of epithelial barrier function and endothelial dysfunction enhances post-radiation inflammation, inhibits repopulation of the epithelial surface, and promotes adverse tissue remodeling (fibrosis).

A number of clinical, preclinical, and basic research studies performed in our laboratory point to deficient levels of TM as a particularly important aspect of radiation-induced endothelial dysfunction and to the involvement of the TM-protein C system in the pathogenesis of both acute and chronic intestinal radiation toxicity [35-39]. TM is a transmembrane glycoprotein, located on the luminal surface of endothelial cells in most normal blood vessels. Thrombin, when bound to TM, loses its pro-coagulant activities and its ability to activate cellular thrombin-receptors (proteinase-activated receptors) and instead acquires the ability to activate protein C. Activated protein C (APC) limits further thrombin generation and counteracts thrombin's many coagulant, inflammatory, and fibroproliferative effects [40]. APC also has potent intrinsic anti-inflammatory and cytoprotective properties [41]. Moreover, TM itself exerts protein C independent anti-inflammatory effects by its ability to bind high mobility group box 1 (HMGB1) protein [42, 43]. A diagram of the coagulation system and the protein C system is shown in Figure 3.

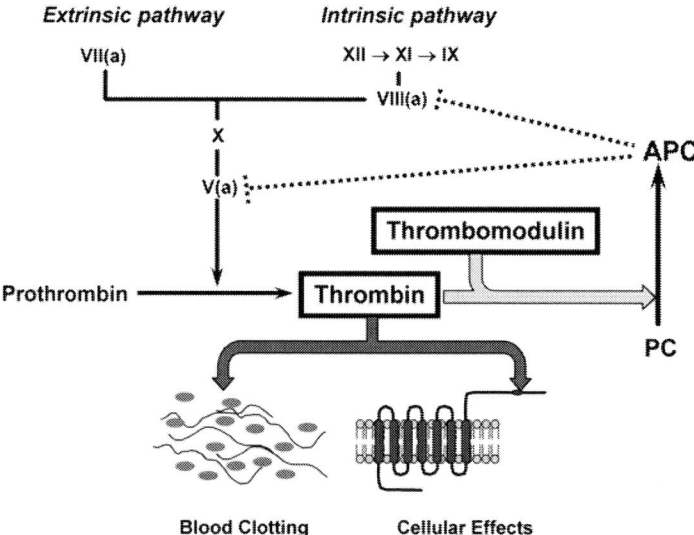

Figure 3. The coagulation cascade and the thrombomodulin-thrombin-protein C system. Simplified schematic representation of the coagulation "cascade" with the intrinsic, extrinsic, and common pathways. Note that thrombomodulin, located on the luminal surface of normal endothelial cells, forms a complex with thrombin, which is then "converted" from a pro-coagulant into an anticoagulant with the ability to activate protein C. Activated protein C (APC) limits further thrombin generation by feedback into the intrinsic and common coagulation pathways.

Deficient TM levels become apparent within hours after irradiation and do not recover, but remain low throughout the chronic phase of injury. The underlying mechanisms of reduced TM expression and activity are multiple: First, cytokines that are upregulated during the radiation response (eg, interleukin 1 [IL1], TNFα, and transforming growth factor β [TGFβ]), downregulate TM [44, 45]. Second, inflammatory mediators cause shedding of TM from the endothelial cell membrane [46]. Third, TM is inactivated by oxidation of a specific methionine (Met388) that is crucial for TM's ability to bind thrombin and activate protein C [47]. In accordance with this model, we found increased levels of enzymatically active thrombin in irradiated intestine, while inhibition of thrombin reduced intestinal radiation toxicity [48], and that radiation, by directly oxidizing Met388, impairs the ability of TM to form a complex with thrombin, thereby reducing the ability to activate protein C [49].

Increased formation of thrombin likely also plays a role in intestinal radiation toxicity. Thrombin removes fibrinopeptides A and B from fibrinogen (to generate fibrin) and also activates platelets, thus forming the fibrin-platelet clot. In addition to being a coagulation factor, thrombin is also an important regulator of cell proliferation, inflammation, and tissue remodeling. For example, thrombin mediates lipopolysaccharide-induced tissue injury [50] and regulates endothelial permeability [51], inflammation [52, 53], and production of TGFβ1 [54] by mechanisms that are independent of coagulation. Thrombin also increases production of platelet-activating factor (PAF), PAF-mediated neutrophil adhesion to endothelial cells, and smooth muscle cell migration and proliferation. Specific inhibitors of thrombin decrease smooth muscle cell proliferation, migration, and collagen production both *in vitro* [55] and *in vivo* [56]. Moreover, studies in our laboratory demonstrate that direct thrombin inhibition ameliorates intestinal radiation toxicity [48].

Thrombin exerts its cellular effects by activating proteinase activated receptors (PARs) on the cell surface. PARs are a 4-member subgroup of the G-protein coupled receptor family that are activated by proteolytic cleavage of the extracellular aminoterminal end. After being cleaved by specific proteinases, the new amino-terminal end activates the ligand binding site on the receptor by a so-called tethered ligand mechanism. Thrombin activates PAR1, PAR3, and PAR4, but PAR1 is the most relevant receptor in inflammation and fibrosis. PAR1 activation promotes endothelial permeability [51], chemotaxis of neutrophils [52] and monocytes [53], production of TGFβ1 [54], as well as proliferation, migration, and collagen production by fibroblasts and smooth muscle cells [55-58]. Studies in our laboratory show that intestinal radiation injury is associated with a striking upregulation of PAR1 in endothelium, smooth muscle cells, and myofibroblasts, particularly in areas of fibrosis [35]. Moreover, experiments in PAR1 knockout mice and with a small molecule inhibitor of PAR1 activation have confirmed a role for PAR1 in certain aspects of intestinal radiation injury (unpublished data).

To summarize (and somewhat simplify) how endothelial dysfunction affects the development of intestinal radiation injury: thrombin is pro-coagulant, pro-inflammatory, and pro-fibrogenic, while the net effects of the TM-protein C pathway is anti-coagulant, anti-inflammatory, and anti-fibrogenic. A pathophysiological model for how dysfunction of the TM-protein C pathway may be involved in intestinal radiation tissue toxicity has been proposed and is depicted in Figure 4 [35]. As discussed below, several compounds that interfere with the TM-protein C pathway have already demonstrated promising protective properties in preclinical models of total body irradiation exposure.

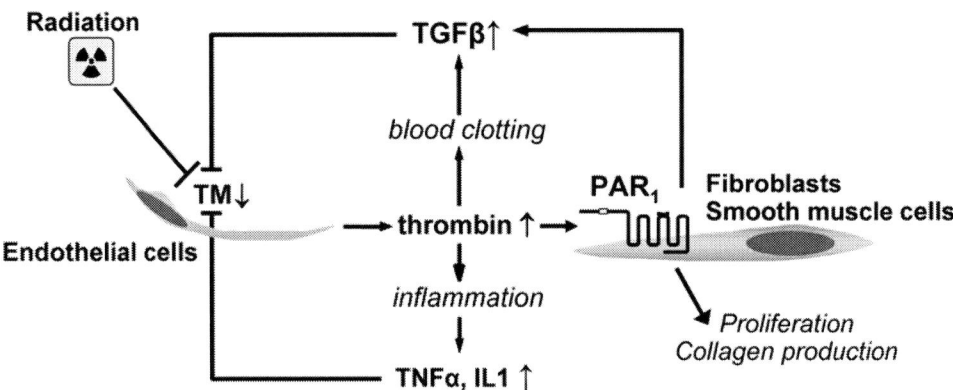

Figure 4. Probable mechanism linking radiation-induced endothelial dysfunction to chronic inflammation and progressive intestinal fibrosis via chronic activation of proteinase activated receptor 1 (PAR1). Radiation causes deficiency of thrombomodulin (TM) on the luminal surface of endothelial cells, leading to insufficient "scavenging" of locally formed thrombin. Thrombin exerts pro-coagulant, pro-inflammatory, and fibro-proliferative effects on various cell types in the irradiated tissue. Feed-back by cytokines, notably transforming growth factor β (TGFβ), interleukin 1 (IL1), and tumor necrosis factor α (TNFα), sustains the endothelial TM deficiency, thus sustaining the process that leads to intestinal toxicity.

Neuroimmune Interactions

The nervous system of the intestine is the second largest in the body, with more neurons than the spinal cord. Of the various components of the enteric nervous system, sensory (afferent) nerves may be particularly important in the context of radiation toxicity. Sensory nerves were traditionally thought of simply as recipients of various stimuli and conveyors of these stimuli from the periphery to the central nervous system or some peripheral neural circuitry; that is, they were assumed to act in a purely unidirectional manner. However, recent research has clearly documented that sensory enteric neurons also have a number of important local effector functions, that they are involved in maintaining the integrity of the intestinal mucosa, and that there are important interactions between sensory nerves and various cell types of the immune system.

Subdiaphragmatic vagotomy reduces the early radiation-induced intestinal inflammatory response [59]. Moreover, sensory nerve ablation by capsaicin pretreatment augments most types of acute GI injury, including experimental inflammatory bowel disease and acute intestinal toxicity after whole-body irradiation or localized irradiation [60, 61], indicating a protective role of sensory nerves in intestinal radiation injury.

While afferent nerves are required for normal mucosal homeostasis, inappropriate stimulation of these nerves causes neurogenic inflammation and structural injury. Substance P and calcitonin gene-related peptide (CGRP) are widely distributed in sensory nerve endings in the GI tract and are presumed to be major neurotransmitters in capsaicin-sensitive neurons. Several lines of evidence support a role for substance P and CGRP in GI inflammation and injury repair processes [62, 63]. Recent studies support the notion that both neuropeptides may be a target for prophylactic and/or therapeutic strategies and that substance P exacerbates intestinal radiation injury, while CGRP ameliorates intestinal radiation toxicity [64].

While the enteric nervous system has prominent interactions with many different cell types of the immune system, the interactions with mast cells appear to be particularly important. Mast cells exhibit close (almost synaptic) anatomical and functional associations with sensory nerve endings [65] and bidirectional interactions between mast cells and afferent nerves are critical for maintaining mucosal homeostasis and ensuring an appropriate response to injury. Hence, sensory nerves regulate the activation threshold of mast cells and thereby control the release of mast cell mediators. Conversely, signaling from mast cells to enteric nerves by histamine and/or nerve growth factor is critical for afferent nerve function and for the neurogenic intestinal defense against injury [66, 67].

Recent evidence suggests that mast cells and the interaction of mast cells with the enteric nervous system play critical roles in the intestinal radiation response. Mast cells are part of the innate immune system that provides the first line of defense against tissue damage. In addition to their critical role in immunoglobulin E (IgE)-dependent, histamine-mediated hypersensitivity, mast cells release and modulate cytokines, growth factors, chemokines, and other mediators, which in turn regulate a vast array of important biological processes.

Injury to the intestinal mucosa is associated with activation and degranulation of resident mucosal mast cells (MMC). Mast cell degranulation contributes to mucosal inflammation in inflammatory bowel disease models and after intestinal irradiation [68, 69]. On the other hand, studies in mast cell-deficient mice and rats have demonstrated that resident MMCs also play a critical physiological role in host defense [70, 71] and that their absence strikingly exacerbates acute radiation injury in the intestinal mucosa [72]. In contrast to MMCs, connective tissue mast cells (CTMCs) appear to play an important role in fibrogenesis, as unequivocally demonstrated in experiments in mast cell-deficient rats, which develop minimal intestinal wall fibrosis [72]. The importance of interactions between mast cells and the enteric nervous system is evident from the observation that the effect of sensory nerve ablation on most parameters of intestinal radiation injury are blunted in mast cell-deficient animals [61].

The mast cell-derived protease tryptase is a main activator of PAR2, a receptor that is expressed in normal intestine and mediates many inflammatory, mitogenic, and fibroproliferative responses [73]. Activation of PAR2 also appears to be important in several other aspects of GI pathophysiology, including the regulation of intestinal ion secretion and absorption [74, 75], nociception [76], motility [77], and inflammation [78, 79]. Recent preclinical evidence from our laboratory suggests that PAR2 activation is also a significant contributor to intestinal radiation toxicity [80, 81].

Preventive and Therapeutic Interventions

Countermeasures against radiation are generally categorized into pre-exposure interventions and post-exposure interventions. Pre-exposure countermeasures (radioprophylactic or radioprotective interventions) are those that either enhance the resistance/tolerance of normal tissues to radiation or interfere directly with the initial radiochemical events. Post-exposure countermeasures, on the other hand, are interventions that interfere with downstream pathophysiological manifestations of radiation by preventing or reducing the progression of radiation damage or by facilitating the resolution of radiation injury. The distinction between pre-exposure and post-exposure countermeasures is relevant to development of radiation countermeasures for use by the military as opposed to in a civilian mass casualty situation. Radioprotective or radioprophylactic countermeasures are a critical requirement for military personnel, first responders, and rescue and cleanup workers. Such interventions may include, but are by no means limited to, strategies aimed at interfering with radiation-specific mechanisms of injury, such as for example the administration of antioxidants, free radical scavengers, or other cytoprotective agents. In contrast, in the mass casualty situation agents are needed that can be administered within hours to days after radiation exposure. This category therefore includes strategies aimed at ameliorating radiation injury at the pathophysiological, cellular, or molecular level; or even those aimed at treating (reversing) established complications. Regardless of the application, a useful medical countermeasure against radiation should ideally fulfill most of the criteria listed in Table 1.

In the following sections, a number of highly diverse approaches aimed specifically at ameliorating intestinal radiation injury will be discussed.

Free Radical Scavengers and Antioxidants
Tissue injury in response to low linear-energy-transfer radiation is largely mediated by the action of reactive oxygen species. Therefore, various antioxidants and free radical scavengers have been investigated as potential protective strategies.

Table 1. Characteristics of the "ideal" radioprotective compound

- Effective
- Safe (few side effects *and* drug interactions)
- Stable and easy to produce
- Timing of administration not critical
- No abuse potential
- Useful in all operational environments (military operations, homeland defense, radiation accidents)
- Favorable logistics (stable in the field, low weight/cube)
- Useful in combined injury situations

The most thoroughly studied radioprotective agent is the aminothiol amifostine (WR2721, Ethyol), a free radical scavenger, developed after the Second World War to prevent radiation injury to troops on the nuclear battlefield. Amifostine reduces the severity of early and delayed radiotherapeutic injuries at several anatomical sites, including the intestine [82-85]. However, the many trials that have been undertaken have been limited in size due to the cost of amifostine and side effects such as hypotension and nausea. In fact, the performance-degrading toxicities of amifostine preclude its use in military personnel, first responders, and cleanup personnel. Moreover, because of the narrowness of the time-window during which amifostine must be administered relative to radiation exposure, this compound is also not useful as a radiation countermeasure for civilian use.

A number of other antioxidants, free radical scavengers, and cytoprotective compounds have undergone testing to assess their efficacy as modifiers of intestinal radiation responses. For example, the L-cysteine prodrug, ribose-cysteine, which stimulates glutathione biosynthesis, affords protection against small- and large-bowel injury in rats and pigs [83, 86]. Several compounds extracted from natural products with antioxidant properties reduce injury from total body radiation exposure. Propylthiouracil (PTU), used to treat hyperthyroidism, protects against radiation-induced tissue injury, possibly because of reduced thyroid activity resulting in a reduced oxidant state in combination with direct antioxidant and immunomodulatory effects of PTU [87].

Superoxide dismutase (SOD), the class of enzymes that converts superoxide to hydrogen peroxide, has been the subject of active investigation for many years. SOD exists in three main forms: mitochondrial manganese SOD (MnSOD), cytoplasmic copper-zinc SOD (Cu/ZnSOD), and extracellular SOD (EC-SOD). Gene therapy with MnSOD in lung, esophagus, and intestine ameliorates several aspects of radiation toxicity in these organs [88-90]. Administration of Cu/ZnSOD does not affect structural radiation injury after abdominal irradiation in mice, but does reduce inflammation [91]. Small molecule compounds that mimic the effects of SOD and/or catalase have been developed and show efficacy, but their ability to specifically protect from intestinal radiation lethality after total body irradiation remains to be determined [92-94].

Tirilazad, a lazaroid or 21-aminosteroid, is a steroid-like compound that, while lacking corticosteroid and mineralocorticoid effects, localizes within cell membranes and inhibits lipid peroxidation. Tirilazad, applied topically in the intestine, is highly protective against radiation toxicity, but the drug does not confer protection when administered systemically

[95]. Similarly, topical application of other inhibitors of lipid peroxidation also protects against experimental intestinal radiation toxicity is protective whether given as oral pretreatment or as a brief topical application [96]. Probucol, another antioxidant that inhibits the formation of peroxides, confers intestinal protection in rats when given either intraluminally or systemically [97]. Interestingly, oral administration of melatonin, leading to increased plasma levels of this hormone, protects against radiation-induced intestinal injury, possibly due to its radical scavenging properties and its stimulatory effects on antioxidant enzymes and the cellular DNA repair machinery [98]. Melatonin also reduces lethality after total body irradiation [99].

Among the nutritional antioxidants, there has been particular interest in the use of vitamin A [100] and vitamin E (tocols) [101-103]. The beneficial effects of vitamin E in the healing of irradiated wounds suggest that these compounds may also be of benefit in some combined injury situations [104]. While there are minor differences in antioxidant properties among the tocols (i.e., the α, β, γ, and δ tocopherols and the α, β, γ, and δ tocotrienols), there are major difference among these compounds in their affinity to endothelial cells and in their ability to inhibit the enzyme hydroxyl-methyl-glutaryl-coenzyme A (HMG-CoA) reductase. Hence, further discussion of tocols as radioprotective agents has been included below under the subheading "Endothelial oriented strategies".

Curcumin, a naturally occurring phytochemical from turmeric, is another nutritional antioxidant that has been subject to investigation as a radioprotective agent [105], although there is some doubt as to whether curcumin confers protection against radiation-induced lethality after total body irradiation [106]. Similar to vitamin E, curcumin has also been shown to accelerate wound healing after irradiation and hence could be of use in certain types of combined injury [107, 108].

Modulators of Cytokines, Growth Factors, or Chemokines

Cytokines are soluble signaling proteins produced by a variety of cell types that regulate a vast array of cellular functions including growth, differentiation, chemotaxis, mediator release, and gene expression. Consequently, cytokines have been extensively studied as potential radiation-response modifiers in tumors and normal tissues. In the acute setting, the focus has mainly been on anti-inflammatory and enterotrophic cytokine manipulations, while fibrogenic cytokines, especially TGFβ, have been the target in strategies aimed at reducing intestinal radiation fibrosis [25, 109].

IL1 has a wide range of biological activities. The 2 distinct forms of IL1 (IL1α and IL1β) are derived from different genes, the amino acid sequences are only 20% homologous, but both IL1s bind to the same receptor and have similar biological properties. Both also have modest and highly schedule-dependent radioprotective effects in mouse intestine [110, 111].

Interleukin 7 (IL7), which plays critical roles in the development of B and T cells, also influences the function of mature NK cells and monocytes/macrophages. In the intestine, IL7 protects intraepithelial lymphocytes (IELs) from undergoing apoptosis [112]. It may also protect the intestinal stem cell compartment from radiation, as demonstrated indirectly by the increased crypt-cell sensitivity of IL7-receptor knockout mice to whole-body irradiation [113].

Interleukin 11 (IL11), in addition to its hematopoietic and immunomodulating activities, also serves to protect and restore the GI mucosa. Administration of IL11 protects mice against the intestinal effects of total-body irradiation [114-116]. It is possible that at least part of the protective effect is simply the result of induction of transient cell cycle arrest [117], somewhat similar to TGFβ, which is assumed to protect intestinal crypt cells by inhibiting their progression through G1 [118]. Despite these encouraging preclinical results, systemic administration of IL11 to humans has been hampered by severe side effects, including fluid retention and multisystem organ failure. In contrast, oral delivery of an enteric-coated formulation of recombinant human IL11 (rhIL11) does not lead to systemic distribution of rhIL11 in rats or human subjects and is thus not associated with the toxicity seen after systemic administration [119, 120]. A recent study showed significant protection against early intestinal radiation injury when human recombinant IL11 was administered once-daily directly into the intestinal lumen of rats [121], suggesting that oral administration of an enterosoluble form of IL11 may be a promising radiation countermeasure.

Interleukin 15 (IL15) is widely expressed by epithelial cells, stromal cells, and immune cells. Because IL15 shares some biological properties with IL2 (which actually promotes, rather than ameliorates, mucositis), it is not known whether inhibition or stimulation of IL15 activities is beneficial in the context of radiation. However, IL15 promotes survival of intraepithelial lymphocytes (IEL), inhibits epithelial expression of interleukin 8 (IL8) and monocyte chemoattractant protein 1 (MCP1) [122, 123], and stimulates proliferation of intestinal epithelial cells [124]. While IL15 has not been systematically studied in radiation injury, it confers an impressive degree of protection against the intestinal toxicity of irinotecan (CPT-11), a chemotherapeutic agent that is notorious for causing GI toxicity, mainly due to dose-limiting diarrhea [125].

The angiogenic growth factors, acidic fibroblast growth factor (aFGF; FGF1), basic fibroblast growth factor (bFGF; FGF2), and vascular endothelial growth factor, have all been shown to be radioprotective in the small intestine of mice exposed to total-body irradiation [15, 126]. The mechanisms of protection are unclear. The many documented effects of bFGF include protection of endothelial cells from apoptosis, enhanced repair of DNA damage, and increased proliferation and enhanced restitution of intestinal epithelium. It remains to be determined whether the enteroprotective effect of bFGF is primarily a direct effect on epithelial cells [127], secondary to reduced endothelial cell apoptosis [15], or a combination of the two.

The keratinocyte growth factors, KGF1 (FGF7) and KGF2 (FGF10), are two other members of the FGF superfamily in which there has been significant interest. In contrast to aFGF and bFGF, which activate several FGF receptors, KGF only activates the receptor FGFR2IIIb in epithelial cells and hence may have greater target cell specificity. Recombinant human KGF1, administered either subcutaneously or intravenously to mice before single-dose, total-body or fractionated abdominal irradiation, increased crypt survival and LD50 [128, 129]. There is some evidence suggesting that recombinant human KGF1 can also reduce intestinal radiation mucositis [130], although there are some questions related to expression of functional KGF receptors in the gut.

Stem cell factor (SCF, mast cell growth factor, or c-Kit ligand) functions to promote stem/progenitor cell survival, proliferation and differentiation, adhesion, activation, and migration/chemoattraction. SCF is a less effective radioprotectant in the gut than most of the other cytokines discussed in this section, but appears to confer some protection in the proximal intestine in the mouse model [129, 131].

The growth hormone (GH)/insulin-like growth factor 1 (IGF1) axis plays a critical role in the growth, development, and restitution of many different organ systems, including intestine.

Both GH and IGF1 are generally considered growth-promoting. Rats fed a high-protein diet and receiving daily subcutaneous administration of recombinant human GH beginning 3 days before irradiation showed increased mucosal height, increased crypt cell proliferation, and reduced mortality and epithelial apoptosis 2-7 days after an "intestinal" LD50 (12 Gy) of abdominal radiation [132]. GH has also been shown to enhance anastomotic healing in irradiated bowel [133]. Although IGF1 was enteroprotective after abdominal irradiation in rats when the growth factor was administered by mini-osmotic pumps [134], short-term systemic administration of IGF1 did not reduce intestinal injury in a mouse model of localized irradiation of kidney and surrounding bowel [135].

Several other cytokines have growth-promoting effects on the intestinal mucosa, including, for example, epidermal growth factor/ transforming growth factor α (EGF/TGFα) and hepatocyte growth factor. Although concerns about tumor protection or tumor growth promotion would likely preclude their use in cancer patients, these cytokines could be useful in accidental radiation exposure and in the radiation terrorism situation, and therefore investigation of their use in these scenarios may be indicated.

Chemokines are technically considered members of the cytokine superfamily, but have unique and rather distinct effects. The name originates from the combination of "chemotaxis" and "cytokine." The central concept of chemokines is their ability to induce directed migration of cells, such as inflammatory cells, to sites of tissue injury. Depending on the situation, this can have both beneficial and detrimental effects. Macrophage inflammatory protein 1α (MIP1α) is a chemokine with a wide range of biological activities. MIP1α plays potential roles in monocyte chemotaxis in tissue responses to injury, including radiation injury. BB-10010, a MIP1α analogue, administered 3 hours before total-body irradiation of mice, conferred a statistically significant (albeit unimpressive in magnitude) protection in terms of increased crypt survival [136].

Enterotrophic Interventions

The goal of enterotrophic (growth-promoting) strategies in intestinal radiation protection is to increase the resistance of the mucosa to radiation injury and/or to enhance its capacity for recovery. Enterotrophic strategies fall into one of the following three categories: nutrients, GI peptides, and cytokines (discussed in the previous section).

The category of enterotrophic nutrients includes a variety of substances and compounds, such as fiber, short-chain fatty acids, and certain amino acids, for example, glutamine and arginine. In general, glutamine supports mucosal structure and recovery. Glutamine ameliorates intestinal radiation toxicity after abdominal irradiation in some studies [137-139], but other authors have been unable to confirm a significant protective effect in similar models [140]. Notably, a large-scale randomized clinical trial in radiation therapy patients showed no benefit of glutamine for the reduction of gastrointestinal radiation injury [141]. Oral arginine supplementation has also been shown to enhance mucosal recovery and bacterial clearance after abdominal irradiation [142], although this finding also does not appear to be uniformly reproducible [143].

There are numerous GI peptide hormones that have potent enterotrophic activities. In addition to GH (discussed in the previous section), this category includes, for example, neurotensin, cholecystokinin, bombesin, peptide YY, and glucagon-like peptide-2. While these peptides have protective effects in various types of intestinal injury, they have not yet been subjected to systematic testing in radiation injury.

Anti-inflammatory Strategies

Probably as a result of the complex role of inflammation in radiation injury, the use of traditional anti-inflammatory drugs to ameliorate radiation injury has been generally disappointing. Acetylsalicylic acid (aspirin) may ameliorate intestinal radiation toxicity to some extent [144], while other nonsteroidal anti-inflammatory drugs do not appear to be effective at all [145]. Sulfasalazine may be of some benefit in the reduction of acute radiation-induced intestinal side effects [146]. In contrast, salicylic acid derivatives, developed specifically for therapy of inflammatory bowel disease, while having potent anti-inflammatory effects, are not only ineffective, but likely exacerbate intestinal radiation injury [147-150]. The immunomodulator orazipone, on the other hand, did reduce intestinal radiation injury after localized irradiation in a rat model, although the exact mechanism by which this broad-based locally acting immunomodulator ameliorates radiation enteropathy remains to be elucidated [151]. It is possible that future agents, targeted to specific aspects of the inflammatory process, may prove more effective in modifying the intestinal radiation response.

Many studies have assessed modification of cyclo-oxygenase (COX) activity or components of the arachidonic acid cascade in the context of radiation responses in normal tissues, including intestine. Inhibition of COX2, for instance, protects against intestinal radiation injury [152]. Other protective agents are prostaglandin E (PGE) and its synthetic analogues, although the exact mechanisms by which these compounds confer cytoprotection are still not known. In animal studies, PGE2 is radioprotective in the intestine [153, 154]. Oral administration of enprostil (a PGE2 analogue) or luminal application of misoprostol (a PGE1 analogue) protects against intestinal radiation toxicity [155, 156]. Misoprostol and a prostacyclin analogue (iloprost) were toxic when given separately, but a combination of the two compounds conferred synergistic radiation protection with considerable amelioration of toxicity [157].

Interventions Targeting Intraluminal Contents

Breakdown of the mucosal barrier during the acute phase of radiation injury exposes subepithelial tissues to the detrimental actions of the contents of the intestinal lumen. The significance of the intestinal contents in acute radiation-induced mucosal damage has been recognized for a century. Not surprisingly, modifications of the various intraluminal factors have been explored as strategies to ameliorate intestinal radiation injury.

A possible role for intestinal bacteria in the development of the acute intestinal radiation response was already proposed in 1906 [158]. Subsequently, the role of the bacterial flora has been extensively studied in germ-free animal models [159-161], as well as in models involving more or less selective "decontamination" with different antimicrobial agents [162-165]. These studies suggest that protection is likely conferred by two different mechanisms. In germ-free animals, the epithelial cell proliferation rate is lower than in normal animals, survival after abdominal irradiation is directly related to cellular transit time [160], and enteral infusion of bile acids restores both proliferation rate and radiosensitivity to control levels [161]. In other words, the relative radioresistance of germ-free animals seems to be the result of a lack of bile salt-deconjugating bacteria. On the other hand, treatment of conventional animals with antibiotics against the aerobic flora before or after irradiation increases survival without significant changes in epithelial cell transit time or excretion of deconjugated bile salts [162]. In contrast to the benefits of reducing the intraluminal aerobic flora, antimicrobials that reduce the anaerobic flora may be detrimental in the total body irradiation situation and should be avoided. Careful selection of antibiotic treatment regimen has been shown to protect lethally irradiated canines [166]. A combination of oral and parenteral antibiotics may reduce bacterial translocation and confer considerable protection. In the clinical situation, it is likely that the proper balance in the bacterial flora is optimal in terms of minimizing radiation toxicity. Hence, there is significant interest in probiotic therapies as a way to enhance the resistance of the gut to irradiation and/or to minimize intestinal radiation toxicity [167].

Among the various intraluminal factors, pancreatic enzymes exert a particularly strong influence on development of intestinal radiation toxicity [168]. Reducing pancreatic enzyme secretion by surgical or dietary methods attenuates acute mucosal injury and increases survival after abdominal irradiation in dogs [169-171]. Pancreatic duct occlusion in rats confers protection both against early radiation mucositis and delayed intestinal radiation fibrosis [172]. Moreover, the reduced levels of intestinal injury seen in dogs fed an elemental diet before and during pelvic irradiation appear to be at least partly due to feedback inhibition of the exocrine pancreas [173]. The flavonoid morin, which does not only have anti-oxidant properties, but also stimulates DNA repair and inhibits trypsin activity, protects against radiation-induced lethality and intestinal injury [174].

The most clinically relevant method of reducing intraluminal pancreatic secretions in patients may be by administration of synthetic somatostatin receptor analogues. These drugs are primarily used in the treatment of patients with acromegaly and as a therapeutic agent in patients with various neuroendocrine tumors, notably carcinoid. However, somatostatin analogues also act as "universal gastrointestinal inhibitors" and are used for a number of indications in gastroenterological disorders and gastrointestinal surgery, such as, intractable diarrhea, short gut syndrome, pancreatic and enterocutanous fistulae, pancreatitis, and bleeding esophageal varices. Because of their strong inhibitory effect on gastrointestinal secretion, somatostatin analogues result in a "pharmacological, reversible exocrine pancreatectomy." Somatostatin analogues are extremely well tolerated and the maximal tolerated dose (MTD) in humans has not been reached, even though patients with neuroendocrine tumors have received doses in excess of 100,000 µg/day. Short-term administration of the somatostatin analogue, octreotide, markedly ameliorates mucosal radiation injury in the small bowel [175-177]. Our laboratory is currently investigating a novel somatostatin analog, SOM230, with superior metabolic stability and broader affinity to somatostatin receptors compared to octreotide, in the total body irradiation model. Studies to date indicate that SOM230 ameliorates structural (mucosal) intestinal radiation injury, decreases lethality, and prolongs post-radiation survival time when administered either before and after, or only after irradiation [178].

Endothelial Oriented Strategies

As discussed above, radiation induces a plethora of changes in the microvascular endothelium. Some of these changes are transient but may be mechanistically involved in the development of various aspects of acute intestinal radiation toxicity. Other changes are more sustained and may play direct roles in radiation fibrosis and in the mechanisms of chronicity of injury. The post-radiation shift in the thrombohemorrhagic balance toward procoagulation and the accompanying cellular effects of thrombin are particularly promising targets for modulation.

Administration of "traditional" antithrombotics, such as heparin, warfarin, or acetylsalicylic acid, confers some, albeit inconsistent, protection against radiation injury in some organs, including intestine. Recent studies have also shown that inhibition of ADP-induced platelet aggregation with clopidogrel, as well as direct thrombin inhibition with hirudin, markedly reduce acute and chronic intestinal radiation injury in a rat model [48, 179]. When these agents are administered in effective doses, however, their use is also associated with a significant risk of bleeding complications, and thus the potential for clinical use is likely limited, particularly in the combined injury situation, where optimal hemostasis may be critical [180]. Nevertheless, these agents may have still have potential application as adjuvant therapies together with other radioprotective agents. In contrast, restoring the TM-protein C pathway or blocking PAR1 presents more attractive and presumably safer alternatives by which to prevent or reduce radiation-induced endothelial dysfunction and its downstream detrimental effects.

Recently, the cholesterol-lowering drugs, statins, have emerged as a promising intervention for counteracting radiation-induced endothelial dysfunction. Statins are among the most commonly prescribed drugs in the Western world and extremely safe. Statins lower cholesterol by inhibiting the conversion of HMG-CoA to mevalonic acid, the rate-limiting step in cholesterol biosynthesis. In addition, by decreasing the generation of various mevalonate pathway intermediates, statins reduce the isoprenylation of small GTP-binding proteins (eg, Rho, Ras, Rac) and other proteins, resulting in effects that are unrelated to lipid-lowering. Through these pleiotropic effects, statins influence a vast array of metabolic and physiological processes, including cell proliferation, apoptosis, immune function, inflammation, coagulation, and fibrinolysis. The vascular endothelium is a major effector cell compartment for the pleiotropic effects of statins. The mechanism underlying most of these effects is related to increased expression and enhanced activity of endothelial nitric oxide synthase (eNOS). Statins prominently upregulate endothelial TM *in vitro*, in an eNOS-dependent manner [181, 182] by a mechanism that involves S-nitrosylation, dissociation of heat shock protein 90 (HSP90) from heat shock factor 1 (HSF1), and binding of HSF1 to specific heat shock elements in the TM promoter [183]. Statins ameliorate gut toxicity *in vivo* after localized irradiation of exteriorized small intestine in mice and after localized, fractionated small bowel irradiation in rats [184, 185], as well as lung injury in mice after irradiation of the chest [186]. The use of statins as radiation response modifiers after total body irradiation is currently under investigation. Interestingly, modulation of nitric oxide has been shown to ameliorate the hematopoietic radiation syndrome in mice [187] and eNOS is absolutely required for appropriate hematopoietic progenitor cell mobilization and recovery after myelosuppressive insults [188]. Hence, the fact that most of the pleiotropic statin effects, including the regulation of TM, are eNOS-dependent, provides a strong rationale for testing statins in hematopoietic injury as well.

As mentioned in the section on antioxidants, tocols (tocopherols and tocotrienols) protect progenitor cells in the GI tract and hematopoietic system from the effects of ionizing radiation by virtue of their antioxidant properties and by preventing endothelial dysfunction. While comparative studies of antioxidant activity of tocols suggest that their antioxidant properties are relatively similar [189, 190], there are substantial differences among tocols in terms of their radioprotective efficacies. Hence, we have evidence to suggest that γ tocotrienol, an unsaturated analogue of tocopherol, is significantly more potent as a radiation prophylactic agent than other tocols (estimated dose-reduction factor >1.3). An important feature that distinguishes γ tocotrienol from other tocols relates to its ability to inhibit HMG-CoA reductase [191]. Hence, compared to tocopherols, tocotrienols accumulate in endothelial cells to levels that are 25-95-fold greater [192] and are 10-fold more effective in reducing adhesion molecule expression [193]. The HMG-CoA reductase inhibitory activity of γ tocotrienol is 30-fold greater than that of α tocotrienol [194]. This feature places γ tocotrienol in a unique position among the tocols. Ongoing studies support the notion that much of the radioprotective effect of γ tocotrienol is attributable to HMG-CoA reductase inhibition (unpublished data). A recent study showed that the mechanism by which γ tocotrienol reduces the activity of HMG-CoA reductase is by triggering ubiquitination of the enzyme, resulting in endoplasmic reticulum associated degradation by 26 S proteasomes. Hence, there are interesting possibilities for combining γ tocotrienol with statins to take advantage of the potential synergy from increasing enzyme degradation and inhibiting enzyme activity simultaneously.

The phosphodiesterase inhibitor pentoxifylline, in addition to exhibiting antioxidant properties, has a variety of other biochemical, immunomodulatory, anti-cytokine, vascular, and rheologic effects. While the initial impetus for investigating this compound in the context of radiation injury was its presumed rheological properties [195, 196], other effects are more likely to be responsible for its efficacy, particularly its endothelial effects. Hence, pentoxifylline is one of relatively few drugs that has been shown to strongly upregulate endothelial TM [197, 198] and downregulate tissue factor expression [199]. In the context of radiation toxicity, pentoxifylline has been used, mostly together with vitamin E, to treat established radiation-induced fibrosis and found to be effective in some studies [200, 201]. The use of pentoxifylline to prevent early radiation toxicity in general and, specifically in the gut, is unclear. However, because pentoxifylline also appears to have benefits in trauma, shock, and critical care [202-204], it may be of particular benefit in the combined injury situation.

Neuroimmune Modulation

Accumulating evidence shows that interactions between the enteric nervous system and various cells of the intestinal immune system are critically important regulators of the intestinal response to injury, including radiation injury. As a result, modulation of these interactions is emerging as a strategy for ameliorating acute radiation toxicity.

Early evidence supporting a role for the nervous system as regulator of the radiation response was derived from observations that atropine ameliorated post-radiation villus morphology and reduced crypt cell depletion in the mouse, thus suggesting involvement of parasympathetic effector sites [205]. More recently, the previously discussed interactions between sensory (afferent) nerves and various types of immune cells, notably mast cells, have been studied most extensively and appear to hold the most promise in terms of the development of medical countermeasures against radiation.

As discussed above, the 2 primary neuropeptides released by sensory nerve endings in the gut are substance P and CGRP. Substance P exerts its effects via the neurokinin 1 (NK1) receptor. Small molecule NK1 receptor antagonists have been shown to reduce substance P-induced production of TNFα and TGFβ by mast cells and ameliorate some aspects of acute

GI toxicity after whole-body irradiation [206]. An NK1 receptor antagonist (GR203040) has been shown to ameliorate radiation-induced intestinal injury in a ferret model [207]. More recently, the NK1 receptor antagonist SR140333 has been shown to reduce intestinal radiation injury in a rat model of localized irradiation, while the substance P analog GR73632 exacerbates injury [64]. Moreover, administration of CGRP ameliorates intestinal radiation injury whereas a CGRP antagonist exacerbates injury. Hence, to the extent that findings from a model of localized intestinal radiation exposure can be extrapolated to the total body irradiation situation, these observations indicate that substance P and CGRP exert opposing effects during the intestinal radiation response, with substance P being detrimental and CGRP beneficial.

Intestinal Dysfunction in Burns, Trauma, Sepsis, and Multiple Organ Dysfunction

The intestine may sustain direct injury as part of blunt or penetrating traumatic injury, as well as is in the context of barotrauma as seen in blast injury. Discussions of these types of injuries and their management may be found in standard and specialized surgical textbooks. The following sections will review the concept of the intestine as a pro-inflammatory organ in conditions that do not directly affect the macro-anatomical integrity of the bowel, and subsequently discuss interventions aimed at minimizing the pathophysiological impact of intestinal dysfunction in burn injury, trauma, sepsis, and MODS.

Mechanisms and Pathophysiology

The intestine plays a critical role in the development of systemic pathophysiological manifestations and complications after burn, trauma, and in sepsis. The reduction in intestinal blood flow that occurs under these circumstances is believed to be the key event that triggers loss of intestinal barrier function and thus changes the gut into a pro-inflammatory organ.

The digestive and absorptive functions and the barrier functions of the intestine are equally important. Hence, while the intestine is responsible for uptake of essential nutrients from the body's external environment (the intestinal lumen), it also separates the external environment from the interior of the body. Because the combined surface area of the gastrointestinal tract is more than 200 times larger than the surface of the skin, the epithelial lining of the gut clearly constitutes the body's most extensive and important barrier to the exterior.

The intestinal barrier is formed by the intestinal epithelial cells, connected to each other by tight junctions. The tight junctions serve as an adjustable, semi-permeable barrier that regulates the para-cellular passive diffusion of solutes across the intestinal mucosa. The intestinal epithelial cells with their tight junctions and mucus layer, form the first line defense against the luminal bacteria, toxins, digestive enzymes, and other macromolecules. The second line defense is formed by the immune system. Any condition that increases intestinal permeability and/or compromises the integrity of the mucosal immune system will exacerbate tissue injury.

Intestinal ischemia or hypo-perfusion is one of the most common causes of deficient intestinal barrier function. While intestinal ischemia can be caused by arterial obstruction or venous outflow obstruction, it occurs more often as a condition of relative ischemia caused either by an absolute decrease in intestinal perfusion or by an inability to increase blood flow in response to increased metabolic demands.

Burn injury, blunt or penetrating trauma, sepsis, and MODS are all clinical conditions where intestinal hypo-perfusion and a decreased intestinal barrier functions plays an important role in the development of complications. All of these conditions are associated with a state of hypovolemia, either induced by blood loss (trauma) or fluid sequestration in extravascular tissues (trauma, burn injury, sepsis, MODS). The decrease in circulating blood volume induces a redistribution of blood flow to maintain oxygen delivery to critical organs like the brain and the heart. At the same time, there is compensatory vasoconstriction in the splanchnic circulation. If, under these conditions, the intestinal blood flow is no longer sufficient to fulfill the metabolic needs of the bowel, breakdown of the epithelial barrier occurs.

It was previously believed that translocated bacteria and endotoxin from the intestinal lumen are the direct causes of the distant organ injury that is seen in conditions of trauma, burn or sepsis. The translocated bacteria and toxins were thought to reach the systemic circulation via the portal vein or the lymphatic system and that, after entering the bloodstream, the bacteria would be transported to distant organs where they would cause additional damage. This theory was supported by studies conducted in rodents, where bacteria were found in portal blood and in the liver after burn, trauma and hemorrhagic shock [208]. However, subsequent research in human patients failed to reproduce these findings and thus the role of the gut during the development of the systemic inflammatory response syndrome (SIRS) and MODS had to be reevaluated [209]. As a result, the prevailing view is now that the gut itself is transformed into a pro-inflammatory organ during conditions associated with intestinal hypo-perfusion and bacterial translocation [210, 211].

Intestinal hypo-perfusion and subsequent reperfusion elicit the production of large amounts of free radicals and other oxygen-derived cytotoxic products. These toxic oxygen species cause tissue injury either directly by damaging the intestinal barrier or indirectly by inducing the production of pro-inflammatory factors, including cytokines, chemokines, and other mediators, by endothelial cells or activated leukocytes. Gut-derived IL6 is believed to be a critical mediator in the development of intestinal reperfusion injury and subsequent distant organ injury. IL6 is important in the induction of the acute phase response to injury and can promote detrimental inflammatory responses. High concentrations of gut-derived IL6 are associated with an adverse clinical outcome [212]. Other pro-inflammatory cytokines that are produced in the gut in ischemia/reperfusion injury include IL1, IL8, and TNFα.

Besides a production site of chemokines, intestinal tissue appears to be an important priming bed for activated polymorphonuclear leukocytes (PMNs). High numbers of PMNs are present in gut tissue after hypoperfusion and PMNs themselves are an important source of cytotoxic reactive oxygen metabolites. Primed PMNs, as well as other pro-inflammatory factors, may reach the systemic circulation through the intestinal lymphatics to contribute to a systemic inflammatory response, eventually resulting in failure of other organs like the lungs, liver, and kidneys. A schematic representation of the event leading to MODS is shown in Figure 5.

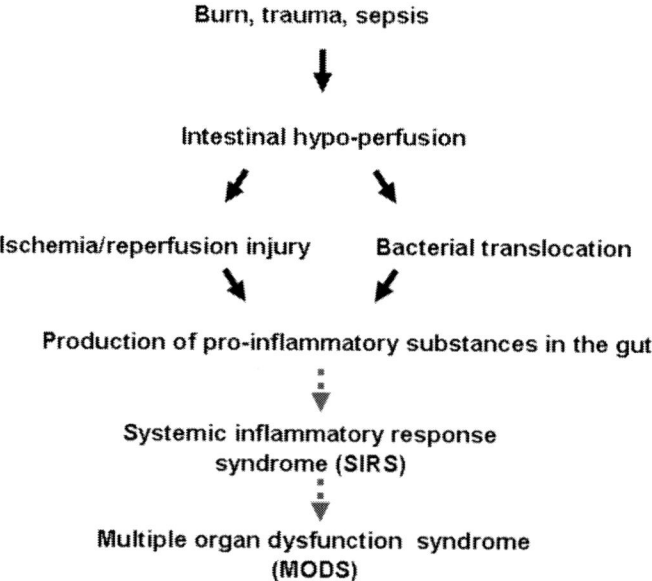

Figure 5. Diagram the central role of the gastrointestinal tract in the pathogenesis of MODS in the context of burn injury, trauma, or sepsis.

Preventive and Therapeutic Interventions

A variety of preventive and therapeutic strategies have been shown to be beneficial in attenuating gut-dysfunction related to burn, trauma, and sepsis.

Resuscitation

Adequate and prompt resuscitation is the first and most important intervention to prevent intestinal injury after burn, trauma, or sepsis. The choice of fluid continues to be a topic of debate. Both crystalloids and colloids have been shown to be effective. Fluid replacement should be used to correct hypovolemia and to increase cardiac output. However, it is probably at least as important, perhaps even more important, to adjust resuscitation to parameters reflecting the splanchnic circulation instead of the systemic circulation [213]. Hence, survival can be improved by the use of normalization of gastric mucosal pH, assessed by gastric tonometry, as endpoint for resuscitation.

Research has shown that oral resuscitation in burn patients can be used to prevent complications. In the mass casualty situation, the availability of intravenous fluids and supplies is often insufficient [214]. Therefore, resuscitation with oral fluids, such as the widely available World Health Organization Oral Rehydration Solution (WHO ORS), would be a way to prevent delays in fluid therapy.

Vasoactive Drugs

Splanchnic perfusion may also be improved by the use of vasoactive drugs like dopexamine, dobutamine, and dopamine. These drugs may be useful to selectively augment splanchnic perfusion and microcirculation independent of their cardiac effects [215]. However, not all studies using these compounds during shock have shown beneficial effects and the evidence supporting their use is conflicting. Nevertheless, the current consensus is that low-dose dopexamine can be considered to improve splanchnic perfusion in trauma, burn, and sepsis patients.

Changing the Gut Flora

Several strategies have been developed with the aim to change the gut flora in order to decrease sepsis caused by pathogenic enteric microbes. The aim of these strategies is to suppress intestinal colonization with pathogenic bacteria and to promote the growth of non-pathogenic, beneficial bacteria.

In selective gut decontamination (SGD), topical, non-absorbable antibiotics combined with systemic antibiotics are used to decrease the numbers of luminal pathogens, mostly aerobic, gram-negative bacteria. The aim of SGD is to selectively reducing the content of harmful microbes, while not affecting the commensal anaerobic flora. While SGD has been proven to be useful in preventing pulmonary infections in critically ill patients, there is no evidence for a clear reduction in mortality in humans [216, 217]. Moreover, some investigator have raised valid concerns about the development of antibiotic resistance with the use of SGD [218].

The intake of probiotics and prebiotics may be an alternative strategy to regulate luminal bacterial colonization. Probiotics are microorganisms that survive the passage trough the stomach and subsequently colonize the intestine to improve the microbial balance. Lactobacilli and bifidobacteria are the most commonly used probiotics.

Prebiotics are non-digestible carbohydrates, which are used by endogenous bacteria in the colon. They selectively stimulate the growth of beneficial endogenous microbes. Another possible beneficial effect of prebiotics is shortening of the GI transit time, which may also contribute to attenuate bacterial translocation [219]. Several animal studies have shown positive effect of prebiotics, but there is little evidence from large randomized controlled trials that support the use of prebiotics in intestinal failure in humans [220].

Finally, it is important to limit the occurrence of intestinal overgrowth by pathogenic enteric bacteria by critically evaluating the need for interventions that are known to increase bacterial overgrowth. Such interventions include overuse of acid suppressing medication and broad spectrum antibiotics [221].

Nutrition

The early start of enteral nutrition after burn injury and trauma has proven to reduce infectious complications and it is generally recommended to begin enteral feeding 24 to 48 hours after injury [222]. Enteral nutrition is clearly superior to parenteral nutrition in preventing complications. Compared to parenteral nutrition, enteral nutrition also appears to have a more potent effect on the maintenance of gut mucosal integrity. Evidence suggests that parental nutrition increases the stress response and impairs local intestinal immunity. Conversely, studies conducted in surgical patients demonstrate that enteral nutrition is associated with better regulation of the inflammatory response than parenteral nutrition [223]. Nevertheless, there is still insufficient evidence in favor of enteral over parenteral nutrition when mortality is used as the endpoint.

Nutrients such as glutamine, arginine and omega-3 polyunsaturated fatty acids are claimed to have immune enhancing effects. Therefore, intestinal function and immune responses in the trauma patient and in burn injury may be further improved by the use of special feeding formulas containing immunonutrients [224]. Glutamine is probably the most studied immunonutrient and many, but not all studies have shown a beneficial effect of glutamine in various types of injury. Glutamine is a conditionally essential amino acid that serves as the main "fuel source" for intestinal epithelial cells. Because glutamine has trophic effects on the mucosa it is thought that glutamine supplementation may enhance the epithelial barrier function of the intestine. Glutamine also has antioxidant properties and promotes the immune response [225]. The amino acid, arginine, is the precursor of nitric oxide and has a wide variety of potential beneficial effects. Conditions such as trauma, burn injury and sepsis are associated with increased arginine breakdown and may lead to an arginine deficient state [226]. Under such circumstances arginine supplementation may be beneficial.

Conclusion

The previous view that normal tissue radiation injuries depend only on the extent of radiation-induced killing of target cells has been supplanted. Instead, it is now well recognized that the mechanism by which normal tissue injury occurs is a combination of cytocidal effects (clonogenic and apoptotic cell death), functional (non-cytocidal) effects, and secondary effects (reactive and downstream cellular or tissue phenomena). Moreover, the traditional and somewhat artificial notion that the hematopoietic, gastrointestinal, and cardiovascular radiation syndromes are separate entities has been replaced by the more logical recognition that total body radiation exposure affects all organ systems and, therefore, the resulting toxicity is more appropriately viewed as a radiation-induced MODS.

In the event of a nuclear/radiological terrorist scenario, combined injury is likely to occur in a high proportion of casualties. Combined injury is complicated, unpredictable, and multifaceted. Therefore, there is a clear need for an improved understanding of the pathophysiology underlying the interactions between radiation and other types of tissue injury, as well as the mechanisms that determine the absence or presence of synergy.

The intestine occupies a key position in the pathophysiology of MODS, whether from radiation or from physical trauma or sepsis. The GI tract is the largest reservoir of microorganisms in the body, constitutes the largest immune system in the body, and contains more neurons than the spinal cord. The GI tract plays an important role in the response to total body radiation exposure, as well as in the response to the physical tissue damage that is likely to occur in a combined injury situation. The involvement of the GI tract in both radiation and traumatic injuries strongly points to prevention of gastrointestinal dysfunction as a key element in the effective management of combined injury victims. There is currently an unmet need to develop effective medical countermeasures against combined injury and to develop medical and surgical treatment algorithms for use in the combined injury situation. In this regard, interventions that target common pathophysiological mechanisms may be particularly promising.

References

[1]   Ledney, GD; Exum, ED; Jackson, WE. Wound-induced alterations in survival of 60Co irradiated mice: importance of wound timing. *Experientia* 1985 41, 614-616.

[2]   Smith, WW; Alderman, IM; Gillespie, RE. Increased survival in irradiated animals treated with bacterial endotoxins. *Am J Physiol* 1957 191, 124-130.

[3]   Smith, WW; Alderman, IM; Schneider, C; Cornfield, J. Sensitivity of irradiated mice to bacterial endotoxin. *Proc Soc Exp Biol Med* 1963 113, 778-781.

[4]   Smith, WW; Alderman, IM; Gillespie, RE. Hematopoietic recovery induced by bacterial endotoxin in irradiated mice. *Am J Physiol* 1958 192, 549-556.

[5]   Smith, WW; Brecher, G; Fred, S; Budd, RA. Effect of endotoxin on the kinetics of hemopoietic colony-forming cells in irradiated mice. *Radiat Res* 1966 27, 710-717.

[6]   Messerschmidt, O. Combined effects of radiation and trauma. *Adv Space Res* 1989 9, 197-201.

[7]   Quastler, H; Lanzl, EF; Keller, ME; Osborne, JW. Acute intestinal radiation death. Studies on roentgen death in mice, III. *Am J Physiol* 1951 164, 546-556.

[8]   Osborne, JW. Prevention of intestinal radiation death by removal of the irradiated intestine. *Radiat Res* 1956 4, 541-546.

[9]   Terry, NHA; Travis, EL. The influence of bone marrow depletion on intestinal radiation damage. *Int J Radiat Oncol Biol Phys* 1989 17, 569-573.

[10]   Monti, P; Wysocki, J; van der Meeren, A; Griffiths, NM. The contribution of radiation-induced injury to the gastrointestinal tract in the development of multi-organ dysfunction syndrome or failure. *Br J Radiol* 2005 Suppl. 27, 89-94.

[11]   Carr, KE. Effects of radiation damage on intestinal morphology. *Int Rev Cytol* 2001 208, 1-119.

[12]   Fajardo, LF; M Berthrong; RE Anderson. Radiation pathology. Oxford University Press: New York, 2001.

[13]   Hauer-Jensen M, Wang J, Denham JW. Mechanisms and modification of the radiation response of gastrointestinal organs. In: Milas L, Ang KK, and Nieder C, eds. Modification of Radiation Response: Cytokines, Growth Factors, and Other Biological Targets. Heidelberg: Springer Verlag, 2002:49-72.

[14]   Denham, JW; Hauer-Jensen, M; Peters, LJ. Is it time for a new formalism to categorise normal tissue radiation injury? *Int J Radiat Oncol Biol Phys* 2001 50, 1105-1106.

[15]   Paris, F; Fuks, Z; Kang, A; Capodieci, P; Juan, G; Ehleiter, D; Haimovitz-Friedman, A; Cordon-Cardo, C; Kolesnick, R. Endothelial apoptosis as the primary lesion initiating intestinal radiation damage in mice. *Science* 2001 293, 293-297.

[16]   Ch'ang, HJ; Maj, JG; Paris, F; Xing, HR; Zhang, J; Truman, JP; Cardon-Cardo, C; Haimovitz-Friedman, A; Kolesnick, R; Fuks, Z. ATM regulates target switching to escalating doses of radiation in the intestines. *Nat Med* 2005 11, 484-490.

[17]   Schuller, BW; Rogers, AB; Cormier, KS; Riley, KJ; Binns, PJ; Julius, R; Hawthorne, MF; Coderre, JA. No significant endothelial apoptosis in the radiation-induced gastrointestinal syndrome. *Int J Radiat Oncol Biol Phys* 2007 68, 205-210.

[18]   Crawford, PA; Gordon, JI. Microbial regulation of intestinal radiosensitivity. *Proc Natl Acad Sci U S A* 2005 102, 13254-13259.

[19] Richter, KK; Fagerhol, MK; Carr, JC; Winkler, JM; Sung, C-C; Hauer-Jensen, M. Association of granulocyte transmigration with structural and cellular parameters of injury in experimental radiation enteropathy. *Radiat Oncol Invest* 1997 5, 275-282.

[20] Hayashi, T; Kusunoki, Y; Hakoda, M; Morishita, Y; Kubo, Y; Maki, M; Kasagi, F; Kodama, K; Macphee, DG; Kyoizumi, S. Radiation dose-dependent increases in inflammatory response markers in A-bomb survivors. *Int J Radiat Biol* 2003 79, 129-136.

[21] Wang, Y; Meng, A; Lang, H; Brown, SA; Konopa, JL; Kindy, MS; Schmiedt, RA; Thompson, JS; Zhou, D. Activation of nuclear factor kappaB In vivo selectively protects the murine small intestine against ionizing radiation-induced damage. *Cancer Res* 2004 64, 6240-6246.

[22] Smith, F; Smith, WW; Andrews, HL; Grenan, MM. Effect of parenteral injections of particulate matter on survival of x-irradiated animals. *Am J Physiol* 1955 182, 396-399.

[23] Langberg, CW; Hauer-Jensen, M; Sung, C-C; Kane, CJM. Expression of fibrogenic cytokines in rat small intestine after fractionated irradiation. *Radiother Oncol* 1994 32, 29-36.

[24] Linard, C; Ropenga, A; Vozenin-Brotons, MC. Abdominal irradiation increases inflammatory cytokine expression and activates NF-kappaB in rat ileal muscularis layer. *Am J Physiol* 2003 285, G556-G565.

[25] Zheng, H; Wang, J; Koteliansky, VE; Gotwals, PJ; Hauer-Jensen, M. Recombinant soluble transforming growth factor-β type II receptor ameliorates radiation enteropathy in the mouse. *Gastroenterology* 2000 119, 1286-1296.

[26] Zheng, H; Wang, J; Letterio, JJ; Ou, X; Hauer-Jensen, M. Dissociation of early and delayed intestinal radiation toxicity in TGF-β1 heterozygous mice. *Radiation Research Society* 2002 49, 103.

[27] Langley, RE; Bump, EA; Quartuccio, SG; Medeiros, D; Braunhut, SJ. Radiation-induced apoptosis in microvascular endothelial cells. *Br J Cancer* 1997 75, 666-672.

[28] Law, MP. Vascular permeability and late radiation fibrosis in mouse lung. *Radiat Res* 1985 103, 60-76.

[29] Dunn, MM; Drab, EA; Rubin, DB. Effects of irradiation on endothelial cell-polymorphonuclear leukocyte interactions. *J Appl Physiol* 1986 60, 1932-1937.

[30] Hallahan, D; Clark, ET; Kuchibhotla, J; Gewertz, BL; Collins, T. E-selectin gene induction by ionizing radiation is independent of cytokine induction. *Biochem Biophys Res Commun* 1995 217, 784-795.

[31] Svanberg, L; Åstedt, B; Kullander, S. On radiation-decreased fibrinolytic activity of vessel walls. *Acta Obstet Gynecol Scand* 1976 55, 49-51.

[32] Verheij, M; Dewit, LGH; van Mourik, JA. The effect of ionizing radiation on endothelial tissue factor activity and its cellular localization. *Thromb Haemost* 1995 73, 894-895.

[33] Jahroudi, N; Ardekani, AM; Greenberger, JS. Ionizing radiation increases transcription of the von Willebrand factor gene in endothelial cells. *Blood* 1996 88, 3801-3814.

[34] Rubin, DB; Drab, EA; Ts'ao, C; Gardner, D; Ward, WF. Prostacyclin synthesis in irradiated endothelial cells cultured from bovine aorta. *J Appl Physiol* 1985 58, 592-597.

[35] Wang, J; Zheng, H; Ou, X; Fink, LM; Hauer-Jensen, M. Deficiency of microvascular thrombomodulin and upregulation of protease-activated receptor 1 in irradiated rat intestine: possible link between endothelial dysfunction and chronic radiation fibrosis. *Am J Pathol* 2002 160, 2063-2072.

[36] Richter, KK; Fink, LM; Hughes, BM; Sung, C-C; Hauer-Jensen, M. Is the loss of endothelial thrombomodulin involved in the mechanism of chronicity in late radiation enteropathy? *Radiother Oncol* 1997 44, 65-71.

[37] Richter, KK; Fink, LM; Hughes, BM; Shmaysani, HM; Sung, C-C; Hauer-Jensen, M. Differential effect of radiation on endothelial cell function in rectal cancer and normal rectum. *Am J Surg* 1998 176, 642-647.

[38] Wang, J; Hauer-Jensen, M. Radiation toxicity and proteinase activated receptors. *Drug Dev Res* 2003 60, 1-8.

[39] Hauer-Jensen, M; Fink, LM; Wang, J. Radiation injury and the protein C pathway. *Crit Care Med* 2004 32, S325-S330.

[40] Esmon, CT; Taylor, FB; Snow, TR. Inflammation and coagulation: linked processes potentially regulated through a common pathway mediated by protein C. *Thromb Haemost* 1991 66, 160-165.

[41] Mosnier, LO; Gale, AJ; Vegneswaran, S; Griffin, JH. Activated protein C variants with normal cytoprotective but reduced anticoagulant activity. *Blood* 2004 104, 1740-1744.

[42] Conway, EM; van de Wouwer, M; Pollefeyt, S; Jurk, K; van Aken, H; de Vriese, A; Weitz, JI; Weiler, H; Hellings, PW; Schaeffer, P; Herbert, J-M; Collen, D; Theilmeier, G. The lectin-like domain of thrombomodulin confers protection from neutrophil-mediated tissue damage by suppressing adhesion molecule expression via nuclear factor κB and mitogen protein kinase pathways. *J Exp Med* 2002 196, 565-577.

[43] Abeyama, K; Stern, DM; Kawahara, K; Yoshimoto, Y; Tanaka, M; Uchimura, T; Ida, N; Yamazaki, Y; Yamada, S; Yamamoto, Y; Yamamoto, H; Iino, S; Taniguchi, N; Maruyama, I. The N-terminal domain of thrombomodulin sequesters high-mobility group-B1 protein, a novel antiinflammatory mechanism. *J Clin Invest* 2005 115, 1267-1274.

[44] Conway, EM; Rosenberg, RD. Tumor necrosis factor suppresses transcription of the thrombomodulin gene in endothelial cells. *Mol Cell Biol* 1988 8, 5588-5592.

[45] Ohji, T; Urano, H; Shirahata, A; Yamagishi, M; Higashi, K; Gotoh, S; Karasaki, Y. Transforming growth factor beta1 and beta2 induce down-modulation of thrombomodulin in human umbilical vein endothelial cells. *Thromb Haemost* 1995 73, 812-818.

[46] Boehme, MWJ; Deng, Y; Raeth, U; Bierhaus, A; Ziegler, R; Stremmel, W; Nawroth, PP. Release of thrombomodulin from endothelial cells by concerted action of TNF-α and neutrophils: in vivo and in vitro studies. *Immunology* 1996 87, 134-140.

[47] Glaser, CB; Morser, J; Clarke, JH; Blasko, E; McLean, K; Kuhn, I; Chang, RJ; Lin, JH; Vilander, L; Andrews, WH; Light, DR. Oxidation of a specific methionin in thrombomodulin by activated neutrophil products blocks cofactor activity. *J Clin Invest* 1992 90, 2565-2573.

[48] Wang, J; Zheng, H; Ou, X; Albertson, CM; Fink, LM; Herbert, J-M; Hauer-Jensen, M. Hirudin ameliorates intestinal radiation toxicity in the rat: support for thrombin

inhibition as strategy to minimize side effects after radiation therapy and as countermeasure against radiation exposure. *J Thromb Haemost* 2004 **2**, 2027-2035.

[49]   Ross, CC; MacLeod, SL; Plaxco, JR; Stites, WEl; Froude, JW; Fink, LM; Hauer-Jensen, M. Direct inactivation of endothelial thrombomodulin by ionizing radiation (Abstr.). *Radiation Research Society* 2006 53, 111.

[50]   Moulin, F; Pearson, JM; Schultze, AE; Scott, MA; Schwartz, KA; Davis, JM; Ganey, PE; Roth, RA. Thrombin is a distal mediator of lipopolysaccharide-induced liver injury in the rat. *J Surg Res* 1996 65, 149-158.

[51]   DeMichele, MAA; Minnear, FL. Modulation of vascular endothelial permeability by thrombin. *Semin Thromb Hemost* 1992 18, 287-295.

[52]   Bizios, R; Lai, L; Fenton, JW; Malik, AB. Thrombin-induced chemotaxis and aggregation of neutrophils. *J Cell Physiol* 1986 128, 485-490.

[53]   Bar-Shavit, R; Kahn, A; Fenton, JW; Wilner, GD. Chemotactic response of monocytes to thrombin. *J Cell Biol* 1983 96, 282-285.

[54]   Yamabe, H; Osawa, H; Inuma, H; Kaizuka, M; Tamura, N; Tsunoda, S; Baba, Y; Shirato, K; Onodera, K. Thrombin stimulates production of transforming growth factor-beta by cultured human mesangial cells. *Nephrol Dial Transplant* 1997 12, 438-442.

[55]   Noda-Heiny, H; Sobel, BE. Vascular smooth muscle cell migration mediated by thrombin and urokinase receptor. *Am J Physiol* 1995 268, C1195-C1201.

[56]   Ragosta, M; Barry, WL; Gimple, LW; Gertz, SD; McCoy, KW; Stouffer, GA; McNamara, CA; Powers, ER; Owens, GK; Sarembock, IJ. Effect of thrombin inhibition with desulfatohirudin on early kinetics of cellular proliferation after balloon angioplasty in atherosclerotic rabbits. *Circulation* 1996 93, 1194-1200.

[57]   Dabbagh, K; Laurent, GJ; McAnulty, RJ; Chambers, RC. Thrombin stimulates smooth muscle cell procollagen synthesis and mRNA levels via a PAR-1 mediated mechanism. *Thromb Haemost* 1998 79, 405-409.

[58]   Chambers, RC; Dabbagh, K; McAnulty, RJ; Gray, AJ; Blanc-Brude, OP; Laurent, GJ. Thrombin stimulates fibroblast procollagen production via proteolytic activation of protease-activated receptor 1. *Biochem J* 1998 333, 121-127.

[59]   Linard, C; Marquette, C; Clarencon, D; Galonnier, M; Mathieu, J; Pennequin, A; Benderitter, M; Gourmelon, P. Acute ileal inflammatory cytokine response induced by irradiation is modulated by subdiaphragmatic vagotomy. *J Neuroimmunol* 2005 168, 83-95.

[60]   Picard, C; Wysocki, J; Griffiths, NM; Linard, C. Sensory nerve ablation modulates abdominal irradiation effects in the rat (Abstr.). *International Congress of Radiation Research* 1999 11, 159.

[61]   Wang, J; Zheng, H; Kulkarni, A; Ou, X; Hauer-Jensen, M. Regulation of early and delayed radiation responses in rat small intestine by capsaicin-sensitive nerves. *Int J Radiat Oncol Biol Phys* 2006 64, 1528-1536.

[62]   Koon, HW; Pothoulakis, C. Immunomodulatory properties of substance P: the gastrointestinal system as a model. *Ann N Y Acad Sci* 2006 1088, 23-40.

[63]   Holzer, P. Implications of tachykinins and calcitonin gene-related peptide in inflammatory bowel disease. *Digestion* 1998 59, 269-283.

[64] Wang, J; Qiu, X; Kulkarni, A; Hauer-Jensen, M. Calcitonin gene-related peptide and substance P regulate the intestinal radiation response. *Clin Cancer Res* 2006 12, 4112-4118.

[65] Skofitsch, G; Savitt, JM; Jacobowitz, DM. Suggestive evidence for a functional unit between mast cells and substance P fibers in the rat diaphragm and mesentery. *Histochemistry* 1985 82, 5-8.

[66] Frieling, T; Cooke, HJ; Wood, JD. Neuroimmune communication in the submucous plexus of guinea pig colon after sensitization to milk antigen. *Am J Physiol* 1994 267, G1087-G1093.

[67] Leon, A; Buriani, A; Dal Taso, R; Fabris, M; Romanello, S; Aloe, L; Levi-Montalcini, R. Mast cells synthesize, store, and release nerve growth factor. *Proc Natl Acad Sci USA* 1994 92, 3739-3743.

[68] Stein, J; Ries, J; Barrett, KE. Disruption of intestinal barrier function associated with experimental colitis: possible role of mast cells. *Am J Physiol* 1998 274, G203-G209.

[69] Sedgwick, DM; Ferguson, A. Dose-response studies of depletion and repopulation of rat intestinal mucosal mast cells after irradiation. *Int J Radiat Biol* 1994 65, 483-495.

[70] Echtenacher, B; Mannel, DN; Hultner, L. Critical protective role of mast cells in a model of acute septic peritonitis. *Nature* 1996 381, 75-77.

[71] Malaviya, R; Ikeda, T; Ross, E; Abraham, SN. Mast cell modulation of neutrophil influx and bacterial clearance at sites of infection through TNF-α. *Nature* 1996 381, 77-80.

[72] Zheng, H; Wang, J; Hauer-Jensen, M. Role of mast cells in early and delayed radiation injury in rat intestine. *Radiat Res* 2000 153, 533-539.

[73] MacFarlane, SR; Seatter, MJ; Kanke, T; Hunter, GD; Plevin, R. Proteinase-activated receptors. *Pharmacol Rev* 2001 53, 245-282.

[74] Mall, M; Gonska, T; Thomas, J; Hirtz, S; Schreiber, R; Kunzelmann, K. Activation of ion secretion via proteinase-activated receptor-2 in human colon. *Am J Physiol* 2002 282, G200-G210.

[75] Cuffe, JE; Bertog, M; Velazquez-Rocha, S; Dery, O; Bunnett, NW; Korbmacher, C. Basolateral PAR-2 receptors mediate KCl secretion and inhibition of Na^+ absorption in the mouse distal colon. *J Physiol* 2002 539, 209-222.

[76] Coelho, AM; Vergnolle, N; Guiard, B; Fioramonti, J; Bueno, L. Proteinases and proteinase-activated receptor 2: a possible role to promote visceral hyperalgesia in rats. *Gastroenterology* 2002 122, 1035-1047.

[77] Linden, DR; Manning, BP; Bunnett, NW; Mawe, GW. Agonists of proteinase-activated receptor 2 excite guinea pig ileal myenteric neurons. *Eur J Pharmacol* 2001 431, 311-314.

[78] Fiorucci, S; Mencarelli, A; Palazzetti, B; Distrutti, E; Vergnolle, N; Hollenberg, MD; Wallace, JL; Morelli, A; Cirino, G. Proteinase-activated receptor 2 is an anti-inflammatory signal for colonic lamina propria lymphocytes in a mouse model of colitis. *Proc Natl Acad Sci USA* 2001 98, 13936-13941.

[79] Miike, S; McWilliam, AS; Kita, H. Trypsin induces activation and inflammatory mediator release from human eosinophils through proteinase-activated receptor-2. *J Immunol* 2001 167, 6615-6622.

[80] Wang, J; Zheng, H; Hollenberg, MD; Wijesuriya, SJ; Ou, X; Hauer-Jensen, M. Up-regulation and activation of proteinase-activated receptor 2 in early and delayed

radiation injury in the rat intestine: influence of biological activators of proteinase-activated receptor 2. *Radiat Res* 2003 160, 524-535.

[81] Wang, J; Qiu, X; Hollenberg, MD; Hauer-Jensen, M. Activation of proteinase-activated receptor 2 potentiates the intestinal radiation response (Abstr.). *Radiation Research Society* 2006 53.

[82] Ito, H; Meistrich, ML; Barkley, T; Thames, HD; Milas, L. Protection of acute and late radiation damage of the gastrointestinal tract by WR-2721. *Int J Radiat Oncol Biol Phys* 1986 12, 211-219.

[83] Caroll, MP; Zera, RT; Roberts, JC; Schlafmann, SE; Feeney, DA; Johnston, GR; West, MA; Bubrick, MP. Efficacy of radioprotective agents in preventing small and large bowel radiation injury. *Dis Colon Rectum* 1995 38, 716-722.

[84] Delaney, JP; Bonsack, ME; Felemovicius, I. Radioprotection of the rat small intestine with topical WR-2721. *Cancer* 1994 74, 2379-2384.

[85] Ben-Joseph, E; Han, S; Tobi, M; Vargas, BJ; Stamos, B; Kelly, L; Biggar, S; Kaplan, I. Intrarectal application of amifostine for the prevention of radiation-induced rectal injury. *Semin Radiat Oncol* 2002 12, 81-85.

[86] Rowe, JK; Zera, RT; Madoff, RD; Fink, AS; Roberts, JC; Johnston, GR; Feeney, DA; Young, HL; Bubrick, MP. Protective effect of RibCys following high-dose irradiation of the rectosigmoid. *Dis Colon Rectum* 1993 36, 681-688.

[87] Sener, G; Kabasakal, L; Atasoy, BM; Erzik, C; Velioglu-Ogunc, A; Cetinel, S; Contuk, G; Gedik, N; Yegen, BC. Propylthiouracil-induced hypothyroidism protects ionizing radiation-induced multiple organ damage in rats. *J Endocrinol* 2006 189, 257-269.

[88] Epperly, MW; Travis, EL; Sikora, C; Greenberger, JS. Magnesium superoxide dismutase (MnSOD) plasmid/liposome pulmonary radioprotective gene therapy: modulation of irradiation-induced mRNA for IL-I, TNF-α, and TGF-β correlates with delay of organizing alveolitis/fibrosis. *Biology of Blood & Marrow Transplantation* 1999 5, 204-214.

[89] Stickle, RL; Epperly, MW; Klein, E; Bray, JA; Greenberger, JS. Prevention of irradiation-induced esophagitis by plasmid/liposome delivery of the human manganese superoxide dismutase transgene. *Radiat Oncol Invest* 1999 7, 204-217.

[90] Guo, H; Wolfe, D; Epperly, MW; Huang, S; Glorioso, JC; Greenberger, JS; Blumberg, D. Gene transfer of human manganese superoxide dismutase protects small intestinal villi from radiation injury. *J Gastrointest Surg* 2003 7, 229-236.

[91] Molla, M; Gironella, M; Salas, A; Closa, D; Biete, A; Gimeno, M; Coronel, P; Pique, JM; Panes, J. Protective effect of superoxide dismutase in radiation-induced intestinal inflammation. *Int J Radiat Oncol Biol Phys* 2005 61, 1159-1166.

[92] Kumar, KS; Vaishnav, YN; Weiss, JF. Radioprotection by antioxidant enzymes and enzyme mimetics. *Pharmac Ther* 1988 39, 301-309.

[93] Rong, Y; Doctrow, SR; Tocco, G; Baudry, M. EUK-134, a synthetic superoxide dismutase and catalase mimetic, prevents oxidative stress and attenuates kainate-induced neuropathology. *Proc Natl Acad Sci USA* 1999 96, 9897-9902.

[94] Vujaskovic, Z; Batinic-Haberle, I; Rabbani, ZN; Feng, QF; Kang, SK; Spasojevic, I; Samulski, TV; Fridovich, I; Dewhirst, MW; Anscher, MS. A small molecular weight catalytic metalloporphyrin antioxidant with superoxide dismutase (SOD) mimetic properties protects lungs from radiation-induced injury. *Free Radical Biol Med* 2002 33, 857-863.

[95]   Felemovicius, I; Bonsack, ME; Griffin, RJ; Delaney, JP. Radioprotection of the rat intestinal mucosa by tirilazad. *Int J Radiat Biol* 1998 73, 219-223.

[96]   Delaney, JP; Bonsack, M; Hall, P. Intestinal radioprotection by two new agents applied topically. *Ann Surg* 1992 216, 417-422.

[97]   Bonsack, ME; Felemovicius, I; Baptista, ML; Delaney, JP. Radioprotection of the intestinal mucosa of rats by probucol. *Radiat Res* 1999 151, 69-73.

[98]   Monobe, M; Hino, M; Sumi, M; Uzawa, A; Hirayama, R; Ando, K; Kojima, S. Protective effects of melatonin on gamma-ray induced intestinal damage. *Int J Radiat Biol* 2005 81, 855-860.

[99]   Vijayalaxmi; Meltz, ML; Reiter, RJ; Herman, TS; Kumar, KS. Melatonin and protection from whole-body irradiation: survival studies in mice. *Mutation Res* 1999 425, 21-27.

[100] Beyzadeoglu, M; Balkan, M; Demiriz, M; Tibet, H; Dirican, B; Oner, K; Pak, Y. Protective effect of vitamin A on acute radiation injury in the small intestine. *Radiat Med* 1997 15, 1-5.

[101] Empey, LR; Papp, JD; Jewell, LD; Fedorak, RN. Mucosal protective effects of vitamin E and misoprostol during acute radiation-induced enteritis in rats. *Dig Dis Sci* 1992 37, 205-214.

[102] Felemovicius, I; Bonsack, ME; Baptista, ML; Delaney, JP. Intestinal radioprotection by vitamin E (alpha-tocopherol). *Ann Surg* 1995 222, 504-510.

[103] Kumar, KS; Srinivasan, V; Toles, R; Jobe, L; Seed, TM. Nutritional approaches to radioprotection: Vitamin E. *Mil Med* 2002 167, 57-59.

[104] Taren, DL; Chvapil, M; Weber, CW. Increasing the breaking strength of wounds exposed to preoperative irradiation using vitamin E supplementation. *Int J Vitam Nutr Res* 1987 57, 133-137.

[105] Okunieff, P; Xu, J; Hu, D; Liu, W; Zhang, L; Morrow, G; Pentland, A; Ryan, JL; Ding, I. Curcumin protects against radiation-induced acute and chronic cutaneous toxicity in mice and decreases mRNA expression of inflammatory and fibrogenic cytokines. *Int J Radiat Oncol Biol Phys* 2006 65, 890-898.

[106] Inano, H; Onoda, M. Radioprotective action of curcumin extracted from Curcuma longa LINN: inhibitory effect on formation of urinary 8-hydroxy-2'-deoxyguanosine, tumorigenesis, but not mortality, induced by gamma-ray irradiation. *Int J Radiat Oncol Biol Phys* 2002 53, 735-743.

[107] Jagetia, GC; Rajanikant, GK. Curcumin treatment enhances the repair and regeneration of wounds in mice exposed to hemibody gamma-irradiation. *Plast Reconstr Surg* 2005 116, 515-528.

[108] Jagetia, GC; Rajanikant, GK. Role of curcumin, a naturally occurring phenolic compound of turmeric in accelerating the repair of excision wound, in mice whole-body exposed to various doses of gamma-radiation. *J Surg Res* 2004 120, 127-138.

[109] Richter, KK; Langberg, CW; Sung, C-C; Hauer-Jensen, M. Increased transforming growth factor β (TGF-β) immunoreactivity is independently associated with chronic injury in both consequential and primary radiation enteropathy. *Int J Radiat Oncol Biol Phys* 1997 39, 187-195.

[110] Wu, SG; Miyamoto, T. Radioprotection of the intestinal crypts of mice by recombinant human interleukin-1 alpha. *Radiat Res* 1990 123, 112-115.

[111] Hancock, SL; Chung, RT; Cox, RS; Kallman, RF. Interleukin 1 beta initially sensitizes and subsequently protects murine intestinal stem cells exposed to photon radiation. *Cancer Res* 1991 51, 2280-2285.

[112] Yada, S; Nukina, H; Kishihara, K; Takamura, N; Yoshida, H; Inagaki-Ohara, K; Nomoto, K; Lin, T. IL-7 prevents both capsase-dependent and -independent pathways that lead to the spontaneous apoptosis of i-IEL. *Cell Immunol* 2001 208, 88-95.

[113] Welniak, LA; Khaled, AR; Anver, MR; Komschlies, KL; Wiltrout, RH; Durum, S; Ruscetti, FR; Blazar, BR; Murphy, WJ. Gastrointestinal cells of IL-7 receptor null mice exhibit increased sensitivity to irradiation. *J Immunol* 2001 166, 2923-2928.

[114] Potten, CS. Protection of the small intestinal clonogenic stem cells from radiation-induced damage by pretreatment with interleukin 11 also increases murine survival time. *Stem Cells* 1996 14, 452-459.

[115] Potten, CS. Interleukin-11 protects the clonogenic stem cells in murine small-intestinal crypts from impairment of their reproductive capacity by radiation. *Int J Cancer* 1995 62, 356-361.

[116] Orazi, A; Du, X; Yang, Z; Kashai, M; Williams, DA. Interleukin-11 prevents apoptosis and accelerates recovery of small intestinal mucosa in mice treated with combined chemotherapy and radiation. *Lab Invest* 1996 75, 33-42.

[117] Peterson, RL; Bozza, MM; Dorner, AJ. Interleukin-11 induces intestinal epithelial cell growth arrest through effects on retinoblastoma protein phosphorylation. *Am J Pathol* 1996 149, 895-902.

[118] Potten, CS; Booth, D; Haley, JD. Pretreatment with transforming growth factor β-3 protects small intestinal stem cells against radiation damage in vivo. *Br J Cancer* 1997 75, 1454-1459.

[119] Tseng, CM; Albert, L; Peterson, RL; Bouchard, P; Dorner, AJ; Keith, J, Jr.; Khor, SP. In vivo absorption properties of orally administered recombinant human interleukin-11. *Pharm Res* 2000 17, 482-485.

[120] Cotreau, MM; Stonis, L; Strahs, A; Schwertschlag, US. A multiple-dose, safety, tolerability, pharmacokinetics and pharmacodynamic study of oral recombinant human interleukin-11 (oprelvekin). *Biopharm Drug Dispos* 2004 25, 291-296.

[121] Boerma, M; Wang, J; Burnett, AF; Santin, AD; Roman, JJ; Hauer-Jensen, M. Local administration of interleukin-11 ameliorates intestinal radiation injury in rats. 2007 67, 9501-9506.

[122] Lai, YG; Gelfanov, V; Gelfanova, V; Kulik, L; Chu, CL; Jeng, SW; Liao, NS. IL-15 promotes survival but not effector function differentiation of CD8+ TCRalphabeta+ intestinal intraepithelial lymphocytes. *J Immunol* 1999 163, 5843-5850.

[123] Lugering, N; Kucharzik, T; Maaser, C; Kraft, M; Domschke, W. Interleukin-15 strongly inhibits interleukin-8 and monocyte chemoattractant protein-1 production in human colonic epithelial cells. *Immunology* 1999 98, 504-509.

[124] Reinecker, HC; MacDermott, RP; Mirau, S; Dignass, A; Podolsky, DK. Intestinal epithelial cells both express and respond to interleukin 15. *Gastroenterology* 1996 111, 1706-1713.

[125] Cao, S; Black, JD; Troutt, AB; Rustum, YM. Interleukin 15 offers selective protection from irinotecan-induced intestinal toxicity in a preclinical animal model. *Cancer Res* 1998 58, 3270-3274.

[126] Okunieff, P; Mester, M; Wang, J; Maddox, T; Gong, X; Tang, D; Coffee, M; Ding, I. In vivo radioprotective effects of angiogenic growth factors on the small bowel of C3H mice. *Radiat Res* 1998 150, 204-211.

[127] Houchen, CW; George, RJ; Sturmoski, MA; Cohn, SM. FGF-2 enhances intestinal stem cell survival and its expression is induced after radiation injury. *Am J Physiol* 1999 39, G249-G258.

[128] Farrell, CL; Bready, JV; Rex, KL; Chen, JN; DiPalma, CR; Whitcomb, KL; Yin, S; Hill, DC; Wiemann, B; Starnes, CO; Havill, AM; Lu, Z-N; Aukerman, SL; Pierce, GF; Thomason, A; Potten, CS; Ulich, TR; Lacey, DL. Keratinocyte growth factor protects mice from chemotherapy and radiation-induced gastrointestinal injury and mortality. *Cancer Res* 1998 58, 933-939.

[129] Khan, WB; Shui, C; Ning, S; Knox, SJ. Enhancement of murine intestinal stem cell survival after irradiation by keratinocyte growth factor. *Radiat Res* 1997 148, 248-253.

[130] von Bultzingslowen, I; Brennan, MT; Spijkervet, FK; Logan, R; Stringer, A; Raber-Durlacher, JE; Keefe, D. Growth factors and cytokines in the prevention and treatment of oral and gastrointestinal mucositis. *Support Care Cancer* 2006 14, 519-527.

[131] Leigh, BR; Khan, W; Hancock, SL; Knox, SJ. Stem cell factor enhances the survival of murine intestinal stemm cells after photon irradiation. *Radiat Res* 1995 142, 12-15.

[132] Vazquez, I; Gomez-de-Segura, IA; Grande, AG; Escribano, A; Gonzalez-Gancedo, P; Gomez, A; Diez, R; De Miguel, E. Protective effect of enriched diet plus growth hormone administration on radiation-induced intestinal injury and on its evolutionary pattern in the rat. *Dig Dis Sci* 1999 44, 2350-2358.

[133] Silver, DF; Simon, A; Dubin, NH; Wheeless, CR. Recombinant growth hormone's effects on the strength and thickness of radiation-injured ileal anastomoses: a rat model. *J Surg Res* 1999 85, 66-70.

[134] Howarth, GS; Fraser, R; Frisby, CL; Schirmer, MB; Yeoh, EK. Effects of insulin-like growth factor-I administration on radiation enteritis in the rat. *Scand J Gastroenterol* 1997 32, 1118-1124.

[135] Nieder, C; Cai, L; Weber, WA; Schill, S; Andratschke, N; Schwaiger, M; Molls, M. Evaluation of insulin-like growth factor-1 in a mouse model of long-term abdominal radiation toxicity. *Anticancer Res* 2007 27, 183-187.

[136] Arango, V; Ettarh, RR; Holden, G; Moriarty, M; Brennan, PC. BB-10010, an analog of macrophage inflammatory protein-1α, protects murine small intestine against radiation. *Dig Dis Sci* 2001 46, 2608-2614.

[137] Klimberg, VS; Souba, WW; Olson, DJ; Salloum, RM; Hautamaki, RD; Plumley, DA; Mendenhall, WM; Bova, FJ; Khan, SR; Hackett, RL; Bland, KI; Copeland, EM. Prophylactic glutamine protects intestinal mucosa from radiation injury. *Cancer* 1990 66, 62-68.

[138] Campos, FG; Waitzberg, DL; Mucerino, DR; Goncalves, EL; Logulo, AF; Habr-Gama, A; Rombeau, JL. Protective effects of glutamine enriched diets on acute actinic enteritis. *Nutricion Hospitalaria* 1996 **11**, 167-177.

[139] Giris, M; Erbil, Y; Oztezcan, S; Olgac, V; Barbaros, U; Deveci, U; Kirgiz, B; Uysal, M; Toker, GA. The effect of heme oxygenase-1 induction by glutamine on radiation-induced intestinal damage: the effect of heme oxygenase-1 on radiation enteritis. *Am J Surg* 2006 191, 503-509.

[140] McArdle, AH. Elemental diets in treatment of gastrointestinal injury. *Advances in the Biosciences* 1994 94, 201-206.

[141] Kozelsky, TF; Meyers, GE; Sloan, JA; Shanahan, TG; Dick, SJ; Moore, RL; Engeler, GP; Frank, AR; McKone, TK; Urias, RE; Pilepich, MV; Novotny, PJ; Martenson, JA. Phase III double-blind study of glutamine versus placebo for the prevention of acute diarrhea in patients receiving pelvic radiation therapy. *J Clin Oncol* 2003 21, 1669-1674.

[142] Gurbuz, AT; Kunzelman, J; Ratzer, EE. Supplemental dietary arginine accelerates intestinal mucosal regeneration and enhances bacterial clearance following radiation enteritis in rats. *J Surg Res* 1998 74, 149-154.

[143] Hwang, JM; Chan, DC; Chang, TM; Tsao, TY; Tsou, SS; Lu, RH; Tsai, LM. Effects of oral arginine and glutamine on radiation-induced injury in the rat. *J Surg Res* 2003 109, 149-154.

[144] Mennie, AT; Dalley, VM; Dinneen, LC; Collier, HOJ. Treatment of radiation-induced gastrointestinal distress with acetylsalicylate. *Lancet* 1975 2, 942-943.

[145] Stryker, JA; Demers, LM; Mortel, R. Prophylactic ibuprofen administration during pelvic irradiation. *Int J Radiat Oncol Biol Phys* 1979 5, 2049-2052.

[146] Kilic, D; Egehan, I; Ozenirler, S; Dursun, A. Double-blinded, randomized, placebo-controlled study to evaluate the effectiveness of sulphasalazine in preventing acute gastrointestinal complications due to radiotherapy. *Radiother Oncol* 2000 57, 125-129.

[147] Freund, U; Scholmerich, J; Siems, H; Kluge, F; Schafer, HE; Wannenmacher, M. Unwanted side-effects in using mesalazine (5-aminosalicylic acid) during radiotherapy. *Strahlenther Onkol* 1987 163, 678-680.

[148] Baughan, CA; Canney, PA; Buchanan, RB; Pickering, RM. A randomized trial to assess the efficacy of 5-aminosalicylic acid for the prevention of radiation enteritis. *Clin Oncol* 1993 5, 19-24.

[149] Martenson, JA; Hyland, G; Moertel, CG; Mailliard, JA; O'Fallon, JR; Collins, RT; Morton, RF; Tewfik, HH; Moore, RL; Frank, AR; Urias, RE; Deming, RL. Olsalazine is contraindicated during pelvic radiation therapy: results of a double-blind randomized clinical trial. *Int J Radiat Oncol Biol Phys* 1996 35, 299-303.

[150] Resbeut, M; Marteau, P; Cowen, D; Richaud, P; Bourdin, S; Dubois, JB; Mere, P; N'Guyen, T. A randomized double blind placebo controlled multicenter study of mesalazine for the prevention of acute radiation enteritis. *Radiother Oncol* 1997 44, 59-63.

[151] Boerma, M; Wang, J; Richter, KK; Hauer-Jensen, M. Orazipone, a locally acting immunomodulator, ameliorates intestinal radiation injury: a preclinical study in a novel rat model. *Int J Radiat Oncol Biol Phys* 2006 66, 552-559.

[152] Keskek, M; Gocmen, E; Kilic, M; Gencturk, S; Can, B; Cengiz, M; Okten, RM; Koc, M. Increased expression of cyclooxygenase-2 (COX-2) in radiation-induced small bowel injury in rats. *J Surg Res* 2006 135, 76-84.

[153] Hanson, WR; Thomas, C. 16,16-Dimethyl Prostaglandin E2 increases survival of murine intestinal stem cells when given before photon radiation. *Radiat Res* 1983 96, 393-398.

[154] Tomas-de la Vega, JE; Banner, BF; Hubbard, M; Boston, DL; Thomas, CW; Straus, AK; Roseman, DL. Cytoprotective effect of prostaglandin E2 in irradiated rat ileum. *Surg Gynecol Obstet* 1984 158, 39-45.

[155] Keelan, M; Walker, K; Cheeseman, CI; Thomson, ABR. Two weeks of oral synthetic E2 prostaglandin (enprostil) improves the intestinal morphological but not the absorptive response in the rat to abdominal irradiation. *Digestion* 1992 53, 101-107.

[156] Delaney, JP; Bonsack, ME; Felemovicius, I. Misoprostol in the intestinal lumen protects against radiation injury of the mucosa of the small bowel. *Radiat Res* 1994 137, 405-409.

[157] Kumar, KS; Srinivasan, V; Palazzolo, D; Kendrick, JM; Clark, EP. Synergistic protection of irradiated mice by a combination of iloprost and misoprostol. *Adv Exp Med Biol* 1997 400B, 831-839.

[158] Krause, P; Ziegler, K. Experimentelle Untersuchungen ueber die Einwirkung der Roentgenstrahlen auf tierische Gewebe. A. Uebersicht ueber die in der Litteratur niedergelegten Angaben ueber die Wirkung der Roentgenstrahlen auf innere Organe. *Fortschr a d Geb d Roentgenstr* 1906 10, 126-182.

[159] Bealmear PM, Holtermann OA, Mirand EA. Radiation pathology and treatment. In: Coates ME and Gustafsson BE, eds. The germ-free animal in biomedical research. Laboratory Animals Ltd.: London, 1984:413-434.

[160] Wilson R, Bealmear P, Matsuzawa T. Acute intestinal radiation death in germfree and conventional mice. In: Sullivan MF, ed. Gastrointestinal radiation injury. Excerpta Medica Foundation: Amsterdam, 1968:148-158.

[161] Mastromarino, AJ; Wilson, R. Increased intestinal mucosal turnover and radiosensitivity to supralethal whole-body irradiation resulting from cholic acid-induced alterations of the microecology of germfree CFW mice. *Radiat Res* 1976 66, 393-400.

[162] Mastromarino, AJ; Wilson, R. Antibiotic radioprotection of mice exposed to supralethal whole- body irradiation independent of antibacterial activity. *Radiat Res* 1976 68, 329-338.

[163] Spratt, JS; Heinbecker, P; Saltzstein, SL. The influence of succinylsulphathiazole (Sulfasuxidine) upon the response of canine small intestine to irradiation. *Cancer* 1961 14, 862-874.

[164] Toorop-Bouma AG, Van der Waaij D. The effect of selective decontamination of the GI-tract of mice on the survival of intestinal mucosa during X-irradiation. In: Wostmann BS, ed. Germfree research. Alan R. Liss, Inc.: New York, 1985:271-273.

[165] Geraci, JP; Jackson, KL; Mariano, MS. Effect of pseudomonas contamination or antibiotic decontamination of the GI tract on acute radiation lethality after neutron or gamma irradiation. *Radiat Res* 1985 104, 395-405.

[166] Kumar, KS; Srinivasan, V; Toles, RE; Miner, VL; Jackson, WE; Seed, TM. High-dose antibiotic therapy is superior to a 3-drug combination of prostanoids and lipid A derivative in protecting irradiated canines. *J Radiat Res* 2002 43, 361-370.

[167] Salminen, E; Elomaa, I; Minkkinen, J; Vapaatalo, H; Salminen, S. Preservation of intestinal integrity during radiotherapy using live Lactobacillus acidopheles cultures. *Clin Radiol* 1988 39, 435-437.

[168] Morgenstern, L; Hiatt, N. Injurious effect of pancreatic secretions on postradiation enteropathy. *Gastroenterology* 1967 53, 923-929.

[169] Sokol, AB; Lipson, LW; Morgenstern, L; Hiatt, N. Protection against lethal irradiation injury by pancreatic enzyme exclusion. *Surg Forum* 1967 18, 387-389.

[170] Morgenstern, L; Patin, CS; Krohn, HL; Hiatt, N. Prolongation of survival in lethally irradiated dogs. *Arch Surg* 1970 101, 586-589.

[171] Rachootin, S; Shapiro, S; Yamakawa, T; Goldman, L; Patin, S; Morgenstern, L. Potent anti-protease from Ascaris lumbricoides: Efficacy in amelioration of post-radiation enteropathy (Abstr.). *Gastroenterology* 1972 62, 796.

[172] Hauer-Jensen, M; Sauer, T; Berstad, T; Nygaard, K. Influence of pancreatic secretion on late radiation enteropathy in the rat. *Acta Radiol Oncol* 1985 24, 555-560.

[173] McArdle, AH; Wittnich, C; Freeman, CR; Duguid, WP. Elemental diet as prophylaxis against radiation injury. *Arch Surg* 1985 120, 1026-1032.

[174] Parihar, VK; Prabhakar, KR; Veerapur, VP; Priyadarsini, KI; Unnikrishnan, MK; Rao, CM. Anticlastogenic activity of morin against whole body gamma irradiation in Swiss albino mice. *Eur J Pharmacol* 2007 557, 58-65.

[175] Wang, J; Zheng, H; Sung, C-C; Hauer-Jensen, M. The synthetic somatostatin analogue, octreotide, ameliorates acute and delayed intestinal radiation injury. *Int J Radiat Oncol Biol Phys* 1999 45, 1289-1296.

[176] Wang, J; Zheng, H; Hauer-Jensen, M. Influence of short-term octreotide administration on chronic tissue injury, transforming growth factor β (TGF-β) overexpression, and collagen accumulation in irradiated rat intestine. *J Pharmacol Exp Ther* 2001 297, 35-42.

[177] Olgac, V; Erbil, Y; Barbaros, U; Oztezcan, S; Giris, M; Kaya, H; Bilge, H; Guler, S; Toker, G. The efficacy of octreotide in pancreatic and intestinal changes: radiation-induced enteritis in animals. *Dig Dis Sci* 2006 51, 227-232.

[178] Fu, Q; Schmid, HA; Boerma, M; Qiu, X; Wang, J; Hauer-Jensen, M. A novel somatostatin analogue, SOM230 (pasireotide), increases survival after total body irradiation (Abstr.). *International Congress of Radiation Research* 2007 13, 135.

[179] Wang, J; Albertson, CM; Zheng, H; Fink, LM; Herbert, J-M; Hauer-Jensen, M. Short-term inhibition of ADP-induced platelet aggregation by clopidogrel ameliorates radiation-induced toxicity in rat small intestine. *Thromb Haemost* 2002 87, 122-128.

[180] Boegelein, K; Reichenbach-Klinke, KE; Messerschmidt, O. Untersuchungen über Kombinationsschäden. 28. Mittelung. Störungen im Hämostasesystem bei Strahlen- und Kombinationsschäden. *Strahlenther* 1980 156, 430-436.

[181] Shi, J; Wang, J; Zheng, H; Ling, W; Joseph, J; Li, D; Mehta, JL; Ponnappan, U; Lin, P; Fink, LM; Hauer-Jensen, M. Statins increase thrombomodulin expression and function in human endothelial cells by a nitric oxide-dependent mechanism and counteract tumor necrosis factor alpha-induced thrombomodulin downregulation. *Blood Coagul Fibrinolysis* 2003 14, 575-585.

[182] Masamura, K; Oida, K; Kanehara, H; Suzuki, J; Horie, S; Ishii, H; Miyamori, I. Pitavastatin-Induced Thrombomodulin Expression by Endothelial Cells Acts Via Inhibition of Small G Proteins of the Rho Family. *Arterioscler Thromb Vasc Biol* 2003 23, 512-513.

[183] Fu, Q; Wang, J; Qiu, X; Fink, LM; Hauer-Jensen, M. Mechanisms of transcriptional regulation of endothelial cell thrombomodulin by statins (Abstr.). *Radiation Research Society* 2006 53, 106.

[184] Wang, J; Qiu, X; Zheng, H; Joseph, J; Ponnappan, U; Mehta, JL; Fink, LM; Hauer-Jensen, M. Effect of statins on endothelial thrombomodulin in vitro and the intestinal radiation response in vivo (Abstr.). *Radiation Research Society* 2004 51, 37.

[185] Wang, J; Boerma, M; Fu, Q; Kulkarni, A; Fink, LM; Hauer-Jensen, M. Simvastatin ameliorates radiation enteropathy development after localized, fractionated irradiation by a protein C-independent mechanism. *Int J Radiat Oncol Biol Phys* 2007 68, 1483-1490.

[186] Williams, JP; Hernady, E; Johnston, CJ; Reed, CM; Fenton, B; Okunieff, P; Finkelstein, JN. Effect of administration of lovastatin on the development of late pulmonary effects after whole-lung irradiation in a murine model. *Radiat Res* 2004 161, 560-567.

[187] Liebmann, J; DeLuca, AM; Coffin, D; Keefer, LK; Venzon, D; Wink, DA; Mitchell, JB. In vivo radiation protection by nitric oxide modulation. *Cancer Res* 1994 54, 3365-3368.

[188] Aicher, A; Heeschen, C; Mildner-Rihm, C; Urbich, C; Ihling, C; Technau-Ihling, K; Zeiher, AM; Dimmeler, S. Essential role of endothelial nitric oxide synthase for mobilization of stem and progenitor cells. *Nat Med* 2003 9, 1370-1376.

[189] Suarna, C; Hood, RL; Dean, RT; Stocker, R. Comparative antioxidant activity of tocotrienols and other natural lipid-soluble antioxidants in a homogeneous system, and in rat and human lipoproteins. *Biochim Biophys Acta* 1993 1166, 163-170.

[190] Yoshida, Y; Niki, E; Noguchi, N. Comparative study on the action of tocopherols and tocotrienols as antioxidant: chemical and physical effects. *Chem Phys Lipids* 2003 123, 63-75.

[191] Qureshi, AA; Burger, WC; Peterson, DM; Elson, CE. The structure of an inhibitor of cholesterol biosynthesis isolated from barley. *J Biol Chem* 1986 261, 10544-10550.

[192] Naito, Y; Shimozawa, M; Kuroda, M; Nakabe, N; Manabe, H; Katada, K; Kokura, S; Ichikawa, H; Yoshida, N; Noguchi, N; Yoshikawa, T. Tocotrienols reduce 25-hydroxycholesterol-induced monocyte-endothelial cell interaction by inhibiting the surface expression of adhesion molecules. *Atherosclerosis* 2005 180, 19-25.

[193] Theriault, A; Chao, JT; Gapor, A. Tocotrienol is the most effective vitamin E for reducing endothelial expression of adhesion molecules and adhesion to monocytes. *Atherosclerosis* 2002 160, 21-30.

[194] Pearce, BC; Parker, RA; Deason, ME; Qureshi, AA; Wright, JJ. Hypocholesterolemic activity of synthetic and natural tocotrienols. *J Med Chem* 1992 35, 3595-3606.

[195] Dion, MW; Hussey, DH; Osborne, JW. The effect of pentoxifylline on early and late radiation injury following fractionated irradiation in C3H mice. *Int J Radiat Oncol Biol Phys* 1989 17, 101-107.

[196] Dion, MW; Hussey, DH; Doornbos, JF; Vigliotti, AP; Wen, BC; Anderson, B. Preliminary results of a pilot study of pentoxifylline in the treatment of late radiation soft tissue necrosis. *Int J Radiat Oncol Biol Phys* 1990 19, 401-407.

[197] Ohdama, S; Takano, S; Ohashi, K; Miyake, S; Aoki, N. Pentoxifylline prevents tumor necrosis factor-induced suppression of endothelial cell surface thrombomodulin. *Thromb Res* 1991 62, 745-755.

[198] Seigneur, M; Dufourcq, P; Belloc, F; Lenoble, M; Renard, M; Boisseau, MR. Influence of pentoxifylline on membrane thrombomodulin levels in endothelial cells submitted to hypoxic conditions. *J Cardiovasc Pharmacol* 1995 25(S2), S85-S87.

[199] Leclerc, NE; Haan-Archipoff, G; Lenoble, M; Beretz, A. Inhibitors of phospodiesterase (Pentoxifylline, Trequinsin) inhibit apical and subcellular matrix expression of tissue

factor in cultured human endothelial cells. *J Cardiovasc Pharmacol* 1995 25(S2), S88-S91.

[200] Delanian, S; Porcher, R; Balla-Mekias, S; Lefaix, JL. Randomized, placebo-controlled trial of combined pentoxifylline and tocopherol for regression of superficial radiation-induced fibrosis. *J Clin Oncol* 2003 21, 2545-2550.

[201] Okunieff, P; Augustine, E; Hicks, JE; Cornelison, TL; Altemus, RM; Naydich, BG; Ding, I; Huser, AK; Abraham, EH; Smith, JJ; Coleman, N; Gerber, LH. Pentoxifylline in the treatment of radiation-induced fibrosis. *J Clin Oncol* 2004 22, 2213.

[202] Akgür, FM; Zibari, GB; McDonald, JC; Granger, DN; Brown, MF. Effects of dextran and pentoxifylline on hemorrhagic shock-induced P-selectin expression. *J Surg Res* 1999 87, 232-238.

[203] Boldt, J; Müller, M; Heyn, S; Welters, I; Hempelmann, G. Influence of long-term continuous intravenous administration of pentoxifylline on endothelial-related coagulation in critically ill patients. *Crit Care Med* 1996 24, 940-946.

[204] Coe, DA; Freischlag, JA; Johnson, D; Mudaliar, JH; Kosciesza, SA; Traul, DK; Chiang, PC; Cambria, RA; Seabrook, GR; Towne, JB. Pentoxifylline prevents endothelial damage due to ischemia and reperfusion injury. *J Surg Res* 1997 67, 21-25.

[205] Carr, KE; Bullock, C; Ryan, SS; Mc Alinden, MG; Boyle, FC. Radioprotectant effects of atropine on small intestinal villus shape. *J Submicrosc Cytol Pathol* 1991 23, 569-577.

[206] Esposito, V; Linard, C; Wysocki, J; Griffiths, NM; Mathe, D. A substance P receptor antagonist (FK 888) modifies gut alterations induced by ionizing radiation. *Int J Radiat Biol* 1998 74, 625-632.

[207] Alfieri, AB; Gardner, CJ. Effects of GR203040, an NK1 antagonist, on radiation- and cisplatin-induced tissue damage in the ferret. *Gen Pharmacol* 1998 31, 741-746.

[208] Baker, JW; Deitch, EA; Li, M; Berg, RD; Specian, RD. Hemorrhagic shock induces bacterial translocation from the gut. *J Trauma* 1988 28, 896-906.

[209] Moore, FA. The role of the gastrointestinal tract in postinjury multiple organ failure. *Am J Surg* 1999 178, 449-453.

[210] Deitch, EA. Bacterial translocation or lymphatic drainage of toxic products from the gut: what is important in human beings? *Surgery* 2002 131, 241-244.

[211] Deitch, EA; Forsythe, R; Anjaria, D; Livingston, DH; Lu, Q; Xu, DZ; Redl, H. The role of lymph factors in lung injury, bone marrow suppression, and endothelial cell dysfunction in a primate model of trauma-hemorrhagic shock. *Shock* 2004 22, 221-228.

[212] Biffl, WL; Moore, EE. Splanchnic ischaemia/reperfusion and multiple organ failure. *Br J Anaesth* 1996 77, 59-70.

[213] Ivatury, RR; Simon, RJ; Havriliak, D; Garcia, C; Greenbarg, J; Stahl, WM. Gastric mucosal pH and oxygen delivery and oxygen consumption indices in the assessment of adequacy of resuscitation after trauma: a prospective, randomized study. *J Trauma* 1995 39, 128-134.

[214] Michell, MW; Oliveira, HM; Kinsky, MP; Vaid, SU; Herndon, DN; Kramer, GC. Enteral resuscitation of burn shock using World Health Organization oral rehydration solution: a potential solution for mass casualty care. *J Burn Care Res* 2006 27, 819-825.

[215] Asfar, P; De Backer, D; Meier-Hellmann, A; Radermacher, P; Sakka, SG. Clinical review: influence of vasoactive and other therapies on intestinal and hepatic circulations in patients with septic shock. *Crit Care* 2004 8, 170-179.

[216] Krueger, WA; Unertl, KE. Selective decontamination of the digestive tract. *Curr Opin Crit Care* 2002 8, 139-144.

[217] Rotstein, OD. Pathogenesis of multiple organ dysfunction syndrome: gut origin, protection, and decontamination. *Surg Infect (Larchmt)* 2000 1, 217-223.

[218] Nathens, AB; Marshall, JC. Selective decontamination of the digestive tract in surgical patients: a systematic review of the evidence. *Arch Surg* 1999 134, 170-176.

[219] Gatt, M; Reddy, BS; Macfie, J. Review article: bacterial translocation in the critically ill - evidence and methods of prevention. *Aliment Pharmacol Ther* 2007 25, 741-757.

[220] Quigley, EM; Quera, R. Small intestinal bacterial overgrowth: roles of antibiotics, prebiotics, and probiotics. *Gastroenterology* 2006 130, S78-S90.

[221] Kollef, MH. Prevention of hospital-associated pneumonia and ventilator-associated pneumonia. *Crit Care Med* 2004 32, 1396-1405.

[222] Kattelmann, KK; Hise, M; Russell, M; Charney, P; Stokes, M; Compher, C. Preliminary evidence for a medical nutrition therapy protocol: enteral feedings for critically ill patients. *J Am Diet Assoc* 2006 106, 1226-1241.

[223] Takagi, K; Yamamori, H; Toyoda, Y; Nakajima, N; Tashiro, T. Modulating effects of the feeding route on stress response and endotoxin translocation in severely stressed patients receiving thoracic esophagectomy. *Nutrition* 2000 16, 355-360.

[224] Montejo, JC; Zarazaga, A; Lopez-Martinez, J; Urrutia, G; Roque, M; Blesa, AL; Celaya, S; Conejero, R; Galban, C; Garcia, dL; Grau, T; Mesejo, A; Ortiz-Leyba, C; Planas, M; Ordonez, J; Jimenez, FJ. Immunonutrition in the intensive care unit. A systematic review and consensus statement. *Clin Nutr* 2003 22, 221-233.

[225] Melis, GC; ter Wengel, N; Boelens, PG; van Leeuwen, PA. Glutamine: recent developments in research on the clinical significance of glutamine. *Curr Opin Clin Nutr Metab Care* 2004 7, 59-70.

[226] Luiking, YC; Poeze, M; Dejong, CH; Ramsay, G; Deutz, NE. Sepsis: an arginine deficiency state? *Crit Care Med* 2004 32, 2135-2145.

In: Global Terrorism Issues and Developments
Editor: Rene A. Larche, pp. 101-120

ISBN: 978-1-60021-930-6
© 2008 Nova Science Publishers, Inc.

Chapter 3

DISTRIBUTION OF FEDERAL ANTI-TERRORISM FUNDS TO STATES IN THE UNITED STATES: A COMPARISON OF POPULATION, INCOME, AND SIMPLE VULNERABILITY INDICATORS WITH INFRASTRUCTURE APPLICATIONS

Michael Greenberg
Rutgers University and the Center for Risk and Economic Analysis of Terrorism Events (CREATE) supported by the U.S. Department of Homeland Security, USA

Rae Zimmerman
New York University and the Center for Risk and Economic Analysis of Terrorism Events (CREATE) supported by the U.S. Department of Homeland Security, USA

Abstract

We conduct a need-based method of allocation of United States Department of Homeland Security (DHS) funds to states and local governments based on the distribution of sources of electric power generation and compare the results of using this method with the distribution of population and per capita income. We also examine the impact of weighting the spatial distribution of our electric power sources by geographical area, which is a surrogate for vulnerability to terrorist attack. Results show strong correlations between DHS grants, population distribution, energy consumption and energy generation, although the last two are less correlated with the distribution of funds than is population. When area is used as surrogate for vulnerability, then the correlations decline. There is a weak relationship with per capita income. Each approach produces slightly different winners and losers with regard to anti-terrorism funding. Efforts to develop the science required to make risk and vulnerability based allocations is discussed.

Introduction

The United States Department of Homeland Security (DHS) was formally established on November 25, 2002 (Homeland Security Act, Public Law 107-296) in the aftermath of the 9/11 terrorist attacks on the United States. An amalgam of all or parts of 22 federal agencies/departments, the DHS role is to protect the homeland against internal threats, and to respond to natural disasters, manage immigration, stop illegal drugs from crossing United States borders, and protect navigable waterways (Office of Management and Budget, 2005; U.S. Department of Homeland Security, 2006a,b, 2007a). The Department's budget exceeds $45 billion and has been steadily growing; in comparison, the 2001 fiscal year aggregate budget for the 22 organizations merged into DHS was less than half of the current DHS budget. The funds are deployed for a wide range of activities, such as preventing potentially dangerous people from crossing into the United States; screening cargo; protecting critical infrastructure, such as the electricity generating system, tunnels and bridges; guarding hazardous facilities (e.g., chemical plants, rail shipments); increasing our emergency response capacity; and enhancing DHS' management and operations, including communication capacity (U.S. Department of Homeland Security, 2006a,b, 2007a,b).

One of the key functions of DHS is to allocate a very large budget to protect the Nation and its assets. The allocation process has been scrutinized by government committees, interest groups, expert panels and the media. Considerable debate and controversy has occurred over the approach to allocation. Some critics cite shortcomings and attribute them to the unusual internal political environment that the agency faced (Glasser and Grunwald, 2005) and the difficulty and extraordinary diversity of some of the tasks left to it, such as protecting America's critical infrastructure. The range of criticisms of the DHS role in general is broad and ongoing, many of which affect the allocation process. For example, here is a short list of recently reported responsibilities the agency has faced and continues to face: granting union rights to DHS employees (e.g., airport screeners); understanding the potential negative impact of passport rules on the travel industry; granting asylum to victims of terrorism; developing forger-proof drivers licenses; avoiding unfair profiling of Arab immigrants; and preventing fraud in expenditures associated with Hurricane Katrina and Rita (Arkin, 2006; Associated Press, 2007; Editors, 2007; Eggen, 2005; Macfarquhar, 2006; Swarns, 2006).

Protecting critical infrastructure is a key DHS mission. To begin the allocation process for critical infrastructure, DHS established what it considered a preliminary data base of critical national assets, which came under criticism by the media for including some trivial security risks, such as a popcorn manufacturing facility, a groundhog zoo, and other less critical facilities in the list (Lipton, 2006a,b).

Overall, the new department has faced an unprecedented organizational challenge, with 184,000 employees, multiple missions, and has faced inordinate scrutiny. Perhaps, the goal of accomplishing this mandate so quickly was unrealistic, leaving little room to cope with the allocation of large sums of money quickly. In some cases DHS has been able to act immediately, and was praised for its efforts to thwart a terrorist plot to hijack airplanes (Hsu and Goo, 2006; Lipton, 2006a,b).

In response to these criticisms and especially the charge that it has not matched grants to vulnerability in risk, and instead uses archaic formulas (see below) that are unrelated to need, DHS has continued to emphasize a risk-based decision-making process (U.S. DHS 2006a,b).

Stepping back from the controversy, this chapter examines three broad questions related to the allocation of funds to states and local governments to inform the allocation process.

1. What is the geographical distribution of funds from DHS to states?
2. How is this distribution compare to common funding distribution factors, specifically population and income, used by other programs?
3. How would the distribution change if vulnerability, measured by electrical generating capacity, is used to distribute the funds? How would it change, if the size and location of the geographical area to protect also are taken into account?

The paper is divided into four sections. The first section lays the groundwork for the answer to second question by presenting information about how the federal government has historically distributed funds to states and local governments. The next section describes the data and methods we use. This section is followed by a presentation of the results, emphasizing the differences among the allocation approaches. The final part examines efforts to move toward a vulnerability and risk-based approach that emphasizes the importance of protecting infrastructure.

Context: Commonly Used Allocation Criteria

The federal government has been redistributing funds and resources to states and local governments through grants, programs, land allocations, and taxing policies since the birth of the nation. The basis for distribution policies has included social justice, politics, competition, revenue-sharing, and needs. Each of these provide lessons for the resource allocation systems for security.

Social Justice

The literature provides insights into these distribution policies, concentrating on the last half century. For example, one heated debate about equity has arisen between those that viewed reallocations from affluent to poor states as counterproductive because these reallocations, they argued, were a disincentive for labor to move to areas where there is opportunity. In other words, it is bad national policy to help poor states (Scott, 1950). In contrast, others argued that it is proper public policy to focus on equity, national interest, and the provision of minimum levels of public services in policy formation (Buchanan, 1952). This debate has been revisited many times and was especially hotly engaged during the Ronald Reagan presidency (Fainstein and Fainstein, 1995; Fainstein and Markusen, 1993). This social justice debate is not the most critical one for the distribution of DHS funds, but it will be examined in this paper because of its historical importance.

Political/Bureaucratic

A second debate has focused on the role of elected officials, bureaucracies, and needs in allocating funds to states and local governments. In 1950, federal grants were $2.2 billion, but by the mid-1980s they exceeded $100 billion (Stein, 1981), or about 20% of Federal domestic expenditures at that time. The fiscal stakes have become higher, and research accordingly has expanded. During the 1970s, scholars observed that elected officials with seniority on key committees used their influence to make sure that their home districts received a disproportionate amount of aid (Anagnoson, 1980, 1982; Anderson and Pearson, 1968; Arnold, 1979; Ferejohn, 1974; Strom, 1975). A classic example was asserted by the late Jack Anderson and Drew Pearson's comment (1968) that Senator Strom Thurmond in his senior role in the United States Congress used his position to allocate so much defense money to the state of South Carolina that the state would sink under the weight of it. Pork barrel politics, in short, were claimed to be major criterion for distributing funds.

This assertion was challenged by those who argued that agencies have taken over the task from elected officials. Furthermore, these authors (Anagnoson, 1980, 1982; Gilbert and Specht, 1974), among others, asserted that these allocations were equally ineffective, and that the agencies allocated funds in ways that would lead Congress to increase their budget rather than address needs in efficient ways (Arnold, 1979).

Competition

When agencies tried competitive grants in order to target areas of need, often they were criticized for leaving out less populous places that could not afford the resources to develop a competitive proposal (Porter et al., 1973; Stein, 1979). The need for matching funds and expertise to prepare proposals reduced the funding chances of smaller, less politically connected governments.

Revenue-sharing

Richard Nixon's "new federalism" model of the early 1970s changed the allocation process. Revenue-sharing began to overcome the advantages of size and political access. Stein (1981) found that compared to 1967, federal grants distributed during the mid-1970s started reaching less populated communities for the first time. He praised this program because data showed that needy small communities were receiving grants.

Need-based

New federalism may increase access and hence procedural equity, but DHS's mandate is to focus on vulnerable and risky locations, or in other words, it requires a more targeted needs – based approach. Needs based approaches were commonly used to allocate environmental protection grants, and needs assessments were common in the wastewater area as a basis for funding by U.S. Environmental Protection Agency (EPA). Yet, it is possible that needs based and revenue-sharing distributions of funds may produce similar results, that is, the same set of places get almost the same amount of money. For example, the EPA's brownfield's pilot program was targeted to communities that had brownfield sites, fiscal distress, and a poor population (Greenberg and Hollander, 2006). The program provided modest grants of up to $200,000 to local governments. The grants were competitive, and the money was to be used to study and develop plans to cleanup and reuse contaminated sites. Research shows that the initial set of grants disproportionately were won by more populous cities with large proportion of minority residents. After a few years, less populous cities that tended to be less minority began to capture the grants. In short, after a decade, hundreds of cities with a large proportion of poor minority people and brownfield sites received grants. The commonality among all the cities was that they had brownfield sites. In addition, some very small cities with a single brownfield site were distressed because they were not receiving pilot grants. The Environmental Protection Agency made in our opinion, a clever adjustment by providing $50,000 grants to needy communities that had only one brownfield site. In other words, the program tried to find a way to support many communities, not just those with the resources to able to put together a strong proposal.

Sometimes the supposedly needy are reluctant to engage with the federal government in the grant process. For example, during the late 1970s, it was apparent that some hazardous waste sites threatened water supplies, and in some instances represented an eminent public hazard. The federal government passed the Comprehensive Environmental Response Compensation and Liability Act (CERCLA, or Superfund), which was to provide funding for controlling the most hazardous sites in the United States. In order to receive federal support, states were required to write a proposal that required a collection of data and apply the formula to determine the risk of sites in their states (Committee on Remedial Action Priorities, 1994). States like Massachusetts, Michigan, New Jersey, New York, and Pennsylvania submitted many applications, and consequently received much of the initial federal support (Greenberg and Anderson, 1984). In contrast, initially the state of Louisiana, a state with many hazardous waste sites, submitted no applications. Likewise, Tennessee and North Carolina should have had more priority sites based on their industrial structure. We know that New Jersey deliberately spent a good deal of money on-site investigations in order to receive as much federal money as possible. We believe that states like Louisiana, Tennessee, and North Carolina chose not to make the effort, at least during the initial years of the program. The point is that some needy states are more aggressive than others in competing for needs based competitive grants. These two examples are consistent with the findings of other studies (Rich, 1989).

Comparison of Different Allocation Schemes

The sharp distinction theorists sometimes make in the literature between pure forms of revenue-sharing and targeting based on need is not so apparent in the actual allocation formulas. Many programs are hybrids, that is, they use elements of revenue sharing and targeting. Most use a combination of data; some use survey data, other census data and others use a combination of data sets. For example, the United States Department of Agriculture

(2007) targets funds to states based on estimated farm income from survey data. The United States Environmental Protection Agency (2005) provides resources for states to improve drinking water quality. It uses drinking water infrastructure surveys. Both of these funding mechanisms rely on survey data. Both, in short, rely primarily on a single data source, albeit complicated surveys have limitations of internal validity. The United States Department of Housing and Urban Development (2007) distributes community development block grant program funds to states based on a formula that takes into account population, poverty, age of housing, and amount of overcrowded housing. States must have a plan to distribute the funds to localities. The National Oceanic and Atmospheric Administration (2007) provides funds to states for enhancing their coastal zones. The formula includes coastal population in shoreline mileage. However, the states must have a plan of action and the ability to provide matching funds. Both of these, in short, use multiple criteria, and different data sets. A final example is the U.S. Department of Health and Human Services (2007), which allocates TANF funds (Temporary Assistance for Needy Families) to states based on historical expenditure and on state median family income. This approach has been adjusted because low income states typically receive fewer funds. Consequently, part of the allocation is set aside for supplemental grants to these under funded states.

Overall, the only commonality we find among these allocation methods is that they have been modified, often multiple times, as more information becomes available and as priorities shift. They all depend on accurate data, and they struggle with variations in data quality and quantity.

As a new federal department, DHS had much less experience at distributing funds than its counterparts, and has been under great pressure to distribute funds based on need and more recently risk, a goal that its federal counterparts with many more years of experience are still trying to achieve. The DHS started with a high level of complexity because of its roots in 22 different organizations. These had to be untangled and consolidated under DHS. The results obviously do not satisfy everyone, nor frankly after a few years should they be expected to.

The initial DHS funding formula guarantees a minimum level to every state (general revenue sharing); funds were not based on vulnerability and critical infrastructure as suggested by the 9/11 Commission (National Commission, 2004). A sample of DHS's programs illustrates the complexity of matching funds to targets. The State Homeland Security Program (SHSP) and Law Enforcement Terrorism Prevention Program (LETPP) provide base allocations to states according to the USA Patriot Act formula, with the remainder allocated based on relative risk and anticipated effectiveness of proposed solutions. The Urban Area Security Initiative (UASI) allocates based on analysis of relative risk and effectiveness of proposed remedy. Data include presence of critical infrastructure, vulnerability, population, population density, law enforcement capacity, mutual aid agreements, and several other criteria. Metropolitan Medical Response System grants (MMRS) distribute funds equally among 124 MMRS jurisdictions. Citizen Corps Program funds are allocated based on the USA Patriot Act, with the remainder allocated based on population. Out of the total of $1.7 billion allocated in FY2006, two elements of the allocation process stand out: population size and the Patriot Act. Relative risk and effectiveness of proposed remedy are much more difficult to assess. Every state receives 0.75% and every territory 0.25% under the Patriot Act formula. For 50 states and five territories, this implies almost 40% is allocated off the top. During the first years, the remainder has been allocated based on population. What these imply is that the states with the most population (California, New York, Florida, Illinois, and Texas) should get much of the money but states like Alaska, North Dakota, Vermont, and Wyoming receive a lot per capita. Thus, each of these programs reflects a mix of criteria, and allocations to individual types of assets introduces yet another set of criteria.

Data and Methods

As part of ongoing research conducted by CREATE (Center for Risk and Economic Analysis of Terrorism Events), we gathered published DHS grant distribution funds for fiscal year 2006 (US Department of Homeland Security, 2006, 2007a,b). The District of Columbia, the Virgin Islands, American Samoa, Guam and the North Mariana Islands were excluded from the analysis. The United States Census and estimates was our source of population, per capita income and other population characteristics, and area size data (as a basis for density measures) (Pearson Education, 2007a,b). As a key example of the infrastructure dimension, we also gathered information about electricity generation by state and electricity consumption by state (U.S. DOE, EIA, 2001, 2007). Simple correlation methods were initially used to examine initial relationships among these variables, and regressions provided a basis for more detailed analysis.

Results

As part of its over $45 billion budget, DHS distributed almost $1.6 billion to the fifty states. The Urban Areas Security Initiative (UASI) accounted for $664 million, or 42 percent of the total. We separated it from the others because the criteria are specifically related to infrastructure. The remaining programs account for 58% of the total. The answers to the three questions are addressed below. The ranking system used in the paper ranks the highest recipient of funds, most populous, most densely populated, and most of any other characteristic as 50 and a state that received the least amount of funds, was the least populated, and was the least densely populated as 1.

Question 1: Geographical Distribution of Funds

As guaranteed by the Patriot Act formula, every state received some funds, with three states California, New York and Florida receiving over $100 million and 11 states (Alaska, Arkansas, Maine, Mississippi, Montana, New Hampshire, New Mexico, Rhode Island, South Dakota, Utah, and Wyoming) receiving less than $10 million (Table 1).

The per capita distribution is notably different, as expected. Seven states received more than $10 per capita (Alaska, Delaware, Hawaii, Nebraska, North Dakota, Vermont, and Wyoming). In contrast, Arkansas, Minnesota, Mississippi, and Tennessee, and Virginia received less than $3.00 per capita. The correlation between total dollars received and per capita received was an insignificant r=-0.028. In other words, the two main factors in the allocation have been acting independently.

Table 1. Allocations of Funds to States and Local Governments, FY06

State name	Total allocation, FY06, $, Millions (1)	RANK, (1)	Per capita allocation, FY06, $ (2)	RANK (2)	Urban initiative allocation, Millions, FY06, $ (3)	RANK (3)
Alabama	15.6	24	3.42	9	0	11.5
Alaska	8.3	8.5	12.58	47	0	11.5
Arizona	20.2	28	3.40	8	3.9	23
Arkansas	8.3	8.5	2.99	5	0	11.5
California	232.0	50	6.42	32	136.3	50
Colorado	21.1	30.5	4.52	19	4.4	27.5
Connecticut	13.5	19.5	3.85	13	0	11.5
Delaware	10.3	12	12.26	45	0	11.5
Florida	100.1	48	5.63	27	53.5	48
Georgia	44.4	42	4.90	22	18.7	43
Hawaii	12.9	16	10.08	44	4.8	29
Idaho	11.8	15	8.25	39	0	11.5
Illinois	90.4	47	7.08	35	52.3	47
Indiana	21.1	30.5	3.37	7	4.4	27
Iowa	13.5	19.5	4.55	20	0	11.5
Kansas	14.3	22	5.22	25	0	11.5
Kentucky	24.1	33	5.78	28	8.5	33
Louisiana	30.4	36	6.73	34	8.4	32
Maine	7.8	3.5	5.91	29	0	11.5
Maryland	24.3	34	4.34	17	9.7	38
Massachusetts	41.2	39	6.44	33	18.2	40
Michigan	46.9	43	4.63	21	18.6	42
Minnesota	13.4	18	2.61	3	4.3	26
Mississippi	8.5	11	2.91	4	0	11.5
Missouri	42.9	41	7.40	38	18.4	41
Montana	7.9	5.5	8.40	40	0	11.5
Nebraska	21.7	32	12.33	46	8.3	31
Nevada	20.5	29	8.47	41	7.8	30
New Hampshire	7.9	5.5	6.03	31	0	11.5
New Jersey	52.0	45	5.96	30	34.3	45
New Mexico	8.3	8.5	4.30	16	0	11.5
New York	183.7	49	9.54	42	128.2	49
North Carolina	30.5	37	3.51	11	9	35
North Dakota	10.8	13	16.88	49	0	11.5
Ohio	41.3	40	3.60	12	17.6	39
Oklahoma	19.5	27	5.49	26	4.1	24
Oregon	18.0	26	4.95	23	9.4	37
Pennsylvania	49.3	44	3.97	15	24.4	44
Rhode Island	7.8	3.5	7.22	36	0	11.5
South Carolina	14.7	23	3.45	10	0	11.5
South Dakota	7.7	1.5	9.87	43	0	11.5
Tennessee	13.8	21	2.32	2	4.2	25
Texas	89.9	46	3.93	14	35	46
Utah	8.3	8.5	3.36	6	0	11.5
Vermont	10.9	14	17.58	50	0	11.5
Virginia	16.9	25	2.23	1	0	11.5
Washington	32.2	38	5.12	24	9.2	36
West Virginia	13.3	17	7.31	37	0	11.5
Wisconsin	24.4	35	4.40	18	8.6	34
Wyoming	7.7	1.5	15.1	48	0	11.5

Question 2: Population-based Factors and the Distribution of Funds

The correlation between total funding and total population was $r=0.928$ ($p<.01$). Nine of the 10 states that received the most funds were among the 10 most populated states. For example, California, New York, Florida, Illinois and Texas ranked 1-5 in receipts (Table 1) and 1, 3, 4, 5, and 2 in population (Table 2), respectively. The only notable deviation at the top was the state of Missouri, which ranked number 41 in dollars received and number 33 in population.

These results are not surprising because these populated and densely developed states received a disproportionate amount of the UASI allocations. Seventy percent of the UASI allocation went to California, New York, Florida, Illinois, Texas, New Jersey, and Pennsylvania which account for a substantial portion of the U.S. population.

While it is true that the UASI funds went disproportionately to populous urban states, it is also true that other funds disproportionately went to populated states. Indeed, the correlation between non-urban initiative funding and population was 0.967 ($p<.01$). The correlation between the urban allocations (42%) and the other allocations (58%) was $r=0.909$ ($p<.01$).

Some states, notably Alabama, Arizona, Iowa, Kansas, South Carolina and Virginia were much more successful at receiving allocations when those were not directly associated with urban security.

We found a weak negative correlation ($r=-0.255$, $p=0.07$) between per capita distribution of DHS funds and population. The relationship between per capita state income and per capita receipt of DHS funds was $r=0.109$ ($p=0.452$). Some states with the highest per capita grants from DHS were among the states with the highest per capita incomes: California, Delaware, Massachusetts, New Jersey, and New York. Other affluent states, however, did not receive a large share of funds, most notably Connecticut, Colorado, Maryland, Minnesota, and Virginia.

Overall, the allocation of funds to states is strongly associated with the distribution of population, and weakly associated with per capita income. It clearly fits the historical pattern of federal funding to states based on the principles of new federalism. The Patriot Act requirement that sends a minimum share to each state leads to a weaker correlation with population than otherwise would be the case and to complaints from elected officials from populated states who complain that it is illogical and unfair to give small states like Wyoming more per capita than large states like California (Feinstein 2003).

Table 2. Population and Per Capita Income by State

State name	Population , 2005 (1)	RANK (1)	Per capita Income, 2005, $1,000 (2)	RANK (2)
Alabama	4.56	28	29.2	10
Alaska	0.66	4	35.6	35
Arizona	5.94	34	30.3	13
Arkansas	2.78	19	26.9	3
California	36.13	50	37	40
Colorado	4.67	29	37.9	43
Connecticut	3.51	22	47.8	50
Delaware	0.84	6	37.1	41
Florida	17.79	47	33.2	28
Georgia	9.07	42	31.1	15.5
Hawaii	1.28	9	34.5	32
Idaho	1.43	12	28.2	7
Illinois	12.76	46	36.1	37
Indiana	6.27	36	31.3	17.5
Iowa	2.97	21	32.3	23
Kansas	2.74	18	32.8	26
Kentucky	4.17	25	28.5	9
Louisiana	4.52	27	24.8	1
Maine	1.32	11	31.3	17.5
Maryland	5.6	32	41.8	47
Massachusetts	6.4	38	44.3	49
Michigan	10.12	43	33.1	27
Minnesota	5.13	30	37.4	42
Mississippi	2.92	20	25.3	2
Missouri	5.8	33	31.9	21
Montana	0.94	7	29.4	12
Nebraska	1.76	13	33.6	30.5
Nevada	2.42	16	35.9	36
New Hampshire	1.31	10	38.4	44.5
New Jersey	8.72	41	43.8	48
New Mexico	1.93	15	27.6	5
New York	19.25	48	40.5	46
North Carolina	8.68	40	30.6	14
North Dakota	0.64	3	31.4	19
Ohio	11.46	44	32.5	24.5
Oklahoma	3.55	23	29.3	11
Oregon	3.64	24	32.1	22
Pennsylvania	12.43	45	34.9	33
Rhode Island	1.08	8	36.2	38
South Carolina	4.26	26	28.4	8
South Dakota	0.78	5	31.6	20
Tennessee	5.96	35	31.1	15.5
Texas	22.86	49	32.5	24.5
Utah	2.47	17	28.1	6
Vermont	0.62	2	33.3	29
Virginia	7.57	39	38.4	44.5
Washington	6.29	37	35.4	34
West Virginia	1.82	14	27.2	4
Wisconsin	5.54	31	33.6	30.5
Wyoming	0.51	1	36.8	39

Question 3: Vulnerability, Risk, and the Distribution of Funds

Targeting funds to states with critical and vulnerable infrastructure is a challenge because many different kinds of infrastructure exist, and a vulnerability in risk associated with each is site-specific or specific to a user area linked to a facility. This section examines the results of using very simple measures of vulnerability to allocate funds to states. Our water supply and sewerage systems, roads and railroads, bridges and tunnels, airports, electricity generation and other infrastructure systems constitute the core of critical infrastructure. Each of these infrastructures has its own special vulnerability.

Disruption of electrical supply hurts the economy and public, and is usually the first infrastructure system that sets off a chain reaction of disruption through many others. Research shows that abrupt cutoff of the supply directly impacts energy-dependent businesses, and then ripples through the economy to affect every sector of the economy and individual (Greenberg, Mantell, et al., 2007; Greenberg, Lahr, Mantell, 2007) and the restoration of infrastructure services after electric power outage may take much longer than the restoration of electricity (Zimmerman and Restrepo, 2006). The same assertion can be made for other basic services, such as water, sewerage, and gasoline. Nevertheless, a policy-maker would certainly want to include the electrical supply as one measuring stick for vulnerability of places. Although we have the data by county for the United States, for purposes of this paper the data were aggregated to the state level.

We correlated the geographical distribution of DHS grants with the distribution of electricity generation by state. In addition, arguably, electricity consumption is a good surrogate for infrastructure in general. Accordingly, we correlated DHS grants with the geographical distribution of electricity consumption. Correlations between DHS allocations on the one hand, and energy generation in year 2000 and energy consumption in the year 2000 were r=0.641 (p<.01) and r=0.758 (p<.01), respectively.

The overall positive association is due to the fact that most of the populace, urban, and heavily industrialized states also generate and consume a great deal of electricity. As indicated in Table 3, these include California (rank 49), Florida (rank 47), Illinois (rank 46), New York (rank 44), Pennsylvania (rank 48), and Texas (rank 50). Each of these states ranks approximately the same in DHS grants, population, and electricity generation. Indeed, the overall correlation between population and energy generation was r=0.820 (p<.01) and r=0.902 (p<.01) with electricity consumption.

If DHS grants were based on electrical generation capacity (assuming that translates directly into vulnerability for infrastructure), then Alabama, Arkansas Indiana, South Carolina Tennessee, West Virginia and Wyoming would receive a larger allocation of funds. In each of these states the rank for electricity generation was 10 or higher than their rank for a grant allocation. For example, as shown in Table 3 for energy generation and Table 2 for allocations, Alabama ranked number 42 in generation and number 24 in grant allocations, South Carolina ranked 36 in generation and 23 in grants, West Virginia 33 versus only 17, and Wyoming 23 versus 1.5.

At the opposite end of the spectrum were states that would have received fewer allocations, if funding was based on electricity generation. These include Delaware, Hawaii, Maryland Massachusetts Missouri, Nebraska, Nevada, New Jersey, and Vermont, each of which ranked at least 10 higher in grants than in electricity generation.

Next we modified our electricity generation analysis by adding area to protect. The ideal circumstance for a terrorist is for all the capacity to be geographically concentrated in a single location and not to be protected. There is a Star Trek movie, *Star Trek VI: the Undiscovered Country,* in which in the year 2293 the unrepentant Klingon Empire is brought to its knees, more specifically to the negotiating table, when the single site it depends upon for its energy supply is destroyed. The United States, of course, has its electrical generation capacity distributed across the country. Nevertheless, the movie's message should not be forgotten. If your eggs are in a few baskets, then you had better protect them.

Operationally this means that if two states produce exactly the same amount of electricity, the state that is 1/10th the size will get additional funds because it is more vulnerable on the basis of the density of electricity generation assets. Colorado is about twice as large as Alabama. If the same electricity generation assets were located in both states, Alabama's would be considered to be more vulnerable because of its higher density and presumed vulnerability. How much more it should get is clearly debatable, and we do not mean to say that that is literally what should be done. In this case, as an experiment, we divided the electricity generation by the square root of the land area of the state.

It can also be argued that it easier to protect one large or several large complexes in multiple dispersed sites. In other words, Colorado should receive more security funds than Alabama because its locations presumably are more dispersed, although one cannot tell that from aggregated state data. We operationalized the idea of more area to protect implies more vulnerability by multiplying electrical generation capacity by the square root of land area.

Reiterating that the correlations between allocations to the states and population size was r=0.928 (p<.01), the correlation of DHS allocations with electricity generation was r=0.641 (p<.01); it was r=0.517 (p<.01) with electricity generation/square root of land area; and r=0.569 (p<.01) with electricity generation, multiplied by square root a land area. Thus, when land area is taken into account (regardless of the way it is taken into account) the correlations decline relative to what they were with population size, but are still in the positive direction.

Table 3 shows that some states are not markedly impacted by adding land area to electricity generation as surrogates for vulnerability, for example, Alabama, Arkansas, California, Florida, Georgia, Hawaii, Illinois, Indiana, Iowa, Kansas, Kentucky, Louisiana, Maine, Minnesota, Mississippi, Missouri, Nebraska, New York, North Carolina, Ohio, Oklahoma, Pennsylvania, South Carolina, Tennessee, Texas, Utah, Vermont, Virginia, and Wisconsin. Other states are notably impacted. Assuming that small space increases vulnerability for an individual state, implies that Connecticut, Delaware, Maryland, Massachusetts, New Hampshire, New Jersey, and Rhode Island would receive a larger share of the funds than if they were just allocated on the basis of electricity generation. All of these are relatively small East Coast states.

New Jersey, for example, received almost $52 million, or 3.26% of the total allocation. If its allocation had been based on estimated 2005 population, on electricity generation, on electricity generation divided by square root of land area, or on electricity generation multiplied by square root of land area, then its share would have been $46.9 million (2.94%), $24.4 million (1.53%), $60.6 million (3.8%), and $8.29 million (0.52 percent), respectively. These are notable differences depending on how one incorporates state land area as a factor.

Table 3. Electricity Generation and Land Area as Allocation Factors

State name	Electricity generation, megawatt hours, 2000 (1)	RANK (1)	Electricity consumption trillion BTU, (2)	RANK (2)	Rank electricity generation/ sq. root of land area (3)	Rank electricity generation x sq. root of land area (4)
Alabama	124,405,340	42	1977	34	41	39
Alaska	6,156,525	3	627	14	1	11
Arizona	88,946,577	32	1216	25	26	41
Arkansas	43,875,766	20	1084	21	23	18
California	208,082,483	49	8519	49	38	49
Colorado	44,165,546	21	1200	24	14	25
Connecticut	32,967,570	13	863	18	33	6
Delaware	5,987,451	2	303	5	12	2
Florida	191,815,840	47	3944	43	49	48
Georgia	123,877,413	41	2770	40	37	42
Hawaii	10,593,403	6	265	4	8	4
Idaho	11,910,442	7	511	9	3	9
Illinois	178,496,081	46	4418	46	48	46
Indiana	127,819,516	43	2778	41	25	37
Iowa	41,542,010	19	1099	22	22	17
Kansas	44,815,905	22	1036	19	18	23
Kentucky	93,006,083	35	1868	33	35	33
Louisiana	92,865,635	34	3965	44	32	36
Maine	14,047,947	8	561	10	6	7
Maryland	51,145,380	24	1520	28	34	13
Massachusetts	38,697,881	18	1723	31	30	10
Michigan	104,209,594	38	3122	42	28	45
Minnesota	51,423,339	25	1688	30	21	28
Mississippi	37,614,563	17	1144	23	20	15
Missouri	76,593,939	30	1659	29	27	35
Montana	26,451,828	10	595	12	5	19
Nebraska	29,109,863	11	584	11	9	14
Nevada	35,484,915	15	633	15	10	21
New Hamp.	15,031,499	9	329	6	17	5
New Jersey	58,085,215	28	2707	39	44	12
New Mexico	34,022,020	14	621	13	7	22
New York	138,079,075	44	4620	47	42	44
North Carolina	122,274,356	40	2502	38	40	38
North Dakota	31,311,196	12	365	7	11	16
Ohio	149,060,280	45	4002	45	46	43
Oklahoma	55,571,957	27	1401	26	24	27
Oregon	51,789,975	26	1080	20	19	31
Pennsylvania	201,687,980	48	4780	48	50	47
Rhode Island	5,971,545	1	250	3	16	1
South Carolina	93,346,240	36	1477	27	39	32
South Dakota	9,697,337	5	246	2	2	8
Tennessee	95,838,584	37	2026	35	36	34
Texas	377,742,365	50	11589	50	47	50
Utah	36,609,074	16	718	16	13	20
Vermont	6,303,014	4	165	1	4	3
Virginia	77,189,370	31	2304	37	29	30
Washington	108,236,880	39	2174	36	31	40
West Virginia	92,865,176	33	744	17	43	26
Wisconsin	59,644,417	29	1800	32	25	29
Wyoming	45,494,280	23	417	8	15	24

States like Arizona and Colorado, Michigan, Missouri, Montana, Nevada, New Mexico, Oregon, South Dakota would receive more funds if a large area implied greater vulnerability. These are almost all large Western states. Their allocations would be increased by assuming that vulnerability increases with areas to protect.

Discussion

Before summarizing the findings of this research and considering their implications, it is important to note the limitations. We used fiscal year 2006 allocation data, and these data represent only a small share of DHS' budget. Annual summaries of where all DHS dollars were spent in all by state and country would allow analysts to follow the inter-state and inter-national flow of DHS funds. For example, where were Coast Guard and immigration service funds spent? With regard to vulnerability, electricity generation is one important infrastructure system. Many other systems such as water, sewer, communication, we assume would be more strongly associated with population than electricity generation. But dams and others would not be market-oriented.

Area to protect is a naive indicator of vulnerability. Law enforcement, other institutional capacities, and existing hardened structures, which are site-specific, are much preferred indicators of vulnerability. In other words, two identical infrastructure systems can be markedly different in vulnerability because one has already invested a good deal in security and the other has not.

With these caveats noted, the FY 2006 allocation of funds from the DHS to states and local governments follows the classic pattern of allocating with a minimum to each state and then much of the rest based on population distribution. This means that California, New York, Florida, Illinois, and Texas each received >$90 million, whereas Wyoming, South Dakota, Alaska, and other less populous states each received less than $10 million. Some less populous and poor states received a higher amount per capita but others did not. The allocations do not appear to disproportionately benefit less poor states.

A criticism aimed at these allocations is that they do not protect vulnerable attributes, that is, more dollars should go to protect critical infrastructure. We used electricity generation as a surrogate for a critical and vulnerable system, and then we added area. The association with population distribution remained but decreased when we added area. If electricity generation was used to allocate funds, then many Northeastern states, which tend to be high consumers with generation occurring beyond their borders, would receive less and Alabama, Arkansas, Indiana, Montana, South Carolina, West Virginia, and Wyoming would receive more. If a small area increases vulnerability, then New Jersey, Connecticut, Massachusetts, Delaware, and a few others would secure more resources. But if more space to protect implies greater vulnerability, then they would receive considerably less. States like California, New York, Florida and Illinois which are populous, produce and consume a good deal of electricity, are not significantly affected by modifications based on area.

The DHS year 2006 budget statement called for "concentrating Federal funds for States and homeland security assistance programs on the highest threats, vulnerabilities, and needs" (U.S. DHS, 2006b: p.151) and added that "nearly half of these funds have been allocated according to Congressionally-mandated formulas that bear little relation to need and risk"

(U.S. DHS, 2006b: p. 156). The statement asserts that money will henceforth be allocated to fill in what it calls "critical gaps" in state and local terrorism prevention and preparedness capabilities.

This statement signals a growing importance of a critical infrastructure database. Earlier we noted that the first version of this data base was mocked by some (Arkin, 2006). However, given the commitment to vulnerability and risk by DHS, the data base will become more central to decision-making. The authors have personal experience with federal and state data bases for Superfund and brownfields, and each of these data bases had errors in the first version that were eventually corrected. For example, we visited an almost brand new factory that had been mislabeled as a Superfund site, and we visited several homes that had been misaddressed as brownfield sites. We also visited sites that we believe had deliberately been mislabeled by local governments seeking cleanup funds. Over time, with patience and field work, blatant errors will be corrected.

Using a list of potentially vulnerable sites to compare risk is a more daunting task. In the case of Superfund sites, the Environmental Protection agency used an algorithm to choose 400 sites initially from among tens of thousands for designation and support. The algorithm was imperfect, and some communities learned how to fool it by adding some key data (Committee, 1994), whereas it missed other sites that probably should be on the list.

At the micro geographical scale, CREATE researchers are testing methods to allocate limited funds across asset of threats or assets. The goal is to prevent, protect, or improve response and recovery. The approach involves risk and economic analyses. The approach is being tested in California where critical facilities are chemical plants, dams, and selected other commercial facilities (Kleinmuntz et al., 2006). At the local, state and national and geographical scales, Greenberg, Lahr, and Mantell (2007) proposed a national scale effort, beginning with states gathering data about their three most potentially serious risks, and then the federal government aggregating and further analyzing these data, using it for planning and potentially for allocating funds.

Infrastructure is an important basis for allocating resources for security. This has been recognized in well over a dozen laws, executive orders, strategies and plans and is firmly embedded in federal security policy (Zimmerman, 2006; Zimmerman and Restrepo, 2006). Infrastructure provides a basis for resource allocation from a number of different perspectives having to do with its properties that make these systems not only vulnerable to attack but also having the potential to produce adverse consequences when they are attacked. Three key factors are critical inputs to resource allocation: (1) interdependencies among infrastructures both spatially and functionally, (2) susceptibility to failure, and (3) the consequences of both interdependencies and failures in terms of economic and social impacts.

Interdependence among infrastructures plays a key role in vulnerability to attack. Interdependencies can occur where several infrastructures are located in close proximity to one another (whether of the same type or different types) and where one infrastructure depends upon another in order to function (Zimmerman, 2005). Under such conditions, vulnerabilities arise when the destruction of one facility can result in the destruction of others, (Zimmerman, 2004) and thus, are potential candidates for protective resources. Concentrations of a single type of infrastructure allow little room for adaptation or flexibility in the face of disruptions due to terrorist attacks or natural disasters. Functional interdependencies can in many cases be more catastrophic, arguing for targeting resources in such cases. The most notable example was the August 2003 U.S.-Canada blackout, which not only shutdown many infrastructure services dependent on electric power, but when power was restored water systems in Cleveland and Detroit took an estimated 2-3 times longer than the time power was restored to come back on line and in NYC transit took 1.3 times as long and traffic signals took 2.6 times as long because of the need to reset equipment (Zimmerman and Restrepo, 2006). Analytical methods and measures such as these are easily applicable to any type of infrastructure as a means of providing inputs for prioritizing for resource allocation.

Failure rates are another type of input for resource allocation in that they reflect vulnerability and consequences of a failure regardless of the cause. In the U.S. electric power outages have been increasing regardless of season, and since the mid-1990s have been increasing in duration as well, with a dramatic rise of 30-40% between 2002-2005 (Simonoff, Restrepo, and Zimmerman, 2007). These changes appear to be largely the result of increases in weather-related events as causal factors. Extreme weather and other natural hazards (Federally-declared major disasters) have been increasing at a rate of close to 2.7% per year over a fifty year period from 1950 to 2000 (Simonoff et al., 2007).

Economic impacts are critical inputs to policy resource allocation policy. Some of the consequences of outage events described above, in particular, economic consequences, provide important guides for resource allocation. In the oil and gas sector, for example, research conducted by NYU researchers on impacts on property values indicates an increase in the dollar value of property damages, with the greatest increases occurring from natural gas transmission lines (Restrepo, Simonoff and Zimmerman 2006). Economic impacts of electric power outages are computable in terms of expected business loss for specific regions, seasons, and outage cause by estimating customers affected by an outage from regression modeling, converting it to number of people affected, and combining it with the average gross domestic product per person and the predicted duration estimated from regression modeling (Zimmerman, et al., 2007). The approach is adaptable to different geographic scales.

Acknowledgements and Disclaimer

This research was supported by the United States Department of Homeland Security through the Center for Risk and Economic Analysis of Terrorism Events (CREATE), Grant number EMW-2004-GR-0112. However, any opinions, findings, and conclusions or recommendations in this document are those of the authors and do not necessarily reflect views of the United States Department of Homeland Security. The authors thank the support of Graduate Research Assistant, Alison M. Culpen for her assistance with organizing some of the databases for this work.

References

Anagnoson, J.T. (1982) Federal grant agencies and Congressional election campaigns. *American Journal of Political Science.* 26(3):547- 561.

Anagnoson, J.T. (1980) Politics in the distribution of federal grants: the case of economic development administration, in *Political Benefits*, Rundquist, B., ed., Lexington, MA: Lexington Books.

Anderson, J., and Pearson, D. (1968) *The Case Against Congress.* New York: Simon and Schuster.

Arkin, W. (2006) The Department of Homeland Security's unlimited "priorities." *Washington Post, Early Warning.* July 13.
http://blog.washingtonpost.com/earlywarning/2006/07/the_department_of_homeland_sec.html. Accessed November 19, 2007.

Arnold, D. (1979) *Congress and the Bureaucracy: a Theory of Influence.* New Haven: Yale University Press.

Associated Press (2007) Senate backs union rights for airport screeners. *New York Times.* March 7, A14.
http://www.nytimes.com/2007/03/07/washington/07screeners.html?ex=1336017600&en= aa50c815f60ff27a&ei=5124&partner=permalink&exprod=permalink.
Accessed November 19, 2007.

Buchanan, J. (1952) Federal grants and resource allocation. *The Journal of Political Economy.* 60(3): 208-217.

Committee on Remedial Action Priorities for Hazardous Waste Sites for Remedial Action Priorities, National Research Council. (1994) *Ranking Hazardous Waste Sites for Remedial Action.* Washington, D.C.: National Academy Press.

Editors. (2007). Shutting out terrorisms' victims. *New York Times.* March 9.
http://www.nytimes.com/2007/03/09/opinion/09fri1.html?ex=1331096400&en=1de8a8e5 dcd4a400&ei=5124&partner=permalink&exprod=permalink. Accessed March 14, 2007.

Eggen, D. (2005) Homeland Security is faulted in audit. *Washington Post.* December 29, A01.

Fainstein, S. and Fainstein, N. (1995) A proposal for urban policy in the 1990s. *Urban Affairs Review.* 30(5): 630-634.

Fainstein, S. and Markusen, A. (1993) Bridging the social and economic development gap. *University of North Carolina Law Review.* 71, June: 1463-1486.

Feinstein, D. (2003). Citing lack of funding for California, Senator Feinstein seeks changes in Homeland Security Funding. www.Feinstein.senate.gov/03/releases/r-homeland-funding-7-7-25.03.htm. Accessed November 19, 2007.

Ferejohn, J. (1974) *Pork Barrel Politics: Rivers and Harbors Legislation, 1947 – 1968.* Stanford, CA: Stanford University Press.

Gilbert, N., and Specht, H. (1974) Picking winners: federal discretion and local experience as bases for planning grant allocation. *Public Administration Review.* 34(6):565-574.

Glasser, S. and Grunwald, M. (2005) Department's mission was undermined from start. *Washington Post.* December 22, A01.

Greenberg, M. and Anderson, R. (1984) *Hazardous Waste Sites: the Credibility Gap.* New Brunswick, NJ: Center for Urban Policy Research.

Greenberg, M. and Hollander, J. (2006) The EPA's brownfield pilot program as a worthwhile federalist environmental innovation. *American Journal of Public Health.* 96(2): 277-281.

Greenberg, M., Lahr, M., and Mantell, N. (2007) Understanding the economic costs and benefits of catastrophes and their aftermath: a review and suggestions for the US federal government. *Risk Analysis.* 27(1): 83-96.

Greenberg, M., Mantell, N., Lahr, M., Felder, F., and Zimmerman, R. (2007) Short and intermediate economic impact of a terrorist-initiated loss of electric power: case study of New Jersey. *Energy Policy*. 35(1): 722-733.

Hsu, S. and Goo, S.K. (2006) Homeland security department praised for its response. *Washington Post*. August 11, A13.

Kleinmuntz, D. von Winterfeldt, D., Willlis, H., and Bowman, H. (2006) *Risk-based research allocation for infrastructure protection*. Paper presented at Society for Risk Analysis Annual Meeting. Baltimore, MD. December 4.

Lipton, E. (2006a) Homeland security department gets better grades in 2nd major test. *New York Times*. August 14. *www.nytimes.com/2006/08/14/washington/14chertoff.html*. Accessed November 19, 2007.

Lipton, E. (2006b) U.S. Can't Protect All Targets, Chertoff Says. *New York Times*. September 13. *http://www.nytimes.com/2006/09/13/washington/13chertoff.html*. Accessed November 19, 2007.

Macfarquhar, N. (2006) Suits seeks data on immigration profiling of Arabs. *New York Times*. October 18, A20. *http://www.nytimes.com/2006/10/18/washington/18arab.html#*. Accessed November 19, 2007.

National Commission on Terrorist Attacks Upon the United States (2004). *The 9/11 Commission Report*. *http://www.gpoaccess.gov/911/pdf/fullreport.pdf*. Accessed November 19, 2007.

National Oceanic and Atmospheric Administration (NOAA) (2007) *Coastal Zone Enhancement*. *http://www.legislative.noaa.gov/Legislation.cama.html*. Accessed January 17, 2007.

Office of Management and Budget, Executive Office of the President (2005) Department of Homeland Security. *http://www.whitehouse.gov/omb/budget/fy2005/homeland.html*. Accessed March 7, 2007.

Pearson Education, Inc. (2007a) Population by state, July 1, 2005. Fact Monster/Information please database. *http://www.factmonster.com/ipka/A0004986.html*. Accessed March 14, 2007.

Pearson Education, Inc. (2007b) Per capita personal income by state. Info please database. *http://www.infoplease.com/ipa/A0104652.html*. Accessed November 19, 2007.

Porter, D.O., Warner, D.C. and Porter, T.W. (1973) *The Politics of Budgeting Federal Aid: Resource Mobilization by Local School Districts*. Beverly Hills, CA: Sage.

Restrepo, C.E., Simonoff, J.S., and Zimmerman, R. (2006) *Analyzing vulnerabilities in the oil and gas sector from incident data*. Paper presented at the Los Alamos National Laboratories Risk Symposium 2006 – Risk Analysis for Homeland Security and Defense: Theory and Application. Santa Fe, NM. March 21.

Rich, M. (1989). Distributive politics and the allocation of federal grants. *The American Political Science Review*. 83(1): 193-213.

Scott, A. (1950) A note on grants in federal countries. *Economica*. 17: 418.

Simonoff, J.S., Restrepo, C.E., and Zimmerman, R. (2007) Risk Management and Risk Analysis-Based Decision Tools for Attacks on Electric Power. *Risk Analysis*. 27(3): 547-570.

Simonoff, J.S., Restrepo, C.E., Zimmerman, R., and Naphtali, Z.S. (2007) Spatial and temporal distribution of electricity and oil and gas pipeline failures in the United States:

A state level analysis, in *Critical Infrastructure Protection: Issues and Solutions*, E. D. Goetz and S. Shenoi, eds. New York: Springer.

Stein, R. (1979) Federal categorical aid: equalization and application process. *Western Political Quarterly*. 32(4): 396-408.

Stein, R. (1981) The allocation of federal aid monies: a synthesis of demand-side and supply-side explanations. *American Political Science Review*. 75(2): 334-343.

Strom, G. (1975) Congressional policy making: a test of a theory. *Journal of Politics.* 37(3): 711-735.

Swarns, R. (2006) Travel industry seeks delay on new passport rules at US borders. August 18. http http://www.nytimes.com/2006/08/18/washington/18immig.html. Accessed

United States Department of Agriculture (2007) Principles. *http://www.usda.gov/wps/portal/ !ut/p/_s.7_0_A/7_0_10B?navid=SEARCH&q=agriculural+resource+managemnt+surve y&site=usda.* Accessed March 17, 2007.

United States Department of Energy, Energy Information Administration (2000) State Energy Data 2000: Consumption. "Table S1. Energy Consumption Estimates by Source and End-Use Sector, 2000 (Trillion Btu)" Washington, D.C.: U.S.DOE.

United States Department of Energy, Energy Information Administration (2007). Electric Power Annual 2006-Data Tables 1990-2006 Net Generation by State by Type of Producer by Energy Source (EIA-906) October 2007. *http://www.eia.gov/cneaf/ electricity/epa/epa_sprdshts.html. Accessed November 21*, 2007.

United States Department of Health and Human Services (2007). TANF *http://www.acf.hhs.gov/prgrams/ofa/funds2.htm#eligibility.* Accessed January 17, 2007.

United States Department of Homeland Security (2007a) *DHS fact sheet. http://www. dhs.gov/xnews/releases/pr-1170702193412.shtm.* Accessed March 7, 2007.

United States Department of Homeland Security (2007b) Homeland Security Grants Program Allocations FY 2006. *http://www.dhs.gov/xlibrary/assets/grants_st-local_fy06.pdf.* Accessed March 14, 2007.

United States Department of Homeland Security, Office of Grants and Training (2006a) *Discussion of the FY 2006 Risk Methodology and the Urban Areas Security Initiative.* Washington, DC: U.S. DHS. *http://www.iowahomelandsecurity.org/asp/CoEM_FR/ Grant/FY06_UASI_ProgramPaper.pdf.* Accessed November 19, 2007.

United States Department of Homeland Security (2006b) *The Budget Year for Fiscal 2006.* Washington, DC: 151-166.

United States Department of Housing and Urban Development (2007) State Administered CDBG. *http://www.hud.gov/offices/cpd/communitydevelopment/programs/stateadmin/.* Accessed January 17, 2007.

United States Environmental Protection Agency (2005) *Drinking Water Infrastructure Needs Survey and Assessment*, Third Report to Congress. EPA 816-R-05-001. Washington, D.C.: EPA.

Zimmerman, R. (2006) Critical infrastructure and interdependency, Chapter 35 in *The McGraw-Hill Homeland Security Handbook*, D.G. Kamien. ed. New York, NY: The McGraw-Hill Companies, Inc.

Zimmerman, R. (2004) Decision-making and the Vulnerability of Critical Infrastructure, *Proceedings of IEEE International Conference on Systems, Man and Cybernetics*, W. Thissen, P. Wieringa, M. Pantic, and M. Ludema, eds. The Hague, The Netherlands: Delft University of Technology.

Zimmerman, R. (2005) Social implications of infrastructure network interactions, in *Sustaining Urban Networks: The Social Diffusion of Large Technical Systems,* O. Coutard, R. Hanley, and R. Zimmerman, eds. London, UK: Routledge.

Zimmerman, R. and Restrepo, C.E. (2006) The next step: Quantifying infrastructure interdependencies to improve security. *International Journal of Critical Infrastructures.* 2(2/3): 215-230.

Zimmerman, R., Restrepo, C.E., Simonoff, J.S. and Lave, L.B. (2007) Risk and economic cost of a terrorist attack on the electric system, Chapter 14 in *The Economic Costs and Consequences of Terrorism*, H.W. Richardson, P. Gordon and J.E. Moore II, eds. Cheltenham, UK: Edward Elgar Publishers.

In: Global Terrorism Issues and Developments
Editor: Rene A. Larche, pp. 121-139

ISBN: 978-1-60021-930-6
© 2008 Nova Science Publishers, Inc.

Chapter 4

INJUSTICE: ACTING OUT INTERNAL TERRORIST STATES OF MIND THROUGH VIOLENCE AND THE POSSIBILITIES OF PREVENTION

Raman Kapur

Threshold, McBrien House, Belfast BT15 5GB, UK

Abstract

A well known assumption in all human conflicts is the capacity of every human being to inflict destructiveness on our fellow man. In war, these murderous impulses are justified through political authority. However, for the individual terrorist, a complex set of emotional processes are triggered which are often based in a feeling of injustice, real or imagined, against the enemy which is usually a national or international government. This paper uses concepts from Kleinian psychoanalysis to illustrate how the mind can powerfully be convinced that revenge and retaliation are the only ways to correct a perceived wrong. An appraisal of this specific threat in any society could help contain the destructive consequences of terrorism and also provide major clues as to the prevention of such actions. As in the consulting room, such acting out can only be prevented by those in authority taking seriously the grievances of the terrorist state of mind and act to repair real or imagined psychic injures which pose a threat to society today.

Introduction

Inflicting violence onto others is a common occurrence in everyday life. This violence can take on psychic (Kapur, 2005) or physical forms (Kapur & Campbell, 2004) where the mind becomes so convinced of the infliction of cruelty and sadism that nothing can stop its tragic consequences on other human beings. Using key concepts from Kleinian psychoanalysis, this paper will describe how the mind can be persuaded through internal propaganda of the necessity of violence and importantly, how this propaganda can be wittingly or unwittingly fuelled by real acts of injustice that convince the individual that the only way to seek redress for perceived wrongs is to murder someone's soul or life. All of these reflections are taken from my own clinical work as a psychoanalytic clinician working with individuals and groups for over 25 years in psychiatric settings and also as someone who has lived through the 'troubles' in Northern Ireland for 2 periods of time (1969-1980 and 1990 – 2007) in my adult life. I will now describe key theoretical concepts from the work of Melanie Klein which I think is one of the most relevant and helpful theories to understand and hopefully prevent, human destructiveness.

Unconscious Phantasy

"A phantasy represents the particular content of the urges or feelings (e.g. wishes, fears, anxieties, triumphs, love or sorrow) dominating the mind at that moment. In early life, there is indeed a wealth of unconscious phantasies which take specific form in conjunction with the catharsis of particular body zones. Moreover, they rise and fall in complicated patterns according to the rise and fall and modulation of the primary instinct – impulses which they express. The world of phantasy shows the same protean and kaleidoscopic changes as the contents of a dream. These changes occur partly in response to external stimulation and partly as a result of the interplay between the primary instinctual urges themselves". (Isaacs, 1952-2002, p.83 / 84).

In my clinical work and professional work, I have come across many examples of destructive phantasies, which as Isaac's suggests, contain important insights into the internal world and thus, internal objects (Segal 1982/86) of the patient. One patient, a 40 year old single lady, who suffered from manic depression described to me her deep anxiety on taking the couch, rather than the chair for our analytical work, as being terrified that I would have a rope in my possession and strangle her from where I was sitting. For this patient, her phantasy of me and my imagined actions gave important clues as to her internal world. Not only did she clearly feel under threat from me, but had relocated in me potentially murderous and sadistic feelings which resided in her own mind. Something within her was strangling the life out of her and my work was to verbalise these internal processes and anxieties and ensure that my interpretative work remained free of any persecutory or 'noose tying' words that would only reinforce such a tragic internal world. Within the consulting room, I certainly felt, in the counter-transference her enormous anxiety that I would take her life.

In the troubled world of Northern Ireland (Kapur & Campbell, 2004) there are many day-to-day examples of where phantasies of persecution, retaliation and collapse dominate the everyday lives of people exposed to over 35 years of horrific violence. One of the most well known images of the troubles is the Drumcree dispute which started in 1996. At Drumcree, residents from the Nationalist community refused to allow the 'traditional' parade of Orangemen to pass through 'their area', which they saw as both an invasion of their territory and a demonstration of triumph and dominance of the larger Protestant population over the minority Catholic community. While, for the Protestant community, the march represented their expression of rights of access to the 'Queens Highway'. The massive public exposure of this incident in the print and broadcast media in Northern Ireland potentially left two predominant phantasies in the minds of its people. For Catholics, a fear that their minds would be invaded, taken over and dominated by the Protestant Community. For Protestants, a fear that their control of their own internal space or territory would shrink, thus eventually pushing them out of Northern Ireland. In respect of the latter, there is an often cited story of how the Catholics could push the Protestants so far back they would spill over the coastlines and swim across the Irish sea back to Scotland were they originated.

Both sets of phantasies have a potentially significant effect on day-to-day human relations. In particular, once they become lodged as primitive feelings in the mind of both groups, they create a huge barrier to trust and intimacy as there is often the state of mind of 'destroy or be destroyed' or 'shoot first and ask questions later'. As such, the first move is defensive or offensive rather than exploratory with a view to fulfilment and satisfaction in day-to-day human relations. It is only through the repeated exposure to good, non-persecutory experiences that such internal phantasies can be modified to lessen the fears of human relationships.

Paranoid–Schizoid and Depressive Positions

The central idea behind Melanie Klein's description of this state of mind is to highlight the power of suspicion and mistrust which can drive people into states of withdrawal with hostility emerging as to the only way to relate to the outside world. Paula Heimann describes this paranoid style of relating well:

> "Psychopathology of every day life abounds in examples of paranoid delusions. We are all apt to feel at times, that is always rains when we have planned to spend a day out of doors, that the bus is going in the opposite direction to ours, always comes first, that some unfortunate experience we have had was directly due to somebody's ill will or at leas to fate. Usually, however, this type of paranoid delusion is easily corrected. On second thoughts, we remember many occasions when the weather was mind, when our bus came immediately, or even when we were particularly lucky and we know that our unpleasant experiences are not caused by enemies, personal or impersonal, but result from other factors, including our own errors of judgement and other imperfections.
>
> Following this line of thought we come to discern a rising scale of sincerity in delusional attitudes. There is the momentary reaction 'Damn that fool!' Ascending the scale, there is the mood which may persist for some hours – 'I knew everything would go wrong with me and it has!'. Neither of these leads, as yet, to harmful consequences; both are entirely compatible with sound mental health. Next in severity might be a paranoid state lasting for days or weeks or more. Finally, there is the psychosis in which the person's life is totally determined by his belief in a persecution, the delusion having become permanent, and the focus of a rigid system". (1955, p.240)

Table 1 details the characteristics of both of these states of mind as developed from the work of Melanie Klein.

The essence of the paranoid-schizoid position is a deep distrust of human relationships. This negative spiral can persuade the patient that the only way to relate to the world is to withdraw and control people around them. One patient described this to me as 'dead safe'; there was a certainty about what was going to happen next though the sacrifice was growth and creativity which can emerge from uncertainty. A state of mind that is intolerable for someone that occupies the paranoid-schizoid position. Klein would place particular emphasis on the mother-infant bond as being the blueprint for all other human relations and, if this goes wrong, there is a much greater chance of paranoid-schizoid functioning. In object relations terminology, there is a significant absence of a good internal object. Segal 1981/1986 offers this definition of a good object:

> "The good part-object is usually applied to the breast or penis and it is experienced in the depressive position in relationships to good experiences. It is felt as a source of life, love and goodness, but it is not ideal. Its bad qualities are recognised and it may be experienced as frustrating in contrast to the ideal object; it is felt to be vulnerable to attacks, and therefore, it is often experienced as damaged or destroyed. The good breast and the good penis are felt as belonging respectively to the good mother and the good father, but they may be experienced before the whole-object relationship is fully established". (p.127)

In other words, the infant or child should have predominantly good experiences of both parents as symbolised by the penis or breast which, in reality, should be providing good experiences to either parent sexually and to the child, emotionally, If this source of goodness is developed through adulthood the hope is that each of us can hold onto a sense of goodness that can help us to relate to ourselves and others in a benevolent way. This creates a sense of trust and safety in the depressive position (see Table 1) where there is value placed on creativity, growth and new ideas, compared to the destructiveness of the paranoid-schizoid position. Furthermore, in the more positive state of mind of the depressive position, there is an experience of creative and equal coupling.

> One of the key elements of the paranoid-schizoid position I have described elsewhere is how envy can act like a terrorist, striking without warning and failing to take personal responsibility for actions (Kapur, 2004). Envy is one of Klein's most powerful ideas in understanding destructiveness in human relationships; she writes in 1957, in her seminal paper 'Envy and Gratitude';
> "I have for many years been interested in the earliest sources of two attitudes that have always been familiar – envy and gratitude. I have arrived at the conclusion that envy is a most potent factor in undermining feelings of love and gratitude at their root, since it affects the earliest relation of all, that to the mother… . I consider that envy is an oral-sadistic and anal-sadistic expression of destructive impulses, operative from the beginning of life, and that it has a constitutional basis". (p.176)

Table 1. Characteristics of the Paranoid-Schizoid and Depressive Positions

Paranoid-Schizoid	Depressive
Paranoia / distrust	Trust & Safety
Splitting into good & bad	Good & bad in everyone
Destructiveness	Creativity
Dysfunctional / hierarchical parental couple	Creative / equal couple
Envy	Pride in self and others
Attacks on links	Creation of links
Others are numbers, part of things	Concern for the fullness of other Human beings
Hatred of reality	Acceptance of reality
Manic defence (control, triumph & contempt)	Relating thoughtfully with concern for self/others
Persecutory guilt	Reparative guilt
Blame game	Personal responsibility

And she adds in the same paper:

> "One is reminded of the saying 'to bite the hand which feeds one', which is almost synonymous with biting, destroying and spoiling the breast. My work has taught me that the first object to be envied is the feeding breast, for the infant feels that is possesses everything he desires and that it has an unlimited flow of milk, and love which the breast keeps for its own gratification. This feeling adds to his sense of grievance and hate, and the result is a disturbed relation to the mother. If envy is excessive, this, in my view, indicates that paranoid and schizoid features are abnormally strong and that such an infant can be regarded as ill". (p.182/3)

Many destructive acts can be explained by envy which often arises when there is a significant incongruity between the recipient of the attack and the person launching the attack. Clinically, this is often seen in the attacks the patient makes on the links to the therapist (Bion, 1959, Kapur, 1993) or that individuals make on the organisational breast (Kapur, forthcoming). As Klein states, this incongruity relates to the envious person feeling they are deprived of the resources of the other person and the only way to eradicate this feeling is with a spoiling attack on the other object.

In contrast, in the depressive position, there is pride attached to the achievement of self and others. Feelings of goodness are experienced in relation to the achievements of other people. Also, if the person is receiving good experiences from others, this can be accepted with feelings of gratitude.

Within the paranoid-schizoid position, human beings become dehumanised and are reduced to numbers. This is what Klein refers to as 'part-objects', where people are experienced in a fragmented, hostile, persecutory and gratifying way. Usually, Klein refers to these part-objects relations with the terms 'breast' and 'penis', but essentially the concept refers to a distant and controlling relationship with sexualised or aggressive phantasies dominating the relationship. In contrast, in the depressive position, people are experienced as 'whole objects' or human beings which leads to a humanisation of relationships. Segal's (1981/6) definition of this is:

> ".. the perception of another person as a person. The perception of the mother as a whole object characterises the depressive position. The whole object contrasts both with the part-object and with objects split into ideal and persecutory parts. Ambivalence and guilt are experienced in relation to whole-objects". (p.128)

This important transition from part to whole object relations triggers the onset of reparative guilt and the capacity for concern. This is a central feature of the therapeutic process which persuades the individual that the other person is a human being and thus, the onslaught of destructive attacks which inflict real harm. It is important here to differentiate between manic and time reparation, as the former is a false hope of deeper psychological change. Segal (1981/6) describes this very clearly:

> "Non-manic and manic reparation differ, however, in important respects. Reparation proper can hardly be considered a defence, since it is based on the recognition of psychic reality, the experiencing of the pain that this reality causes and the taking of appropriate action to retrieve it in phantasy and reality. It is, infact, the very reverse of a defence, it is a mechanism important both for the growth of the ego and its adaptation to reality.

"Manic reparation is a defence in that its aim is to repair the object in such a way that guilt and loss are never experienced. An essential feature of manic reparation is that it has to be done without acknowledgement of guilt, and therefore, under special conditions. For instance, manic reparation is never done in relation to primary objects of internal objects, but always in relation to more remote objects; secondly, the object in relation to which reparation is done must never be experienced as having been damaged by oneself; thirdly, the object must be felt as inferior, dependent and, at depth, contemptible. There can be no true love for the object or esteem for the object or objects that are being repaired, as this would threaten the return of true depressive feelings". (p.95/96)

An indepth analysis of this process in clinical work and everyday life is essential to discover whether any real change is occurring. A powerful mechanism of change in this process is the individual accepting responsibility for their actions in the spirit of learning from experience rather than a persecutory guilt or 'blame game' scenario where self and others are presented for their actions. This state of mind requires considerable thought and concern for others. In other writings, Winnicott (1979) has referred to the depressive position as developing a capacity for concern for the other person which, if completed fully, triggers internal and external changes that re-instate value in a good object that can bring goodness to others, rather than the destructiveness of manic repair which is destined only to repeat the previous mistakes.

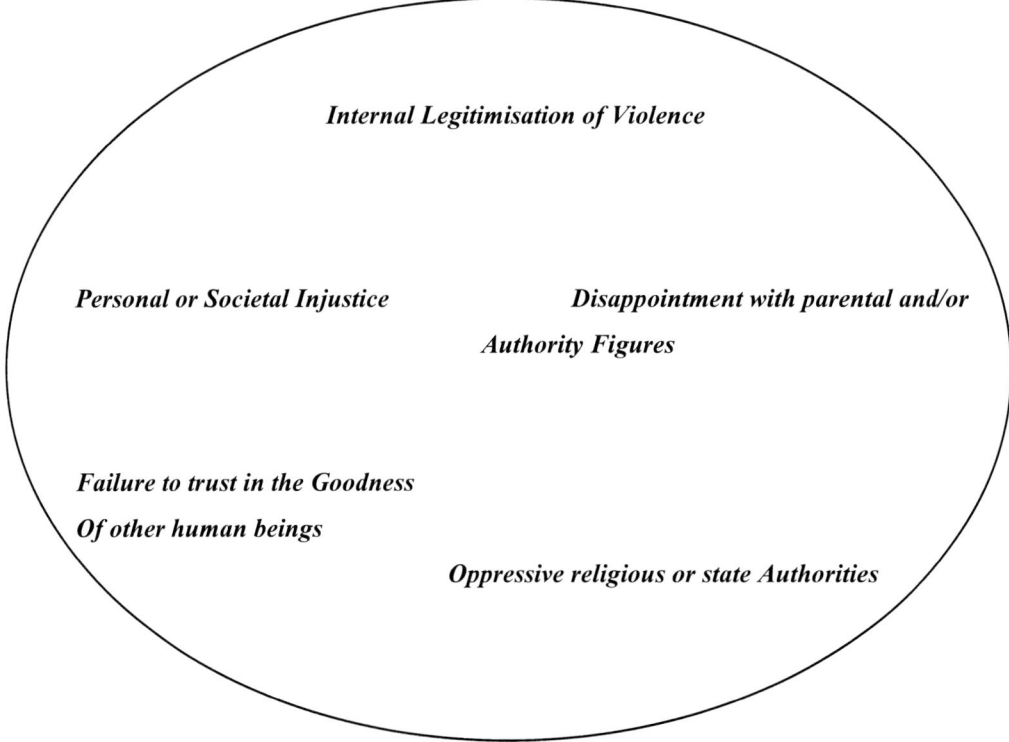

Figure 1.

I shall now describe the terrorist state of mind, using the words of terrorists from Northern Ireland and elsewhere (Iraq and Afghanistan) using the above theoretical framework. I will then describe 3 psychic scenario's which illustrate how these internal terrorist states of mind are acted out through violence and what work authorities can do to assess these threats, analyse the consequences of such actions and prevent such horrific acts of human violence occurring in the future.

Terrorist State of Mind

Figure 1 describes key themes of the internal world of a terrorist. Here, I have tried to highlight characteristics of a potential terrorist so that the risks of such attacks occurring can be assessed by politicians, psychologists and others in authority. For too long, authorities have been reactive rather than proactive in their response to terrorism. However, as medical knowledge teachers us 'prevention is better than cure' and thus, it is the responsibility of governments to become aware of societal flaws that can become the breeding ground for terrorist states of mind. I will now analyse these themes.

Personal or Social Injustice

"My mother's tales were versions of Irish history: she told us of the priests' who had died to preserve our Catholic faith when the Cromwellians had hunted them down, decapitated them, and placed their heads on spikes outside towns and churches. She aroused a sense of anger in me about the wrongs done to us by the British, the atrocities, the penal laws, the theft of our estates – although she never mentioned the word 'republicanism'. For her, the fight against the British had been a fight to preserve faith, not a fight to create a nation. She encouraged me to feel, none the less that the injustice of partition, the division of Ireland, was yet another wrong inflicted on Catholics by Protestants. She passed on the Catholic faith in a way which passed on the idea of resistance to an enemy". (Collins, 200 , p.36)

So wrote the ex-IRA terrorist (or freedom fighter) Eamon Collins in describing the reasons behind his violence. This social injustice is echoed by many terrorists where they powerfully adopt views which generate their terrorist behaviour. As described earlier, the powerful role of phantasy can distort reality to such an extent that the injustice may be invented or exaggerated. Nevertheless, the effects are the same. A state of mind is created which believes that a wrong has to be corrected by violence. This is an observation taken too lightly by politicians yet it ranks as one of the fundamental reasons for 'ordinary people' adopting violence as a way of 'getting even'. Importantly, this experience of injustice is multiplied when governments wittingly or unwittingly collude with acts of injustice. Conn Hallinan, writing on the reasons behind September 11th, points to the injustice of the Bush administration;

"There is a law in politics almost as old as the business itself. When one lays claim to the moral high ground, goes the saying, one should be 'as the Caesar's wife; above reproach'. The Bush administration's inattention to that pact of wisdom is likely to cause it no end of trouble, as it tries to cobble together an international coalition against terrorism".

When the United States' new United Nations' Ambassador, John Negropante, rose to praise that body's September 28 resolution on terrorism, reminding delegates that the action 'obligates all member states to deny financing, support and safe haven for terrorists'. His remarks were greeted with studied silence by Latin American delegates. It is hard to cheer when you're gritting your teeth.

Twenty years ago, Negroponte was financing and supporting terrorist death squads in Honduras and providing 'safe haven' for the Contras, who used to sabotage and murder in their efforts to overthrow the Sandinista regime in Nicaragua". (2002, p.59)

To prevent acts of terrorism governments have to take seriously how their actions can fuel feelings of injustice that impel people towards acts of violence. Minimizing experiences of injustice from those in authority lessens the possibility of such terrorism occurring. Also, in my own personal observations of people involved in terrorist acts in Northern Ireland, the identity and excitement associated with violence often masks troubled personal relationships. Often, unhappy marriages and poor family relationships are covered over by the distraction of a common enemy which can act as a receptacle of bad feelings within the personal situations of people caught up with violence. Personal injustices may become covered by social injustices and with the conviction that a feeling of being wronged can be corrected through terrorism.

Internal Legitimisation of Violence

"The destructive omnipotent way of living like Simon often appears highly organised, as if one were dealing with a powerful gang dominated by a leader, who controls all the members of the gang to see that they support one another in making the criminal destructive work more effective and powerful. However, the narcissistic organisation not only increases the strength of the destructive narcissism, and the deadly force related to it, but it has a defensive purpose to keep itself in power and so maintain the status quo. The main aim seems to be to prevent the weakening of the organisation and to control the members of the gang so that they will not desert the destructive organisation and join the positive parts of the self or betray the secrets of the gang to the Police, the protecting super-ego, standing for the helpful analyst, who might be able to save the patient. Frequently, when a patient of this kind makes progress in analysis and wants to change, he dreams of being attacked by members of the Mafia or adolescent delinquents, and a negative therapeutic reaction sets in". (Rosenfeld, 1987, p.111-112)

So writes Herbert Rosenfeld in his analysis of a patient. The same applies to a terrorist state of mind where there is enormous propaganda to convince the individual that violence is a legitimised action. Within contemporary terrorism linked to Islam and Muslim religions, there is the promise to the suicide bomber of many virgins to greet them through the gates of eternal peacefulness. Religious writing and political beliefs can so easily be hijacked to provide this internal authority necessary for acts of violence. Of course, this internal state of mind is made worse through bad authority figures who utter words of hate and paranoia and who can provide blind followers with plenty of evidence that killing others, in service of their cause, is perfectly legitimate. Here, it is again critical that governments proactively minimise these influences to lessen the possibilities of often vulnerable individuals acting out the instructions of an idealised authority figure.

Disappointment with Parent and/or Authority Figures

As stated above, the acting out of violence can be traced to earlier disappointments in the individual's life. Unknown to the individual, they may be attempting to correct previous disappointments or persecutions in their own personal history. An analysis of the personal idiosyncrasies of terrorists often reveals these issues. Eamon Collins, quoted earlier writes of his mother:

> "Kathleen Cumiskey was born in Crossmaglen in 1929, the only girl in a family of nine boys. She attended a number of convent schools where she picked up a good knowledge of history, the Irish language and – what most impressed me – the piano. But I remember most clearly her love of God, the Catholic God, and her determination to instil her religious faith in her children. Not a day went by without some words of instruction from her about the Roman Catholic Church". (1997, p.30)

Could it be that the overly religious atmosphere of a Catholic home predisposed Collins to a deep disappointment of authority figures which became projected on to a similarly oppressive British state? While this formulation may seem wild and speculative, what needs to be taken seriously to prevent terrorism is the identification of personal vulnerabilities in terrorists which may contribute to such violence. How could this take place? Society, and in particular, religious and educational authorities, have to minimise the influence of oppressive regimes that inevitably will leave people feeling disappointed. Theoretically, in this paranoid-schizoid style of thinking, there is an idealisation of oppressive authority which ultimately may act as a breeding ground for a violent reaction against all forms of authority, particularly those that resemble such persecutory experiences.

Michael Stone, a loyalist (Protestant) terrorist describes his own personal history, which can provide an alternative analysis of how earlier disappointments can contribute to terrorism, he writes:

> "I came into the world on 2nd April 1955 in Lordswood Hospital, Harborne, Birmingham, the first-born child of Mary Bridget and Cyril Stone. I am a British citizen and proud to be one. I have always cherished my nationality. My family history is complex, but it forms the backbone of my identity. I have two sets of parents; my biological mother and father, Mary Bridget O'Sullivan and her husband Cyril Alfred Stone, and the parents who raised me as their own, Margaret and John Gregg............ Mary Bridget and Cyril met in the UK and were married at Caxton Hall Registry Office, London in 1953. She was just eighteen and he, just twenty one when they exchanged vows. The union lasted only two years, enough time for Mary Bridget to decide motherhood and marriages weren't for her. She walked out on her husband and new baby in September 1955, when I was just five months old ...... My mother (Margaret Gregg) resented Mary Bridget for abandoning her baby and walking out on her family". (2003, p.2/3)

While Stone does go on to describe his positive experiences of being brought up by his 'foster parents', the reality was that he never knew his biological mother, who may have been Catholic, he adds;

> "I am not interested in Mary Bridget's religion and religious persuasion is not an issue for me. She may have been a Roman Catholic or she may not have been. It doesn't matter". (p.4)

But does it matter? Could Stone's violence and hatred against Catholics be a primitive reaction to being discarded by a potentially Catholic mother? As a baby he was abandoned and rejected by the breast of a Catholic mother – is it too far fetched to suggest that this could explain some of his deep hatred of Catholics? Michael Stone was a notorious member of a loyalist murder gang who would often on his own initiative kill Catholics at random. He is best known for his shooting and bombing spree at Milltown Cemetery where he attacked a funeral with the aim of murdering as many Catholics as possible. Again, while these interpretations are highly speculative, they point to a very important piece in the psychic jigsaw of a state of mind, namely, the possibility that what may be acted out is a deeper disappointment with early authority figures that potentially leaves individuals with a reason to hate. As stated, a preventative ingredient would be for society to take seriously the impact of abandoning and rejecting experiences on individuals. Another possible effect of a preponderance of these experiences is to propel individuals to join terrorists groups, thus giving them a sense of belonging they missed in the early family unit.

Oppressive Religious or State Authorities

Segal (1995) highlights the projective processes which maintain the existence of oppressive states when she writes:

> "A political grouping, such as Facism or Communism, can combine the army mentality with the religious mentality, bringing about guiltless destruction. The same can happen when the group called the National gets ruled by Nationalism. Members of a group are brought together because they share common interests and common anxieties ……… political groups contain psychotic fears and mechanisms. At its simplist, the rich man or the oppressor unable to face guilt about his destructive greed or ambition joins others in denying the guilt in two ways; one is the creation of a joint group super-ego and the other is the projection of destructiveness and guilt into the poor and oppressed, creating a red monster of communism or the black – and – red monster amongst depressed coloured populations. The poor, on the other hand, feel helpless, vengeful and envious; and they too resort to projection and self-idealisation – as in the Marxist idealisation of the proletariat. The proletarian dictatorship would be good and constructive because the poor and oppressed and guiltless, as though that group were immune from the human factors of greed, persecution etc". (p.195/6)

The capacity to oppress or become authoritarian can be understood through these projective processes as they exist in the paranoid-schizoid state of mind. Central to the oppressive or authoritarian act is the belief that it is for the good of the oppressed: the dominant state takes on a view that they know what is best for the population who are regulated to a sub-serviant position. When this hierarchical state is established there then emerges, as described by Hanna Segal, a disavowal of mental states that maintain this destructive status quo.

In such states, those in political authority take away any individuality or responsibility from the ordinary citizen as they are perceived to be unable to be part of a democratic process that gives them the capacity to think intelligently about how good or bad authority can be. In turn, the citizen in such an oppressed state accepts this passive position, which conveniently, allows them to passively exist and takes away the discomfort of protesting and rallying against such an oppressive regime. This infantile dependent relationship has a perverse status quo, but ultimately denies the individual his right for full expression and allows authoritarian states to exist with accountability to a social conscience which is expressed through an effective democratic system.

Cohen (2001 in explaining the states of denial about the German concentration camps writes:

> "People knew vaguely what was happening, but just as vaguely didn't care … . Even if one looked away, asked no questions, and refrained from talk in public, a dull awareness remained … . Like not having an inquiring mind, the phrases 'better not to know more' and 'dull awareness' stand out". (p.149)

This passive acceptance leaves individuals with a feeling of oppression and persecution. For a terrorist state of mind, we can locate this in the state being the terrorist or citizens, legitimately feeling they are 'freedom fighters' as they wish to liberate society from authorities that refuse to allow thought and inquiry which are so necessary for healthy states of mind.

Failure to Trust in the Goodness of Other Human Beings

> "The internalisation of good parents and the identification with them underlie loyalty towards people and causes and the ability to make sacrifices for one's convictions. Loyalty towards what is loved or felt to be right implies (which are never entirely eliminated) and turned towards those objects which endanger what is felt to be good". (p.269)

So writes Melanie Klein on the characteristics of good mental health; there has to be a fundamental trust in the goodness of human beings, particularly those in authority. However, when terrorist minds become formed, as described above, early bad experiences of authority are repeated throughout the individuals life. This familiar pattern can be seen in all types of psychiatric disorders and is a universal feature of all psychopathologies. What Melanie Klein highlights, and is crucial for the understanding of terrorist state of minds, is that the terrorist has given up hope that goodness will overcome their perceived or imagined injustice. There is a retreat to badness and destructiveness, either as a way of correcting a perceived injustice or for destroying goodness in others that cannot be tolerated. Individuals who have a 'good enough' experience of authority are able to engage with democratic processes that trust positive change as a result of good deeds and actions. Prevention of terrorist acts could be aimed at maximising the possibility of good experiences from those in authority, so reducing the possibility that individuals will turn to terrorist acts as a way of changing society. If authority figures can take seriously the views of others then constructive change can follow rather than perpetuating destructiveness by devaluing genuinely held views and grievances of every day life.

I will now use the above theoretical framework to analyse three states of mind and describe how preventive measures could be adopted to minimize such acting out.

Three Psychic Scenarios

Low Cast Fenians

"The Civil Rights movement developed out of the Homeless Citizens League, formed to protest against what was judged to be the unfair discrimination of houses by the local Council in Dungannon, County Tyrone. The League accused the Unionist controlled Council of favouring Protestant applicants for public sector housing, with the result that many Catholic families remained in over-crowded, unsanitary accommodation. So successful was the League in highlighting these grievances that it became the basis from which a wider campaign against similar injustices elsewhere was launched in 1966, under the banner of the Campaign for Social Justice in N. Ireland. The campaign was initially conducted through the publication and widespread circulation of information and statistical data highlighting allegations of discrimination against the Roman Catholic – Nationalist community in employment, public housing allocations and electoral law and practices.

> Unionist and Government circles attempted to ignore or dismiss the campaign 'as typical of the scurrilous propaganda put out by a small section of the community whose avowed intention is to overthrow the constitution of Northern Ireland'.
> The new Labour Government in Great Britain followed the line of it's Conservation predecessor almost to the letter, arguing that since allegations of injustice pertained to matters under the direct jurisdiction of the Northern Ireland Government, it would be improper for the British Government to intervene, Prime Minister, Harold Wilson's Private Secretary, made this point quite bluntly in reply to correspondence with the campaign when he wrote in 1965, 'The matters about which you allege discrimination are talking within the field of responsibility of the Northern Ireland Government and Parliament. This being so, he thinks it would be wrong for him to seek to intervene'. (Farren & Mullvihill, 2000, p27)

We see here all the ingredients for a terrorist state of mind and the subsequent acting out of violence acts. The creation of the Civil Rights movement was a direct result of real injustice in society. In reality, people were being denied equal and fair access to opportunities within a so called democratic system. In Government, and therefore throughout the authority structures in N. Ireland, there were real experiences of injustice. Many Catholic families would have seen their children go to mainland Britain or the USA to find work they were being denied in their own country. This led to the inevitable splitting up of families and a genuine sense of grievance that ordinary rights where being denied. Here, the ingredients for the propagation of terrorist states of mind were being laid by these fundamental flaws in society. As highlighted in Figure 2, personal and societal injustice coupled with a disappointment with authority figures was rife. The conditions for poor mental health, as defined by the above object relations theory, were impacting on the Catholic minority population all of the time. Constantly, this part of the population were being exposed to experiences that could only decrease their trust in authority, and thus the goodness of other human beings.

These experiences left the minority Catholic population feeling like second class citizens or at the bottom of the binary religious system in N. Ireland. It is essential here to take seriously the effects of this day to day treatment of Catholics in society. One personal account of a young female Catholic working in the predominately Protestant newspaper, the 'Newsletter' in the 1970s talks of her daily humiliation by the security officer

> "Every morning, without fail, the security man would stop me, no one else and empty my handbag all the time. Right in front of everyone, he picked me out….. time and time again and made sure I knew he was an Orangeman and I had to know my place as a second class citizen. Paradoxically, I only got the job because an English woman, who didn't care about religion and was only worried whether I got my work done, gave me the job on merit. Also, my name was difficult to place as either Catholic or Protestant, so I got away with it". (Personal Communication)

In Kleinian terminology, one of the most delicate and valuable objects belonging to a woman was emptied with its contents exposed to the gaze of onlookers and a male Protestant in his attempt to devalue and empty any precious contents of this individual's identity. After all, is it not the handbag that contains, and can represent all the sensitive elements of female (vaginal) sexuality i.e. personal and private possessions and experiences that belong to the female identity and can only be given with the full authority of the woman rather than being violently intruded upon and emptied by the enemy, a Protestant phallus or Orangeman.

Symbolically, this incident and the example of societal discrimination highlighted above represents a denial and intrusion of goodness on the Catholic state of mind. Furthermore, when noting the Government's response to societal discrimination, Harold Wilson conveniently turned a 'blind eye' and said it would be wrong to intervene. The parental father was denying the abuse of the Northern Ireland governmental mother against it's vulnerable child, the catholic minority. This could only sow the seeds of the terrorist state of mind described in Figure 2. So what preventative measures could be put in place?

Firstly, as stated throughout this chapter, Governments and those in authority have to take seriously the grievances of the minority. The 'brushing aside' or 'sweeping under the carpet' of injustices is a critical ingredient in the aetiology of terrorism and must be addressed by politicians' and those in positions of authority otherwise, two things are bound to occur. There will be a omnipresence of bad experiences with authority that will embed a paranoia in everyday life that will lead to the inevitable acting out of internal states of mind. Next, in Kleinian theory, people will simply feel that living in the 'paranoid-schizoid' situation is normal and have little or no experience of good experiences as represented in the depressive position. The capacity for concern will rarely flourish in everyday life and people will be reduced to part-object human relations with little or no value placed on humanity and people being treated equally.

Secondly, care and attention must be given not to intrude and evacuate an other person's state of mind as represented in the 'hand bag' incident. Abuse, in all forms is characterised by a violent intrusion in the sensitive and vulnerable parts of others. Society, and particular those in authority have to uphold, wherever possible, the values of the depressive position so minimising experiences of violent intrusion which can only further propagate terrorist state of minds. When a society is split, as Northern Ireland is, it takes a tremendous effort from those in authority to correct previous 'wrongs'. Genuine reparation, as described earlier in this chapter, can only take place when there is a recognition of the damage done through the treatment of someone else as a second class citizen and a genuine wish to treat the other person as an equal human being who has been on the receiving end of horrific abuse. This, in turn, decreases the likelihood of us all being the victim of terrorism.

My Queen my Country

Michael Stone, the notorious loyalist terrorist writes of his identification with the British state,

> "My family were good, working class loyalists who were loyal to the Crown, loyal to their Queen, loyal to their identity and loyal to British nationality". (p9)

And later he adds,

> "I told the (Parliamentary) Committee that what I did, I did in the name of my Britishness. I told them what I did because I am a British citizen". (p288)

The internal justification for acts of destruction has a powerful internal structure which can powerfully legitimise violence. In the case of Michael Stone and many other loyalists, the identity of being loyal to the Queen allowed many murderous attacks to occur on innocent victims. This overvaluation of Britishness allows the individual to 'borrow' authority and permission to carry out such acts. In many occasions, and Michael Stone seemed to illustrate this characteristic, his strength covered over a paranoid structure which had a deep distrust in early family life. In his recollections of his 'adopted parents', there emerges an idealisation of them.

> "I have two sets of parents, my biological mother and father, Mary Bridget O'Sullivan and her husband Cyril Alfred Stone, and the parents who raised me as their own, Margaret and John Gregg… .
> Margaret and John are the only parents I have ever known. Margaret was the best mother a young boy could wish for" … . (2003, p1 & 2)

However, regardless of what developmental perspective we take on the mind of Michael Stone, it is near impossible to believe that his replacement parents, and in particular, his mother was the best a 'young boy could wish for' His dedication to murderous acts and absolute hatred of Catholics must have had some aetiology on personal disappointments in his earlier life. I had speculated above that the rejection by his Catholic mother may have left him with these negative feelings towards Catholics. However, it may also be equally true that the idealisation of his adoptive parents, particularly his mother, disguised a deep seated resentment about life.

The acts committed by Stone and legitimised through his own internal loyalty to the Queen verged on barbaric. In his infamous attack on Republican political leaders and innocent Catholics at Milltown Cemetery in Belfast, he writes,

> "The priest was finishing his service, I could hear a woman wailing. Protestant women have cried like this too, saying goodbye to a husband, lover and friend. A woman volunteer began the oration and again, I held back. They were soldiers and they deserved a soldier's farewell… . I wanted to panic the crowd. I needed to confuse them, I wanted them to start running in fear. The grenades would do that. I moved towards the Republican plot and took out two grenades with five second fuses. I pulled the split pins and lobbed both grenades over the heads of the mourners, straight at Martin McGuinness and Gerry Adams, who were 50 metres away… . I took out the Browning and fired 3 shots directly into the air". (2003, p141)

In this description Stone does fluctuate, as highlighted by the 2-way arrow in the theoretical designation of a paranoid ⇌ schizoid depressive position, between a respect for the humanness of his victims, 'Protestant women have cried like this too' and 'They were soldiers and deserved a soldiers farewell' to the dehumanisation of the very same people when grenades were thrown into the crowd of people. His internal justification of his murderous acts 'For Queen and Country' had allowed him to change, within seconds, his feelings about exactly the same people.

The power of this internal propaganda and the speed at which the mind is convinced that these dehumanising acts are necessary is remarkable, and must be understood fully to prevent terrorist acts. Within the paranoid-schizoid state of mind, the depth of hatred is so strong that it eradicates feelings of goodness and humanity. This hatred, unwittingly, can be fuelled by disappointment or persecuting authority figures and this political leaders, who convince individual and vulnerable citizens that taking the life of others, and in the case of suicide bombers, is justified out of some payment of loyalty to political beliefs. If Governments actively justify such terrorist propaganda, which can so easily become internalised via terrorist groups i.e. in Stone's case a commitment to British values has become hijacked by loyalist groups to commit murder, then there is a greater likelihood that terrorist acts may occur.

As such, if Governments can take a pride in nationalism but be careful that it is communicated to others in such a way that exposes a sense of goodness rather than badness. Again, in respect of Michael Stone he comments in the Milltown atrocity that a elite police force were nearby, both to spy on the Republican funeral, but also to protect mourners. So paradoxically, he is killing others for 'Queen and Country', yet the police force which should uphold law and order actually were in danger of being attacked by him as they came to protect the mourners. It was convenient for Stone to use his loyalty to Queen and Country to justify his acts, yet when the forces of Queen and Country where protecting innocent mourners he was prepared to attack them. He could not tolerate that a civilised and 'sane' 'Queen and Country' is about preventing violence to everyone, not just to be used in a 'mad' way to legitimise murder.

In analysing the work of Stone we see a deeply ingrained personality structure that is preoccupied with destruction of Catholics, who became his enemy. His early years, and then being part of a terrorist paramilitary group, maximised the negative internal influences for Stone to carry out his crimes. There was a paucity of good experiences, he was constantly exposed to acts of destruction. In his murder of the Catholic, Patrick Brady, he writes:

"In my paramilitary life I had a ritual, I never looked at newspapers and I never watched television reports. The radio was my only source of news. Mid-morning bulletins confirmed Patrick Brady's death, and that same day the UFF claimed responsibility for the murder in a telephone call to Downtown Radio. I tried to look at Brady's death in a detached way. He was a soldier and I was a soldier, and in war soldiers die. I didn't want to expose myself to the human aspect, the grieving widow and the weeping children, because that's when it becomes real... . When you take a man's life you lose part of yourself and part of your humanity forever". (p.72)

In reflecting on his destructive past, Stone was able to reflect on the inhumanity of his deeds, but there wasn't enough goodness in his personal history to mitigate against his violence. Again, with prevention in mind, Governments' have to pay serious attention to the possibility that a preponderance of negative experiences can only fuel the flames of destruction. Poor living conditions along with economic deprivations, whether it be on the Falls or Shankill Roads of Belfast, the Gaza or the back streets of Baghdad, these can only act as breeding grounds for negative states of mind that leaves individuals feeling that terrorism is the natural next stage in their lives.

White Might is Right

"There is a direct linkage between the terrible events of September 11 and the politics represented by the United Nations World Conference Against Racism held in Durban, South Africa, only days prior to the terrorist attacks. The U.S. Government in Durban opposed the definition of slavery as "a crime against humanity". It refused to acknowledge the historic and contemporary effects of colonialism, racial segregation and apartheid on the under-development and oppression of the non-European world.

> It polemically manipulated the charge of anti-Semitism to evade discussions concerning the right of self-determination for the Palestinian people. The world's subaltern masses represented at Durban sought to advance a new global discussion about the political economy of racism – and the United States insulted the entire international community. Should we therefore be surprised that Palestinian children celebrate in the streets of their occupied territories when they see televised images of our largest buildings being destroyed?" Marble, 2002 (p.153)

Western Governments rarely understand the negative impacts of crushing opposition and alternative views through 'White brute force'. The history of the world, as highlighted in the above quote points to the unconscious and conscious influences on global relationships. White power, whether it is represented through Western Governments' or the USA, have a legacy of being in a powerful position over non-Whites. There is often an implicit assumption that 'White' is not only stronger, it has to be 'right' by the virtue of its legacy. This assumption permeates not only global politics but everyday human relationships. In my own professional work, I have encountered such views (Kapur, 2005). However, for me as a Professional and a Writer, my capacity to protest is through my work. For the individual on the streets of Baghdad or Gaza, protest is through violence.

When such injustice if felt strongly the opportunity to legitimise terrorism through religion is massive. This is where Islamic teachings are hijacked by terrorists to justify their hatred of White Americans and others who they see as the enemy. Sahih Al-Bakhari, quoting from a collection of sayings and deeds from the Prophet Mohammed, writes of his apostle, Huraia, as saying:

> "I have been sent with the shortest expressions bearing the widest meanings, and I have I have been made victorious with terror, and while I was sleeping, keys of the world were brought to me and put in my hand". (Vol. 4, Book 52, No.220)

An interpretation of this quote for the persecuted in Iraq could be the adoption of terror to achieve access to the treasures of the world; whatever that may be. Real experiences of injustice in the outside world coupled with the legitimisation of extreme interpretations of religion is a deadly cocktail in the transition of a 'normal' human being to a terrorist.

Governments' have to take this seriously to minimise terrorist acts occurring in everyday life. Minds that are primed to commit acts of terrorism will use many different pieces of news to justify their actions. A further example of this is the lack of understanding from the American administration to see the dangers of this. U.S. Secretary of State, Madeline Albright's infamous reply to a question posed on a USA TV programme points to this lack of awareness:

> *Interviewer:*" We have heard that half a million children have died because of sanctions against Iraq. It means that more children died here than died in Hiroshima. And is the price worth it?"
>
> *Madeline Albright:* "I think this is a very hard choice, but eh price – we think the price is worth it".

Here, people can see and hear very real acts of injustice. Is one White life worth 100, 200, or 300 non-Whites lives? Over 3000 people were killed in September 11; well over this number of children die from starvation in Africa every year. If powerful Politicians' project this White superiority in their political and public lives, then they must realise how a state of mind ready to act out terrorism will use these stories as evidence for their own destructive acts onto White people. All the characteristics of the 'paranoid-schizoid' mind again take over. Envy can also be acted out on White authority. For example, one interpretation of the twin tower attacks, is a non-White envious attack on the two White Phallic objects that represented 'White is might is right'. By collapsing these twin towers, Muslims demonstrated that they can ht America where it hurts and leave the White world with feelings of helplessness and impotence. Surely, Governments' in authority can act more wisely to prevent potential terrorists feeding in the 'Klu Klux Clan' implications of unwise comments by politicians. A mind ready to carry out a terrorist act often just requires one more piece of information to legitimise killing other human beings.

Conclusion

When terrorist events occur, many people tend to stand back and believe that the events have no connection to their day-to-day life in the world we live in. Unfortunately, for the terrorist acting out his state of mind through destructive acts, he sees a very clear link between his conviction that terrorist acts have to be committed and a feeling of injustice perceived to reside in society, which includes you and me. As highlighted in Figure 2, and described in this chapter, there are many experiences that go into the minds of terrorists and a common thread tends to be a feeling of injustice, keenly felt and often originating in people in authority, failing to deliver good enough experiences whereby their grievances can be understood.

To prevent terrorist acts, people in authority have to take seriously grievances that constitute the reasons why such acts occur. In the three themes highlighted in this paper, I have pointed to universality of disappointment and injustice felt by people involved and/or associated with terrorism. While these issues are sometimes acknowledged by those with power, they are often given cosmetic value, with no real attempts to address the root causes of injustice. The cure – a serious recognition that an emotional injury has occurred and a genuine effort by society, and thus Governments', to put things right. This visible act of reparation decreases the likelihood that people will commit terrorist acts as they will feel their voices have been heard. This visibility is crucial to minimise terrorist threats. However, people 'on the ground' have a responsibility to minimise the possibility that injustices and grievances will not be acted out by acknowledging their own de-humanisation and demonisation of minority groups who are connected with terrorist groups. In the current climate of Islamic terrorism, we can see many examples of this where public opinion forms negative views of Muslims, so increasing the likelihood of injustice and thus acts of terrorism. If Politicians and people on the ground brush aside and ignore real injustices then we can't be surprised to see further terrorist atrocities, where people who commit these acts are desperate to be heard. Humanising our day-to-day and political relations decreases the terrorist threat and thus keeps us all safe in our global village of today.

References

[1]   Ali-Bakhari, S., *Collection of Saying and Deeds of the Prophet Mohammed*, vol. 4, Book 52, No. 220.

[2]   Bion, W.R. (1959). Attacks on Linking. *International Journal of Psychoanalysis*, 40, p.308-315, also in *Second Thoughts* (6th Ed.) London, Karnac, 2004, p.93-110.

[3]   Cohen, S. (2001). *States of Denial: Knowing about Atrocities and Suffering*. Malden, USA.

[4]   Collins, E. (1997) *Killing Rage*. London, Grants Books.

[5]   Farren, S. & Mullvihill, R.F. (2000). *Paths to a Settlement in Northern Ireland*. New York. Oxford University Press.

[6]   Hallinan, C. (2002). The U.S. Terrorists in Burbach, R. & Clarke, B. (Eds). *September 11 and the U.S. War: Beyond the Curtain of Smoke*. San Francisco, City Lights Books, p.59-60.

[7]   Heimann, P. (1956) Dynamics of Transference Interpretations. *International Journal of Psychoanalysis*, 37, p.303-310.

[8]   Isaacs, S. (1952). The Nature and Function of Phantasy. In, Klein, M., Heimann, P., Isaacs, S. & Riviere, J. *Developments in Psychoanalysis*. London, Karnac, p.67-121.

[9]   Kapur, R. (1993). The Effects of Group Interpretations with the Severely Mentally Ill. *Group Analysis*. 26, p.411-432.

[10] Kapur, R. & Campbell, J. (2004). *The Troubled Mind of Northern Ireland; An Analysis of the Emotional Effects of the Troubles*. Karnac, London.

[11] Kapur, R. (2005). Dealing with Damage: The Desire for Psychic Violence to Soothe Psychic Pain. *Psychotherapy and Politics International*, 3, (3), p.180-193.

[12] Klein, M. (1960). On Mental Health, in *Melanie Klein: Envy and Gratitutde and Other Works*. London, Hogarth Press, P.268-274.

[13] Marble, M. (2002). The Failure of U.S. Foreign Policies, in Burbach, R. & Clarke, B. (Eds). *September 11 and the U.S. War: Beyond the Curtain of Smoke*. San Francisco, City Lights Books, p.152-154.

[14] Rosenfeld, H.R. (1987). *Impasse and Interpretation: Therapeutic and Anti-therapeutic Factors in Psychoanalytic Treatment of Psychotic, Borderline and Neurotic Patients*. Hove, Brunner- Routledge.

[15] Segal, H. (1986) (5th Ed.). *Introduction to the Work of Melanie Klein:* London, Hogarth Press.

[16] Segal, H. (1995). From Hiroshima to the Gulf War and After: A Psychoanalytic Perspective in Elliott, A. & Frosh, S. (Eds) *Psychoanalysis in Contexts*. London, Routledge, P.191-204.

[17] Stone, M. (2003) *None Shall Divide Us*. Wales, John Blake.

[18] Winnicott, D. (1963). The Development of the Capacity for Concern in *Maturational Procecsses and the Facilitating Environment*. London, Hogarth Press.

In: Global Terrorism Issues and Developments
Editor: Rene A. Larche, pp. 141-148

ISBN: 978-1-60021-930-6
© 2008 Nova Science Publishers, Inc.

Chapter 5

ALCOHOL RELAPSES ASSOCIATED WITH THE WORLD TRADE CENTER ATTACKS: FURTHER FINDINGS

William H. Zywiak[1,2,], Robert L. Stout[1,2], Robert M. Swift[2], Robert J. Schneider[3] and Donald S. Shepard[4]*

[1]Decision Sciences Institute, Pacific Institute for Research and Evaluation, Providence, RI, USA
[2]Center for Alcohol and Addiction Studies, Brown University, Providence, RI, USA
[3]Behavioral Health, Harvard Vanguard Medical Associates, Braintree, MA, USA
[4]Schneider Inst. for Health Policy, Heller School, Brandeis University, Waltham, MA, USA

Abstract

In the present chapter we build upon our previous research (Zywiak et al., 2003a) by adding results from the control group to the previously examined case monitored group. We also examine healthcare utilization following 9-11, types of relapse, and 12 months of post 9-11 Timeline Followback data. Our earlier results suggested a relapse rate of 42% for clients recently completing an inpatient detoxification. In the present chapter with a larger sample size we now estimate that 40% relapsed. These results suggest an increased burden on the regional healthcare system. Predictor analyses suggest that relapses were more likely for older clients, and for clients not cohabiting nor married. Twelve-month outcome data suggest that drinking following 9-11 was related to drinking a year later. Follow-up calls from formal treatment programs following disasters, and publicity for cost-effective mutual-help meetings following disasters are recommended. Further, prospective studies with larger samples, with repeated assessments across a number of domains are recommended to advance knowledge regarding general reactions and individual differences in reactions to man-made and natural disasters.

---

[*] To whom correspondence should be addressed at Decision Sciences Institute, P.I.R.E., 120 Wayland Avenue, Suite 7, Providence, Rhode Island 02906; email: zywiak@pire.org

Keywords: alcohol; relapse; disaster; trauma; terrorism

Introduction

Research examining alcohol relapses associated with the man-made disasters on September 11, 2001 [i.e., the destruction and loss of life associated with the attacks on the World Trade Center (WTC) and the Pentagon, and the plane crash in Shanksville, PA] may inform optimizing the response to future man-made and natural disasters, as well as informing more generally theories of relapse. Miller and Heldring (2004) conducted an integrative literature review of 29 studies with 3 goals: to examine the prevalence of psychological symptoms just after September 11, 2001 (9-11), to examine temporal parameters of these symptoms (in relation to 9-11), and to examine correlates of symptom severity and resilience. Miller and Heldring report that the literature as a whole yielded equivocal findings regarding alcohol and drug use following 9-11. Some researchers found increases in alcohol, tobacco, and marijuana use within the New York City (NYC) region, but some studies of people in the region did not find these increases. Similar mixed findings were reported for heroin and cocaine use. In general, an increase in symptom prevalence was most common in and around NYC, and not always found at more distal locations. However, Silver et al. (2004) reported an increase in symptom prevalence even for people more than 1000 miles away from NYC.

Our earlier prospective case report (Zywiak et al., 2003) of clients enrolled in the case monitoring protocol (Stout, Rubin, Zwick, Zywiak, & Bellino, 1999) and receiving a case monitoring telephone contact both before and after 9-11 was one of the studies reviewed by Miller and Heldring. In our earlier study we found that 42% of the case monitored clients relapsed between these two telephone contacts. The case monitoring protocol is based on the Rogerian client-centered approach and consists of telephone calls on a tapered schedule, about once a month for more than a year. In addition to providing social support, during these calls the case monitor queries with open-ended questions the current clinical status of the client. The case monitor then rates the clinical status on a 5-point scale where, 1 is "No Use, No Risk," 2 is "No Use, Instability," 3 is a "Slip," and 4 is "Use without Negative Consequences," and 5 is "Use with Negative Consequences." We reported in the earlier paper that the clinical status of the case monitored clients was statistically worse post 9-11 [t(11) = 2.72, p < .05]. These clients were recruited from clinics in Boston, MA and Providence, RI, both within 250 miles of NYC. Two of the strengths of our earlier study were the prospective assessment of drinking status, as well as fairly short contact intervals. The respective contacts were on average 25 days before, and 43 days after 9-11.

Method

In this chapter we present additional prospective data as well as additional longitudinal data. The sample consists of case monitored and control participants that completed a baseline research interview (and were randomized) before 9-11. Data presented include data from the baseline interview and the 12-month follow-up. A number of interviews and surveys were administered at the 12-month follow-up. These included the Timeline Followback, the Health

Care Data Interview, and the Reasons for Drinking Questionniare. Additionally, data from the 24-month Timeline Followback were examined.

The Timeline Followback (TLFB) interview yields a continuous calendar of drinking data, with standard drink units consumed since the baseline interview. Sobell, Sobell, Klajner, Pavan, and Basian (1986) have shown this to be a reliable method for collecting drinking data. Formal and informal healthcare service utilization was assessed with the Health Care Data Interview (Larson, Shepard, Zwick, & Stout, 1997; Zywiak et al., 1999). If a client relapsed after being recruited, they were asked to complete the Reasons for Drinking Questionnaire for that relapse (Zywiak, Connors, Maisto, & Westerberg, 1996). Strengths of the data presented here include the TLFB and the long-term follow-up. Miller and Heldring (2003) reported that few long-term follow-ups addressing the mental health effects of 9-11 have been published. One of the weaknesses is the small sample size. While we conduct some statistical tests, in some instances descriptive analyses alone are presented.

Clients were some of the first participants recruited for a large randomized clinical trial of Extended Case Monitoring. To be eligible for this study, clients had to be currently insured with private health insurance, and must have had this insurance for at least 8 of the last 12 months, as health care cost is a primary outcome measure in this randomized clinical trial. Other eligibility requirements included an age of at least 18 and no greater than 65, residential stability, access to a telephone where s/he could be regularly reached, and a current DSM-IV alcohol dependence diagnosis [as determined by the Structured Clinical Interview for DSM-IV Disorders (First, Spitzer, Gibbon, & Williams, 1995) administered by the research interviewers.]

Twenty-eight clients were recruited before 9-11. The first client was recruited in early May 2001. Twenty-four of the 28 clients (86%) completed a 12-month follow-up. Four of these relapsed prior to 9-11, leaving 20 clients with 12 months of outcome data. [A relapse was defined as any alcohol consumption following discharge from inpatient detoxification. Please see Miller (1996) for a discussion of different ways to define relapse.] Relapses are hypothesized to be associated with 9-11-01 if the relapse occurred on or after 9-11-01 and before 01-11-02 (i.e., within four months). Eight of 20 (40%) participants relapsed within this window. The first four relapses occurred within 30 days of 9-11, the fifth within 60 days, the sixth within 90 days, and seventh and eighth within 120 days. (The next relapse following the eighth occurred another 98 days later, lending some support to our intention to study relapses that were associated with 9-11.) In particular, two relapses occurred on 9-11 and the third on the 13th. Regarding the number of standard drink units consumed on the first day of the relapse, this ranged from 4.8 standard drink units to 40.6 standard drink units (a potentially lethal quantity). The mean was 16.4 (SD = 12.9) and the median was 11 standard drink units. The duration of the relapses was clearly defined in all but one case. Seven of the eight relapses consisted of a string of continuous drinking days followed by a long period of uninterrupted abstinence. These relapses ranged from one to 14 days in length with a mean of 9.3 days (SD = 5.5) and a median of 11 days. The eighth relapse consisted of drinking four days a week, which turned into drinking everyday months later.

In addition to proximity to NYC, Miller and Heldring reported that demographic characteristics were associated with symptom increases following 9-11. As part of our research design we used urn randomization (Stout, Wirtz, Carbonari, & Del Boca, 1994) to ensure that our experimental and control groups were equivalent on four demographic variables. These variables were gender, living situation, ethnicity, and treatment history.

Using these variables to describe the sample of 20, the sample was 30% female, 55% married or cohabiting, 30% on their first detoxification treatment episode, and 10% minority (5% of the sample was Latino and 5% were multiracial). In addition to the four urn variables we also examined age, since this is another demographic variable that has been found to be associated with increased symptoms following 9-11 (Miller & Heldring, 2004). The average age of our sample (on 9-11-01) was 50.1 years (SD = 9.2, median = 49.5, range from 35 to 65).

For each of the four dichotomous demographic variables a chi-square analysis between that variable and presence versus absence of a 9-11 relapse was conducted. For the continuous variable age, a t-test was conducted. Please see Table 1.

Our power to detect associations is of course limited by the small sample size. Married (or cohabiting) may have served as a protective factor (27% versus 56% relapsing). Treatment history (one or more prior detoxification) was associated with worse outcome (50% versus 17% relapsing). Being older was associated with a greater likelihood of relapse [mean ages 54.4 (SD = 8.86) versus 47.4 (SD = 8.64)]. Descriptively, splitting marital status into finer categories, we found that 60% of the divorced clients (n = 5) relapsed, 50% of those never married (n = 4) relapsed, 33% of those currently married (n = 9) relapsed and 0% of those remarried (n = 2) relapsed. Regarding living situation, 75% of those living alone (n = 5) relapsed, 67% of those living with family (n = 3) relapsed, 27% of those living with a partner (n = 11) with or without children relapsed, and 0% of those living with friends (n = 2) relapsed. Admittedly, these percentages are based on very small sample sizes.

A logistic regression with relationship status (dichotomous), treatment history, and age all entered to predict relapse suggested that age was the only predictor (one tail p = .03; treatment history p = .108, relationship status p = .349; R^2 = .290). In an attempt, to further clarify these results, we determined that age was not related to treatment history (one-tail p = .230) nor relationship status (one-tail p = .446). Given the number of variables in this analyses and the small sample size, the logistic regression is best viewed as an example of a statistical approach that would be appropriate with a sample size that was at least twice as large.

For the seven relapses with a clear ending point, age was correlated with the length of the relapse (r = .71; one tail p = .037). Age was not correlated with the number of drinks consumed on the first drinking day (one tail p = .146). Regarding the four dichotomous demographic variables, men had more drinks on the first day of the relapse than women [20.1 versus 5.1; t(5) = 2.84, one tail p = .018] although there was no gender difference in the length of the relapse. Relationship status was not related to the number of drinks consumed nor the length of the relapse. Treatment history and minority status had too few cases (only one treatment novice relapsed; no minorities relapsed) to permit conduct of t-tests.

Table 1. Predictors of Relapse in Pre 9-11 group (n = 20)

Variable	test value	one-sided p
Gender	kappa = .074	n.s.
Relationship status	kappa = .275	.0995
Ethnicity	kappa = .190	n.s.
Treatment history	kappa = .304	.0815
Age	t = 1.789	.0450

Table 2. Long-term effects of relapsing between 9-11-01 and 01-10-02

Measure	Relapsed M (SD)	Not Relapsed M (SD)	(df) t-value	one-tail p
Percent days abstinent:	63.4 (48.8)	100 (0)	t(7) = 2.12	.036
Weekly volume:	28.4 (46.4)	0 (0)	t(7) = 2.03	.041
Drinks per drinking day:	4.3 (6.6)	0 (0)	t(7) = 2.25	.030

Examining the healthcare utilization of those that relapsed following 9-11, 38% entered inpatient detoxification shortly after the relapse. Twenty-five percent had already been attending, and continued to attend mutual-help groups. (The group relapsing consisted of 50% case monitored clients, and 50% control clients.)

From our entire sample of 301, the Reasons for Drinking Questionniare (Zywiak et al., 1996; Zywiak, Westerberg, Connors, & Maisto, 2003b) was administered for 115 cases for their first drink within 12-months of randomization. Mean item scores for each of three factors (negative affect, social pressure, craving/cued factors) were used to classify the types of relapses. Overall rates for type of relapse were: 53% negative affect relapses, 32% craving/cued relapses, and 15% for social pressure relapses. For those relapsing between 9-11 and 1-11-02, 57% were negative affect relapses, 29% were craving/cued relapses, and 14% were social pressure relapses, equivalent to the types of relapses for the sample as a whole.

We also examined the 24-month TLFB for those 20 clients that are the focus of this chapter. Nineteen of the twenty clients (95%) completed the 24-month assessment. Four of these drank during the two weeks starting with September 11, 2002. We examined a period of whole weeks (2.0) to control for weekend drinking. For those 19 with data, the average percent days abstinent was 84.6 (SD = 35.7, minimum = 0), the average weekly volume was 11.9 (SD = 32.3, maximum = 129.6), and the average drinks per drinking day was 1.8 (SD = 4.67; maximum = 18.5).

Comparing those who had a 9-11 relapse to those that had not, we found that those that had a 9-11 relapse were more likely to be drinking a year hence (50%) than those that had not (0%). Using square-root transformations to normalize weekly volume, and drinks per drinking day, we also found statistical differences between those that had relapsed between 09-11-01 and 01-10-02 on drinking measures 12 months after 9-11. Please see Table 2.

Discussion

There are several main findings of this study. Our estimate of the number of clients relapsing (40%) is in line with our earlier estimate of 42%. All of these clients had completed inpatient detoxification recently (between May and August 2001). Of special interest is that 15% relapsed between 9-11 and September 13, 2001, inclusive. This is a comparatively large proportion in a short interval anchored to the actual calendar. Given the distance from NYC we could hypothesize that there were many alcohol dependent clients in early recovery in the New England and Tri-State Region (NY, NJ, and CT) that relapsed on 9-11 and the weeks that followed. Thirty-eight percent of those relapsing completed another inpatient detoxification. Detoxification programs may have been flooded with potential clients shortly after 9-11. Increased healthcare utilization would have also been associated with increased healthcare costs. Mutual-help groups, of course, offer an effective and cost-effective aid to alcohol dependent clients (e.g., Kelly, Stout, Zywiak, & Schneider, 2006).

Results suggest that it may have been useful for detoxification programs within 250 miles of the World Trade Center to make follow-up calls to recent patients since they may have had a greater likelihood of relapse. Since resources are often constrained in healthcare settings, it may have been more useful to focus on recent patients that were 50 or more years old.

Results suggest that older clients were more likely to relapse, and when they did relapse, these relapses were longer, reflecting some convergent validity. These results are in line with Chen, Chung, Chen, Fang, and Chen (2003) who found that emotional distress following 9-11 was related to age in a curvilinear manner for residents in Chinatown in Manhattan. In particular, they found that those in their 50s had the greatest emotional distress, followed by those in their 40s, followed by those in their 60s. Those under 20 exhibited the lowest level of distress. Chen et al. (2003) hypothesized that this finding may have reflected that residents in their 50s may have had more economic responsibility for their families. This economic hypothesis is bolstered by the drop in the stock market on and following 9-11.

Results suggesting that clients with a partner were less likely to relapse are in line with stress-buffering models of social support (Cohen & Wills, 1985). Partners may have helped the clients process the events of 9-11. Partners may have ameliorated negative affect. Two people rather than one in the home, may have increased the likelihood that the duration of viewing explicit news coverage of 9-11 would have been reduced. In other words, the probability of someone realizing that repeated viewing of planes crashing into the World Trade Center may not be particularly healthy would increase as a function of the number of people in the room. Marital status being related to symptom severity following 9-11 was also reported by Miller and Heldring (2004) in their review of the literature.

Results suggesting a link between drinking on or shortly after 9-11 and drinking a year hence are consistent with theories of alcohol being using to dampen hyperarousal symptoms associated with trauma or secondary trauma, and alcohol's interference with cognitive processing and the extermination of the fear response (Conrod & Stewart, 2003). Further, we speculate that the autonomic arousal associated with withdrawal from alcohol (e.g., tachycardia) may accentuate hyperarousal associated with posttraumatic stress disorder. This may further increase alcohol consumption to reduce these symptoms. On the other hand, the correlation between drinking at one point following treatment and a subsequent point following treatment has been found in other studies (Maisto, Clifford, Stout, & Davis, 2007), and may be more reflective of the stability of drinking patterns then the long-term effects of stressor or trauma induced relapses.

Some findings from our study are more speculative given the sample size. As was true for the larger sample, most of the relapses were negative affect relapses. This suggests that medications targeting craving (e.g., naltrexone) may not be effective in the midst of stressors, for clients receiving inpatient detoxification.

There are a number of strengths in our methodology. Clients were already enrolled prior to 9-11, eliminating biases that may arise when participants are enrolled in a study to examine the effects of 9-11 after the event. The Timeline Followback yields rich data especially when studying temporal patterns. Our study is unusual in that most of the clients were followed up for a year after 9-11-01.

There are also a number of caveats. The most notable is the small sample size. The small sample size permits only the detection of the largest effect sizes, and some of these findings may be spurious as well. Further, weaker relationships can not be detected using this small sample size, so null findings should be treated very cautiously. Defining relapses as being associated with 9-11 if they were within 4 months of 9-11, may have included some false-positive relapses. Several domains of theoretical importance were not adequately assessed. For example, it would have been useful to distinguish between secondary traumatization (e.g., death of a friend due to the attacks) versus tertiary traumatization (e.g., repeated exposure to video coverage of planes crashing into towers, people jumping from buildings, etc.). Of the eight 9-11 relapsers, we know that one knew one of the victims on one of the planes flown into the World Trade Center. There may have also been some psychological proximity in that many if not all of the clients would have flown out of Logan International Airport at some point in their lives (the departure point for two of the four hijacked planes).

In summary, a number of interesting results are presented, but these are tempered by the small sample size. The results presented here are best viewed in the context of the greater 9-11 research literature. We also did not assess all relevant domains. For instance, future studies examining the relationship between a disaster and alcohol relapse could assess a number of parameters regarding exposure to the event. These include the actual proximity to the event, proximity to the event through ones social network, proximity to the event through ones travel and residence history, and duration of exposure to the event through the media. Further, in addition to using the Timeline Followback or similar measure, other life stressors, coping strategies (see e.g., Silver, Holman, McIntosh, Poulin, & Gil-Rivas, 2002), negative affect, and PTSD symptoms should also be assessed prospectively and longitudinally.

Acknowledgements

This research was funded by the National Institute on Alcohol Abuse and Alcoholism Grant No. R01 AA09907 "Extended Case Monitoring for Alcoholics: Health Costs." We thank Pamela Dwight, Nazia Khan, Amy Lagasse, Joy LaGrutta, Constance Lawson, and Winston Trefry for their assistance with this research. This chapter is dedicated to the past, present, and future members of the FDNY and NYPD.

References

Chen, H., Chung, H., Chen, T., Fang, L., & Chen, J.-P. (2003). The emotional distress in a community after the terrorist attack on the World Trade Center. *Community Mental Health Journal, 39*, 157-165.

Cohen, S. & Wills, T. A. (1985). Stress, social support, and the buffering hypothesis. *Psychological Bulletin, 98*, 310-357.

Conrod, P. J. & Stewart, S. H. (2003). Experimental studies exploring functional relations between posttraumatic stress disorder and substance use disorder. In P. Ouimette and P. J. Brown (Eds.) *Trauma and Substance Abuse: Causes, Consequences, and Treatment of*

Comorbid Disorders. (pp. 57-71). Washington, DC: American   Psychological Association.

First, M. B., Spitzer, R. L., Gibbon, M., & William, J. B. W. (1995). *Structured Clinical Interview for DSM-IV.* Washington, D. C.: American Psychiatric Press.

Kelly, J. F., Stout, R., Zywiak, W., & Schneider, R. (2006). A 3-year study of addiction mutual-help group participation following intensive outpatient treatment. *Alcoholism: Clinical and Experimental Research, 30,* 1381-1392.

Larson, M. J., Shepard, D. S., Zwick, W., & Stout, R. (1997). Validity of health care utilization reporting systems [abstract]. *Alcoholism: Clinical and Experimental Research, 21 (3), Suppl.,* 36A: 195,

Maisto, S. A., Clifford, P. R., Stout, R. L., & Davis, C. M. (2007). Moderate drinking in the first year after treatment as a predictor of three-year outcomes. *Journal of Studies on Alcohol, 68,* 419-427.

Miller, A. M & Heldring, M. (2004). Mental health and primary care in a time of terrorism: Psychological impact of terrorist attacks. *Families, Systems, & Health, 22,* 7-30.

Miller, W. R. (1996). What is relapse? Fifty ways to leave the wagon. *Addiction, 91* (Supplement), S15-S27.

Silver, R. C., Poulin, M., Holman, E. A., McIntosh, D. N., Gil-Rivas, V., & Pizarro, J. (2004). Exploring the myths of coping with a national trauma: A longitudinal study of responses to the September 11th Terrorist Attacks. *Journal of Aggression, Maltreatment, and Trauma, 9,* 129-141.

Silver, R. C., Holman, E. A., McIntosh, D. N., Poulin, M., & Gil-Rivas, V. (2002). Nationwide longitudinal study of psychological responses to September 11. *Journal of the American Medical Association, 288,* 1235-1244.

Sobell, M. B., Sobell, L. C., Klajner, F., Pavan, & Basian, E. (1986). The reliability of a timeline method for assessing normal drinker college students' recent drinking history: Utility for alcohol research. *Addictive Behaviors, 24,* 17-35.

Stout, R. L., Wirtz, P. W., Carbonari, J. P., and Del Boca, F. K. (1994). Ensuring balanced distribution of prognostic factors in alcohol treatment outcome research. *Journal or Studies on Alcohol (Supplement 12),* 70-75.

Stout, R. L., Rubin, A., Zwick, W., Zywiak, W., & Bellino, L. (1999). Optimizing the cost-effectiveness of alcohol treatment: A rationale for extended case monitoring. *Addictive Behaviors, 24,* 17-35.

Zywiak, W. H., Connors, G. J., Maisto, S. A., & Westerberg, V. S. (1996). Relapse research and the Reasons for Drinking Questionnaire: A factor analysis of Marlatt's relapse taxonomy. *Addiction, 91* (Supplement), S121-S130.

Zywiak, W., Larson. M. J., Lawson, C., Rubin, A., Zwick, W., Stout, R. L. (1999). Test-retest reliability of the health care data form [Abstract]. *Alcoholism: Clinical and Experimental Research, 23 (5) Suppl.,* 134A: 769.

Zywiak, W. H., Stout, R. L., Trefry, W. B., LaGrutta, J. E., Lawson, C. C., Khan, N., Swift, R. M., & Schneider, R. J. (2003a). Alcohol relapses associated with September 11, 2001: A case report. *Substance Abuse, 24,* 123-128.

Zywiak, W. H., Westerberg, V. S., Connors, G. J., & Maisto, S. A. (2003b). Exploratory findings from the Reasons for Drinking Questionnaire. *Journal of Substance Abuse Treatment, 25,* 287-292.

In: Global Terrorism Issues and Developments
Editor: Rene A. Larche, pp. 149-164

ISBN 978-1-60021-930-6
© 2008 Nova Science Publishers, Inc.

Chapter 6

MAJOR HAZARD PLANT: RISK ASSESSMENT AND THE THREAT OF TERRORISM

Robin Hankin[1] *and Michael N. Coster*[2]
[1] The University of Auckland
currently at The National Oceanography Centre, Southampton
[2] AWT New Zealand Limited
AWT House 131 New North Road, Eden Terrace
P.O. Box 109-601 Newmarket, Auckland

Abstract

We consider the risk to major hazard plant from terrorists deliberately causing catastrophic industrial accidents: here we focus on loss-of-containment events of toxic or flammable substances such as chlorine or LPG.

The local population is clearly at risk from such catastrophic events and fatalities may number in the hundreds or thousands: this represents a significant "weapon" in the hands of terrorist groups.

Risk assessment of major hazard plant typically neglects the possibility of terrorist attack; we discuss possible reasons for this. We argue that terrorism may usefully be treated as a rational behaviour and in doing so it becomes possible to assess the risks it causes. We outline a basic risk assessment methodology for terrorism and analyse the vulnerability of major hazard plant to terrorist attack: we identify eight factors (access, security, opacity, secondary hazard, robustness, law enforcement response, victim profile, and political value) that might be used as a starting point for more formal risk assessment and management.

1. Introduction

We consider the risk to major hazard plant from terrorists deliberately causing catastrophic industrial accidents: here we focus on loss-of-containment events of toxic or flammable substances such as chlorine [19], hydrogen fluoride [42], or LPG [21].

1.1. Risk Assessment of Major Industrial Hazards

The purpose of risk assessment is to determine the probabilities and consequences of certain undesirable events, and to judge their acceptability to society. Attention usually focuses on quantifying the human suffering or death caused by accidents occurring within a specific industrial activity. As large scale chemical installations have the potential to release large quantities of harmful substances [2], risk assessment is frequently used to assess the acceptability of such installations [22].

In the context of risk assessment, 'hazard' is defined as 'the possibility of harm', while 'risk' is defined as 'the chance of bad consequences'. Risk and hazard are thus different concepts: a risk is a hazard with an associated frequency of realization.

Recently, the risk posed to populations living or working near such a 'major hazard site' has become the object of public and legislative concern [22]. This risk is primarily due to the possibility of a release of toxic or flammable material into the atmosphere.

Many industrial processes use liquefied gases which are hazardous (that is, potentially harmful). This class of substances is therefore important to a risk assessment as an accidental release may harm large numbers of people.

If the gas is flammable it may ignite immediately after loss of containment, forming a flash fire or vapour cloud explosion. A 'BLEVE' (Boiling Liquid Expanding Vapour Explosion) may form if sufficient heat is supplied to the containing vessel [22]. However, if the gas fails to ignite, either because the gas is of low flammability or there is no source of ignition, a drifting cloud is formed. Such a drifting cloud may cause harm by its toxicity, or by drifting and igniting [53].

2. Terrorism and Major Industrial Hazards

Many process industry facilities report that the number of local people likely to be affected by such catastrophic events number in the hundreds or thousands [50]. This represents a significant "weapon" in the hands of terrorist groups.

One agency reports the dangers as follows:

> a terrorist interested in harming large numbers of persons might prefer to attempt to engineer a chemical disaster using conventional means to attack an industrial plant or storage facility, rather than develop and use an actual chemical weapon. In this way, significant technical and resource hurdles could be overcome, as well as reducing the profile of the terrorist organization to potential detection by intelligence or law enforcement agencies [9].

The United States of America Department of Justice [50] reports that "breaching a containment vessel of an industrial facility with an explosive or otherwise causing a chemical release may appear relatively simple to. . . a terrorist". They concluded that the risk of such action is "real and credible".

Analysis of terrorism is often hampered by its being described as "irrational"; one corollary would be that it is unpredictable. However, we argue that terrorism may usefully be treated as a rational behaviour and in doing so it becomes possible to assess the risks it causes. We outline a basic risk assessment methodology for terrorism and analyse the vulnerability of major hazard plant to terrorist attack: we identify eight factors (access, security, opacity, secondary hazard, robustness, law enforcement response, victim profile, and political value) that might be used as a starting point for more formal risk assessment and management.

In the context of major industrial hazards, risk assessment appears to neglect deliberate, malicious actions such as those of terrorism. The risk posed by such deliberate human activity differs from conventional risk in several ways. One difference is that terrorists may specifically and explicitly endeavour to cause as much harm as possible, in contrast to accidentally released hazards that occur at random. Terrorists may also specifically target vulnerable victims (such as children or the infirm) to add to the psychological impact of an attack.

In particular, a terrorist attack may be calculated to precipitate a major toxic [50] flammable [51], or biologically active [16] release: we refer to this as "secondary hazard". Recent attacks by terrorist groups indicate the increasing danger of terrorists deliberately causing catastrophic industrial accidents [51].

The United States of America Department of Justice [50] described how terrorists or other criminals are likely to view the potential of a chemical release from an industrial facility as a "relatively attractive means of achieving [their] goals"; they point out that breaching a containment vessel of an industrial facility with an explosive or otherwise causing a chemical release may appear relatively simple to a terrorist with a political agenda. Therefore, someone seeking to cause the damage associated with weapons of mass destruction may instead seek to cause a chemical release from an industrial facility.

Terrorists can and do cause equipment to fail in ways that simply do not occur unintentionally: recall that the Union Carbide disaster in Bhopal [47]—undeniably the worst process industrial accident in history—could not have occurred accidentally.

We suggest that terrorist attacks can be viewed as a new failure mode. We follow Burns's analytical framework [4] for discussing terrorism: we draw a general theory from diverse parallel lines of argument, as much of the literature is of necessity anecdotal, and an interdisciplinary approach is needed.

2.1. Defining Terrorism

Studies of terrorism commonly refer to the difficulty of defining what terrorism is, and why it occurs. Jenkins [25] cites a number of other researchers who describe their work as being hampered by the lack of a succinct definition of terrorism. More recent examples would include Eyerman [13], Whittaker [54], and Mahmood [34]. Jenkins goes on to state that a single definition cannot describe the nature, practice and motivation for the activity.

Military theorists, in contrast, have long held that terrorism can usefully be regarded simply as a *tactic* [43]. In the present context, we adapt Rapoport's approach by considering major hazard plant from the perspective of a group planning a terrorist attack. This has two advantages: firstly, one is freed from semantic debates, and secondly, risk assessments are forced to consider the motives and capabilities of relevant terrorist groups explicitly.

2.2. Ethical Concerns

One aim of our research is to construct analysis which simulates that performed by terrorists. As such, we hope to clarify this analysis for the benefit of risk assessors. We do not offer any new information to terrorists—we merely describe a process that terrorists already perform. This chapter does not produce, or reproduce, information that may be useful to terrorists.

3.   Literature Review

3.1. Major Hazard Risk Assessment and Terrorism

Coster [6] presents a comprehensive literature review of major industrial hazard risk assessment, and finds that terrorism is routinely—and almost uniformly—ignored. Here, we give a brief review of the literature on terrorism that appears to be most relevant to risk assessment of major hazard plant; we find that there appear to be systematic distortions that go some way to explaining the absence of terrorism from major hazard risk assessment.

Kletz [27] makes a strong case that the Union Carbide disaster in Bhopal—arguably the worst process industrial accident in history [47]—was almost certainly the result of deliberate sabotage. In a period where the plant was shut down and not operating, water was somehow introduced to the reaction materials (in what was otherwise an inert, stored state) which began a runaway reaction.

Yet despite this, the investigation of that particular case of deliberate sabotage, and indeed sabotage in general, seems to have remained a virtually nonexistent part of conventional risk assessment.

The absence of terrorism from, for example, Pitblado's discussions of human generated faults [40, 41] appears to reflect the focus of risk assessment practitioners on mathematically—or at least statistically—modellable phenomena [40].

This appears to be a significant absence from the field of major hazard risk assessment, and in the light of the serious consequences of terrorism it appears necessary to find some explanation for the absence of this form of analysis.

3.2. Review of Academic Literature on Terrorism

Much literature on terrorism makes reference to the fact that there is a need to come to some understanding of terrorists' motives, but that so far this has not been done [57, 58].

Many commentators observe a tendency amongst both the media and academic workers to describe groups or individuals as "terrorists" and thereafter abandon any further effort to understand or describe their motivation [58]. Crenshaw [8] states that "most sociological thinkers appear to have simply defined terrorism as 'irrationality' and given the issue no further thought". Considering terrorism as irrational is thus not necessarily a useful or justified position: we show that treating terrorism as a rational act, following Jenkins [25], can aid formal risk assessment of this threat. Crenshaw states

> It is important to remember that terrorism has an autonomous logic that is comprehensible, however unconventional... it is essential to understand the ideolo-

gies or worldviews of practitioners of terrorism on their own terms, and not to exclude them from analysis because they appear 'irrational' in a conventional sense

Mahmood [34] compares contemporary treatment of terrorism to that of 'witchcraft', adding that the myth of the 'terrorist' has become 'part of the political drama of our time'. Hyder [24] takes the position that the politics of terrorist groups have not yet been understood and this deficiency prevents decision makers from avoiding policy that creates "pro-terrorist sentiment". His position parallels a body of literature widely criticising US foreign policy [33].

Crenshaw further notes that the idea of the 'new terrorism' (that is, terrorism through weapons of mass destruction) should be critically examined as to whether it has in fact been attempted or made manifest in reality. In this context we note that terrorists may indeed posses this capability through inducing catastrophic releases in the industrial process industries.

Wilkinson [56] adduces the 1995 Tokyo sarin gas attack as an example of new terrorism, but suggests that "such new terrors are *as yet* a less significant problem than the more widely used tactics of bombings and gun attacks" (our italics).

Some researchers argue that the unwillingness to ascribe a logical basis for terrorism is part of a deliberate agenda to demonise terrorism and terrorists. Margold [36] in particular asserts that the notion of government sponsored terrorism is a "reductive trope" used to demonise and obscure the political and cultural agencies of foreign governments.

We do not wish to suggest that the 'analytical sciences' have no contributions to make to a predictively useful understanding of terrorism; indeed Crenshaw describes the need for advances in just this sort of modelling, advocating that we avoid "the attribution of terrorism to personality disorders or 'irrationality' ".

Kegley [26] refers to the notion that 'all terrorists are madmen' as one of the 'myths' that hamper analysis of the phenomenon of terrorism. Jenkins expands upon the need to understand terrorism, stating:

> we must try to *think like terrorists* and see beyond the apparent meaninglessness—even tragic absurdity—of a single terrorist act, to discern its objectives (our italics).

3.2.1. Summary

We surmise that there is a need to come to some understanding of terrorists' motives, and that this approach is absent from conventional major hazard risk assessment.

We thus consider terrorism as an element of public risk exposure. We argue that it is necessary to come to some understanding of terrorism as an instrumental behaviour (following Coster [6] and Coster and Hankin [7]) rather than simply defining it as irrational. We restate that our consideration of terrorism as a rational act is as much utilitarian as it is inferential.

3.3.   Risk Assessment of Terrorism and the Assumption of Good Faith

In risk assessment, it is typically assumed that all actors will do their best to fulfil their designated roles: they act *in good faith*.

Like many assumptions this goes unstated, and appears to go back to the early methodologies of risk assessment; Chicken [5] gives a brief discussion. Kletz, however, acknowledges that 'corner cutting' (where individuals do not strictly adhere to instructions) but, states that it is exists not possible to describe the reasons or likelihood that this will occur.

We follow Coster [6] and consider terrorism to be an extreme form of misbehaviour. As a corollary of the assumption of good faith, we find that conventional major hazard risk assessments typically assume, explicitly or implicitly, that assessing terrorism is not possible. For example,

> We *cannot* estimate the probability that. . . [a worker]. . . will make a conscious decision not to close. . . [a safety valve]. . . either because he considers it unnecessary or because he has made a conscious decision to do so because he wishes to sabotage operations (Kletz [27], p101).

(our italics). Kletz's opinion is essentially the policy of the Institute of Chemical Engineers and their counterpart bodies in the US. As a matter of general rule he states: "Never attribute to malice or other deliberate decision what can be explained by human frailty, imperfection or ignorance".

We find the widespread assumption (in risk assessment and elsewhere) that individuals do not act maliciously. However, recent Australian and New Zealand legislation [46] has begun to question this assumption, requiring that risk assessments consider "political circumstances" and "individual activities" as sources of risk. This would seem to suggest a more thorough analysis of deliberate sabotage and terrorism in risk assessment.

We have argued above that that much of the academic literature which is typically consulted by those conducting risk assessment of major industrial hazards suggests that terrorism cannot be assimilated into the framework of conventional risk assessment.

There are several difficulties associated with including antagonistic hazards in risk assessment of major hazard plant. We suggest two major reasons: the assumption of good faith, and statistical unmanageability. These two factors are in addition to the wider denial of terrorism's rationality discussed above.

3.3.1.   Conventional Statistical Risk Assessment Techniques Applied to Terrorism

In major hazard risk assessment, standard statistical techniques such as Poisson processes [32] appear to be of limited use: catastrophic accidents caused by terrorism are not distributed in the same way accidents due to other causes [1]

---

[1]Whether terrorist attacks are 'random' is an interesting question. Classical probability theory would say 'no': the attacks are planned by the terrorists in a deterministic manner, so nothing is random.

The *likelihood* paradigm espoused by Edwards [12] would say 'yes': there *is* a pattern to the attacks, known to the terrorists, about which we (the risk assessors) are ignorant, implying the use of a uniform support curve.

The subjectivist Bayesian framework would say 'it depends': to the terrorists themselves, an attack is an inevitable event; but risk assessors are not party to this information so they would have to work with an uninformative prior.

It appears to be almost meaningless to study antagonistic hazard from a purely probabilistic point of view when the intent of terrorist attack on any plant is part of a complex political environment of which the plant itself may be a part.

An approach that described any industrial plant as being at a Poisson-distributed risk of being subject to terrorist attack would appear to be unhelpful, especially post hoc.

One strategy open to terrorist groups is to carry out multiple attacks simultaneously [48], confounding the assumptions of independence underlying conventional failure rate analysis [23].

We also find it unhelpful to consider terrorism as an extreme form of some physical process (as one might look at, say, tropical storms), which would allow use of standard statistical techniques such as extreme value theory [17].

It should be noted that Coster considers terrorism as an extreme form of misbehaviour and finds that assessment protocols for industrial sabotage and indeed political direct action all require an understanding of the likely goals and motivation of the antagonistic agents (terrorists or saboteurs).

3.4. Academic Literature

The academic literature on terrorism was reviewed by Harmon [20] and Drake [10]. These accounts include summaries of common terrorist tactics, and descriptions of particularly severe terrorism-related incidents. This literature offers a useful perspective on the scale and nature of resources available to terrorist groups. Jenkins (1990) and Drake (1998) give accounts of the general structure of terrorism-related incidents. We propose that these sources are useful starting points from which to conduct antagonistic risk assessment of major hazards.

Descriptions of contemporary terrorist activity do not appear to be useful in a risk assessment context; workers appear to concentrate on the estimation of the extent and type of resources that particular terrorist groups have available.

One difficulty inherent in this approach is that analysis will be based on historical accounts, whereas terrorist groups are known for using novel and unconventional weapons and techniques [50].

Drake [10] presents two tactics that have a bearing on risk assessment of major hazards: *mass casualty attack* (intended to kill a large number of people, often indiscriminately); and *mass destruction attack* (intended to kill a large number of people and do a lot of damage). Mass casualty attacks usually involve bombings but can involve arson or the indiscriminate use of firearms on crowds [10, 37]. Terrorists typically time attacks when areas are busiest; or attempt to trigger some form of secondary hazard. Terrorists executing their agenda in an intelligent and rational manner will actively seek out releases causing maximal damage, thus distorting the usual frequency-severity curve in which high mortality events are generally less likely than low mortality events [29].

3.5. Phases of Antagonistic Hazard Incidents

In analysing a site with regard for its potential for an antagonistic hazard incident (AHI), it is first necessary to come to some appreciation of how antagonistic hazard incidents occur and the particular dynamics at work in them. Many workers, such as Feldman [14] and Jenkins [25], analyse AHIs in terms of up to 10 phases. However, when considering AHIs from a major hazard risk assessment perspective, the most useful division would be: pre-incursion, incursion, and post-incursion; all are discussed below.

3.5.1. Pre-incursion Phase

This phase refers to the period before an incursion, attack or sabotage attempt occurs; the emphasis is on intelligence-gathering and reconnaissance at the site. Drake [10] and Feldman [14] assert that the next phase of an attack is the insertion of weapons into an area. This most commonly refers to caches of arms for guerrilla attacks in isolated areas or placement of bombs.

3.5.2. Incursion Phase

This is the gaining of access to an industrial site in the prosecution of either sabotage or terrorist attack. During this phase, those committing the incursion are generally liable for some form of legal sanction and may draw a security, police, or military response. It is in this phase that terrorists may use physical violence against on-site security personnel. Unless it is terrorists' intention to establish a barricade-hostage situation [10], they will be under considerable pressure to overpower a security force quickly. In this regard, speed of execution has been a key factor in many terrorist actions [1].

3.5.3. The Post-incursion Phase

Once terrorists have left an industrial site, there are still particular courses of action that may be carried out which may include claims of responsibility, regrouping or further attacks.

Drake identifies the final phase of a terrorist attack as issuing communiques and claims of responsibility. This does not always occur in every attack, especially when part of a larger guerrilla war.

After an attack, new security measures are often put in place with the intention of replacing or augmenting previous security systems; terrorists in particular will attempt to devise strategies to overcome these new measures. We suggest that this is a strong argument for prevention by design (that is, making sites less valuable if attacked) rather than prevention by making sites difficult to hit.

3.6. Instructional Literature

Despite the clandestine nature of terrorist groups, there is a considerable body of open information on how these groups operate. Instructional style literature—much of it freely available—offers insight into these groups' thinking. In making use of such literature, it appears most useful to use it as a source of information on the relationship between antagonistic hazard agents and their intended targets, rather than as the basis for predictive models.

4.   Industrial Sites as Targets for Antagonistic Hazard

Drake [10] describes eight types of targets that may be attacked by terrorists. In the present context, the most relevant division of Drake's typology would be *cathartic* (attacked for expressive or symbolic reasons personal to the terrorist), and *instrumental* (attacked to draw attention to terrorists' political aims and make a statement in and of themselves). From a risk assessment perspective, we would suggest that industrial targets may be instrumental because they increase a terrorist attack's capability to do harm, by way of secondary hazard. The uniform sequential structure of terrorist attacks detailed above, and Drake's analysis of target type, suggest eight factors that are directly relevant to risk assessment. These are discussed below.

We note here that our assessment protocol is distinct from that of military threat assessment. The military "appreciation process" focuses on an analysis of a battlefield situation, with a consequent emphasis on likely enemy capabilities and likely enemy action. This generates two key considerations: the enemy's most likely course of action, and most dangerous course of action. In some ways this parallels standard risk assessment where consideration is given to both high consequence/low frequency, and low consequence/high frequency events.

It would therefore appear that the military appreciation process could form part of a formal risk assessment methodology.

Access is the degree to which the public may innocently gain access to or near a site. Against easily accessible sites, both the pre-incursion and incursion phases are more easily carried out. Because most process industry sites have workplace safety regimes [44], access to them is generally restricted to authorized personnel. As such, the degree of casual access offered to potential terrorists is limited, and this would be expected to lower the risk of attack. However, terrorists making attacks in public spaces face no such restrictions to their movement. This might form a useful benchmark: for a terrorist group to attack an industrial facility it must offer a more effective target than would be achieved by simply attacking some public place. Standard risk management strategies [29, 30, 31, 44] for process industry facilities do not generally recommend a specific access policy. Mecklenburgh [38] discusses access to facilities for emergency services, but without regard to terrorists.

Security is the difficulty of controlling non-authorized access to a site. Since terrorists are able to engage security forces, access control systems that rely on making terrorists' entrance conspicuous may not have the same preventive value that they would have against politically motivated saboteurs.

Also, terrorists are willing to use physical force to overpower manned access control systems (such as security booths). systems have little mitigating effect in an antagonistic context.

Security considerations typically focus on depth and the notion of "layered security" [49] but in the present context, we suggest that security is best considered from the terrorists' perspective.

Informational security systems that enable identification or detection of intruders may be of less use with regard to some threats than others. Some terrorist groups whose personnel have low levels of commitment may be influenced by the presence informational security systems whereas fanatical or highly committed terrorist groups may not be deterred at all by such measures. The Washington Post [52] quotes a British transit security specialist: "Closed-circuit TV works with the IRA, because they don't want to be caught... it wouldn't work with a suicide operator".

Physical security and access control to industrial sites is often a requirement of occupational safety and health legislation [44]. As such, access control systems mean that industrial sites are "harder" targets than public spaces, and this might be expected to reduce the risk of attack.

One must also consider the degree to which terrorists or other intruders such as saboteurs must make themselves conspicuous during the incursion phase of an AHI. This may be a factor both of the site's layout and construction and also of its geographical location. With regard to terrorism, deterrents that rely on an intruder's unwillingness to make themselves conspicuous to security forces may have little value.

Opacity is the ease with which terrorists can gather operational information about a site. An opaque site requires "inside knowledge" to realize a secondary hazard. Sites with complex or poorly understood reaction processes might offer a less intuitive target than sites with some easily recognizable toxic agent stored on site in bulk [50]

Opacity is strongly affected by the security measures in place at a site. As Drake argues, terrorists generally design their plans of attack to exploit perceived weaknesses in the security measures of an installation. As such, if these can be easily or comprehensively investigated (with a plausible covering story if necessary) then they offer less protection from terrorist attack.

We suggest that it is difficult to generalize about the effect of security measures at industrial sites. Disclosure can compromise a site's opacity; this would need to be evaluated in terms of balancing the increased safety offered by open information dissemination against the increased risk of terrorism.

Secondary hazard is the potential for off-site damage, harm or intimidation to members of the public that may be realized by terrorist activity through release of on-site hazardous materials.

Terrorist groups are usually poorly armed and supported and therefore must try to get as much effect from their limited munitions as possible [25]. The process industries offer one situation where extra damage may be caused in the form of stored chemical and radioactive material, waste and fuels, as well as biological waste or biotechnological agents. In this manner, terrorists may use industrial sites as instrumental targets.

Similarly, terrorists without any form of mass destruction weapon may attempt to get the same effect from triggering an industrial accident or loss of containment [50].

Secondary hazards may have a more insidious effect than direct toxicity: the substances released may be "dread", in the sense of Slovic [45]. This is particularly evident when considering radioactive discharge and is discussed from a different perspective under "victim profile" below.

Robustness is the ability of a system to sustain damage safely without a major secondary hazard being triggered. Sites with low robustness, if attacked, are more likely to result in a serious industrial accident.

Conventional assessments of robustness are of limited value in the case of terrorism because they center on *mechanical* failure modes that occur without outside interference. In the case of terrorist attack, failure will be induced by any one of a variety of methods *calculated* to overcome a site's mechanical ability to withstand damage, whereas an accidental failure occurs at random and may or may not be sufficient to cause a catastrophic hazard.

When appreciating robustness from a terro-centric perspective, it is useful to consider the difficulty of transporting sufficient reagents to a position where they can trigger a catastrophic chain reaction.

When considering intentionally-caused releases, Coster and Hankin [7] point out that robustness is more difficult to assess in the case of terrorism than direct action sabotage, because terrorists in general are able to use more vigorous forms of attack than activists: they are less concerned about escape and visibility; and they are willing and able to use dangerous and powerful means such as explosives and/or firearms.

Law enforcement response is the speed and effectiveness with which local police (or equivalent) respond to an AHI. Radical groups may regard targets as more or less amenable if they perceive there will be a stronger or weaker law enforcement (or military) response to an attack.

Law enforcement response is a predictor of target value for terrorists as it may act in several different ways depending on the intentions and doctrine of the terrorist group. For some groups, a strong law enforcement response may be a significant deterrent, and targets may be chosen so that they are isolated from such responses. For other groups, law enforcement personnel may be a secondary or even primary target for terrorist attack, and as such a vigorous law enforcement response may make an installation more, rather than less, attractive. An extreme example of this would be the use of police themselves as targets by Abu Sayaf and the FARC.

The level of law enforcement response to a terror attack is not a factor which is controllable by an industrial facility, nor is it a by-product of the site's operation. As such, it may be useful for site operators and risk managers to be aware of this factor, but it is not one that can easily be managed.

Victim profile is the demographic characteristics of the at-risk (off-site) population. The impact of a terrorist attack can often be greater when the victim pattern is unfair, specifically, when people unconnected with a site or facility are made victims from it [45].

In the absence of a significant secondary hazard (for example, in regard to some facility that deals with benign or stable reagents and processes), the only victims of a terrorist attack are likely to be employees of the plant itself. As such, these individuals have some psychological connection to the site attacked and it becomes easier for the public to associate the victims of the attack with a particular situation. As such, the effect of psychological intimidation of a terrorist attack is reduced and therefore the site would make a relatively unattractive target.

Compare this to a situation where a site with a large inventory of toxic or flammable substances is bordered by (say) schools or medical facilities. Here, the victim profile of those exposed to the attack (and secondary hazard) would add to its value as a target for instrumental terrorism.

Political value is the symbolic power of destroying a target in relation to a terrorist agenda. Terrorists' targets may be chosen because they have some political or social value in themselves. Nuclear power in particular is a status symbol for many governments: attacking nuclear power plants has the effect of demonstrating a government's inability to protect its infrastructure. In general, the process industries would appear to be unlikely to be associated with this type of prestige, and as such we suggest that political value is not a pertinent indicator in many cases.

This may be different in the case of nationalized industries, or facilities operated by organizations with links to a particular country. Examples would include Maoist guerrillas in Nepal attacking foreign-owned industries, notably coca-cola [11, 39].

It is instructive to note that political value of a site as perceived by a terrorist is closely related to the consequence analysis performed in a conventional industrial assessment. We suggest that overlap of this sort is a common occurrence in major hazard risk assessment.

5. Summary

Despite the fact that terrorist attacks may constitute a significant contribution towards process hazard release, it appears that terrorism has been largely neglected as a causative factor.

Whilst there are several possible explanations for this, there appears to be a consistent assumption within the literature that it is not possible to understand these phenomena well enough to effectively categorize the risks associated with them. We argue that it is possible to describe terrorism as an instrumental, and therefore predictable, behaviour. From this standpoint it is possible to analyse terrorist activity from a risk assessment perspective.

In this chapter, we identify eight factors that bear on risk assessment of antagonistic hazards. They are: access, security, opacity, secondary hazard, robustness, law enforcement response, victim profile, and political value. One aspect of major hazard risk assessment that is peculiar to antagonistic hazard and terrorism is the distortion of the usual frequency-severity curve in which high mortality events are generally less likely than low mortality events [29]). Terrorists, executing their agenda in an intelligent and rational manner, will actively seek out releases causing maximal damage.

References

[1] Amnesty International. Getting away with murder: political killings and 'disappearances' in the 1990s. *Amnesty International*, 74:88–89, 1993.

[2] R. E. Britter and J. McQuaid. *Workbook on the Dispersion of Dense Gases*. HMSO, 1988.

[3] J. Burchael. Framing a moral response to terrorism. In C. Kegley, editor, *International terrorism: characteristics, causes and controls*, pages 27–29. St Martin's Press, New York, 1990.

[4] R. Burns. *Introduction to research methods*. Addison Wesley Longman, third edition, 1996.

[5] J. Chicken. *Risk Assessment for Hazardous Installations*. Pergamon Press, 1986.

[6] M. Coster. Antagonistic hazards in risk assessment. Master's thesis, School of Environmental and Marine Sciences, The University of Auckland, 2000.

[7] M. Coster and R. K. S. Hankin. Risk assessment of antagonistic hazards. *Journal of Loss Prevention in the Process Industries*, 16:545–550, 2003.

[8] M. Crenshaw. The psychology of terrorism: an agenda for the 21st Century. *Political Psychology*, 21(2):405–420, 2000.

[9] P. K. Davies and B. M. Jenkins. Deterrence and influence in counterterrorism: a component in the war on al Qaeda. Technical Report DASW01-01-C-0004, RAND National Defence Research Unit, 2002.

[10] C. J. M. Drake. *Terrorists' target selection*. Palgrave, Hampshire, 1998.

[11] K. J. Dudonis and D. P. Schultz. *The counterterrorism handbook: tactics, procedures, and techniques*. CRC Press, 2005. ISBN 0849330238.

[12] A. W. F. Edwards. *Likelihood (expanded edition)*. John Hopkins University Press, 1992.

[13] J. Eyerman. Terrorism and democratic states—soft targets or accessible systems? *International Interactions*, 24(2):151–170, 1998.

[14] A. Feldman. *Formations of violence: the narrative of the body and political terror in Northern Ireland*. University of Chicago Press, Chicago, 1991.

[15] D. Foreman and B. Haywood. *Ecodefense: a field guide to monkeywrenching*. Abbzug Press Chico, California, 1993.

[16] L. Garret. The nightmare of bioterrorism. *Foreign Affairs*, 80(1):75–77, 2001.

[17] Y. Y. Haimes. Risk of extreme events and the fallacy of the expected value. *Control and Cybernetics*, 22(4):7–31, 1994.

[18] Y. Y. Haimes. Risk of extreme events and the fallacy of the expected value. *Control and Cybernetics*, 22(4):7–31, 1994.

[19] R. K. S. Hankin and R. E. Britter. TWODEE: the Health and Safety Laboratory's shallow layer model for dense gas dispersion. Part 1, mathematical basis and physical assumptions, 1999.

[20] C. Harmon. *Terrorism today*. Frank Cass Publishers, Portland, 2000.

[21] Health and Safety Executive. *Canvey: A Second Report*. HMSO, 1981. ISBN 0-11-883618-8.

[22] Health and Safety Executive. *Control of industrial major accident hazards regulations*. HMSO, 1984. ISBN 0-11-047902-5.

[23] N. W. Hurst, R. K. S. Hankin, L. J. Bellamy, and M. J. Wright. Auditing—a European perspective. *Journal of Loss Prevention in the Process Industries*, 7(2):197–200, 1994.

[24] T. Hyder. Kashmir: Self-determination versus state terrorism. *Korean Journal of Defence Analysis*, 14(1):141–174, 2002.

[25] B. Jenkins. International terrorism: characteristics, causes and controls. In C. Kegley, editor, *International terrorism: the other world war*, pages 27–39. St Martin's press, New York, 1990.

[26] C. Kegley, editor. *International terrorism: characteristics, causes and controls*. St Martin's Press, New York, 1990.

[27] T. A. Kletz. *An engineer's view of human error*. Rugby: Institution of Chemical Engineers, third edition, 2001.

[28] D. Knott. Terrorists target U. K. storage sites (oil and gas terminals). *The Oil and Gas Journal*, 91(25):29, June 1993.

[29] F. P. Lees. *Loss prevention in the process industries*, volume 1. Butterworth, Oxford, second edition, 2001.

[30] F. P. Lees. *Loss prevention in the process industries*, volume 2. Butterworth, Oxford, second edition, 2001.

[31] F. P. Lees. *Loss prevention in the process industries*, volume 3. Butterworth, Oxford, second edition, 2001.

[32] B. W. Lindgren. *Statistical Theory*. Collier Macmillan, third edition, 1976.

[33] R. Luckabaugh, E. Fuqua, J. Cangemi, and C. Kowalski. Terrorist behavior and united states foreign policy: who is the enemy. *Psychology*, 34(2):1–15, 1997.

[34] C. Mahmood. Terrorism, myth, and the power of ethnographic praxis. *Journal of Contemporary Ethnography*, 30(5):520–545, 2001.

[35] R. Marcinko. *Rogue warrior, memoirs of a navy SEAL*. New York, USA, 1996.

[36] J. A. Margold. From cultures of fear and terror to the normalization of violence - an ethnographic case. *Critique of Anthropology*, 19(1):63–88, 1999.

[37] C. Marighella. The minimanual of the urban guerilla. Samizdat, 1967.

[38] J. C. Mecklenburgh. *Plant layout: a guide to the layout of process plant and sites*. Leonard Hill Books, Aylesbury, 1973.

[39] United States Department of Defense. *Political violence against Americans*. Diane Publishing, 2001. ISBN 1428965602.

[40] R. Pitblado and R. Turney. *Risk assessment in the process industries*. Institute of Chemical Engineers, 1996.

[41] R. Pitblado, J. Williams, and D. Slater. Quantitative assessment of process safety programs. *Plant Operations Progress*, 9(3):169, 1989.

[42] J. S. Puttock et al. Dispersion models and hydrogen fluoride predictions. *Journal of Loss Prevention in the Process Industries*, 4:16–28, January 1991.

[43] D. C. Rapoport. *Inside terrorist organizations*. Frank Cass Publishers, Oregon, second edition, 2001.

[44] D. Scott and F. Crawley. *Process plant design and operation*. Institute of Chemical Engineers, 1992.

[45] P. Slovic. Perception of risk. *Science*, 236:280–285, 1987.

[46] Standards Association of Australia. *Risk management*. Homebush NSW: Standards Australia; Wellington, NZ: Standards New Zealand, 1995.

[47] S. S. Tachakra. The human cost of Bhopal—'an estimate'. *Journal of loss prevention*, 1(1):3–4, January 1989.

[48] United Press International. 4th plane was headed for the capitol, 12 September 2002. United Press International; p1008255w2088.

[49] United States of America Department of Defense. U. S. Army field manuals collection: Physical security, 2001. FM3-19.30.

[50] United States of America Department of Justice. Assessment of the increased risk of terrorist or other criminal activity associated with posting off-site consequence analysis information on the internet, 2000.

[51] Violence Policy Center. Sitting ducks: the threat to the chemical and refinery industry from 50 caliber sniper rifles, 2003.

[52] Washington Post. Britons know price of averting terrorism at home, September 2001. Page A16.

[53] C. J. Wheatley and D. M. Webber. Aspects of the dispersion of denser-than-air vapours relevant to gas cloud explosions. Technical Report SR/007/80/UK/H; XII/829/84-EN, Safety and Reliability Directorate, Wigshaw Lane, Culcheth, Warrington WA3 4NE, 1984.

[54] D. J. Whittaker, editor. *The terrorism reader*. Routledge, second edition, 2003.

[55] P. Wilkinson. *Terrorist Targets and Tactics : New Risks to World Order*. Center for Security Studies, 1990.

[56] P. Wilkinson. Politics, diplomacy and peace processes: pathways out of terrorism. *Terrorism and Political Violence*, 11(4), 1999.

[57] R. Yandrick. The preventative approach to reducing workplace problems. *Behavioural Healthcare Tomorrow*, 4(5):30–35, 1995.

[58] J. Zulaika and W. Douglas. *Terror and taboo: the follies, fables, and faces of terrorism*. Routledge New York, 1996.

In: Global Terrorism Issues and Developments
Editor: Rene A. Larche, pp. 165-185
ISBN: 978-1-60021-930-6
© 2008 Nova Science Publishers, Inc.

Chapter 7

FREE LABELING OF FACIAL EXPRESSIONS OF EMOTIONS IN CHILDREN SURVIVING THE TERRORIST ATTACK IN BESLAN'S SCHOOL

Sara Scrimin[*], Ughetta Moscardino,
Fabia Capello and Giovanna Axia
Department of Developmental and Social Psychology, University of Padova, Italy

Abstract

Background: The identification of facial emotional expressions is a crucial component of social and emotional development. Although recent studies indicate that terrorism induced trauma has a negative impact on child psychological functioning, no previous studies have ever investigated the effects of terrorism on children's face emotion processing. This study reports pilot information on free labeling of facial expressions of emotions in a group of severely traumatized children surviving the terrorist attack in Beslan 3 months after their school siege. These children were compared with a group of non exposed children matched by age and gender.

Method: Participants were 66 children with a mean age of 9.85 years (SD=1.33) who were either exposed or not exposed to the terrorist attack in Beslan, Russia. Children were tested on free labeling of 10 facial expression stimuli representing happiness, sadness, anger, disgust, fear and surprise. All responses were judged by two raters on valence and specific emotion category.

Results: Children of both groups equally recognized the correct specific category of happiness. However, significant differences were found in responses to negative emotions stimuli. Terrorism exposed children more frequently attributed a negative valence to anger and correctly recognize it whereas non exposed children more frequently attributed a negative valence to fear and identified it correctly. On the contrary, exposed children did not recognize fear. The qualitative analysis of the "non responses" category revealed the presence of other labels that significantly differed between the two groups. For example, terrorism exposed children frequently mentioned suspect and offence, whereas not exposed children often described face stimuli as thoughtful or concentrated.

[*] Corresponding Author: Sara Scrimin, Via Venezia 8, 35131 Padova, Italy. Tel: +39.049.827.6576; Fax: +39.049.827.6511; Email:sara.scrimin@unipd.it

Conclusion: These results suggest that terrorism may impact on children's perception of facial expression of negative emotions. Findings are discussed in terms of their implications for child development; clinical suggestions are given for working with children surviving terrorism.

Keywords: terrorism, children, emotion recognition, PTSD

Introduction

On September 1, 2004 in the Russian town of Beslan in North Ossetia, armed multinational terrorists (Chechens, Ingush) hold hostages about 1200 children and adults in School Number One. It was the first day of school and children, together with their families, were ready to attend the party for the opening school year when a group of masked and armed terrorists took children, parents and teachers hostages. *"We were going to the school party...in Ossetia the beginning of the school year is always a big event: there is music, dancing, and all people in town get together with children to take part in the event. So many of our neighbours come just to see the party, because we live close to the school. Our homes are here, the school just there. There is no security anymore"* (mother of a young boy who survived the siege, ID 7). Terrorists kept the school under siege for three days during which the hostages were left without water, food or medical supplies. They were jammed in hundreds in the school gym, where the heat was unbearable. In these conditions, many children died for dehydration, others drank their urine to survive. *"The first day, the terrorists did not treat us too badly, they gave water to the children, let us go to the bathroom. Then, I do not know what happened, the second day they became an inhuman species. Every minute they fired just over the children's heads, they shouted. It was hell. In the evening of the first day, it was not possible to breathe anymore, people were amassed in the room, sitting one against the other. They did not give water anymore and in that heat, the children started to die, especially the youngest ones"* (mother of a girl, both survivors of the attack, ID 11). The hostages were forced to remain still and were continuously threatened; to demonstrate their intentions, the terrorists repeatedly killed a number of children and adults: *"...terrorists took a group of children in the cafeteria, told them to stand by the window and shout to the soldiers outside the school not to shoot. Then, when all children started shouting, they shoot them from behind and killed them. All."* While children and adults were held as hostages in the school, the entire community (i.e. parents and relatives) were waiting outside the school yard, watching the dead bodies as they were thrown out of the windows and hearing the shooting inside.

The siege ended after shooting broke out between the hostage-takers and Russian security forces on September 3, 2004: the terrorists exploded the mines which were located all around the building, part of the school collapsed and the army had to intervene as a crowd of parents and relatives was trying to enter into the school. *"After the explosion, I was in a state of shock....When I recovered, I saw there, this may be disgusting for you to hear, I saw the mountains of corpses, the dismembered, many were never found anymore. The people, the children were jumping outside the windows, chaotically. In the room there were so many corpses and we were among them, and everywhere explosions, shooting...then, the fire started, the ceiling collapsed, everything was burning, there were more explosions"* (ID 5).

As a consequence of this terrorist attack 394 persons died, among whom 172 were children. In addition, hundreds of others were seriously injured and others are still missing.

The school massacre in Beslan is one of the worst atrocities enacted on a civilian population in Europe in recent history, with an extensive negative impact on the health of children, families, and the entire community (Parfitt, 2004). This is one of the first attacks especially directed to children in their everyday environment. *"When they (the armed terrorists) circled us and when they compelled us to enter into the school, the children did not understand yet that the terrorists were already there, that it was an ambush. The children were scared by the masks, by the shootings and ran, ran and jumped into their school, because they thought that there they would be safe"* (ID 1).

These words, used by a mother to describe how it all began, clearly express the aim of terrorism: attacking civilians in those places that are part of their everyday life and that are thought to be safe. As a matter of fact, using children in their developmental environment as a target for a terrorist attack has strong psychological effects on the entire community, attributing an increased value to the political goals of perpetrators. Terror acts produce devastating injuries, destruction and death, although their ultimate goal is psychological: to create a climate of fear, uncertainty, and vulnerability.

Most definitions of terrorism include only those acts which are intended to create fear or "terror", are perpetrated for an ideological goal, and deliberately target "non-combatants".

The attack in the Ossetian school represents a horrifying example of terrorism directed to those who are the most "innocent" part of a civilian population of non combatants and caused severe physical and psychological effects.

The interest in the psychological effects of trauma caused by terrorism has greatly increased as we are experiencing the world wide proliferation of violence. Terrorism has devastating effects on the community and on both physical and psychological functioning. Several aspects of terrorist attacks result in specific patterns of stressors and reactions caused by the unpredictable, sudden, and indefinite character of these events (Fermont, 2004), all these aspects contribute to qualifying terrorism as a strongly traumatic event.

Research on this issue has reported several severe psychological outcomes in relation to this type of trauma. Specifically, a high incidence of PTSD, as well as other psychological (e.g., high levels of anxiety, depression) and cognitive (e.g., memory impairments, attention deficits and difficulties in concentrating) dysfunctions have been found in both adults and children surviving terrorism. However, no studies have investigated social and emotional functioning in relation to terrorism-induced trauma in children. This is a big lack in the literature considering that terrorism is mostly a community traumatic event, which involves social and emotional interactive dynamics. The identification of facial emotion expression is a crucial component of social and emotional functioning and development. The ability to decode a facial expressions and recognize emotions helps us to cope with threats and opportunities presented by the social world, as well as to interact with others (Vicari, Snitzer, Reilly, Pasqualetti, Vizzotto & Caltagirone, 2000).

This study aims at providing pilot information on the effects of the terrorist attack in Beslan on school-age children's ability to recognize emotions in ambiguous facial stimuli three months post-attack. Understanding how children surviving terrorism recognize facial emotional expressions will enable us to plan specific psychosocial interventions aimed at improving emotional functioning and social interactions.

Effects of Terrorism-induced Trauma on Children

Research on traumatic events such as community violence and terrorist attacks has mainly focused on adults (Fremont, 2004). However, the impact of terrorism on children covers a range of violent acts that include isolated events in countries not at war, *i.e.* the Oklahoma city bombing (Pfefferbaum, Nixon & Krug, 1999), the 9/11 terrorist attacks (Beauchesen, Kelly, Patsdaughter, Pickard, 2002; Schuster, Stein, Jaycox, Collins, Marshall, Elliott, et al., 2001) and repeated terrorist attacks in areas of political conflict, *i.e.* bombing in Israel (Laor, Wolmer, & Cohen, 2001), state terrorism in Guatemala (Miller, 1996) and terrorist activities in Northern Ireland (Cairns & Toner, 1993). Research on the effects of these attacks indicates that children exposed to violence are greatly affected by the experience. Most of these studies focused on the protective and risk factors affecting children's reactions and on those aspects that may lead to the development of PTSD (Neneroff, Bremner, Foa, Mayberg, North, & Stein, 2006; Salomon, & Bryant, 2002). Recent studies indicate that the rates of PTSD in children exposed to terrorist activities range from 28% to 50% (Pfefferbaum et al., 1999; Susser, Jackson, & Hoven, 2001). Even after a short event and even if they are not directly exposed, school-age children can develop negative reactions (Phillips, Prince, & Schiebelhut, 2004) and high rates of post traumatic stress disorder (Pfefferbaum, et al. 1999).

Children who survived the terrorist attack in school Number One in Beslan were all directly involved in the attack and victims of a siege. Seventy-three percent of a sample of these children reported high levels of severe PTSD symptoms three months after the attack (Scrimin, Axia, Capello, Moscardino, Steinberg, & Pynoos, 2006).

The literature on the psychological functioning of children who survived a terrorist attack and developed PTSD symptomatology has mostly focused on behavioural problems, such as irritability or sleep problems (Melville & Lykes, 1992), psychiatric problems including anxiety and depression (Hoge & Pavlin, 2002), and developmental difficulties, such as memory and attention impairments (Beers & De Bellis, 2002; Scrimin et al., 2006). To our knowledge, no previous studies have ever investigated the effects of terrorism-induced trauma and subsequent PTSD on children's ability to recognize emotions.

Identification of Facial Expressions as a Component of Social and Emotional Development

From an evolutionary perspective, emotions are central states shaped by natural selection that enable animals to cope with threats and opportunities presented to them by the physical and social environment. Most of all, the so-called basic emotions (Ekman, 1992) –fear, disgust, anger, joy, sadness and surprise- can be thought of as response-coordination packages sculpted by evolution to meet particular environmental challenges, such as avoiding physical environmental challenges, for example physical harm (fear) and contaminants (disgust).

There is a large body of literature on emotion expression recognition in infancy, providing evidence of remarkable abilities at a very young age (Hiatt, Campos, & Emde, 1979; Trevarthen, 1985; Walker-Andrews, 1997). Children as young as a few months have been shown to be able to discriminate happy and sad faces from surprised faces, and also to discriminate between different intensities (i.e., mild versus intense happy expressions) (see

Nelson & De Haan, 1997 for a review of studies). Furthermore, there is evidence that the facial expressions of others may alter infants' behavioural responses (Sorce, Emde, Campos, & Klinnert, 1985; Serrano, Iglesias, & Loeches, 1995; Montague & Walker-Andrews, 2001). Results of a number of studies on the development of emotion expression recognition have reported that the recognition of emotional expressions improves with age (Boyatzis, Chazan, & Ting, 1993; Odom & Lemond, 1972; Philippot & Feldman, 1990). However, studies indicate that emotion expression recognition does not emerge as one specific stage in development (Camras & Allison, 1985; De Sonneville, Verschoor, Njiokiktjien, Op 't Veld, Toorenaar, & Vranken, 2002; Gross & Ballif, 1991; Smith & Walden, 1998; Vicari et al., 2000). Rather, children's abilities emerge gradually over time, with happiness recognised earliest and with the greatest accuracy, followed by sad or angry expressions, then by expressions of surprise or fear. However, the recognition of basic emotions such as "happiness", "anger", "fear", and "sadness" seems to be fully developed at the age of 6 years while recognition of more complex emotions continues to mature (Markham, & Adams, 1992).

The ability to decode facial expression is an important component of social interaction because of the significant role of facial information in the appropriate modification of social behaviors (Philippot & Fledman, 1990; Vicari, et al., 2000). Thus, emotion identification is crucial for subsequent social interaction and functioning. Abnormalities in emotion expression recognition are associated with psychiatric disorders in adult (Phillips, Drevets, Rauch, & Lane, 2003) and child populations (Blair, 2003).

Emotion Recognition and Trauma in Children

Most of the literature on emotion recognition and the underlying cognitive processes focuses on maltreated, abused and neglected children as these are known risk factors for the development of psychopathology (Herba & Phillips, 2004).

We know that neglected and abused children are not as accurate as well-treated children in recognizing different facial expressions of emotions (Camras, Ribordy, Hill, Martino, Sachs, Spaccarelli, & Stefani, 1990). The studies conducted on abused and neglected children demonstrate that children whose parents reported high levels of hostility directed toward their offspring required less perceptual information to correctly identify facial expressions of anger. In addition, physically abused children required more information to recognize sad facial expressions (Pollak & Sinha 2002). The same authors (Pollak, Cicchetti, Hormoh, & Reeg, 2000) had previously demonstrated that physically abused children had difficulty in recognizing emotions such as sadness and disgust whereas their accuracy in recognizing anger did not differ from non maltreated children. Studies of maltreating families suggest that neglectful and physically abusive parents differ from non maltreating parents because they show less positive emotions (Bungental, Blue, & Lewis, 1990) and more negative emotions (Herrenkol, Herrenkol, Egolf, & Wu, 1991). However, it is not clear whether this pattern may also be found in children surviving terrorism.

While we do not need to learn how to make facial expressions of emotions (they are present by our evolution and occur spontaneously when an emotion is aroused), it is less certain whether the ability to recognize those signals also operates from innate instructions or is instead learned during life. There may be an intermediate ground as well, in which preset instructions may be damaged or destroyed by severely disturbed early experience.

This study examines the possible effects of a very stressful and life threatening traumatic event outside the family context on children's ability to recognize emotions.

More specifically, two questions were addressed: 1. Do terrorism exposed children recognize the correct emotion valence (positive versus negative) differently from non-exposed children? 2. Is there a group difference between exposed and non-exposed children in the ability to identify specific emotions, such as fear or anger (Felmingham, Bryant, & Gordon, 2003; Herba & Phillips, 2004)?

Method

Participants

Participants in this study were 66 children who where either exposed or non exposed to the terrorist attack in Beslan's school. The target group (exposed children) included 18 children (10 boys and 8 girls) with a mean age of 10.23 (SD =2.41) who survived the terrorist attack whereas the control group of 48 children non-exposed to the attack included 26 boys and 22 girls with the same mean age of the exposed children (Mean= 10.15, SD=.95).

Both groups of children came from low to medium income families living in small town communities. No differences were found between the two groups with regard to parents' SES in terms of parents' educational level and employment status.

All exposed children had spent 1-2 months in the Russian pediatric hospital of Moscow, where they were treated for injuries received during the attack. These children had injuries of medium severity level as established by Russian health care professionals, this made the group fairly homogeneous with respect to their physical condition and medical treatment. However, none of these children was on medication, which may have influenced their cognitive functioning at the time of assessment. All exposed children reported high levels of traumatic symptoms. Using cut-off scores established against a structured diagnostic interview (Steinberg, Brymer, Decker, & Pynoos, 2004), 12 children (70%) met full diagnostic criteria for PTSD and the remaining 5 (30 %) met the criteria for sub clinical PTSD as criteria A, B and D were all met. These 5 children suffered from less than 3 avoidance symptoms (Scrimin et al., 2006). Differently from the target group of exposed children, controls did not report PTSD symptoms.

Procedure and Instruments

This study was conducted three months after the terrorist attack in Beslan. Exposed children were recruited during a 40-day stay in Trento, Italy, organised by an Italian non-governmental agency operating in the Russian Children's Clinic and Hospital of Moscow. Children of the non exposed group were recruited and assessed in a school nearby the town of Trento, Italy. Informed consent was obtained from all caregivers, and children gave their assent to participate in the study. Assessments of children included the evaluation of PTSD symptoms, the neuropsychological testing of attention and digit span memory and an emotion recognition task. Children were tested individually in a quiet room especially adapted for this purpose. For children's PTSD evaluation and neuropsychological testing of attention and digit span memory, results and procedure are reported in Scrimin et al. (2006). In addition, interviews were conducted with parents on their daily routines, psychological difficulties after the traumatic event for them and their children. Results on these data are reported elsewhere (Moscardino, Axia, Scrimin, & Capello, 2007).

The emotion recognition task was designed using a specific apparatus and set of stimuli and was performed in a quiet and adequately lit room. To examine the ability of this specific population to recognize the basic negative emotions, 10 face cues were used (drawn from Ekman, 2003, pp.229-242): 2 displaying disgust, 2 sadness, 2 fear, 2 anger, 1 surprise and 1 enjoyment as a control to see whether children could recognize a positive emotion. Images were reproduced in grey scale using Adobe Photoshop. Facial stimuli were presented on a High Vision computer monitor. Each cue appeared on the screen and lasted for 3 seconds; then a blank slide appeared and lasted until the child had described the emotion that was just presented and was ready for the next cue. The child was sitting at a 90 cm from the 20 cm computer screen and was positioned so that the stimuli occurred on the participant's horizontal strait ahead line of sight. For each presented face, a free labeling procedure was used and children were asked to say "How is this person feeling?" (e.g.: Izard, 1971; Markham & Adams, 1992). Although this method is often substituted with forced choice labeling when working with verbal children, recently Widen and Russell (2003) revaluated free labeling as it appears less subject to artefacts of forced choice and thus comes closer to tapping the child's spontaneous specification of the emotion seen in the face. In order to make this method work at its best, we considered various procedure arrangements following Widen and Russel (2003). First, as the child may be overwhelmed or not have enough time to respond, we did not present the subsequent stimulus until the child explicitly said that he/she was ready. Second, a neutral baseline face with no emotion displayed was shown before the beginning of the task so that the children had a stimulus against which to compare the expressions. Third, the child must understand instructions and must not be too shy or intimidated to perform properly. So we spent time before the task playing with the children and getting to know each other. Finally, the child must be able to produce a label on demand; he/she might know the correct emotion category, but not know its label. To understand whether the needed label was available in the child's vocabulary, we checked to see if the label was used elsewhere in the task by the child.

The children were allowed to use any label they chose. Collectively, the 66 children had 660 opportunities to label a face. These opportunities yielded 38 different types of responses plus one category that we labeled "non responses" that included only uninterpretable (silence), nonsensical responses (e.g.: "she's just making a face", "I don't know", "big eyes") or other emotions different from the primary ones ("suspicious", "offended"). For each of the 38 types of responses, two raters made two judgements: (a) valence and (b) specific emotion category. Disagreements were resolved by a third rater who rated only those responses on which the two original raters disagreed.

For the valence ratings, the raters' tasks was to indicate whether the response was positive (e.g.: "happy", "smile"), negative (e.g.: "sad", "angry", "painful", "crying"), or uninterpretable in regard to valence (e.g.: "funny", "looks somewhere away", "a little happy"). Because surprise can be pleasant or unpleasant, "surprised" was not scored for valence. The two original raters agreed on 80% of the response types. In the cases where the two judges disagreed, a third judge rated the response and the valence was determined by the majority.

For the specific emotion category rating, the raters' task was to indicate into which one of the six emotions categories each response fit (happy, sad, angry, surprised, disgusted or scared) or if it was uninterpretable in regard to these six categories. Responses rated correct for the happy category were "happy", "smile"; for the sad category, "sad", "dissatisfied", "painful", "feeling sick", "crying", "exhausted" (see Ekman 2003); for the angry category, "angry", "touchy", "disappointed", "hates", "annoyed by everything"; for the fear category, "scared", "worried"; for the disgust category, "disgusted", "doesn't like anything"; for the surprise category, "surprised", "dazed". Response varied from those presented in syntax or by embedment in a phrase (e.g.: "very scared", "just stopped crying"). The two original raters agreed on the category for 82% of the response types. In cases where the two original judges disagreed, a third judge rated the response and the specific emotion category was determined by majority.

For further analyses, the nonresponse category was analyzed through descriptive statistics to identify the presence of other possible categories which differed between the two groups. The identification of different categories of labels included in the initial "non response" group was thought to allow a better understanding of the different error typologies in exposed and non-exposed children.

Results

Results answer three main questions which correspond to the next three subsections:

1) While describing ambiguous face emotions stimuli, when considering the valence (positive versus negative) of the emotion expressed by the face stimuli, do exposed children perform differently compared to non–exposed children? Specifically, do they recognize the valence of different stimuli significantly less well than controls? 2) When considering the correct specific category of the face stimuli, do exposed children recognize emotions differently compared to non-exposed children? In particular, do exposed children recognize less correct specific categories? 3) Does the qualitative analysis of the "non response" category reveal the presence of other labels that significantly differ between the two groups?

Group Differences in Recognizing the Valence of Different Face Stimuli

Each of the 10 face emotion stimuli was first coded for correct or incorrect valence. A correct- incorrect score was given (0=incorrect, 1= correct) to each label, where correct corresponded to the correct valence attributed by the child to each face emotion stimulus (e.g., negative emotion stimulus labelled by the child with a negative emotion valence label), and incorrect corresponded either to a mismatch between the stimulus emotion valence and the child's label (e.g., positive emotion stimulus labelled by the child with a negative emotion valence label) or to a non response. The proportion of correct valence labels for each of the five main emotions (i.e., happiness, sadness, fear, anger and disgust) was then computed.

Because "surprise" can be pleasant or unpleasant, it was not scored for valence and was left out from this first set of analyses. To test for possible age and gender effects, Pearson's correlations were computed between correct valence proportions and child's age and gender; as no significant relations were found, none of these child's characteristics were used as covariates in group comparison analyses.

Univariate analyses of variance were performed comparing the two groups on the proportions of correct valence labels used. Overall, exposed children were correct (as to stimuli valence) on 57.2% of the 180 trials, and non exposed children were correct in regard to valence on 59.5%, this difference was not significant. Figure 1 displays the proportion of correct valence responses to the 5 different facial expressions in the two groups of traumatized and non traumatized children. Table 1 reports the mean and standard deviations of proportions of correct responses in regard to valence on each facial expression for each of the two groups and the results derived from the group comparison analyses. ANOVAs showed that non exposed children recognized the negative valence of fear significantly more frequently than exposed children, whereas exposed children recognized the negative valence of anger significantly more frequently than the control group.

Table 1. Proportion of correct valence on each facial expression for both exposed and non exposed children

Correct valence						
Type of facial expression	Exposed children		Non-exposed children		Group comparison	
	Mean	SD	Mean	SD	F	p
Happiness	.88	.32	.95	.20	1.09	ns
Sadness	.72	.25	.68	.34	.16	ns
Anger	.86	.23	.63	.28	8.94	.004
Fear	.50	.34	.75	.33	7.48	.008
Disgust	.78	.25	.89	.23	3.25	ns

Group Differences in Recognizing the Correct Specific Category of Different Face Emotion Stimuli

The 10 stimuli were then coded for correct specific category. A correct-incorrect score was given (0=incorrect, 1=correct) to each label, where correct corresponded to the correct specific category given by the child to each face emotion stimulus (e.g., sad face expression stimulus labeled by the child with a label corresponding to sadness), and incorrect corresponded either to a mismatch between the stimulus face specific emotion category and the child's label (e.g., fear face expression stimulus labeled by the child with a label corresponding to sadness) or to a non response. The proportion of correct specific category labels for each emotion was then calculated. To verify if there was an age or gender effect, Pearson's correlations were computed between the proportions of correct specific categories and child's age and gender; as no significant associations were found, none of these child's characteristics were used as covariates in group comparison analyses. Univariate analyses of variance were performed comparing the two groups on the proportion of correct specific categories of each emotion.

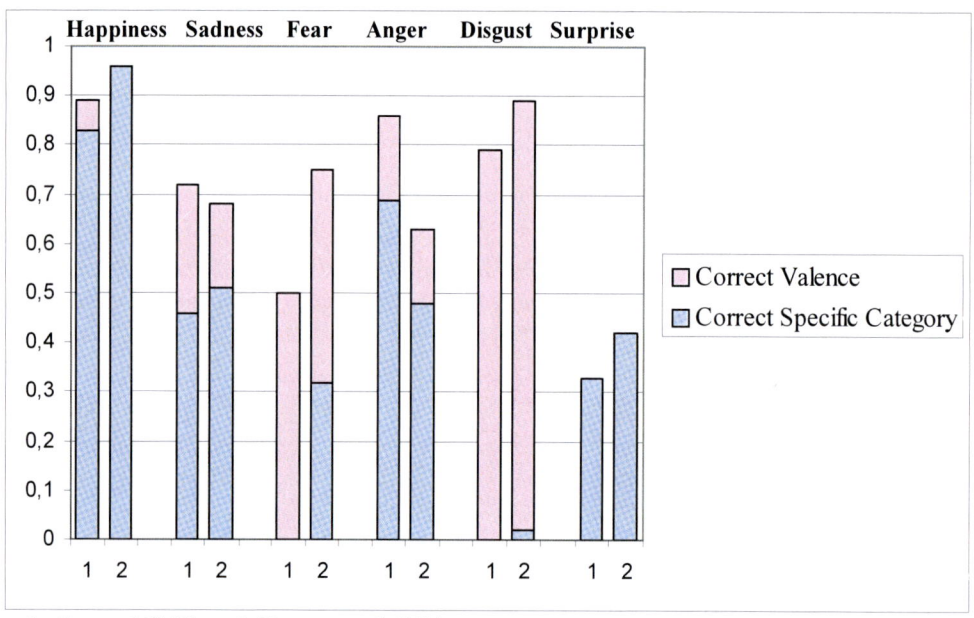

Note: 1= Exposed Children, 2=Non-exposed Children.

Figure 1. Proportion of correct specific category and correct valence responses to the facial expression in the two groups of exposed and non exposed children.

Overall, exposed children were correct (as to specific category) on 32% of the 180 trials, whereas non-exposed children were correct on 38% of the trials, resulting in an overall nearly significant group difference in the ability to recognize the correct specific category, $F(1,65)=3.35$, $p=.07$. Figure 1 displays the proportion of correct specific category responses to the 6 different facial expressions in the two groups of exposed and non-exposed children, and Table 2 reports the proportion of correct responses in regard to specific category on each facial expression for the two groups. In addition, group comparisons are reported showing that non-exposed children recognized fear significantly more frequently than exposed children, who did not recognize it; whereas the exposed children recognized anger significantly more frequently than the control group.

Table 2. Proportion of correct specific emotion category on each facial expression for both exposed and non exposed children

	Correct specific category					
	Exposed children		Non-exposed children		Group comparison	
	Mean	*SD*	*Mean*	*SD*	*F*	*p*
Happiness	.83	.38	.95	.20	2.96	*ns*
Sadness	.46	.29	.51	.31	.38	*ns*
Anger	.69	.25	.48	.40	4.54	.037
Fear	.00	.00	.32	.31	18.41	.0001
Disgust	.00	.00	.03	.10	.76	*ns*
Surprise	.33	.48	.41	.49	.37	*ns*

Qualitative Analyses of the Non-response Category

The last step of our analyses focused on the "non response" category, which was qualitatively analyzed through a description of the proportions of different labels used by the two groups of children to describe face stimuli independently from the emotional expression. When considering the total 660 opportunities that the two groups of children had to label a face, 250 of them (nearly 40%) were categorized in our previous analyses as " non responses" since the labels used by the children could not be grouped under a basic emotion tag. However, a further qualitative analyses allowed us to identify 11 new categories: "offence", "guilt", "suspect", "calm", "bored", "thoughtful", "focusing", "joking", "disappointed" "ordinary", "don't know". Offence was coded when children used the word "offence" or "offended". Guilt included "thinks she had done something wrong" or "she is in trouble", whereas suspect included "knows the person is cheating". Calm was rated when labels were "peaceful", "relaxed" or "cozy", and bored was coded when the child said "boring", "boredom", "yawning" or "sleepy". Thoughtful included "she is thinking of something", "serious" or "seriousness", while focusing included "she is concentrating" or "is paying attention to something very carefully". Joking included "makes silly faces" or "quizzical", whereas disappointed included "frustrated". Ordinary was scored when children said "normal", "nothing special", "plain". The "don't know" category was rated when children either said that they "did not know" or that they "did not see anything". These new categories were rated by two independent judges who agreed on the categories for 73% of the response types. In cases where the two original judges disagreed, a third judge rated the response and the specific category was determined by majority. Figure 2 shows the proportions of free labeling definitions given by children as part of the "non response" category. In addition, if considering group differences in the use of the 11 free labeling definitions used by children, some significant differences can be observed. Specifically, exposed children used significantly more labels grouped as "offence" than control children, $F(1, 65)=9.46$, $p=.003$. In addition, exposed children significantly more often said that they were unable to give an emotional label to the face stimuli, as they made more use of those expressions labeled as "I don't know", $F(1, 65)=6.36$, $p=.014$. In contrast, children from the non-exposed group used more "thinking" expressions, $F(1,65)=15.63$; $p=.0001$ and had a tendency to use more labels related to "focusing", $F(1,65)=2.98$; $p=.089$, compared to the exposed children.

Conclusion

The aim of this study was to asses whether a threatening event outside the family context, as a terrorist attack, may impact on the child's ability to recognize facial emotions. Some pilot information is given on how school-aged children, three months after surviving a terrorist siege in their school, perform differently compared to a group of non exposed peers in recognizing some specific facial emotions stimuli.

Our results show that children in both groups attributed the correct positive valence to happiness, and most of them also recognized this specific emotion, that is children were able to recognize a positive facial expression regardless of being exposed or non-exposed to the terrorist attack. However, when considering negative emotions (i.e., sadness, anger, disgust and fear), significant differences were found in both the recognition of the correct emotion valence and of the correct emotion specific category. Children exposed to the terrorist attack were less accurate in recognizing negative emotions than non-exposed children of the same age, especially fear; however, they were more accurate in recognizing the specific expression of anger.

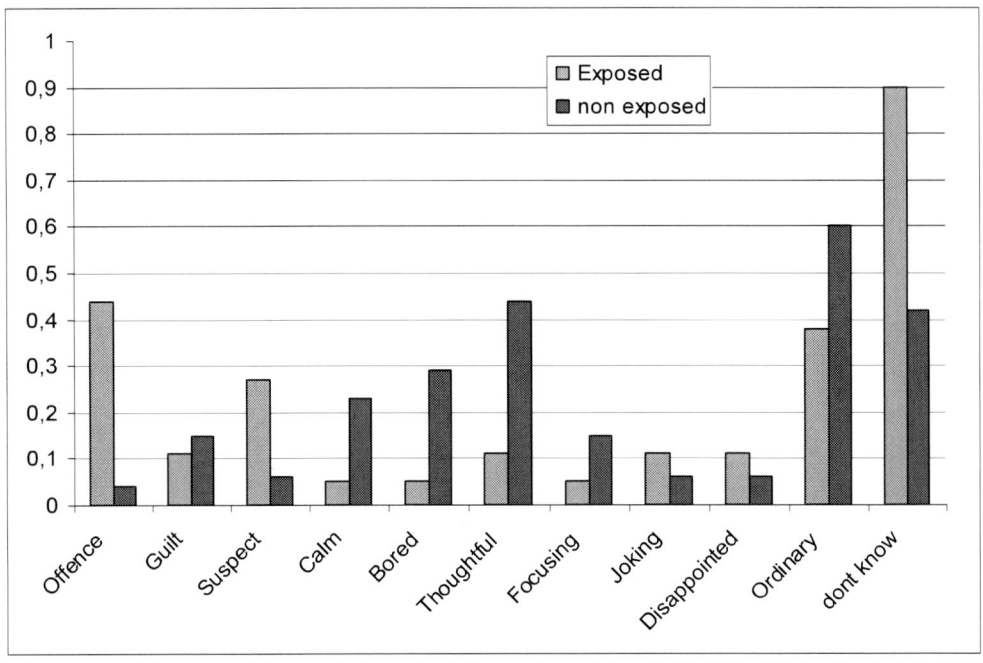

Figure 2. Proportion of new categories emerged from the qualitative analyses of the "non-response" in the two groups of traumatized and non traumatized children.

Ekman and Friesen (1975) stated that recognition of facial expression of emotion develops at different rates, with happiness being learned first, followed by sadness and anger, and more difficult emotions such as fear, disgust and surprise, developing later. Our results provide somehow support to this notion as happiness was the emotion correctly identified the most, irrespective of exposure. Sadness also was accurately recognized; in contrast, fear and disgust were hardly recognized by both groups even if accuracy increased in non-exposed children in recognizing fearful faces creating a significant group difference.

An additional result, confirming previous studies on the development of facial emotion recognition, is related to the expression of anger.

When seeing an angry face, children exposed to terrorism significantly more often attributed a correct negative valence and correct specific category to it than non-exposed children. This finding shows a pattern in terrorism-exposed children that is similar to what it is reported for maltreated and physically abused children. Children whose parents report high levels of hostility directed toward their offspring better correctly identify facial expressions of anger (Pollak & Sinha, 2002; Pollak & Tolley-Schell, 2003). Studies contrasting different types of maltreating families suggest that physically abusive parents interact with their children frequently, but with high rates of verbal and physical aggression directed at them (Bousha & Twentyman, 1984). Therefore, physically abusive environments are likely to include high intensity aggressive outbursts, frequent patterns of aggression, heightened hostility, and increased interpersonal threat (Pollak & Sinha, 2002). Because of threat signals that physically abused children are exposed to in their family environments, anger may become a particularly salient environmental cue for them. Therefore, one possibility is that physically abused children learn to make decisions about the signaling of anger using minimal visual information, thus providing a behavioral advantage for children living in threatening contexts. A similar frightening context was experienced by Beslan's children during the three day-siege. Even if, in the case of the terrorist attack, children experienced aggressive and threatening behaviors towards them only for a relatively short period of time and not as a developmental environment, the severity of these episodes, which included the display of violent acts by the perpetrators that caused the death of many friends and family members, may have contributed to a very similar effect on these children's reactions to angry facial expressions.

A further explanation for this particular ability of Beslan's children to accurately recognize anger may be due to the cultural and socio-political context of this region. Anger and rage are considered in this culture as the appreciated expressions of bravery which is a basic quality that a Ossetian "warrior" must have to fight invaders. Children do not hesitate in labeling facial expressions as part of the anger category as they know that this is an estimate emotion expression in their community. In addition, as anger is considered in this climate a key emotion for survivorship children may have learned its importance very early in life from the family and community.

Last, in relation to the recognition of anger, it should be mentioned that a pattern similar to that of exposed children has also been found in children with ADHD (Cadesky, Mota, & Schachar, 2000). Children with ADHD are less accurate in emotion recognition compared to controls across all emotions except anger. At the time of the assessment, exposed children from our sample displayed patterns of behaviors that resembled those of children with ADHD. Scrimin and colleagues (2006) have found attention deficits in these children, and parents reported disturbing hyper-activity behaviors in their children after the event. Mothers often complained about their children's behaviour: *"...something has changed in him, I can't clearly define what, his personality I guess. He does not live things calmly as before. Now he is hyper-activated: aggressive. For example, before I used to get close to him, talk with him, ...now if just I get near him, he over-reacts and jumps up, starts moving around..."*(ID 3) or *"I don't know how she will be able to get back to her studies. She can't even sit still for a couple of minutes any more. She totally can not concentrate. She is just jumping and running around...before she could sit and make drawings or just read a book...now she just can't" (ID 10).*

In brief, the severe traumatic event of the 3 days terrorist siege experienced in the every-day, and usually safe context of school, may have caused in exposed children a facial emotion recognition pattern that is similar to that of maltreated children. In addition, the high incidence of PTSD that is associated with symptoms similar to those of ADHD patients, such as attention deficits and hyper-activity (Scrimin et al., 2006), may have also contributed to the accuracy of exposed children in recognizing the anger expressions.

As we have previously mentioned, exposed children, with the exception of anger stimuli, did not accurately well recognize negative emotions. This inability was particularly evident for fear facial stimuli. As a matter of fact, when labeling facial fear emotion stimuli, exposed and non-exposed children performed differently both in relation to the correct valence and to the correct specific category. While non-exposed children mostly recognized the correct negative valence of fear, in the group of children exposed to terrorism the attribution of a valence to fear was due to chance, that is in this group the proportion of correct responses in relation to the valence of fear was .50. Yet, the more striking finding was the inability of children surviving the terrorist attack to recognize the specific emotion of fear. None of the fear facial stimuli was correctly labeled by exposed children. The fact that fear was hardly recognized by exposed children in our study is consistent with the pattern seen among other clinical samples of children as well as children in the general population, where fear tends to be the most frequently mystified emotion (McAlpine, Singh; Kendall, & Ellis, 1992). Developmentally, together with surprise and disgust, fear is the most difficult facial emotion expression to master and thus the last to be learned. However, our results differentiate children surviving a terrorist attack from those who have been physically abused. Psychopathological studies have provided evidence that physically abused children, compared with controls, allocate more processing resources when their attention is directed to anger but perform similarly to controls when attending to happy and fearful faces (e.g., Pollak, Klorma, Thatcher, & Cicchetti, 2001). These findings suggest that physically abused children do not have global emotion recognition or affective information-processing problems, but instead display differential processing of emotions that appears to be specific for anger. The same can not be said about children surviving a terrorist attack, as the present preliminary data show that children with this specific trauma report a complete inability to recognize fear. Yet, it is interesting to note here that once again the performance of exposed children resembles to that of children with ADHD. Young patients with attention deficits reported the largest errors in the recognition of fear (Singh, Ellis, Winton, Singh, Leung, & Oswald, 1998). The similarities between children exposed to terrorism and children with ADHD in the recognition of facial expressions of both anger and fear appear to attribute importance to cognitive and behavioral factors, such as attentional performance and hyper-activity that are important symptoms both in ADHD and PTSD. Nevertheless exposed children's responses to fearful faces were not a matter of errors in accuracy, but rather a complete misinterpretation. This is somehow surprising if we consider that often an individual's ability to accurately recognize a facial expression is related to the degree of exposure to that emotion in his/her everyday life, as suggested by Mcalpine, and colleagues (1992). Furthermore, in healthy populations the protection of parents and other adults provided to younger children by limitating their exposure to fear may restrict the children's opportunity to learn about this facial expression. Fear was experienced by these children very strongly during the 3-day terrorist siege in their school as they underwent many and repeated frightful experiences. Through the reports of what happened in those days made by the press (Parfitt, 2004) and the words of mothers who were in the school during the siege, it is clear that children must have been not only scared, but terrified, *"...she was crying, saying "let me go out from here!"* (mother of a 10-year-old girl who was in the school during the attack, ID12), and that they had several fearful experiences. For example, *"when they* (the terrorists) *were taking us inside, when this attack started, I couldn't find my daughter. We were in different places. She told me that there were a lot of people and they demanded silence, the terrorists, but silence was impossible with all those people...no silence. So every now and then...we were sitting or lying on the floor...and they would put a person, a man...and this she can't forget...and shout that if they wouldn't shut up they'd kill him. And this fear she can't forget, she experiences fear again and again. Because they shot that man right there in front of us. He was killed under our eyes".* (ID 9)

However, this same emotion is not recognized by exposed children during a face emotion stimuli presentation three months after the event. Yet, we also know that in this sample, 70% of children had clinical PTSD and the remaining had a sub clinical PTSD (Scrimin et al., 2006), which is well known to be associated to avoidance symptoms and inhibition of emotions that may reactivate the process of re-experiencing the traumatic event. The bad performance of these children in the process of attributing the correct emotion label to fear may be caused by aspects related to PTSD. Thus, avoidance symptoms may also contribute to explain -at least in part- the inability of these severely traumatized children to recognize fearful emotional expressions because they repeatedly experienced them.

A further comment on the non-use of the fear label by Beslan's children could be related to some cultural aspects. If on one hand the identification and use of emotion such as anger, are well appreciated by the Ossetian proud culture (Moscardino et al., 2007) the same can not be said for emotions such as fear. Children are taught not to be fearful and scared but to be brave and strong. Consequently our young participants might have avoided to use and learn expressions such as fear that are not approved by their parents. As a confirmation of this possible explanation we identified the labels used to describe these faces by children surviving the attack as including "guilt", "sadness" and with the most frequently categories used being "anger" and "offence" together with "I don't know".

It should also be mentioned that the inability to recognize fear in these children supports the neurophysiological data from adults with PTSD (Felmingham et al., 2003). The literature based on fMRI and event-related potentials (ERPs) reports that adults with PTSD mainly show difficulties in recognizing fearful and in some cases angry facial expressions in static images, but have no or relatively little difficulties in recognizing other emotions such as disgust, happiness and sadness (Adolphs, Gosselin, Buchanan, Tranel, Schyns, & Damasio, 2005; Felmingham et al., 2003; Killgore, Oki, & Yurgelun,-Todd, 2001; Pizzigalli, Lehmann, Hendrick, Regard, Pascual-Marqui, & Davidson, 1999; Thomas, Drevets, Whalen, Eccard, Dahl, Ryan, & Casey 2001) thus demonstrating that trauma may impact on the neural basis of emotion. As a consequence, one may hypothesize a heightened cortical ERP response to fearful faces also in children surviving terrorism with PTSD, further studies should address this issue.

The exposed and non-exposed group comparison revealed no differences in the accurate recognition of sadness, and inaccuracy related to disgust facial expressions. Yet, important differences were found in response to angry and fearful facial expressions. Further groups differences were also found in additional analyses of the tags used by the two groups of children during the free labeling procedure.

A qualitative analysis was performed on those labels grouped under the "non response" category. Frequently children used particular labels to define a facial emotional expression that could not be categorized under the well-known basic emotions (i.e., happiness, sadness, anger, fear, disgust and surprise). These alternative tags or expressions used by children may allow to gather additional relevant information. As a matter of fact, from what we initially classified as "non response" we were able to derive further significant group differences. Specifically, exposed and non-exposed children used very different classes of words and sentences during the free labeling procedure to describe which facial emotion stimuli they were seeing.

A first group difference, probably caused by the exposed children's high levels of distress, was related to the presence of more expressions with a negative valence in children surviving the Beslan terrorist attack compared to non-exposed children. Namely, whereas children surviving the terrorist attack in Beslan's school used labels such as rage, offence, suspect, disappointment and don't know, non-exposed children used more labels that were grouped into the categories of calm, bored, focusing, thoughtful and ordinary. Thus indicating that non exposed children used labels that are typical of children, such as bored or ordinary when they did not correctly identify the facial expression. In some other cases, non-exposed children used labels that might be associated with a typical school script where children are asked to pay attention, think about issues and focus on them. On the other hand, exposed children used labels that were mostly associated with rage or other related words, such as suspect or offence, that might be related to an everyday context of fear, lack of safety and insecurity. The use of these labels may be caused by the trauma and the psychological reaction to it. This possible interpretation may also help us to explain the significantly higher presence of disappointment, as a display of dissatisfaction, and also "don't know", as a signal of insecurity and lack of self confidence expressed through the explicit statement that they did not know the "correct" answer.

Another possible explanation of this qualitative group difference may be related to specific cultural and socio-political aspects. Even if cross-cultural studies of emotion recognition have been one of several central sources of evidence in favor of emotional universality, in our sample there is clearly a difference in the labels used freely by children. As a matter of fact, the use of terms such as "suspect" and "offence" in Beslan's children might be caused not only by the traumatic experience of the attack, but also by the social, cultural and political context and the specific patterns of reactions that might be related to terrorism.

As some may know, Beslan is a town located in the Republic of North Ossetia-Alania, one of the smallest, most densely-populated and multi-cultural republics in the Russian Federation. People from Beslan narrate that the Alans were a brave people of warriors whose salient characteristics included physical and moral strength, along with an exceptional courage and modesty. These cultural aspects are still valued by Ossetian people (Moscardino et al, 2007) and are relevant for social and community life as well as for the way parents socialize their children to express and recognize emotional expressions. In this culture, children learn from an early age to restrain emotional expressions which may display their weaknesses, such as fear (Isaenko & Petschauer, 1999). However, other emotions such as rage and offence are valued. Thus, the significant use of "offence" and "suspect" tags emerging from the free labeling procedure may be incentivated by the fact of being appreciated. In addition, the great importance given to offence may be due to the cultural role of it in this proud people. There is a strong relation between anger and offence, as warriors may be expected to take off easily and react. These children are used to associate offence to a immediate reaction of anger and rage. Suspect is also a crucial theme for this population, because there is a history of fight and suspect between Ossetia and its neighbours countries, i.e., Chechnya and Ingushetia, two Muslim republics. It may also partly derive from the lack of protection and the general political conditions of their home country. The feelings of being "abandoned" and "betrayed" by the government emerged in several caregivers' accounts (Moscardino et al, 2007). Indeed, as Lynch notes, "Russian responses during the Beslan attack displayed problems of coordination among different kinds of troops, a lack of preparation and planning, and a failure to secure the area to prevent the escape of terrorists or interference with local vigilantes. " (Lynch, 2005, p. 157).

The pediatric population at risk for developing PTSD as a consequence of collective violence is a world-wide increasing problem. This population is not only at risk for long and short term learning disabilities due to cognitive impairments (Scrimin et al., 2006), but it may also be compromised in emotional and social functioning. The difficulties of children exposed to a terrorist attack in discriminating among basic emotional expressions such as fear and the response bias for angry facial cues may make it difficult for these children to effectively recognize and respond appropriately to the social signals conveyed by others. According to this view, differences in recognition, understanding , and discrimination of facial expressions between exposed and non-exposed children of the same age provide promising insight into why children surviving terrorism may develop many social and emotional problems. Problems may arise in relation to the interaction with peers and the community life (Herba & Phillips, 2004).

The present results may help clinicians to focus their attention on specific aspects of emotional functioning in children surviving terrorism. In particular, it is suggested here that care should be taken in helping children to recognize and verbally express fear. Recognizing such emotions may be the first step to address PTSD symptoms induced by this specific type of trauma. Clinicians may address those emotions that have been most intensely experienced by children during a violent attack and help them to express, reframe and constructively re-elaborate them. This can be done by collaborating with teachers and social workers to organize psycho-educational groups with children finalized at helping children to increase their awareness of frightening emotions. It is worth noting that in response to terrorism, working with groups and classes might be suggested as many children and adults are involved and psychological interventions with single individuals may not always be the most effective approach in communities affected by terrorism. Finally, interventions with traumatized populations in non-Western countries require a culturally sensitive approach that appropriately considers the cultural measuring of emotions. Free labeling may be a useful technique to understand the verbal meanings of and values about emotion in any given culture.

It should be noted that this is a pilot study providing preliminary information on the emotion recognition abilities of children surviving an extremely life-threatening event. As such, results must be taken with caution. The limited sample size prevents us from generalizing our findings. A further limit may be that only a free labeling procedure was used. It should be noted, however, that at the time of the assessment, children were still highly traumatized and we did not feel like pressing them too much or too long with psychological testing for ethic reasons.

The next step of this study is a further data collection in Beslan that will allow us to gather information on a much larger sample including an Ossetian control group and to plan a on site psycho-educational intervention.

References

Adolphs, R., Gosselin, F., Buchanan, T., Tranel, D., Schyns, P., & Damasio, A. (2005). A mechanism for impaired fear recognition after amygdala damage. *Nature, 433,* 68-72.

Beauchesene, M.A., Kelly, B.R., Patsdaughter, C.A., & Pickard, J. (2002). Attack on America: children's reaction's and parent's responses. *Journal of Pediatric Health,* 16, 213-221.

Beers, S.R., & De Bellis, M.D. (2002). Neuropsychological Function in Children With Maltreatment-Related Posttraumatic Stress Disorder. *American Journal of Psychiatry,* 159, 483-486.

Blair, R.J.R. (2003). Facial expressions, their communicatory functions and neuro-cognitive substrates. *Philosophical transactions of the royal society of London: B series,* 358, 561-572.

Bousha, D.M., & Twentyman, C.T. (1984). Mother-child Interactional Style in Abuse, Neglect, and Control Groups: Naturalistic Observations in the Home. *Journal of Abnormal Psychology,* 93, 106-114.

Boyatzis, C.J., Chazan, E., & Ting, C.Z. (1993). Preschool children's decoding of facial emotions. *Journal Genetic Psychology,* 154, 375-382.

Bungental, D., Blue, J., & Lewis, J. (1990). Caregiver beliefs and dysphoric affect directed to difficult children. *Developmental Psychology,* 26, 631-638.

Cadesky, E.B., Mota, V.L., & Schachar, R.J. (2000). Beyond words: How do children with ADHD and/or conduct problems process nonverbal information about affect? *Journal of the American Academy of Child and Adolescent Psychiatry,* 39, 1160-1171.

Cairns, E., & Toner, I. (1993). Children and political violence in northern Ireland: from riots to reconciliation. In: *The psychological effects of was and violence on children,* Leavit L, Fox N, eds. Hillsdale, NJ: Earlbaum, 215-230.

Camras, L.A., & Allison, K. (1985). Children's understanding of emotional facial expressions and verbal labels. *Journal of Nonverbal Behavior,* 9, 84–94.

Camras, L.A., Ribordy, S., Hill, J., Martino, S., Sachs, V., Spaccarelli, S., & Stefani, R. (1990). Maternal facial Behavior and the recognition and production of emotional expression by maltrated and nonmaltrated children. *Developmental Psychology,* 26, 304-312.

De Sonneville, L.M.J., Verschoor, C.A., Njiokiktjien, C., Op 't Veld, V., Toorenaar, N., & Vranken, M. (2002). Facial identity and Facial emotions: Speed, Accuracy, and Processing Strategies in Children and Adults. *Journal of Clinical and Experimental Neuropsychology,* 27, 200-213.

Ekman, P. (1992). An argument for basic emotions. *Cognition and Emotion,* 6, 169-200.

Ekman, P. (2003). Emotions revealed. New York: Henry Holt and Company, Owl Book.

Ekman, P., & Friesen, W.V. (1975). *Unmasking the face. A guide to recognizing emotions from facial clues.* Englewood Cliffs, New Jersey: Prentice-Hall.

Felmingham, K.L., Bryant, R.A., & Gordon, E. (2003). Processing angry and neutral faces in post-traumatic stress disorder: an event related potentials study. *Neuroreport,* 14, 777-780.

Fremont, W.P. (2004). Childhood reactions to terrorism-induced trauma: a review of the past 10 years. *Journal of the American Academy of Child and Adolescent Psychiatry,* 43, 381-392.

Gross, A.L., & Ballif, B. (1991). Children's understanding of emotion from facial expressions and situations: a review. *Developmental Review,* 11, 368–98.

Herba, C., & Phillips, M. (2004). Annotation: Development in facial expression recognition from childhood to adolescence: behavioural and neurological perspectives. *Journal of Child Psychology and Psychiatry*, 45, 1185-1198.

Herrenkol, R., Herrenkol, E., Egolf, B., & Wu, P. (1991). The developmental consequences of child abuse. In R Starr & D. Wolfe (Eds.), *The effects of child abuse and neglect* (pp.57-81). New York: Guilford Press.

Hiatt, S., Campos, J., & Emde, R. (1979). Facial patterning and infant emotional expression: Happiness, surprise, and fear. *Child Development*, 50, 342-53.

Hoge, C.H., & Pavlin, J.A. (2002). Psychological sequelae of September 11. *New English Journal of Medicine*, 347, 443-445.

Isaenko, A.V., & Petschauer, P.W. (1999). Traditional civilization in the North Caucasus: Insiders and outsiders. In K. Nader, N. Dubrow & B. H. Stamm (Eds.), *Honoring differences: Cultural issues in the treatment of trauma and loss*. Philadelphia, PA: Brunner/Mazel.

Izard, C.E. (1971). The face of emotion. New York: Appleton Century Crofts.

Killgore, W.D.S, Oki, M., & Yurgelun-Todd, D.A. (2001). Sex differences in amygdale activation during the perception of facial affect. *Neuroreport*, 12, 2543-2547.

Laor, N., Wolmer, L., & Cohen, D.J. (2001). Mothers' functioning and children's symptoms 5 years after a SCUD missile attack. *American Journal Psychiatry, 158*, 1020-1026.

Lynch, D. (2005). 'The enemy is at the gate': Russia after Beslan. *International Affairs, 81*, 141-161.

Markham, R., & Adams, K. (1992). The effect of type of task on children's identification of facial expressions. *Journal of Nonverbal Behaviour, 16,*21-39.

McAlpine, C., Singh, N.N., Kendall, K.A., & Ellis, C.R. (1992). Recognition of facial expressions of emotion by persons with mental retardation: A matched comparison study. *Behavior Modification, 16*, 543–558

Melville, M.B., & Lykes, M.B. (1992). Guatemalan Indian children and the sociocultural effects of government-sponsored terrorism. *Social Science and Medicine, 34*, 533-548.

Miller, K.E., (1996). The effect of state terrorism and exile on indigenous Guatemalan Refugee children: mental health assessment and an analysis of children's narratives. *Child Development, 67*, 89-106.

Montague, D.P.F., & Walker-Andrews, A.S. (2001). Peekaboo: A new look at infants' perception of emotion expressions. *Developmental Psychology*, 37, 826-838.

Moscardino, U., Axia, G., Scrimin, S., & Capello, F. (2007). Narratives from caregivers of children surviving the terrorist attack in Beslan: issues, of health, culture, and resilience. *Social Science and Medicine*, 64, 1776-87.

Nader, K., Dubrow, N., & Stamm, B. H. (Eds.) (1999). *Honoring differences: Cultural issues in the treatment of trauma and loss*. Philadelphia, PA: Brunner/Mazel.

Nelson, C.A., & De Haan, M. (1997). A neurobehavioral approach to the recognition of facial expressions in infancy. In: J.A. Russel and J.M. Fernandez-Dols, Editors, *The Psychology of Facial Expression*, Cambridge University Press, pp. 176–204

Neneroff, C.B., Bremener, J.D., Foa, E.B., Mayberg, H.S., North, C.S., & Stein, M.B. (2006). Posttraumatic stress disorder: a state of the science review. *Journal of Psychiatry Research*, 40, 1-21.

Odom, R.D., & Lemond, C.M. (1972). Developmental differences in the perception and production of facial expressions. *Child Development*, 43, 359-369.

Parfitt, T. (2004). How Beslan's children are learning to cope. *Lancet*, 364 (9450): 2009-2010.

Pfefferbaum, B., Nixon, S.J., Krug, R.S., (1999). Clinical needs assessment of middle and high school students following the Oklahoma City bombing. *American Journal of Psychiatry.* 156, 1069-1074.

Philippot, P., & Fledman, R.S. (1990). Age and social competence in preschoolers decoding of facial expression. *British Journal Social Psychology,* 29, 43-53.

Phillips, D., Prince, S., & Schiebelhut, L.. (2004). Elementary school children's responses 3 months after the September 11 terrorists attack: a study in Washington, DC. American. *Journal of Orthopsychiatry,* 27 (4), 509-528.

Phillips, M.L., Drevets, W.C., Rauch, S.L., & Lane, R. (2003). Neurobiology of emotion perception I: The neural basis of normal emotion perception. *Biology Psychiatry,* 54, 505-514.

Pizzagalli, D.A., Lehmann, D., Hendrick, A.M., Regard, M., Pascual-Marqui, R.D., & Davidson, R.J.(2002). Affective judgments of faces modulate early activity (approximately 160 ms) within the fusiform gyri. *Neuroimage,* 16, 663-77.

Pollak, S.D. & Tolley-Schell, S.A.(2003). Selective attention to facial emotion in physically abused children. *Journal of Abnormal Psychology*, 112, 323-338.

Pollak, S.D., & Sinha, P. (2002). Effects of early experience on children's recognition of facial displays of emotions. *Developmental Psychology,* 38, 784-791.

Pollak, S.D., Cicchetti, D., Hormoh, K., & Reeg, A. (2000). Recognizing emotion in faces: developmental effects in child abuse and neglect. *Developmental Psychology,* 36, 679-688.

Pollak, S.D., Klorman, R., Thatcher, J.E., & Cicchetti, D. (2001). P3b reflects maltreated children's reactions to facial displays of emotion. *Psychophysiology*, 38, 1-8.

Salmon, K., & Bryant, R.A. (2002). Posttraumatic stress disorder in children. The influence of developmental factors. *Clinical Psychology Review, 22*, 163-188.

Schuster, M.A., Stein, B.D., Jaycox, L.H., Collins, R.L., Marshall, G.N., Elliott, M.N., Zhou, A.J., Kanouse, D.E., Morrison, J.L., & Berry, S.H. (2001). A national survey of stress reactions after the September, 11, 2001, terrorist attacks. *New England Journal of Medicine, 345,* 1507-1512.

Scrimin, S., Axia, G., Capello, F., Moscardino, U., Steinberg, A.M., & Pynoos, R.S. (2006). Posttraumatic reactions among injured children and their caregivers 3-months after the terrorist attack in Beslan. *Psychiatry Research*, 141, 333-336.

Serrano, J.M., Iglesias, J., & Loeches, A. (1995). Infants' responses to adult static facial expressions. *Infant Behavior and Development,* 18, 477–482.

Singh, S.D., Ellis, C.R., Winton, A.S.W., Singh, N.N., Leung, J.P., & Oswald, D.P. (1998). Recognition of Facial Expressions of Emotion by Children with Attention-Deficit Hyperactivity Disorder. *Behaviour Modifications*, 22(2), 128 - 142.

Smith, M., & Walden, T. (1998). Developmental trends in emotion understanding among a diverse sample of African-American Preschool children. *Journal of Applied Developmental Psychology*, 177-197.

Sorce, J.F., Emde, R.N., Campos, J. & Klinnert, M.D. (1985). Maternal emotional signalling: Its effect on the visual cliff behaviour of one-year-olds. *Developmental Psychology,* 21, 195-200.

Steinberg, A.M., Brymer, M.J., Decker, K.B., & Pynoos, R.S. (2004). The University of California at Los Angeles Post-traumatic Stress Disorder Reaction Index. *Current Psychiatry Reports, 6,* 96-100.

Susser, E., Jackson, H., & Hoven, C. (2001). Terrorism and mental health in school: the effects of September 2001 on New York city school children.

Thomas, K.M., Drevets, W.C., Whalen, P.J., Eccard, C.H., Dahl, R.E., Ryan, N.D., & Casey, B.J. (2001). Amygdala response to facial expressions in children and adults. *Biology Psychiatry*, 49, 309-316.

Trevarthen, C. (1985). Facial expressions of emotions in mother-infant interaction. *Human Neurobiology, 4,* 21-32.

Vicari, S., Snitzer, Reilly, J., Pasqualetti, P., Vizzotto, A., & Caltagirone, C. (2000). Recognition of facial expression of emotions in school age children: the intersection of perceptual and semantic categories. *Acta Pediatrica*, 89, 836-845.

Walker-Andrews, A.S. (1997). Infants' perception of expressive behaviours: Differentiation of multimodal information. *Psychological Bulletin*, 121, 437-456.

Widen, S.C., & Russell, J.A. (2003). A closer look at preschoolers' freely produced labels for facial expressions. *Developmental Psychology,* 39, 114-128.

In: Global Terrorism Issues and Developments
Editor: Rene A. Larche, pp. 187-212

ISBN: 978-1-60021-930-6
© 2008 Nova Science Publishers, Inc.

Chapter 8

THE TRANSGENERATIONAL EFFECTS OF TRAUMA FROM TERROR: A DEVELOPMENTAL MODEL

Marsha Kaitz[1,*], Richard Ebstein[1],
Stephen V. Faraone[2] and David Mankuta[3]
[1]Department of Psychology, Hebrew University, Jerusalem, Israel
[2]Departments of Psychiatry and of Neuroscience & Physiology,
SUNY Upstate Medical University, Syracuse, NY, USA
[3]Hadassah Hospital and Hebrew University Medical School, Jerusalem, Israel

Abstract

In this paper, we focus on the impact that trauma from terror can have on parents and parenting and the vicarious effects that can be passed on to children. Central to the paper is a discussion of a "transmission model" that casts trauma-related disturbances in the home and care giving environment as primary transmitters of transgenerational effects. Primary tenets of the model are that (1) Parents' trauma from terror affects parenting and the home-environment, (2) Adverse home environments and compromised parenting stress children, and (3) Chronic stress disturbs child development. We also discuss environmental and biological/genetic factors that may moderate the impact of terror-exposure on parents and the risk that can be transmitted to the young. Finally, we suggest alternative models of transmission and directions and challenges of future research.

Keywords: terror, trauma, children, parenting, violence, stress

Introduction

The transgenerational effects of trauma (TET) are demonstrated by the shown impact of trauma experienced by one family member on another family member of a younger

---

[*] Correspondence to Dr. Marsha Kaitz, Department of Psychology, Hebrew University, Jerusalem 91095, Israel, e-mail msmarsha@mscc.huji.ac.il, phone: 972-2-5883372.

generation, whether or not he/she was not directly exposed to the traumatic event(s). In this definition, the operative word is "impact" because the symptoms of primary trauma usually are not the same as the secondary effects that it has on others (Weingarten, 2004). Most often, TET is demonstrated (statistically) by an association between the intensity of parents' symptoms and the symptoms of their children (e.g., Yehuda, Schmeidler, Giller, Sierver, Binder-Brynes, 1998), although TET also can be shown by significant differences between children whose parents experienced trauma and children whose parents did not (e.g., Daud, Skoglund, & Ryedelius, 2005; Yehuda, Schmeidler, Wainberg, Binder-Brynes, & Duvdevani, 1998). In most studies, TET was assessed by participants' ratings on symptom inventories (e.g., Rosenheck, 1986); a few used behavioral measures based on direct observation (e.g., Lyons-Ruth, Yellin, Melnick, & Atwood, 2005), perceptual-cognitive tasks (e.g., Stroop task, Suozzi & Motta, 2004), or biochemical markers of physiological stress (e.g., Yehuda, Halligan, & Grossman, 2001).

In this paper, we focus on the potential risk imposed on children by living with a parent who was traumatized by terror (herein referred to as the "transgenerational effects of trauma from terror", abbreviated TETT). As elsewhere, "terror" is defined as "premeditated, politically motivated violence perpetuated against noncombatant targets by sub-national groups or clandestine agents, usually intended to influence an audience" (Title 22 of the United States Code, Section 2656(d)). As such, terror is an example of political violence and has as its primary aims the spread of fear, retaliation, or the demonstration of strength, in addition to the realization of political goals. The word "terror" reflects the indiscriminate nature and randomness of terror attacks, as well as the inability of "targets" to prevent them or stay out of their way. (See Danieli, Brom, & Sills, 2004 for an in depth discussion of the definition of terror.)

Following others, we refer to trauma as a cascade of psychological and physiological effects that can be "triggered" by exposure to "unthinkable" events or situations, such as those involving actual death or serious injury or a threat to the physical integrity of self or others (e.g., Shalev, 2004). Some persons who suffer from prolonged and intense stress reactions have symptoms consistent with a diagnosis of posttraumatic traumatic stress disorder (PTSD), which includes significant dysfunction, frequent re-experiencing of the traumatic event, persistent avoidance of stimuli associated with trauma, and numbing of feelings. They may have other disorders besides or along side PTSD as well (Abu-Saba, 1999). In all of these cases, the response to trauma is considered pathological, and we refer to such responses as extreme traumatic reactions, trauma disorders, and pathological trauma.

Our focus on the risk for TETT is motivated by forecasts of continuing terror, worldwide, and the large number of children who could be affected by their parents' trauma from terror. To prevent this, it is important to find means for detecting parents and children who may be particularly vulnerable, fostering their resiliency, and treating them effectively. To our mind, these advances are essential, not only for the sake of individuals who were or will be exposed directly or vicariously to terror, but also to stymie the potential for "national traumas", which can change the spirit of whole societies, perhaps, forever (Lifton, 2005; Volkan, 2001, 2002).

Here, we aim to contribute by reviewing and integrating information related to TETT and by piecing together a rudimentary model of transmission to illustrate one route that could carry risk from parents to their children. To illustrate the potential of TETT, we borrow from family-focused research on the effects of war and community violence, on which there is a more extensive literature than there is on terror. Our primary aims are to review current information, discuss the potential dangers of TETT, and underline the need for further information on the topic. We also hope that our discussion furthers consideration of trauma and its sequelae from a psychosocial and relational perspective to account for the broad-based effects that trauma of one family member can have on others, and vise versa.

We acknowledge the similarity of our model and previous considerations of parents as potential pathogens that can levy risk for development disturbances on their children (e.g., Kellerman, 2001; Perry & Pollard, 1998; Pynoos, Steinberg, & Piacentini, 1999; Scheeringa & Zeanah, 2001; Schore, 2001, 2002). Nonetheless, our model is the only one to consider such effects in the special context of terror. We use the word "special" because unlike natural disasters, terror is of human design, has an element of targeted hate, and poses a constant danger; unlike war, it is aimed deliberately at civilians, can not predicted, and occurs during "normal life"; unlike family violence, its source is outside the home; and unlike most accidents, terror can affect masses of people, including those who were directly exposed to it and those who were not. For these reasons, as well as the potential effect that terror can have on all of our lives, we feel that it deserves special attention, preparation, strategies for intervention, and models of its own.

We begin with a review of studies that have focused on the mental health of parents in the aftermath of terror. In the sections that follow, we provide relevant examples of transgenerational research, discuss the primary tenets of our model, and suggest directions for future study.

The Impact of Terror on Parents' Mental Health

A number of studies have described the psychological impact of terror on parents. In almost all of them, the participants were mothers, and their subjective reports indicated that distress in the wake of terror-exposure is high, but decreases within a relatively short period of time for some, but not all individuals. For example, Laor and colleagues sampled mothers who had been exposed to SCUD attacks in Israel during the first Gulf war in 1991 and collected data on their symptoms, via administration of symptom check-lists, 6-months (Laor, Wolmer, Mayes, Golomb, Silverberg, Weizman, & Cohen, 1996), 30-months (Laor, Wolmer, Mayes, Gershon, Weizman, Cohen, 1997), and 5-years after the attacks (Laor, Wolmer, & Cohen, 2001). Results of these studies indicate that the women experienced considerable emotional distress at the first time-point; a proportion ($\approx$ 10%) experienced PTSD symptoms at 30-months, and those who had been displaced from their homes were at particular risk for heightened symptoms out to the 5-year time-point. Variability in reactions to terror is also demonstrated in the study of 52 women who had been close to the World Trade Center on 9/11, during pregnancy. Twenty-six weeks after the attack, four had "probable PTSD"; two were classified with moderate depression and state anxiety scores were above the 75th percentile (Engel, Berkowitz, Wolff, & Yehuda, 2005). Also, in a study on parents who lived in Washington DC at the time of the 9/11 attacks, 74% indicated that they found themselves thinking about the attacks a great deal; 85% indicated that their sense of safety was very much or somewhat shaken; 74% reported intrusive thoughts 3-months post-terror (Phillips, Prince, & Schiebelhut, 2004). Together, these findings, as well as results from broader-based surveys following terror, (e.g., 9/11; Galea, Ahern, Resnick, Kilpatrick, Bucuvalas, Gold, & Vlahov,

2002; Galea, Vlahov, Resnick, Ahern, Susser, Gold, Bucuvalas, & Kilpatrick, 2003; Schlenger, Caddell, Ebert, Jordan, Rourke, Wilson, Thalji, Dennis, Fairbank, & Kulka, 2002; Schuster, Stein, Jaycox, Collins, Marshall, Elliott, Zhou, Kanouse, Morrison, & Berry, 2001; Silver, Holman, McIntosh, poulin, & Gil-Rivas., 2002; Oklahoma bombing; North, Nixon, Shariat, Mallonee, McMillen, Spitznagel, & Smith, 1999; in Israel 2002; Bleich, Gelkopf, & Solomon, 2003; Bleich, Gelkopf, Melamed, & Solomon, 2006); in Spain 1997-2002; Baca, Baca-Garćia, Pérez-Rodrígues, & Cabanas, 2005; in France 1995-1996; Verger, Dab, Lampin, Loze, Deschaseaux-Voinet, Abenhaim, & Rouillon, 2004), demonstrate the varied reactions of persons to terror-exposure and the extreme effects that it can have on some individuals.

Added to these findings, Yehuda and colleagues (Yehuda, Engel, Brand, Seckl, Marcus, & Berkowitz, 2005) reported that women who developed PTSD after direct exposure to the World Trade Center (WTC) attacks on 9/11 had lower (basal) levels of the stress hormone cortisol than did two comparison groups: one group comprised of women who were exposed to the 9/11 attacks but did not develop PTSD and one group comprised of women who never had been exposed to terror. These results and others (on survivors of the Oklahoma bombing; Tucker, Pfefferbaum, North, Kent, Burgin, Parker, Hossain, Jeon-Slaughter, & Trautman, 2007; on Vietnam veterans; Boscarino, 1996, on Holocaust survivors; Yehuda, Golier, & Kaufman, 2005; on survivors of a natural disaster; Goenjian, Yehuda, Pynoos, Steinberg, Tashjian, & Yang, 1996) constitute evidence that trauma disorders are associated with disturbed neural functioning, particularly within the hypothalamic-pituitary-adrenal axis (HPA), which regulates cortisol levels. Cortisol plays a key role in the central nervous system, where it is involved in the modulation of stress, learning, memory, and emotion, in the metabolic system, and in the immune system. Its influence also extends to multiple other systems in the body (review in Miller, Chen, & Zhou, 2007).

Transgenerational Research

The results of many studies demonstrate that children of parents who suffer from trauma disorders are put at risk for disturbances, although there are none that relate to terror, per se. The most relevant have focused on offspring of parents who were severely traumatized by war-experiences, and these include studies of children of Vietnam combat veterans (Rosenheck & Fontana, 1998) and children of Holocaust survivors (e.g., Yehuda et al., 1998; see meta-analysis in van IJzendoorn, Bakermans-Kranenburg, & Sagai-Schwartz, 2003), among others (Danieli, 1998) There are also studies of children of parents who endured repression (e.g., in Chile; Becker & Diaz, 1998; in Argentina; Edelman, Kordon, & Lagos, 1998) or racism as members of indigenous groups such as the Australian Aboriginal people (Raphael, Swan, & Martinek, 1998) and Native Americans (Duran, Duran, Brave Heart, & Yellow Horse-Davis, 1998). In all of these studies, parents' reactions to traumatic events (or their consequences) seem to be associated with disturbances among offspring; despite the fact that they had not been born at the time of the parents' primary traumatic experiences. Across studies, children's disturbances included anxiety, depression, sleeplessness, aggression, eating disorders, and a risk for PTSD; although it is important to point out that not all children of trauma victims, even if pathology is very severe, show such disturbances (see review on offspring of Holocaust survivors in Solomon, 1998) and children's symptoms will depend on their age, gender, and a myriad of other factors (see section on moderators). Nonetheless, the findings do suggest that trauma experienced by parents can have potentially disturbing influences on children, even if they were not exposed to the same traumatic events as their parents, and we suggest that this extends to children whose parents suffer from extreme trauma from terror.

Association studies that demonstrate significant relations between the psychological symptoms of parents and children, who were concurrently exposed to terror, also provide some support for transgenerational effects, although these results may reflect influences from parent to child, child to parent, or both. Nonetheless, findings of strong correlations between parents and children's reactions months after the attacks (Laor et al., 2001; Fairbrother, Stuber, Galea, Fleischman, & Pfefferbaum, 2003) and, in at least one study, findings of increased parent-child associations over time (i.e., from 3 to 9 months after the 1993 World Trade Center bombing; Koplewicz, Vogel, Solanto, Morrissey, Alonso, Abikoff, Gallagher, & Novick, 2002), suggest that care givers and/or the home environs make a significant contribution to these associations (also see Schuster et al., 2001). In fact, one of the predominant predictors for referral of children to counseling after 9/11 was having a parent with PTSD (Stuber, Fairbrother, Galea, Pferfferbaum, Wilson-Genderson, & Vlahov, 2002). Other association studies have used samples of Israeli mothers and children during the 6-day Arab-Israel War (Meijer, 1985), Lebanese mothers and children (Bryce, Walker, Ghorayeb, & Kanj, 1989; Chimienti, Nasr, & Khalifehi, 1989), Palestinian mothers and children (Qouta, Punamäki, & El Sarraj, 2003), Bosnian mothers and children (Smith, Perrin, Yule, & Rabe-Hesketh, 2001), South African mothers and children (Dawes, Tredoux, & Feinstein, 1989), and mothers and children who were refugees from Kosova (Almqvist & Broberg, 2003). In some of these studies, the parent-child association was shown to be moderated by age of the child and the degree of exposure, such that younger children and persons with close exposure to terror were more distressed than older children and persons with more distal exposure; and in some studies, the relation held for some measures of distress but not others (e.g., Laor et al., 1997). Also worth noting is the study of Punamäki, Qouta, El Sarraj, and Montgomery (2006) that describes some Palestinian families as showing complementary patterns (e.g., mother high distress and child low distress).

Significantly, infants of mothers who had PTSD following direct exposure to 9/11, when they were pregnant, showed the same low levels of cortisol as their mothers did. These findings may reflect the impact of extreme stress (via their mother) or genetic and environmental factors shared by parent and child. However, irregardless of the cause, atypical cortisol levels could predict disturbances in development, as has been shown in studies of children living in adverse home-environments (Hart, Jordan, Gunnar, & Cicchetti, 1996), children whose mothers were stressed when they (the children) were very young (Essex, Klein, Cho, & Kalin, 2002), and children of anxiety-disordered mothers (Warren, Gunnar, Kagan, Anders, Simmens, Rones, Wease, Aron, Dahl, & Sroufe, 2003), among others (see review in Gunnar & Vaquez, 2001).

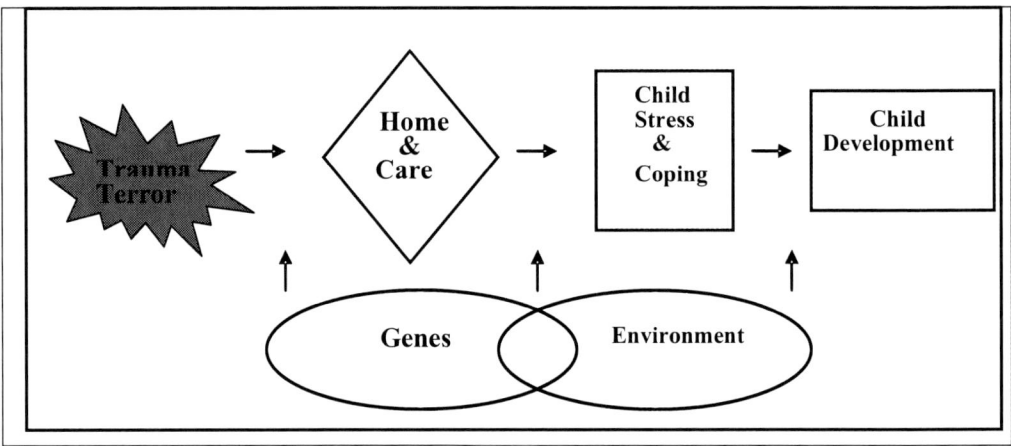

Figure 1. Theoretical model describing one route by which mothers can transmit the trauma of terror to their children.

The Transmission Model

Our model for TETT is illustrated in Figure 1. As shown, it describes processes that link parents' trauma from terror and their children's disturbed development, via the perturbation of neural stress systems and children's capacity to cope with and adapt to environmental challenges. To describe the model, we provide evidence for its basic assumptions, which are: (1) Parents' trauma from terror affects parenting and the home-environment, (2) Adverse home environments and compromised parenting stress children, and (3) Chronic stress disturbs child development. We also discuss moderators of the model, namely psychosocial factors and genes.

Parents' Trauma from Terror Affects Parenting and the Home-environment

The small-scale study of Levy (2006) illustrates vividly the impact that severe trauma from terror can have on mothers, their behavior, and their capacity to fulfill their parenting role. In that study, eight Israeli women who had been pregnant or who had given birth after exposure to terror were interviewed about the influence that their terror experiences had on mothering. Most of the women had endured terrible losses and injury. Without exception, the women espoused heart rending accounts of their emotional pain, although a few also described their traumatic experiences as a source of personal growth. In regards to mothering, the women described overwhelming fears for their children's physical and emotional health and safety, as well as difficulties in caring for their children, particularly when they were sick or in pain. Most of the women described themselves as over-protective; sometimes frenzied; and different, at the core, than they were prior to their experience with terror. Professionals who worked with parents who were victims of 9/11 also have described extreme trauma reactions of some parents who were exposed to terror and their challenges in caring for their children (Coates & Schecter, 2004; Pierce, 2006).

Similarly, effects of trauma on parenting were seen in a study of 1,200 male Vietnam veterans, who were questioned about their parenting attitudes and the functioning of their families (Jordan, Marmar, Fairbank, Schlenger, Kulka, Hough, & Weiss, 1992). Results showed marked problems in marital and family adjustment, parenting skills, and violent behavior among veterans with PTSD compared to those without PTSD. In addition, respondents with PTSD reported that their children presented more problems for them and that they were less satisfied in their parenting role and with their children's development than veterans without PTSD. Over half of those with PTSD scored in the highest category on measures of parental problems. In other research, Silow (1993) studied parents who were Holocaust survivors; almost 50 years after the horror of their experiences, those reporting continuing symptoms of PTSD also reported sustained difficulties in parenting, particularly in regards to their strong need to protect their children. These parents also reported parenting behaviors categorized as high on caring as a result of severe losses. Yehuda et al. (2001) found that offspring of Holocaust survivors reported more emotional abuse and neglect than comparison participants.

In addition to these studies, a broad literature attests to the deleterious impact that depression (review in Reck, Hunt, Fuchs, Weiss, Noon, Moehler, Downing, Tronick, & Mund, 2004) and high levels of anxiety (review in Kaitz & Maytal, 2005) can have on parenting, on parent-child interactions, and on the home-environment; and as noted above, these disorders can be symptoms of pathological trauma. Results of many studies portray depressed and anxious mothers as prone to shows of negative affect, as more intrusive or withdrawn, and as less sensitive to their children during mutual interactions than typical mothers. The translation of PTSD symptoms forecasts similar deficits, given the hyper arousal, proneness to startle, and negatively skewed perceptions that are characteristic of the disorder. In addition, parents with PTSD may find it difficult to sustain emotional availability to their children due to intrusive thoughts and recollections and, in extreme cases, signs that their child is distressed could rekindle trauma-memories, which could seriously disturb parenting by "forcing" the parent to seek refuge in emotional and physical distance from their children (Almquist & Broberg, 2003; Fearon & Mansell, 2001; Pierce, 2006). As so described, some parents who suffer from severe trauma are expected be challenged in their efforts to provide effective and sensitive care to their children, though many variables seem to play a part in determining parental functioning post-terror (see moderators below). Importantly, terror can affect parents' beliefs, concerns, practices, and priorities, even if they are exposed to terror but not severely traumatized by it (Dekel, 2004), and some of the changes may persist months after the attack(s) (Mowder, Guttman, Rubinson, & Sossin, 2006).

An Adverse Home Environment and Compromised Parenting are Stressful to Children

There is strong evidence that adversities within the home and care giving environment can impose stress on children and interfere with the development of tools for coping with it. In one study, parents' sensitivity to their children predicted the severity of their children's symptoms due to violence, a dog bite, or less extreme stressors (e.g., storm, rejection from school) (Rossman, Bingham, & Emde, 1997). In a study of effects of exposure to community violence; children's perception of parental acceptance made a significant contribution to children's (internalizing) symptoms over and above the contribution of violence exposure, and the interaction between exposure and acceptance was also significant (Kliewer, Cunningham, Diehl, Parrish, Walker, Atiyeh, Neace, Duncan, Taylor, & Mejia, 2004). Additionally, there are many studies that tested for an association between parental behavior and children's response to more ordinary stressors. These studies have employed high-risk (e.g., Malaesta-Magai, 1991; Mayes, Bornstein, Chawarska, Haynes, & Granger, 1996; Rubin, Burgess, & Hastings, 2002) and low risk samples (Gable & Isabella, 1992; Spangler, Schieche, Ilg., Maier, & Ackerman, 1994), a variety of stressors (e.g., separation, frustrating situations in Braungart-Rieker & Stifter, 1996; novel stimuli in Nachmias Gunnar, Mangelsdorf, Parritz, & Buss, 1996), and a range of measures (intensity of distress, heart rate in Haley & Stansbury; 2003; vagal tone in Moore & Calkins, 2004; cortisol level in Spangler, Schieche, Ilg, Maier, Maier, & Ackermann, 1994). In these and many other studies, sensitive parental behavior and well-managed parent-child interactions were associated with children's more effective regulation of stress.

Important to the present discussion are several studies that provide evidence that disturbed parenting and adversities in the home environment can mediate the relation between children's exposure to traumatic events and measures of their mental health. Mediation in these studies was demonstrated statistically, by showing (1) significant associations between trauma-exposure, symptoms, and a variable reflecting home or parenting, and (2) evidence that home/parenting accounts for most of the association between exposure and symptoms (Baron & Kenny, 1986). Using this technique, Bat-Zion and Levy-Shiff (1993) found that parents' responses were a central mediating factor for Israeli children's reactions to SCUD missile attacks. Similarly, Punamäki, Qouta, & El Sarraj (1997) interviewed Palestinian children exposed to political violence (in Gaza), and found that children's perceptions of their parents' behavior partially mediated the relation between their exposure to violence and their adjustment. Also relevant are studies, which show that the relation between exposure to community violence and measures of children's adjustment was mediated by adversities within the family (maternal distress in Linares, Heeren, Bronfman, Zuckerman, Augustyn, & Tronick, 2001; Smith et al., 2001; family conflict in Farver, Xu, Eppe, Fernandex, & Schwartz, 2000; Overstreet & Braun, 2000).

These data, among many others, attest to the importance of sensitive parenting for children's normal development, including their capacity to effectively modulate internal and external stress. According to attachment theory (Bowlby, 1969/1982), this important competency develops in the context of well-managed, harmonious, and satisfying parent-child interactions, which are considered to be the foundation of a secure child-parent relationship. Within such relationships, persons are expected to gain emotional strength and feelings of self-efficacy and control, which allow them to cope adaptively with challenges (e.g., Carter, 1998; Hofer, 1994). Conversely, insensitive parenting is expected to foster insecurities, fears, and a sense of helplessness in children, as well as promote the adoption of maladaptive strategies for coping with their own distress and outside stressors.

Sensitive parenting also plays an important role in helping children "digest" and express their feelings, and by doing so, parents help them consolidate coherent cognitions about emotionally-charged experiences (review in Oppenheim, 2006). Parents who do not serve as sensitive guides in these processes or who disallow their children's free expression of their emotions (explicitly or implicitly), either by not expressing feelings themselves (Kellerman, 2001), negatively reinforcing children's espousals, overwhelming their children with "scary stories" or lessons learned from traumatic experiences (e.g., that the world is a dangerous place; Abrams, 1999; Hughes & Chen, 1999; Solomon, 1998), or reenactments (Ancharoff, Munroe, & Fisher, 1998), silence (Auerhahn & Laub, 1998; Apfelbaum, 2000; Felsen, 1998; Kalayjian, Shahinian, Gergerian, & Saraydarian, 1996; Lichtman, 1984; Nagata & Cheng, 2003; Okner & Flaherty, 1989; Solomon, 1998) can promote fearfulness, difficulties in coping with challenges, and general disturbances in their children's ability to adapt to their environment, both inside and outside the home (Kliewer, Lepore, Oskin, & Johnson, 1998).

Chronic Stress Can Disturb Child Development

Traumatic experiences can have long-term consequences on children's development of neural structure and function and their capacity to regulate stress and arousal; and, along with others (e.g., Perry & Pollard, 1998; Perry & Azad, 1999; Pynoos et al., 1999; Scheeringa & Zeanah, 2001; Schore, 2002), we assume that the chronic or recurrent stress of living with a parent who suffers from extreme trauma can put children at risk for some of the same difficulties. If this reasoning is correct, the effects of TETT on young children could be far-reaching; and beyond dysregulation of the HPA axis and extreme stress reactions, we might expect difficulties in the sharing of information by the two hemispheres due to stress-related impact on hemispheric integration, difficulties in executive function (inhibitory behavior and the integration of motor and speech activity with sensory information) due to damage in the prefrontal lobes, deficits in learning and memory due to the impaired neurogenesis in the hippocampus (see King & Laplante, 2005), and a risk for affective disorders due to perturbations of the catecholaminergic system, HPA axis, amgydala, and hippocampus (e.g., Schore, 2002; Perry, Pollard, Blakely, Baker, & Vigilante, 1995). Moreover, these anomalies are expected to deter the development of regulatory skills that are important for success in many domains of development, notably socio-emotional development and learning, which would impose further stress on the individual and may even increase the likelihood of future trauma. Finally, the damage imparted by extreme stress on cardiovascular and immune functioning can lead to physical disease and, in the extreme, premature death (McEwen, 1998; Rosmond, Dallman, & Bjorntorp, 1998; Schnurr & Jankowski, 1999). In fact, a recent HMO retrospective study suggest that childhood trauma (witnessing violence, childhood victimization, and child exposure to severe household dysfunction) are risk factors for ill health (Felitti, Anda, Nordenberg, Williamson, Spitz, & Edwards, Koss, & Marks, 1998), and the same probably holds true for children chronically stressed by living with a parent traumatized by terror (Hagan & The Committee on Psychosocial Aspects of Child and Family Health and the Task Force on Terrorism, 2005).

Moderators of Transmission

Environmental/psychosocial Factors

A number of psychosocial stressors significantly influence the effects that terror-exposure has on adults and children; we assume that these same factors impact the "strength" (and likelihood) of transgenerational transmission and the effects that transmission have on children. In this regard, we presume that some factors exert direct effects on both adults and children (socioeconomic status, integrity of community infrastructure, availability of health services); some factors affect children indirectly through the impact that they have on parenting and the home environment (lack of social support); and most of these factors are likely to impact children both directly and indirectly. Further to this, bidirectional effects from parent to child and child to parent need to be considered since children can levy stress on parents, just as parents can levy stress on children.

Most of the risk factors implicated in terror (and trauma) research impose stress, exacerbate stress, or limit access to coping resources. Among them are factors related to the terror events themselves (e.g., degree of injury, loss, and displacement) and for the proposed model, we would add whether one or both parents are affected and the degree to which daily life is interrupted by attacks or future threats. In addition, demographic factors such as being a member of an ethnic minority (e.g., Bleich et al., 2006), having experienced previous trauma, and having a history of psychological problems have been shown to predict distress, post-terror, among adults (meta-analysis in Brewin, Andrews, & Valentine, 2000; review in Norris, Friedman, Watson, & Bryne, 2002). Studies on children's reactions to war and trauma implicate difficulties in regulating emotions and behavior, a shy and fearful nature, cognitive deficits (Finzi-Dottan, Dekel, Lavi, & Su'ali, 2006), previous experiences of loss and trauma, use of passive and distracting strategies (Punamäki et al., 2001), and difficulties in the social domain as contributors of risk to psychosocial adjustment (see reviews in Fremont, 2004; Joshi & O'Donnell, 2003; Shaw, 2003; Pine, Costello, & Masten, 2005). In addition, child gender may influence the degree and kind of psychological effects that are experienced after a terror attack, with girls more inclined to manifest the spectrum of anxiety symptoms upon exposure and boys, more likely to show disruption in behavioral adaptations (e.g., Qouta, Punamaki, & El Sarraj, 2005). Additionally, family variables, besides those targeted as mediators in the proposed model, are likely to contribute to direct and transgenerational effects of terror, and these include family isolation and family resources (e.g., review in Fremont, 2004). Finally, variables related to the larger social milieu, including community cohesion have been shown to be influential in coping with terror and other kinds of out-of-home violence (e.g., Kaplan Matar, Kamin, Sadan, & Cohen, 2005), and they too are likely to moderate parents' reactions to terror and the secondary effects that parents' trauma from terror can have on their children.

Psychosocial variables can serve, not only as sources of risk, but also as sources of resilience, so that just as social isolation can negatively affect prognosis for adjustment in a context of terror; an effective social network can serve to buffer its effects (e.g., Laor et al., 1997). In relation to the proposed model, support from extended family members, teachers, and friends; good health; competent self-regulation; and social adeptness are likely to buffer transgenerational effects on children in much the same way as they buffer effects of direct exposure to terror (e.g., Joshi & O'Donnell, 2003).

The variables listed do not stand on their own; but rather can covary, cumulate, and interact with one another as well as with other factors such as cultural context. Accordingly, the effects of direct and transgenerational effects may be conceptualized as influenced by a wide set of interacting, contextual domains, including "who the child is", his or her family, neighborhood, and culture and class. This ecological perspective (Bronfenbrenner, 2005) takes account of the wide range and complexities of influences on children, and is useful for explaining development, in general and, related to the present discourse, the impact that terror can have on the young.

Genes

Genetic vulnerabilities are included in our model as moderators of TETT because there is increasing evidence that genes may act to influence people's susceptibility or resistance to stressful experiences (review in Heim & Nemeroff, 2001). For example, recent twin studies are indicating an increased prevalence of PTSD in monozygotic compared to dizygotic twins (Stein, Jang, Taylor, Vernon, & Livesley, 2002; True, Rice, Eisen, Goldberg, Lyons, & Nowak, 1993). Further, in a study that compared startle responses in pairs of Vietnam combat veterans and their noncombat-exposed monozygotic twins, researchers found evidence of more slowly habituating skin conductance startle response in veterans with PTSD and their noncombatant co-twins, compared to veterans without PTSD and their noncombat exposed co-twin (Orr, Metzger, Lasko, Macklin, Hu, Shalev, Pitman, Eisen, Gilbertson, Gillette, Goldberg, Gurvits, Henderson, Keane, Lyons, McFarlane, Paige, True, Tsuang, Weathers, & Yehuda, 2003). Moreover, there is support for the moderate heritability of baseline HPA axis activity (for review see Wüst, Federenko, Van Rossum, Koper, Kumsta, Entringer, & Hellhammer, 2004) and dimensions of temperament (see reviews in Goldsmith & Lemery, 2000), both of which have been associated with atypical reactivity to stress.

Human genomic studies are naming candidate genes that may explain individual variability in the response to stress and trauma, including some genes encoding Corticotropin-releasing hormone (CRH) (Baerwald, Panayi, & Lanchbury, 1996; Gu, Sadler, Daiger, Wells, & Wagner, 1993), which is a key player in HPA-function (e.g., Lesch, Bengel, Heils, Saol, Greenberg, Petri, Benjamin, Muller, Hamer, & Murphy, 1996; Ohara, Nagai, Suzuki, Ochiai, & Ohara, 1998; see Wüst et al, 2004 for a review) and others that have been associated with a risk for anxiety and depression (review in Leonardo & Hen, 2006). There is evidence that some tendencies that may forecast high stress levels in the face of challenges, such as avoidance and the atypical processing of emotional stimuli, have been associated with variants of the serotonin transporter (5-HTT) promoter gene, a COMT polymorphism (Val158Met), and the polymorphism in the promoter of the MAO-A gene (e.g., Smolka, Schumann, Wrase, Grusser, Flor, Mann, Braus, Goldman, Buchel, & Heinz, 2005). In an association study of PTSD, some evidence was found for the involvement of the D2 dopamine receptor gene (DRD2) and dopamine transporter gene SLC6A3 (Segman, Cooper-Kazaz, Macciardi, Goltser, Halfon, Dobroborski, & Shalev, 2002).

Taken together, these findings provide support for the contention that some persons are inherently more susceptible to difficulties in regulating and coping with stress and, in relation to the proposed model, may be more affected by trauma or its transgenerational effects than others. Further to this, it is important to note the cumulating evidence of Gene x Environment interactions on proneness to affective disorders. Of particular relevance are results that demonstrate that the association between stressful/traumatic life events and depression is moderated by the inheritance of variants in the functional 5-HTT polymorphism in the serotonin transport gene, such that persons who had experienced trauma and who had inherited one or two copies of the short allele on the 5-HTT promoter polymorphism had more symptoms of depression, a higher prevalence of clinical depression, and also had more thoughts of suicide than did counterparts homozygous for the long allele (Caspi, Sugden, Moffit, Taylor, Craig, Harrington, McClay, Mill, Martin, Braithwaite, & Poulton, 2003). In terms of our proposed model, the results of these and other studies raise the possibility that persons who are exposed to terror (directly or transgenerationally) and have vulnerable genotypes are more likely to suffer from more severe reactions than persons beset with one of these risk conditions, but not both.

Alternative Explanations and Models of TETT

Our model is only one attempt to integrate findings into a coherent model TETT; there are other models that may be equally plausible, and they also should be considered. Alternative models could consider family context and parenting as moderators rather than mediators; based on the assumption that trauma-transmission is influenced by, but not actually grounded in or forwarded by the quality of parenting and the family environment. Such models have been used to explain the association between parents and children's post-trauma symptoms, in cases in which both parents and children were exposed to the same stressful events (e.g., Bailey, Hannigan, Delaney-Black, Covington, & Sokol, 2006; Foy, Madvig, Pynoos, & Camilleri, 1996; Proctor, 2006; Scheeringa & Zeanah, 2001; Kliewer et al., 2004). Other models for TETT could name parents' and/or their children's regulatory capacity or HPA axis activity as the mediators or moderators, as suggested by the studies of Maughan and Cicchetti (2002) on maltreated youngsters; Kliewer et al. (2004) on children exposed to community violence; and Katz and Gottman (1997) on children faced with high levels of marital conflict. Other candidates might include children's feelings of safety and security, as suggested in the model of traumatic stress proposed by Pynoos, Steinberg, & Wraith (1995) or social-cognitive skills, as suggested by the work of Schwartz and Proctor (2000) on children who witnessed community violence (also see Meiser-Stedman, 2002). Finally, one could consider children's attachment style as a mediator of TETT, based on the assumption that it is the security of the caregiver-child relationship that determines the degree to which children will tolerate and well-regulate stress (e.g., McCarthy & Taylor, 1999).

Directions for Future Research

We have presented a rudimentary model of the TETT in order to discuss its potential and to further research that focuses on processes of transmission that could "carry" effects of parents' trauma from terror to their children (also see Barenbaum, Ruchkin, & Schwab-Stone, 2004; Feerick & Prinz, 2003). In this section, we describe some of the challenges inherent in this kind of research.

Sample

Questions arise as to where to recruit subjects, how to recruit subjects, and which subjects to recruit. As to locale, it is important to consider the differences in sample composition that may result from different methods of or locales for recruitment. Parents recruited from medical stations may generate extreme samples, comprised of parents and children with more severe disorders; those who answer advertisements may reflect a proportion of victims who want to discuss feelings and, perhaps, those who feel good about the manner in which they have coped with their terror-experiences, feel lucky, or have some other agenda as to why they want to participate in study on terror. In setting criteria for participant selection, researchers need to consider whether or not to include nontraditional families (e.g., single parents) that, on one hand, would increase the generalizability of results but, on the other hand, may confound results and skew interpretation. In this regard, researchers need to consider whether to include parents or children who were traumatized by experiences besides terror, those who had mental health issues prior to their exposure to trauma, and/or individuals who are medicated. We add that almost all studies that have examined parenting to children's response to terror (and community violence) have focused on mothers, not fathers; although fathers are affected by terror, contribute to family dynamics, and could be an important source of resiliency or stress for their children in the context of terror (e.g., Punamaki, Qouta, & El Sarraj, 2001).

Definitions and Diagnoses

Difficulties arise in discerning normal and typical reactions to terror from atypical or pathological responses (Yehuda, Bryant, Marmar, & Zohar, 2005). This is because signs of impairment (e.g., fears of leaving the house) may be normal or abnormal; feelings of sadness may be normal or signs of depression; chronic worry may be normal or a sign of generalized anxiety. For parents of infants, diagnoses may be further complicated by the normal disturbances in sleep and eating that often accompany the postpartum period (review in Ross & McLean, 2006). Diagnoses of very young children may be made difficult due to a lack of developmentally appropriate measures (review in Davis & Siegel, 2000). There also are difficulties in measuring and ranking exposure to terror (experiencing, witnessing, and/or hearing about it) and its consequences.

Design

Disentangling transgenerational effects from direct effects that children's own exposure to terror might have on them is a primary difficulty in studies of TETT. The design offered by Laor et al. (2001), in which parents and children are tracked over time so that changes in parents' feelings can be mapped onto changes in their children's feelings, are more informative than studies in which data are obtained at one time-point only; although the interpretation of correlations remains a problem. The Smith et al. (2001) study carried out on families in Bosnia-Herzegovina suggests some important design features, including: (1) the use of independent data from mothers and children regarding their respective symptoms, together with mothers' and teachers' reading of children's symptoms, (2) the assessment of children and mothers' exposure to war-events, (3) the use of different explanatory (symptom-type, extent of exposure) variables so that contribution of these variables on different aspects of child outcome could be examined independently, and (4) the use of structural equation modeling to evaluate the simultaneous effects of exposure and mothers' distress on child's distress while at the same time quantifying and controlling for the effect of mothers' own distress on the ratings of their children (also see Linares et al., 2001). Using these design features, analyses afforded estimates of contributions by mothers' and child's shared exposure and complex family interactions on the association between mothers' and children's symptoms, so although basically correlational, the results afford more detailed information on mediators, moderators, and pathways to outcome.

Other suggestions are offered by previous research. For instance, in Yehuda et al. (2005), participants were mothers exposed to terror and their children, who were born after the event. This "antenatal" design holds promise because it is one way to assure that children were not directly exposed to the terror attack, although shared genes and shared environmental factors can blur readings of transgenerational effects. Also worthy of mention is the study of Dybdahl (2001), in which mothers' and children's symptoms were assessed before and after a 5-month intervention and compared to those of a control group that received only medical attention. This study offers the advantage of a before and after design, plus mothers and children received the benefits of intervention as part of the study.

Measures

To date, parents' and children's feelings as a result of exposure to terror have been mostly limited to rating scales that reflect symptoms closely aligned to or reflecting trauma (PTSD). This is probably the most direct means of assessing distress-level of victims, but may not capture the profile of effects that parents' trauma has on their children. As suggested by our proposed model, measures that reflect children's internal state at rest, stress-elicited responses, or regulatory deficits also may be important correlates.

For elucidating routes of transmission, it will be important to collect information (from multiple informants) on parenting and family functioning, as well as physiological indices (heart, cortisol) of state regulation. Equally important is the collection of information on potential moderating factors, including the degree to which culture and society help families of terror-victims and the degree to which families have access to these resources (Kaplan et al., 2005).

Developmental Issues

Studies of terror-effects on children and parents need to tune methodology to the age of the children studied (also see Beauchesne et al., 2002; Hagan & The Committee on Psychosocial Aspects of Child and Family Health and the Task Force on Terrorism, 2005). To assess young children's feelings, parents may be one source of information, although their readings of their children's emotions are likely affected by parents' own feelings, mood, and experiences. Further, information derived from parents' reports and descriptions are likely to refer to children's behavior within the home, though children may behave differently in school or with their friends than they do with their family.

New methods of eliciting and evaluating young children's narratives offer reliable and valid avenues for accessing young children's thoughts and feelings about terror and the impact that it has on them and their family. One example of such a tool is the MacArthur Story Stem Battery, which offers children a story-stem, which they are asked to complete with the aid of dolls and props (Emde et al., 2004). Coding the narratives and behavior elicited by the story stem centers on themes, coherence, emotional tone; and these measures can afford insight into children's cognitions about their experiences and their state of mind (Emde, Wolf, & Oppenheim, 2003). For older children and adolescence similar techniques may be useful (e.g., Jones & Kafetsios, 2005) in addition to validated symptom check lists, which can be self-administered.

Ethical Considerations

Ethical issues regarding the questioning of victims about their terror-experiences need to be considered, because the discussion of terror may cause persons who were exposed to it considerable distress, especially if they were severely traumatized by the event(s). Accordingly, research on terror-effects needs to be carried out by persons who are sensitive, well-trained, and compassionate; and it also is important that these assistants are provided supportive supervision on a regular basis during the course of the research study. If and how to offer resources to victims and their families, if needed, requires thoughtful consideration. In all studies, approval of design and methods from ethical committees should be mandatory and their recommendations abided by, in full.

Conclusion

There is much to learn about the impact that parents' exposure and trauma from terror has on their family and on their children's development and well-being. For this, badly needed are studies that go beyond surveys and studies of symptom-prevalence in efforts to examine family functioning, parenting, and child development in households in which one parent or both suffer trauma from terror. Simple models such as the one that we propose may serve as a good beginning for examining transmission processes; and as more data become available, such models should be modified and tuned, accordingly. Research paradigms should include genetic testing, biochemical assays, neuroimaging, and behavioral measures in order to gain a comprehensive view of transmission processes and their effect on children. Finally, we need studies on TETT that use prospective measures in order to track effects of transmission as they unfold; and for this, researchers need to commit to such research for many years. Although challenging, studies on TETT are important for understanding how and under what conditions trauma from terror is transmitted from one generation to another, what the effects look like at different ages, and how long term development may be affected. Sadly, these issues are likely to be of critical importance to the health of children, parents, and their families in many countries throughout the world.

Acknowledgement

This work was partially supported by a grant from the Israel Science Foundation (389/05) to the first author.

References

Abrams, M. S. (1999). Transgenerational transmission of terror: Recent contributions from the literature of family systems approaches to treatment. *American Journal of Psychotherapy, 53*, 225-231.

Abu-Saba, M. B. (1999). War-related trauma and stress characteristics of American University of Beirut students. *Journal of Traumatic Stress, 12*, 201-207.

Almqvist, K., & Broberg, A. G. (2003). Young children traumatized by organized violence together with their mothers- The critical effects of damaged internal representations. *Attachment & Human Development, 5*, 367-380.

Ancharoff, M. R., Munroe, J. F., & Fisher, L. M. (1998). The legacy of combat trauma: Clinical implications of transgenerational transmission. In Y. Danieli (Ed.), *International handbook of multigenerational legacies of trauma* (pp.257-276). New York, NY: Plenum Press.

Apfelbaum, E. (2000). And now what, after such tribulations? Memory and dislocation in the era of uprooting. *American Psychologist, 55*, 1008-1017.

Appleyard, K., Egeland, B., van Dulmen, M. H. M., & Sroufe, L. A. (2005). When more is not better: The role of cumulative risk in child behavior outcomes. *Journal of Child Psychology and Psychiatry, 46*, 235-245.

Auerhahn, N. C., & Laub, D. (1998). Transgenerational memory of the Holocaust. In Y. Danieli (Ed.), *International handbook of multigenerational legacies of trauma* (pp. 21-41). New York: Plenum Press.

Baca, E., Baca-García, E., Pérez-Rodrígues, M. M., & Cabanas, M. L. (2005). Short and long-term effects of terrorist attacks in Spain. In Y. Danieli, D. Brom, D., & J. Sills (Eds.), *The trauma of terrorism: sharing knowledge and shared care, An International Handbook* (pp. 157-173). New York: The Haworth Maltreatment & Trauma Press.

Baerwald, C.G., Panayi, G. S., & Lanchbury, J. S. (1996). A new $Xmn1$ polymorphism in the regulatory region of the corticotrophin-releasing hormone gene. *Human Genetics, 97*, 697-698.

Bailey, B. N., Hannigan, J. H., Delaney-Black, V., Covington, C., & Sokol, R. J. (2006). The role of maternal acceptance in the relation between community violence exposure and child functioning. *Journal of Abnormal Child Psychology, 34*, 57-70.

Barenbaum, J., Ruchkin, V., & Schwab-Sone, M. (2004). The psychosocial aspects of children exposed to war: Practice and policy initiatives. *Journal of Child Psychology and Psychiatry, 45*, 41-62.

Baron, R. M., & Kenny, D. A. (1986). The moderator-mediator variable distinction in social psychological research: Conceptual, strategic, and statistical considerations. *Journal of Personality and Social Psychology, 51*, 1173-1182.

Bat-Zion, N., & Levy-Shiff, R. (1993). Children in war: Stress and coping reactions under the threat of Scud missile attacks and the effect of proximity. In L. A. Leavitt & N. A. Fox (Eds.), *The psychological effects of war and violence on children* (pp. 143-161). Hillsdale, NJ: Lawrence Erlbaum Associates, Inc.

Beauchesne, M. A., Kelley, B. R., Patsdaughter, C. A., & Pickard, J. (2002). Attack on America: Children's reactions and parents' responses. *Journal of Pediatric Health Care, 16*, 213-221.

Becker, D., & Diaz, M. (1998). The social process and the transgenerational transmission of trauma in Chile. In Y. Danieli (Ed.), *International handbook of multigenerational legacies of trauma* (pp. 435-446). New York: Plenum Press.

Bleich, A., Gelkopf, M., Melamed, Y., & Solomon, Z. (2006). Mental health and resiliency following 44 months of terrorism: a survey of an Israeli national representative sample. *BMC Medicine, 4*, 21-32.

Bleich, A., Gelkopf, M., & Solomon, Z. (2003) Exposure to terrorism, stress-related mental health symptoms, and coping behaviors among a nationally representative sample in Israel. *JAMA, 290*, 612-20.

Boscarino, J. A. (1996). Posttraumatic stress disorder, exposure to combat, and lower plasma cortisol among Vietnam veterans: findings and clinical implications. *Journal of Consulting and Clinical Psychology, 64*, 191-201.

Bowlby, J. (1969/1982). *Attachment and loss: Vol. 1. Attachment.* New York: Basic Books.

Braungart-Rieker, J. M., & Stifter, C. A. (1996). Infants' responses to frustrating situations: Continuity and change in reactivity and regulation. *Child Development, 67*, 1767-1779.

Brewin, C. R., Andrews, B., & Valentine, J. D. (2000). Meta-analysis of risk factors for posttraumatic stress disorders in trauma-exposed adults. *Journal of Consulting and Clinical Psychology, 68*, 748-766.

Bronfenbrenner, U. (2005). Making human beings human: Bioecological perspectives on human development. Thousand Oaks, CA: Sage Publications Limited.

Bryce, J. W., Walker, N., Ghorayeb, F., & Kanj, M. (1989). Life experiences, response styles and mental health among mothers and children in Beirut, Lebanon. *Social Science & Medicine, 28*, 685-95.

Carter, C. S. (1998). Neuroendocrine perspective on social attachment and love. *Psychoendocrinology, 23*, 779-818.

Caspi, A., Sugden, K., Moffit, T. W., Taylor, A., Craig, I. W., Harrington, H., McClay, J., Mill, J., Martin, J., Braithwaite, A., & Poulton, R. (2003). Influence of life stress on depression: Moderation by a polymorphism in the 5-HTT gene. *Science, 301*, 386-389.

Chimienti, G., Nasr, J., & Khalifehi, I. (1989). Children's reaction to war-related stress II. The influence of gender, age, and mothers' reaction. *International Journal of Mental Health, 21*, 72-86.

Coates, S., & Schecter, D. (2004). Preschoolers' traumatic stress post-9/11: relational and developmental perspective. *Psychiatric Clinics of North America, 27*, 473-489.

Danieli, Y. (Ed). (1998). *International handbook of multigenerational legacies of trauma.* (pp. 623-637). New York, NY, US: Plenum Press.

Danieli, Y., Brom, D., & Sills, J. (2004). The trauma of terrorism: Contextual considerations. In Y. Danieli, D. Brom, & J. Sills (Eds.), *The trauma of terrorism: Sharing Knowledge and shared care, An international handbook* (pp. 19-32). New York: Haworth Maltreatment & Trauma Press.

Daud, A., Skoglund, E., & Ryedelius, P. A. (2005). Children in families of torture victims: Transgenerational transmission of parents' traumatic experiences to their children. *International Journal of Social Welfare, 14,* 23-32.

Davis, L., & Siegel, L. J. (2000). Posttraumatic stress disorder in children and adolescents: A review and analysis. *Clinical Child and Family Psychology Review, 3,* 135-154.

Dawes A., Tredoux, C., & Feinstine A. (1989). Political violence in South Africa: Some effects on children of the violent destruction of their community. *International Journal of Mental Health, 18,* 16-43.

Dekel, R. (2004). Motherhood in a time of terror: Subjective experiences and responses of Israeli mothers. *Affilia, 19,* 24-38.

Duran, E., Duran, B., Brave Heart, M.Y.H., & Yellow Horse-Davis, S. (1998). Healing the American Indian soul wound. In Y. Danieli (Ed.), *International handbook of multigenerational legacies of trauma* (pp. 341-354). New York: Plenum Press.

Dybdahl, R. (2001). Children and mothers in war: An outcome study of a psychosocial intervention program. *Child Development, 72,* 1214-1230.

Edelman, L., Kordon, D., & Lagos, M. (1998). Transmission of trauma: The Argentine case. In Y. Danieli (Ed.). *International handbook of multigenerational legacies of trauma* (pp. 447-465). New York: Plenum Press.

Emde, R. N., Wolf, D.P., & Oppenheim, D. (2003). *Revealing the inner worlds of young children. The MacArthur Story Stem Battery and parent-child narratives.* New York, U.S.A.: Oxford University Press.

Engel, S. M., Berkowitz, G. S., Wolff, G. S., Wolff, M. S., & Yehuda, R. (2005), Psychological trauma associated with the World Trade Center attacks and its effect on pregnancy outcome. *Paediatric and Perinatal Epidemiology. 19,* 334-341

Essex, M. J., Klein, M. H., Cho, E., & Kalin, N. H. (2002). Maternal stress beginning in infancy may sensitize children to later stress exposure: Effects on cortisol and behavior. *Biological Psychiatry, 52,* 776-784.

Fairbrother, G., Stuber, J., Galea, S., Fleischman, A. R., & Pfefferbaum, B. (2003). Posttraumatic stress reactions in New York City children after the September 11, 2001, terrorist attacks. *Ambulatory Pediatrics, 3,* 304-311.

Farver, J. A. M., Xu, Y., Eppe, S., Fernandex, A., & Schwartz, D. (2005). Community violence, family confliect and preschoolers' socioemotional functioning. *Developmental Psychology, 41,* 160-170.

Fearon, R. M. P., & Mansell, W. (2001). Cognitive perspectives on unresolved loss: Insights from the study of PTSD. *Bulletin of the Menninger Clinic, 65,* 380-396.

Feerick, M. M., & Prinz, R. J. (2003). Next steps in research on children exposed to community violence on war/terrorism. *Clinical Child and Family Psychology Review, 6,* 303-305.

Felitti, V. J., Anda, R. F., Nordenberg, D., Williamson, D.F, Spitz, A. M., Edwards, V., Koss, M. P., & Marks, J. S. (1998). Relationship of childhood abuse and household dysfunction to may of the leading causes of death in adults: The Adverse Childhood Experiences Study. *American Journal of Preventive Medicine, 14,* 245-258.

Felsen, I. (1998). Transgenerational transmission of the effects of the Holocaust: The North American research perspective. In Y. Danieli (Ed.), *International handbook of multigenerational legacies of trauma* (pp. 43-68). New York: Plenum Press.

Finzi-Dottan, R., Dekel, R., Lavi, T., & Su'ali T. (2006). Posttraumatic stress disorder reactions among children with learning disabilities exposed to terror attacks. *Comprehensive Psychiatry, 67*, 144-151.

Foy, D. W., Madvig, B. T., Pynoos, R. S., Camilleri, A J. (1996). Etiological factors in the development of posttraumatic stress disorder in children and adolescents. *Journal of School Psychology, 34*, 133-145.

Fremont, W. P. (2004). Childhood reactions to terrorism-induced trauma: A review of the past 10 years. *Journal of American Academy of Child and Adolescent Psychiatry, 43*, 381- 392.

Gable, S., & Isabella, R. A. (1992). Maternal contributions to infant regulation of arousal. *Infant Behavior and Development, 15*, 95-107.

Galea, S., Ahern, J., Resnick, H., Kilpatrick, D., Bucuvalas, M., Gold, J., & Vlahov, D. (2002). Psychological sequelae of the September 11 terrorist attacks in New York City. *New England Journal of Medicine, 346*, 982-987.

Galea. S., Vlahov, Resnick, H., Ahern, J., Susser, E., Gold, J., Bucuvalas, M., & Kilpatrick, D. (2003). Trends of probable post-traumatic stress disorder in New York City after the September 11 terrorist attacks. *American Journal of Epidemiology, 158*, 514-524.

Goenjian, A. K., Yehuda, R., Pynoos, R. S., Steinberg, A. M, Tashjian, M., & Yang R. K, Najarian, L.M., & Fairbanks, L. A. (1996). Basal cortisol, dexamethasone suppression of cortisol, and MHPG in adolescents after the 1988 earthquake in Armenia. *American Journal of Psychiatry, 153*, 929-934.

Goldsmith, H. H., & Lemery, K. S. (2000). Linking temperamental fearfulness and anxiety symptoms: A behavior-genetic perspective. *Biological Psychiatry, 48*, 1199-1209.

Gu, J., Sadler, L., Daiger, S., Wells, D., & Wagner, M. (1993). Dinucleotide repeat polymorphism at the CRH gene. *Human Molecular Genetics, 2*, 85.

Gunnar, M. & Vazquez, D.M. (2001). Low cortisol and a flattening of the expected day-time rhythm: Potential indices of risk in human development. *Development and Psychopathology, 13*, 516-538.

Hagan, J. F. Jr, & The Committee on Psychosocial Aspects of Child and Family Health and the Task Force on Terrorism. (2005). Psychosocial implications of disaster or terrorism on children: A guide for the pediatrician. *Pediatrics, 116*, 787-95.

Haley, D. W., & Stansbury, K. (2003). Infant stress and parent responsiveness: Regulation of physiology and behavior during still-face and reunion. *Child Development, 74*, 1534-1546.

Hart, J., Gunnar, M., Cicchetti, D. (1996). Altered neuroendocrine activity in maltreated children related to symptoms of depression. *Development and Psychopathology, 8*, 201-214.

Heim, C., & Nemeroff, C. B. (2001). The role of childhood trauma in the neurobiology of mood and anxiety disorders: Pre clinical and clinical studies. *Biological Psychiatry, 49*, 1023-1039.

Hofer, M.A. (1994). Early relationship as regulators of infant physiology and behavior. *Acta Paediatrica Supplementum, 397*, 9-18.

Hughes, D., & Chen, L. (1999). The nature of parents' race-related communications to children: A developmental perspective. In C. S. Tamis-LeMonda, & L. Balter (Eds.), *Child psychology: A handbook of contemporary issues* (pp.467-490). New York: Psychology Press.

Jones, L., & Kafetsios, K. (2005). Exposure to political violence and psychological well-being in Bosnian adolescents: A mix method approach. *Clinical Child Psychology and Psychiatry, 10*, 157-176.

Jordan, B. K., Marmar, C. R., Fairbank, J. A., Schlenger, W. E., Kulka, R. A., Hough, R. L., & Weiss, D. S. (1992). Problems in families of male Vietnam veterans with posttraumatic stress disorder. *Journal of Consulting and Clinical Psychology, 60*, 916-926.

Joshi, P. T., & O'Donnell, D. A. (2003). Consequences of child exposure to war and terrorism. *Clinical Child and Family Psychology Review, 6*, 275-292.

Kaitz, M., & Maytal, H. (2005). Interactions between anxious mothers and infants: An integration of theory and research findings. *Infant Mental Health Journal.* (in press).

Kalayjan, A.S., Shahinian, S. P., Gergerian, E.L., & Saraydarian, L. (1996). Coping with Ottoman Turkish genocide: An exploration of the experience of Armenian survivors. *Journal of Traumatic Stress, 9*, 87-97.

Kaplan, .Z, Matar, M.A., Kamin, R., Sadan, T., & Cohen, H. (2005). Stress-related responses after 3 years of exposure to terror in Israel: Are ideological-religious factors associated with resilience. *Journal of Clinical Psychiatry, 66*, 1146-1154.

Katz, L. F., & Gottman, J. M. (1997). Buffering children from marital conflict and dissolution. *Journal of Clinical Child Psychology, 256*, 157-171.

Kellerman, N. P. F. (2001). Transmission of Holocaust Trauma- An integrative view. *Psychiatry, 64*, 256-267.

King, S., & Laplante, D. P. The effects of prenatal maternal stress on children's cognitive development. Project Ice Storm. *Stress, 8*, 35-45.

Kliewer, W., Cunningham, J. N., Diehl, R., Parrish, K. A., Walker, J. M., Atiyeh, C., Neace, B., Duncan, L., Taylor, K., & Mejia, R. (2004). Violence exposure and adjustment in inner-city youth: Child and caregiver emotion regulation skill, caregiver-child relationship quality and neighborhood cohesion as protective factors. *Journal of Clinical Child and Adolescent Psychology, 33*, 477-487.

Kliewer, W., Lepore, S. J., Oskin, D., & Johnson, P. D. (1998). The role of social and cognitive processes in children's adjustment to community violence. *Journal of Consulting and Clinical Psychology, 66*, 199-209.

Koplewicz, H. S., Vogel, J. M., Solanto, M. V., Morrissey, F., Alono, C. M., Abikoff, H., Gallagher, R., & Novick, R. M. (2002). Child and parent response to the 1993 World Trade Center bombing. *Journal of Traumatic Stress, 15*, 77-83.

Laor, N., Wolmer, L., & Cohen, D. J. (2001). Mothers' functioning and children's symptoms 5 years after a SCUD missile attack. *American Journal of Psychiatry, 158*, 1020-1026.

Laor, N., Wolmer, L., Mayes, L. C, Geshon, A., Weizman, R., & Cohen, D. J. (1997). Israeli preschools under Scuds: A 30-month follow-up. *Journal of American Academy of Child and Adolescent Psychiatry, 36*, 349-356.

Laor, N., Wolmer, L., Mayes, L.C., Golomb, A., Silverberg, D. S., Weizman, R., & Cohen, D. J. (1996). Israeli preschoolers under Scud missile attack. A developmental perspective on risk-modifying factors. *Archives of General Psychiatry, 53*, 416-423.

Leonardo, E. D., & Hen, R. (2006). Genetics of affective and anxiety disorders. *Annual Review of Psychology, 57,* 117-37

Lesch, K. P., Bengel, D., Heils, A., Saol, S. Z, Greenberg B D., Petri, S., Benjamin, J., Muller, C. R., Hamer, D.H., & Murphy, D. L. (1996). Association of anxiety-related traits with a polymorphism in the serotonin transporter gene regulatory region. *Science, 274,* 1527-31.

Levy, M. (2006). Maternity in the wake of terrorism: Rebirth or retraumatization? *Journal of Prenatal and Perinatal Psychology and Health, 20,* 221-248.

Lichtman, H. (1984). Parental communication of Holocaust experience and personality characteristics among second-generation survivors. *Journal of Clinical Psychology, 40,* 914-924.

Lifton, R. J. (2005). Americans as Survivors. *New England Journal of Medicine,* 352, 2263-2265.

Linares, L. O., Heeren, T., Bronfman, E., Zuckerman, B., Augustyn, M., & Tronick, E. (2002). A mediational model for the impact of exposure to community violence on early child behavior problems. *ChildDevelopment, 72,* 639-52.

Lyons-Ruth, K., Yellin, C., Melnick, S., & Atwood, G. (2005). Expanding the concept of unresolved mental states: Hostile/Helpless states of mind on the Adult Attachment Interview are associated with disrupted mother-infant communication and infant disorganization. *Development and Psychopathology, 17,* 1-23.

Malatesta-Magai, C. (1991). Emotion expression during infancy. In J. Garber & K. A. Dodge (Eds.), The development of emotion regulation and dysregulation (pp. 303-322). New York: Cambridge University Press.

Maughan, A., & Cicchetti, D. (2002). Impact of child maltreatment and interadult violence on children's emotion regulation abilities and socioemotional adjustment. *Child Development, 73,* 1525-1542.

Mayes, L. C., Bornstein, M. H., Chawarska, K. Haynes, O. M., & Granger, R. H. (1996). Impaired regulation of arousal in 3-month-od infants exposed prenatally to cocaine and other drugs. *Development and Psychopathology, 8,* 29-42.

McCarthy, G., & Taylor, A. (1999). Avoidant/ambivalent attachment style as a mediator between abusive childhood experiences and adult relationship difficulties. *Journal of Child Psychology and Psychiatry, 40,* 465-477.

McEwen, B. S. (1998). Protective and damaging effects of stress mediators. *New England Journal of Medicine, 338,* 171-9.

Meijer, A. (1985). Child psychiatric sequelae of maternal war stress. *Acta Psychiatrica Scandinavia,* 72, 505-511.

Meiser-Stedman, R. (2002). Towards a cognitive-behavioral model of PTSD in children and adolescents. *Clinical Child and Family Psychology Review, 5,* 217-232.

Mertesacker, B., Bade, U., Haverkock, A., & Pauli-Pott, U. (2004). Predicting maternal reactivity/sensitivity: The role of infant emotionality, maternal depressiveness/anxiety, and social support. *Infant Mental Health Journal, 25,* 47-61.

Miller, G. E., Chen, E., & Zhou, E. S. (2007). If it goes up, must it come down? Chronic stress and the Hypothalamic-Pituitary-Adrenocortical Axis in humans. *Psychological Bulletin, 133,* 25-45.

Moore, G.A., & Calkins, S.D. (2004). Infants' vagal regulation in the still-face paradigm is related to dyadic coordination of mother-infant interaction. *Developmental Psychology, 40*, 1068-1080.

Mowder, B. A., Guttman, M., Rubinson, F., Sossin, K. M. (2006). Parents, children, and trauma: Parent role perceptions and behavior related to the 9/11 tragedy. *Journal of Child and Family Studies, 15*, 733-743.

Nachmias, M., Gunnar, M., Mangelsdorf, S., Parritz, R. H. & Buss, K. (1996). Behavioral inhibition: The moderating role of attachment security. *Child Development, 67*, 508-522.

Nagata, D. K., & Cheng, W. J. Y. (2003). Transgenerational communication of race-related trauma by Japanese American former internees. *American Journal of Orthopsychiatry, 73*, 266-278.

Norris, F., H., Friedman, M. J., Watson, P. J., & Byrne, C. N. (2002a). 60,000 disaster victims speak: Part I. An empirical review of the empirical literature, 1981-2002. *Psychiatry, 65*, 207-239.

North, C. S., Nixon, S. J., Shariat, S., Mallonee, S., McMillen, J. C., Spitznagel, E. L., & Smith, E. M. (1999). Psychiatric disorders among survivors of the Oklahoma City bombing. *JAMA, 25, 282*, 755-762.

Ohara, K., Nagai, M., Suziki, Y., Ochiai, M, & Ohara, K. (1998). Association between anxiety disorders and a functional polymorphism in the serotonin transporter gene. *Psychiatry Research, 81*, 277-279.

Okner, D. F., & Flaherty, J. (1989). Parental communication and psychological distress in children of Holocaust survivors: A comparison between the U.S. and Israel. *International Journal of Social Psychiatry, 35*, 265-73

Oppenheim, D. (2006). Child, parent, and parent-child emotion narratives: implications for developmental psychopathology. *Development and Psychopathology, 18*, 771-790.

Orr, S. P., Metzger, L. J., Lasko, N. B., Macklin, M. L., Hu, F. B., Shalev, A. Y., Pitman, R. K., Eisen, S. A., Gilbertson, M. W., Gillette, G. M., Goldberg, J., Gurvits, T. V., Henderson, W. G., Keane, T. M., Lyons, M. J., McFarlane, A. C., Paige, S. R., True, W. R., Tsuang, M. T., Weathers, F. W., Yehuda, R. (2003). Physiologic responses to sudden, loud tones in monozygotic twins discordant for combat exposure: Association with posttraumatic stress disorder. *Archives of General Psychiatry, 60*, 283-288.

Overstreet, S., & Braun, S. (2000). Exposure to community violence and post-traumatic stress symptoms: Mediating factors. *American Journal of Orthopsychiatry, 70*, 263-271.

Perry, B. D., & Azad, I. (1999). Posttraumatic stress disorders in children and adolescents. *Current Opinion in Pediatrics, 11*, 310-321.

Perry, B. D., & Pollard, R. (1998). Homeostasis, stress, trauma, and adaptation. A neurodevelopmental view of childhood trauma. *Child and Adolescent Psychiatric Clinics of North America*, 7, 33-51.

Perry, B. D., Pollard, R. A., Blakely, T. L., Baker, W. L., & Vigilante, D. (1995). Childhood trauma, the neurobiology of adaptation and 'use-dependent' development of the brain: How 'states' become 'traits'. *Infant Mental Health Journal, 16*, 271-291.

Phillips, D., Prince, S., & Schiebelhut, L. (2004). Elementary school children's responses 3 months after the September 11 terrorist attacks: a study in Washington, DC. *American Journal of Orthopsychiatry. 74*, 509-528.

Pierce, M. (2006). Transgenerational transmission of trauma: What we have learned from our work with mother and infants affected by the trauma of 9/11. *International Journal of Psychoanalysis, 87*, 555-557.

Pine, D. S., Costello, J., & Masten, A. (2005). Trauma, proximity, and developmental psychopathology: The effects of war and terrorism on children. *Neuropsychopharmacology, 30,* 1781-1792.

Proctor, L. J. (2006). Children growing up in a violent community: The role of the family. *Aggression and Violent Behavior, 11,* 558-576.

Punamäki, R. L., Qouta, S., & El Sarraj, E. (1997). Relationships between traumatic events, children's gender, and political activity, and perceptions of parenting styles. *International Journal of Behavioral Development, 21,* 91-109.

Punamäki, R. L., Qouta, S., & El Sarraj, E. (2001). Resiliency factors predicting psychological adjustment after political violence among Palestinian children. *International Journal of Behavioral Development, 25,* 256-267.

Punamäki, R. L., Qouta, S., El Sarraj, E., & Montgomery, E. (2006). Psychological distress and resources among siblings and parents exposed to traumatic events. *International Journal of Behavioral Development, 30,* 385-397.

Pynoos, R. S., Steinberg, A. M., Piacentini, J. C. (1999). A developmental psychopathology model of childhood traumatic stress and intersection with anxiety disorders. *Biological Psychiatry, 46,* 1542-1554.

Pynoos, R. S., Steinberg, A. J., & Wraith, R. (1995). A developmental model of childhood traumatic stress. In D. Cicchetti & D. J. Cohen (Eds.). *Manual of developmental psychopathology* (pp. 72-95). New York: John Wiley.

Qouta, S., Punamäki, R. L., & El Sarraj, E. (2003). Prevalence and determinants of PTSD among Palestinian children exposed to military violence. *European Child & Adolescent Psychiatry.* 12, 265-272.

Qouta, S., Punamäki, R. L., & El Sarraj, E. (2005). Mother-child expression of psychological distress in war trauma. *Clinical Child Psychology and Psychiatry, 10,* 135-156.

Raphael, B., Swan, P., & Martinek, N. (1998). Transgenerational aspects of trauma for Australian Aboriginal people. In Y. Danieli (Ed.). *International handbook of multigenerational legacies of trauma* (pp. 327-340). New York: Plenum Press.

Reck, C., Hunt, A., Fuchs, T., Weiss, R., Noon, A., Moehler, E., Downing, G., Tronick, E. Z., & Mund, S. (2003). Interactive regulation of affect in postpartum depressed mothers and their infants: An overview. *Psychopathology, 37,* 272-280.

Rosenheck, R. (1986). Impact of posttraumatic stress disorder of World War II on the next generation. *Journal of Nervous and Mental Disease, 174,* 319-27.

Rosenheck, R., & Fontana, A. (1998). Transgenerational effects of abusive violence on the children of Vietnam combat veterans. *Journal of Traumatic Stress, 11,* 731-742.

Rosmond, R., Dallman, M. F., & Bjontrop, P. (1998). Stress-related cortisol secretion in man: Relation with abdominal obesity and endocrine, metabolic and hemodynamic abnormalities. *The Journal of Clinical Endocrinology & Metabolism, 83,* 1853-1859.

Ross, L. E., & McLean, L. M. (2006). Anxiety disorders during pregnancy and the postpartum period: A systematic review. *Journal of Clinical Psychiatry, 67,* 1285-1298.

Rossman, B. B. R., Bingham, R. D., & Emde, R. N. (1997). Symptomology and adaptive functioning for children exposed to normative stressors, dog attack and parental violence. *Journal of American Academy of Child and Adolescent Psychiatry, 36,* 1089-1097.

Rubin, K. H., Burgess, K. B., & Hastings, P. D. (2002). Stability and social-behavioral consequences of toddlers' inhibited temperament and parenting behaviors. *Child Development, 73,* 483-495.

Scheeringa, MS., & Zeanah, C.H. (2001). A relational perspective on PTSD in early childhood. *Journal of Traumatic Stress, 14,* 799-814.

Schlenger, W. E., Caddell, J. M., Ebert, L., Jordan, B. K., Rourke, K. M., Wilson, D., Thalji, L., Dennis, J. M., Fairbank, J. A., & Kulka, R. A. (2002). Psychological reactions to terrorist attacks: Finds from the National Study of American's Reactions to September 11. *JAMA, 288,* 581-588.

Schnurr, P. P., & Jankowski, M. K. (1999). Physical health and post-traumatic stress disorder: review and synthesis. *Seminars in Clinical Neuropsychiatry, 4,* 295-304. Schore, A.N. (2001). The effects of a secure attachment relationship on right brain development, affect regulation, and infant mental health. *Infant Mental Health Journal, 22,* 7-66.

Schore, A. N. (2002). Dysregulation of the right brain: A fundamental mechanism of traumatic attachment and the psychopathogenesis of posttraumatic stress disorder. *Australian and New Zealand Journal of Psychiatry, 36,* 9-30.

Schuster, M. A., Stein, B. D., Jaycox, L. H., Collins, R. L., Marshall, G. N., Elliott, M. N., Zhou, A. J., Kanouse, D. E., Morrison, J. L., & Berry, S. H. (2001). A national survey of stress reactions after the September 11, 2001, terrorist attacks. *New England Journal of Medicine, 345,* 1507-1512.

Schwartz, D., Proctor, L. J. (2000). Community violence exposure and children's social adjustment in the school peer group: the mediating roles of emotion regulation and social cognition. *Journal of Consulting and Clinical Psychology, 68,* 670-83.

Segman, R. H., Cooper-Kazaz, R., Macciardi, F., Goltser, T., Halfon, Y., Dobroborski, T., & Shalev, A. Y. (2002). Association between the dopamine transporter gene and posttraumatic stress disorder. *Molecular Psychiatry, 7,* 903-907.

Shalev, A. Y. (2004). Further lessons from 9/11: Does stress equal trauma. *Psychiatry, 67,* 174-177.

Shaw, J. A. (2003). Children exposed to war/terrorism. *Clinical Child and Family Psychology Review, 6,* 237-246.

Silow, C. J. (1993) Holocaust survivors: A study of the long-term effects of post-traumatic stress and its relationship to parenting attitudes and behaviors. Ann Arbor, MI: UMI Dissertation services

Silver, R. C., Holman, E. A., McIntosh, D. N., Poulin, M., & Gil-Rivas, V. (2002). Nationwide longitudinal study of psychological responses to September 11. *JAMA, 288,* 1235-1244.

Smith, P., Perrin, S., Yule, W., & Rabe-Hesketh, S. (2001). War exposure and maternal reactions in the psychological adjustment of children from Bosnia-Hercegovina. *Journal Child Psychology and Psychiatry, 42,* 395-404.

Smolka, M.N., Schumann, G., Wrase, J., Grusser, S.M., Flor, H., Mann, K., Braus, D. F., Goldman, D., Buchel, C., & Heinz, A. (2005). Catechol-O-methyltransferase val158met genotype affects processing of emotional stimuli in the amygdala and prefrontal cortex. *Journal of Neuroscience, 25,* 836-842.

Solomon, Z. (1998). Transgenerational effects of the Holocaust: The Israeli research perspective. In Y. Danieli (Ed.), *International handbook of multigenerational legacies of trauma* (pp. 69-83). New York: Springer.

Solomon, Z., Kotler, M., & Mikulincer, M. (1988). Combat-related posttraumatic stress disorder among second-generation Holocaust survivors: Preliminary findings. *American Journal of Psychiatry, 145*, 865-868.

Spangler, G., Schieche, M., Ilg, U., Maier, U., & Ackermann, C. (1994). Maternal sensitivity as an external organizer for biobehavioral regulation in infancy, *Developmental Psychobiology, 27*, 425-437.

Stein, M. B., Jang, K. L., Taylor, S., Vernon, P. A., & Livesley, W. J. (2002). Genetic and environmental influences on trauma exposure and posttraumatic stress disorder symptoms: A twin study. American Journal of Psychiatry, 159, 1675-1681.

Stuber, J., Fairbrother, G., Galea, S., Pferfferbaum, B., Wilson-Genderson, M., & Vlahov, D. (2002). Determinants of counseling for children in Manhattan after the September 11 attacks. *Psychiatric Services, 53*, 815-821.

Suozzi, J. M., & Motta, R. W. (2004). The relationship between combat exposure and the transfer of trauma-like symptoms to offspring of veterans. *Traumatology, 10*, 17-37.

True, W. R., Rice, J., Eisen, S. A, Heath, A. C., Goldberg, J., Lyons, M. J., & Nowak, J. (1993). A twin study of genetic and environmental contributions to liability for posttraumatic stress symptoms. *Archives of General Psychiatry, 50*, 257-265.

Tucker, P. M., Pfefferbaum, B., North, C. S., Kent, A., Burgin, C. E., Parker, D. W., Hossain, A., Jeon-Slaughter, H., & Trautman, R. P. (2007). Physiological reactivity despite emotional resilience several years after direct exposure to terrorism. *American Journal of Psychiatry, 164*, 230-235.

van IJzendoorn, M. H., Bakermans-Kranenburg, M. J., & Sagi-Schwartz, A. (2003). Are children of Holocaust survivors less well-adapted: A meta-analytic investigation of secondary traumatization. *Journal of Traumatic Stress, 16*, 459-469.

Verger, P., Dab, W., Laming, D. L., Loze, Y-Y, Deschaseaux-Voinet, C., Abenhaim, L., & Rouillon, F. (2004). The psychological impact of terrorism: An epidemiologic study of posttraumatic stress disorder and associated factors in victims of the 1995-1996 bombings in France. *American Journal of Psychiatry, 161*, 1384-1389.

Volkan, VD. (2001). Transgenerational transmissions and chosen traumas: An aspect of large-group identity. *Group Analysis, 34*, 79-97.

Volkan, V. (2002). September 11 and societal regression. *Group Analysis, 35*, 456-483.

Warren, S. L., Gunnar, M. R., Kagan, J., Anders, T. F., Simmens, S. J., Rones, M., Wease, S., Aron, E., Dahl, R. E., Sroufe, L. A. (2003). Maternal panic disorder: infant temperament, neurophysiology, and parenting behaviors. *Journal American Academy of Child and Adolescent Psychiatry, 42*, 814-825.

Weingarten, K. (2004). Witnessing the effects of political violence in families: Mechanism of transgenerational transmission and clinical interventions. *Journal of Marital and Family Therapy, 30*, 45-59.

Wüst, S., Federenko, I. S., Van Rossum, E. F. C., Koper, J. W., Kumsta, R., Entringer, S., & Hellhammer, D. H. A. (2004). A psychobiological perspective on genetic determinants of hypothalamus-pituitary- adrenal axis activity. *Annals of the NewYork Academy of Sciences, 1032*, 52-62.

Yehuda, R., Bryant, R., Marmar, C., & Zohar, J. (2005). Pathological responses to terrorism. *Neuropsychopharmacology,* 1-13.

Yehuda, R., Golier, J. A., Kaufman, S. (2005). Circadian rhythm of salivary cortisol in Holocaust survivors with and without PTSD. *American Journal of Psychiatry, 162,* 998-1000.

Yehuda, R., Engel, S. M., Brand, S. M., Seckl, J., Marcus, S. M., & Berkowitz, G.S. (2005). Transgenerational effects of posttraumatic stress disorder in babies of mothers exposed to the World Trade Center attacks during pregnancy, *Journal of Clinical Endocrinology & Metabolism, 90,* 4115-4118.

Yehuda, R., Halligan, S.L., & Grossman, R. (2001). Childhood trauma and risk for PTSD: Relations to transgenerational effects of trauma, parental PTSD, and cortisol excretion. *Development and Psychopathology, 13,* 733-753.

Yehuda, R., Schmeidler, J.,Giller, E. L. Jr., Siever, L. J., & Binder-Brynes, K. (1998a). Relationship between posttraumatic stress disorder characteristics of Holocaust survivors and their adult offspring. *American Journal of Psychiatry, 155,* 841-843.

Yehuda, R., Schmeidler, J., Wainberg, M., Binder-Brynes, K., & Duvdevani, T. (1998b). Vulnerability to posttraumatic stress disorder in adult offspring of Holocaust survivors. *American Journal of Psychiatry, 155,* 1163-1171.

In: Global Terrorism Issues and Developments
Editor: Rene A. Larche, pp. 213-232

ISBN: 978-1-60021-930-6
© 2008 Nova Science Publishers, Inc.

Chapter 9

CHEMICAL TERRORISM: SARIN NERVE GAS AND OTHER TOXIC NERVE AGENTS

Yasuharu Tokuda[*]

Clinical Practice Evaluation and Research Center
St. Luke's Life Science Institute
9-1 Akashi-cho, Chuo City, Tokyo 104-8560 Japan

Abstract

Chemical warfare agents have been employed previously as a weapon of war on several occasions, from World War I to the Gulf War. Among chemical warfare agents, nerve gas "sarin" was used for the first time as a weapon of terrorism in the 1990s. The 1994 Matsumoto sarin attack in Japan was the first chemical terrorism attack against the general public by a religious cult. In the 1995 Tokyo subway sarin attack, the same religious cult released sarin gas into crowded subway commuter trains during the morning rush hour. Twelve passengers died, and about 5500 people were harmed. Sarin is a highly toxic nerve gas that can cause death within minutes or a few hours. The biochemical mechanism of nerve gas involves cholinergic hyperstimulation by inhibition of the crucial enzyme "acetylcholinesterase". Therapy for nerve agent toxicity is divided into three major categories, including decontamination, respiratory support, and antidotes. All of these therapies should be provided simultaneously as soon as possible after the exposure. In this chapter, I will review toxicology, assessment, management, and prevention for chemical terrorism of sarin nerve gas as well as other toxic nerve agents. To minimize the possible catastrophic impact on the public, I will provide recommendations based on detailed analysis of the Tokyo subway sarin attack and a systematic review of the current scientific literature.

Keywords: Chemicals; Emergency medical service; Emergency medical technician; Intoxication; Poisoning; Toxicity; Transport

---

[*] Phone and fax: 81-3-5550-2426

Introduction

Similarly to other weapons of mass destruction, chemical warfare agents are lethal and extremely disabling. Although use of chemical weapons represents a breach of international law as well as a grave violation of human rights, chemical weapons have been employed in conflict, warfare, and terrorism (1, 2). Among chemical weapons, nerve gas agents, such as sarin, have produced serious illnesses and casualties in civilians, military, police, security persons as well as healthcare providers in previous wars and terrorist attacks (3). The mechanisms of toxicity of nerve gas agents block a life-sustaining enzyme acetylcholinesterase, and thus they produce symptoms and signs of generalized cholinergic hyperactivity. The 1995 Tokyo subway sarin poisoning by the Aum Shinrikyo religious cult illustrated the potential impact of nerve gas chemical terrorism in an urban setting (4-8). In that attack, twelve people died and more than 5500 people were harmed.

Under the post-cold war context, few countries exist without the threat of terrorism, in which a nerve gas could be chosen as a mode of indiscriminate attack. If used as offensive weapons under certain meteorological conditions, nerve gas agents could cause large-scale mass casualties (6). Victims may present in enormous numbers and overwhelm local medical resources (7). Hostile use of nerve gas agents could cause significant impacts on emergency medical systems on an unprecedented scale (8). Therefore, healthcare providers need to be familiar with toxicology, assessment, management and prevention for illnesses caused by these agents.

In this chapter, I will summarize the state-of-the art knowledge about nerve agents based on a review of the literature on toxicology and disaster epidemiology regarding nerve gases as well as analysis of the Matsumoto City and the Tokyo subway sarin poisonings, both in Japan. I will also make recommendations in scope to address effective mass casualty management strategies when facing the potential catastrophe related to attacks by toxic nerve agents.

Toxicology

1. Nerve Agents

Nerve agents are the most toxic chemical warfare agents. Most nerve agents were originally produced in a search for insecticides, but because of their extreme toxicity, they were evaluated for military use. They are classified as phosphorus-containing organic chemicals, which are chemically similar to organophosphate pesticides. They exert their biological effects by inhibiting the acetylcholinesterase enzyme, which normally relaxes the activity of acetylcholine, a neurotransmitter (9). Consequently, accumulating acetylcholine at receptor sites creates an acute cholinergic crisis. Death can ensue from respiratory depression within seconds to minutes after exposure if no treatment is provided (2).

Classic nerve agents include tabun (also designated as GA), sarin (GB), soman (GD), cyclosarin (GF), and VX (Table 1). The G-series nerve agents, which were named because German scientists first synthesized them, have the history of beginning with GA in 1936. GB was discovered next in 1938, followed by GD in 1944 and finally, GF in 1949.

Table 1. Selected physical characteristics of nerve agents[*]

Characteristic	Tabun	Sarin	Soman	VX
Color	colorless	colorless	colorless	amber
Taste	tasteless	tasteless	tasteless	tasteless
Odor	fruity	oderless	camphor	oderless
Specific gravity†	1.073	1.089	1.022	1.008
Molecular weight (daltons)	162.3	140.1	182.2	267.4

[*] Based on Agency for Toxic Substances and Disease Registry, Medical management guidelines for nerve agents; tabun (GA); sarin (GB); soman (GD); and VX. Centers for Disease Control and Prevention. 2007

† Specific gravity of water = 1.0.

G-type agents are clear, colorless, and tasteless liquids that are miscible in water and most organic solvents (9). They evaporate approximately at the same rate as water, within 24 hours after deposition on the ground. An exception is cyclosarin which is oily. By their high volatility, a spill of any amount of nerve agents can cause a serious vapor hazard (2). Sarin is odorless and the most volatile nerve agent (Figure 1). Tabun has a slightly fruity odor, and soman has a slight camphor-like odor. VX is the exception, since it is a clear, amber-colored, odorless, and oily liquid. It is miscible with water and soluble in all solvents, and the least volatile nerve agent. With its low vapor pressure, VX is less likely to be a vapor hazard but can be a serious environmental hazard persisting in the environment longer (9, 10).

The US National Advisory Council has proposed acute emergency guideline levels (AEGLs) for several nerve agents including sarin (11). The AEGLs are intended for use in emergency planning, prevention and response. The levels are described as threshold limits for the general public: mild effects, serious adverse effects, and lethality. Further, the limit levels are depicted as air concentrations (mg/m³) applicable for exposure durations of 10 min, 30 min, 1 h, 4 h, and 8 h (12-15). The general population limit for all nerve gases is 0.000003 mg/m³ for 8 hour duration. Table 2 provides the estimated human exposure guideline for nerve agents.

The scale of casualties related to nerve agent poisoning would depend on meteorological factors surrounding the attack site. The potential number of casualties during an attack is determined by whether it occurs in an indoor or outdoor setting and by meteorological conditions such as wind velocity, relative humidity, rainfall precipitation, and temperature (9). Specifically, dispersal of sarin vapor can be significantly diminished by the absence of winds or in a closed indoor setting.

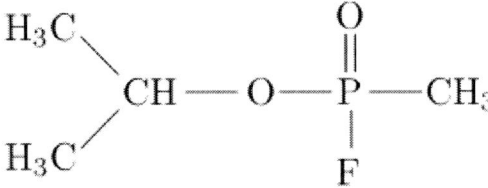

Figure 1. Molecular structure of sarin.

Table 2. Estimated human exposure guideline for nerve agents

| Nerve agent | Vapor (mg/m^3) | | Liquid |
	AEL	EC$_{50}$	ED$_{50}$ (mg/70kg)
Tabun (GA)	0.0001	< 1.7	< 880
Sarin (GB)	0.0001	< 0.8	1,000
Soman (GD)	0.00003	< 0.8	200
VX	0.00001	< 0.3	< 2.5

AEL: The maximum airborne exposure concentration for an 8-hr workday.

EC$_{50}$: The airborne concentration sufficient to induce severe effects in 50% of those exposed for 30 minutes.

ED$_{50}$: The amount of liquid agent on the skin sufficient to produce severe effects in 50% of the exposed population.

Sources: (AEL) Edgewood Safety Office, 1996; (ED$_{50}$) National Research Council; (EC$_{50}$) derived from Ect50 of Committee on Toxicology, 1998.

2. Mechanism of Toxicity

Acetylcholinesterase inhibition accounts for the major life-threatening effects of nerve agent poisoning (9). Acetylcholinesterase is bound to postsynaptic membranes at cholinergic synapses and functions as a turn-off switch to regulate neurotransmission (16). Inhibition of acetylcholinesterase causes the released neurotransmitter, acetylcholine, to accumulate abnormally and to enhance synaptic transmission at neuroeffector junctions (muscarinic effects), at skeletal neuromuscular junctions and autonomic ganglia (nicotinic effects), and also in the central nervous system (17-19). This end-organ hyperstimulation is recognized clinically as cholinergic crisis (20). Initial symptoms depend on the dose and the route of exposure (9).

Sarin (o-isopropyl methylphosphonofluoridate; GB) is a high-potency organophosphate ester (17). It is a clear and colorless liquid with a vapor pressure of 2.1 mm Hg. In the liquid state, it can rapidly penetrate skin and clothing. As a vapor, it can rapidly penetrate the mucous membranes of the eye or be inhaled into the lungs, where it is rapidly absorbed. Unless a nerve agent is removed by specific therapy such as oxime therapy, its binding to cholinesterase is essentially irreversible (21). Erythrocyte acetylcholinesterase activity recovers at about 1% per day. Plasma butyrylcholinesterase recovers more quickly and is a better guide to the recovery of tissue level enzyme activity (2).

Nerve agents also cause tachycardia and hypertension via stimulation of the adrenal medulla. They also appear to bind glutamate N-methyl-d-aspartate (NMDA) receptors directly. Nerve agents also antagonize gamma-aminobutyric acid (GABA) neurotransmission, which in part may mediate seizures and central nervous system neuropathology.

3. Routes of Exposure

Nerve agents are readily absorbed through inhalation, dermal contact, or ingestion (2). Among these three routes, vapor inhalation is the usual route of exposure in both battlefield and terrorist attacks. Nerve agent vapors are heavier than air. Odor does not provide adequate warning of detection. Vapors are not absorbed through the skin except at very high concentrations, but they easily cross the cornea, and produce miosis (22).

The clinical effects of nerve agent exposure are almost identical for vapor and liquid exposure routes if the dose is sufficiently large (9). But the speed and order of symptom onset may differ. The nature and timing of symptoms following dermal contact with liquid nerve agents depend on the exposure dose. The clinical effects following dermal contact may be delayed up to 18 hours, while inhalation symptoms can occur within seconds. As little as one drop of VX on the skin can be fatal and 1 to 10 mL of tabun, sarin, or soman can be fatal. Ingestion of nerve agents is rarely encountered compared to inhalation exposure or skin contact. However, they are readily absorbed from the GI tract and are highly toxic (17).

4. Clinical Manifestations

Exposure to high doses of sarin produces an acute cholinergic syndrome featuring a variety of signs and symptoms affecting mainly the peripheral and central nervous systems (17). Signs and symptoms of nerve agent exposure depend on the type of cholinergic receptor stimulated. Muscarinic signs and symptoms include: pinpoint pupils (one of the earliest signs of sarin exposure) (23); blurred or dimmed vision (24); rhinorrhea; headache; hypersecretion by salivary, lacrimal, sweat, and bronchial glands; nausea; vomiting; diarrhea; crampy abdominal pain; bowel and bladder incontinence; and; dyspnea. Nicotinic signs and symptoms include: skeletal muscle twitching and cramping; weakness and flaccid paralysis; tachycardia; and; hypertension. Central nervous system signs and symptoms include: irritability; ataxia; seizures; and; respiratory depression (9, 18). If the dose is sufficient, death results after generalized convulsions and respiratory arrest (17). Patients who survive exposure to nerve agents may also experience long-term complications (25-28).

Miosis cannot be used as a marker for the severity of nerve agent exposure, because miosis depends on the route and time course of exposure. In inhalational exposures, miosis occurs early. In such exposures, normal pupil size is predictive of low toxicity. However, in dermal exposures at sites distant from the eye, miosis occurs later in the progression of toxicity and depends on whether significant systemic absorption has occurred.

Experience of Sarin Attacks

1. History of Sarin Use

Sarin was first synthesized in 1938 by a German scientist. During World War II, Germany developed it as a chemical weapon but did not use it. However, it was reported that the

Germans tested nerve agents on inmates of concentration camps to investigate their effects and to develop antidotes (29).

Sarin was first used on battlefields during the first Persian Gulf war during 1984-1987 (17). Indirect evidence exists that the Iraqi military used sarin against Kurdish villagers in 1988 as well as during the Iraq-Iran War. In 1988, Iraq used various chemical and cluster bombs including sarin and other toxic nerve agents, and about 70,000 were harmed and over 5,000 died. The poison gas attack on the Iraqi town of Halabja was the largest-scale chemical weapons attack against a civilian population in modern times. The Halabja attack involved multiple chemical agents, including the nerve agent sarin, tabun and VX as well as mustard gas. Estimate of total casualties related to nerve gas agents in the Iraq-Iran war ranges from 20,000 to 100,000.

In 1994 and 1995, the Japanese religious cult Aum Shinrikyo used sarin in two terrorist attacks in Matsumoto and Tokyo (30, 31). Furthermore, sarin is known to be included in the military stockpiles of several nations, including the United States.

2. Matsumoto Sarin Attack

In 1994, sarin was used for chemical terrorism at Matsumoto City in Japan (30, 32). Matsumoto City, located 250km northwest from Tokyo, is a middle-sized city with a population of about 200,000 people, with 80,000 household units. A religious cult released an impure form of sarin using a heater and a fan from a truck for about 10 minutes. Around 600 people were exposed to sarin; 7 were killed; 58 were admitted to hospitals and over 200 were harmed. By the secondary contamination of sarin from the first exposure, 35% of the rescuers were also harmed (33). All of them had started relief activities within 5 hours after the onset of the sarin release. In a two-year follow-up health examination, severely poisoned patients still had some symptoms, such as occasional seizures, palpitation, dyspnea, and low-grade fever (25, 26).

The Matsumoto sarin attack demonstrates the implications of a nerve gas attack in outdoor settings (8). Unlike the previously reported characteristics of sarin, its lethal effect seems to be robust even in an outdoor setting, as seven (1.2%) out of 600 exposed people died with the sarin vapor in the city (30). When the cult group sprayed the diluted sarin, it was humid (95%) with a drizzle and a little wind (0.5m/sec) in a night of early summer (20.4°c). These conditions may have enabled the sarin vapor to maintain its lethal concentration. Additionally, all who died had the windows of their dwellings opened at the time of exposure.

3. Tokyo Subway Sarin Attack

Nine months after the Matsumoto sarin attack, one of the largest chemical terrorism events occurred in Tokyo during Monday morning rush hour, known as the Tokyo subway sarin attack (5, 34, 35). Twelve passengers died and about 5,500 people were harmed. Five members of the same religious cult released sarin by puncturing plastic bags full of sarin liquid with a tip of an umbrella. They brought 10 bags, which contained about 600 ml of 35% diluted sarin liquid, to five different commuter trains on three convergent subway lines. A geographic scheme of sarin-exposed subway stations is shown in Figure 2. Each commuter train was overcrowded with passengers on the way to work as usual. The traveling trains carried some sarin-exposed passengers at a distance in excess of 10 kilometers from the epicenters.

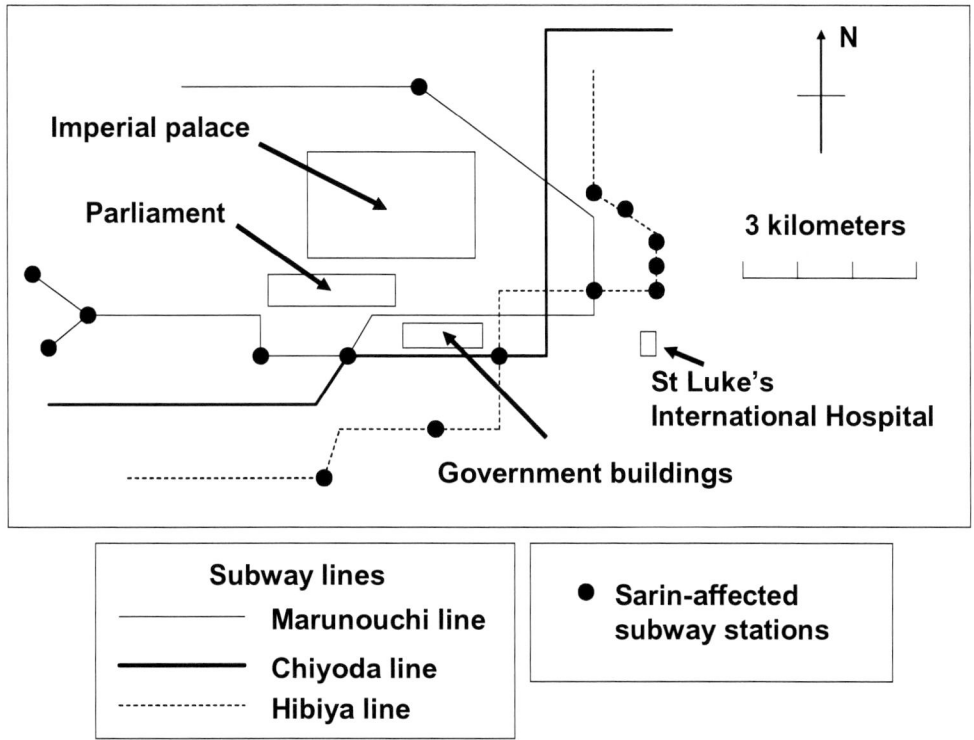

Figure 2. Subway stations exposed to sarin in the metropolitan Tokyo.

In the Tokyo subway sarin attack, sarin exhibited a very strong toxicity because of the indoor settings (5). In the Tokyo subway systems, it took a longer time for the evaporated sarin to be dispersed to the outside of trains and stations, because sarin is heavier than air (9). Thus, in enclosed spaces such as vehicles and theaters, sarin can sustain its lethal concentration for a relatively longer time.

The most common acute symptoms and signs among exposed patients were miosis and associated visual darkness (6). This was described later as "the world going black" (5). Other major symptoms and signs included headache, dyspnea, nausea, ocular pain, blurred vision, vomiting, coughing, muscle weakness, and agitation (5, 34) (Table 3). Secondary contamination of sarin from exposed patients occurred in more than 20% of nurses and resident physicians in a nearby main acute care hospital (St Luke's International Hospital). Some patients who survived exposure to the nerve agent experienced chronic symptoms (28, 36). Approximately 1 year after the Tokyo subway sarin attack, the hospital sent follow-up questionnaires to 606 patients. Of 303 respondents, 46% still had either physical or psychological symptoms: 18.5% had eye symptoms; 11.9% had easy fatigability; and 8.6% had headaches. For self-reported psychological symptoms, 12.9% felt fear of subways, 11.6% had fear concerning escape from the attack, 10.6% reported flashbacks, 7.9% had depression and 7.6% had lack of concentration. Moreover, chronic decline of psychomotor function and memory function were also recognized 7 years after the sarin exposure (37).

4. Emergency Medical Services in the Tokyo Subway Sarin Attack

The Japanese government had not set up any prior comprehensive programs for a chemical disaster before the subway sarin attack (6-8). First, there were no programs for planning decontamination spaces and providing personal protective equipment for emergency medical technicians (32, 33). Consequently, they wore conventional work clothing, instead of protective equipment for chemical agents. As a result, many emergency medical technicians suffered from the secondary exposure of sarin. Of 1363 emergency medical technicians, 135 (9.9%) developed symptoms and signs from the secondary contamination and subsequently received treatment. Most of them had exposure from primary exposed victims in poorly ventilated ambulances during a patient transportation.

Second, there was little cooperation and communication among related organizations (6). The Tokyo Metropolitan Ambulance Control Center was in confusion since incoming information about the chemical disaster exceeded the capacity to manage communications. Emergency medical technicians could not transport the victims properly to available hospitals, since they could not contact hospital staffs.

Third, at the affected site, triage was not performed appropriately by emergency medical technicians (6). The clinical conditions of some patients who were initially triaged as the mild cases became worse on the way to hospitals. Furthermore, the emergency medical technicians arrived at the scenes after the majority of the victims had departed for the nearest hospitals. Triage tags were not used for most patients. According to the report from St. Luke's International Hospital, 35% of patients walked to the hospital, 24% were transported by taxi, and only 7% were transported by ambulances. Two of 3 victims with cardiopulmonary arrest were transported by private vehicles to other distant hospitals.

5. Hospital Emergency Departments in the Tokyo Subway Sarin Attack

Information regarding the causative material was not initially available in the hospital caring for patients in the Tokyo subway sarin attack (7). About 2 hours after the initial exposure, the Tokyo Metropolitan Fire Department misidentified the agent as acetonitrile (methyl cyanide) because their database did not include nerve agents at the time of the attack. Fortunately, the hospital staff largely ignored this misinformation because there were no clinical findings compatible with acetonitrile poisoning among patients. Acetonitrile overdose cause a toxic syndrome of cyanide which is a secondary metabolite of acetonitrile (38). Although the police identified sarin as the culprit agent based on the database of the US National Institute of Standards and Technology 3 hours after the attack, this crucial information was not distributed directly to the hospitals because of a state of communication chaos. Fortunately, one of the emergency physicians of St. Luke's International Hospital quickly consulted a toxicology specialist at an affiliated University via telephone and he received the correct advice that the poison was probably sarin based on the experience of clinical manifestations in patients of the Matsumoto sarin attack (7). Thereafter, the hospital staff was able to better manage more than 500 patients.

The hospitals of Tokyo had not set up a prior disaster program for managing mass casualties (7). As hospitals did not restrict free access to the emergency department, families and friends of patients, coworkers, television crews, and curious onlookers entered the hospital freely and created a state of chaos in the hospitals. As a result, some medical records were scattered and lost during this confused period. However, intra-hospital triage for caring patients was performed relatively well.

Many hospital staff (23%) developed acute poisoning symptoms due to the secondary exposure to sarin for the following reasons (7). First, the hospital provided no chemical-resistant clothing to the staff. The hospital staff simply wore gloves and masks, which were used usually for surgical operations. Second, ventilation was poor in some treatment rooms. About half of the hospital staff working at one of these such rooms in a hospital complained of acute poisoning symptoms. Finally, as there was no room preplanned for decontamination in the hospital, decontamination was not done for most patients.

Management of Nerve Agent Poisoning

1. General Recommendations

Hospitals, local governments and multilevel organizations should coordinate disaster drills and mass casualty planning for potential nerve gas terrorism (4, 39). Local medical centers as well as emergency medical services should be prepared to deal with decontamination procedures and medical treatment of nerve gas poisoning to minimize human casualties (40). Authorized headquarters should provide appropriate personal protective equipments, ventilation devices, and decontamination facilities to prevent secondary exposure to medical staff (41). In addition, rescue teams should report to control stations and ancillary medical facilities about the clinical condition of each patient, the treatment given, and the estimated time of arrival at medical facilities (42). It is critical to consult with control station physicians or regional poison control centers for seeking advice regarding triage when facing multiple numbers of exposed patients.

2. Personal Protective Equipments

Saving live victims is the mission of rescue teams and healthcare institutions, while minimizing harm to rescuers and healthcare providers is also important (42, 43). Emergency medical technicians need to be protected from the secondary exposure to nerve gas agents, while exposed victims should be decontaminated thoroughly. The first responders may absorb nerve gas agents through the skin by touching them or through the lungs by inhaling vapors from contaminated clothes. When entering a scene or when treating victims exposed to liquid nerve agents, rescue personnel must wear as a standard complete clothing including protective suits, heavy butyl rubber gloves, boots, and air-supplied respirators with a self-contained breathing apparatus (44). Figure 3 presents the pictures taken in a drill for 2000

Okinawa Summit and the author is putting on the standard complete clothing. It is also desirable to use de-contaminable gurneys made of monofilament polypropylene fabric which does not absorb chemical agents and non-permeable fiberglass backboards.

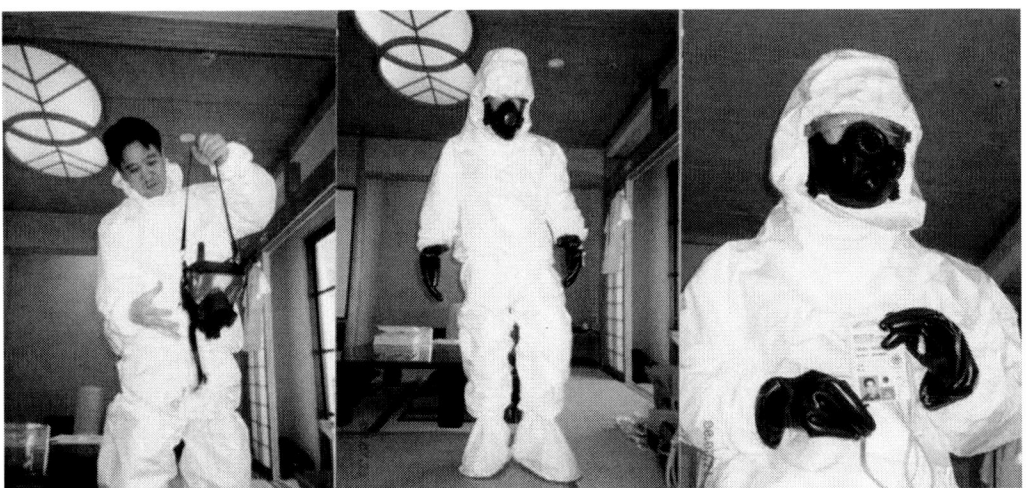

Figure 3. In a drill for 2000 Okinawa Summit, the author (YT) is putting on the standard complete clothing.

Minimizing the exposure duration of rescuers and healthcare providers will minimize their potential hazard. However, a rescuer in standard protective equipment with a self-contained breathing apparatus can be protected for up to 30 minutes in a nerve agent environment (43). Quick entry, rescue, and exit will minimize the hazards to both victims and rescuers, while diligently avoiding any contact with residual contamination will be mandatory.

3. Casualty Triage

Casualty triage for patients exposed to chemical terrorism is based on walking capability, respiratory status, age, and the conventional injuries of each patient (45). Triage officers must know the natural course of a given nerve gas poisoning, the medical resources immediately available, the current and likely casualty flow, and the evacuation capabilities. The Simple Triage and Rapid Treatment (START) system was developed to allow first responders to triage multiple victims within 30 seconds or less, based on three primary observations: Respiration, Perfusion, and Mental Status (45). There are four triage categories: immediate (priority 1), delayed (priority 2), minimal (priority 3), and expectant (priority 4), as shown in Table 3.

1. *Immediate*: casualties who require lifesaving care within a very short time.
2. *Delayed*: casualties with severe injuries who are in need of hospital care, but delay of this care will not adversely affect the outcome.
3. *Minimal*: casualties who can be helped by non-physician medical personnel and will not require hospitalization.

4. *Expectant*: casualties with severe life-threatening injuries who would not survive with optimal medical care.

There are several principles of triage for chemical agent exposures in general (2, 39, 41, 45). First, staff should keep checking triage tags for all patients and survey for evidence of associated trauma. Second, severe cases requiring assisted ventilation should be triaged as immediate. A severe nerve agent casualty who is unconscious, convulsing or postictal, breathing with difficulty or apneic, and possibly flaccid, can survive with appropriate and immediate therapy including ventilation support if the patient still has an intact circulation. Thus, these kinds of patients should be triaged as immediate if that therapy can be provided. Third, if there are chemical exposures which may cause delayed but potentially serious symptoms, triage for including those victims into categories 1 and 2 is considered appropriate to proper medical facilities that can observe and manage any delayed onset symptoms. Lastly, expectant categories in multi-casualty events may include those victims who have experienced a cardiac arrest, respiratory arrest, or continuous seizures immediately after the exposures (46). Unfortunately, limited resources should not be expended on these casualties if there are large numbers of casualties requiring care and transport with minimal or scant resources available (42, 47).

Victim removal from the exposure zone should also be rapidly accomplished (45). If victims can walk, they may be escorted out of the exposure zone to the decontamination zone. Depending on available resources, triage of remaining victims should be performed. Victims who are unable to walk may be removed from the exposure zone using backboards. If these are not available, it is recommended to carefully carry or drag victims to safety areas.

4. Respiratory Support

Management for acute nerve agent poisoning usually includes respiratory support, decontamination, antidotes, and anticonvulsants (2). In severe cases, all of these forms of therapy may be given simultaneously. Patients exposed to nerve agent toxicity should be rapidly assessed for airway, breathing, and circulation (2, 39, 48). Respiratory failure is the principal cause of deaths in nerve agent poisonings. Respiratory failure is caused by increased airway resistance by bronchorrhea and bronchoconstriction, respiratory muscle paralysis, and loss of central respiratory drive.

Early endotracheal intubation and ventilatory support may be needed in treating patients with manifestations of severe toxic reactions (49). Suction is important because large amounts of airway secretions may occur. When rapid sequence intubation strategy is used, succinylcholine should be avoided because it is metabolized by plasma cholinesterase, and therefore it will accumulate in patients with nerve agent poisonings. Atropine can be given before endotracheal intubation as it will improve ventilation support (20).

Table 3. Acute symptoms and signs in the Tokyo sarin attack*

Symptoms and signs	% of patients
Miosis	99.0
Headache	74.8
Dyspnea	63.1
Nausea	60.4
Eye pain	45.0
Blurred vision	39.6
Visual darkness	37.8
Vomiting	36.9
Easy fatigability	36.9
Cough	34.2
Agitation	33.3
Fasciculation	23.4
Convulsion	2.7

* Based on Okumura T, Suzuki K, Fukuda A, et al.
The Tokyo subway sarin attack: disaster management, Part 2: Hospital response. Acad Emerg Med. 1998; 5(6):618-24.

5. Decontamination

The purpose of decontamination is to prevent further absorption of nerve gas agents by victims and to prevent the spread of nerve gas agents to other persons including rescuers and healthcare providers (50). Exposed individuals should be removed from the source of exposure and rapidly decontaminated (48). Even small amounts of the liquid form of a nerve agent contacting the unprotected skin can be severely incapacitating if the victim or responder is not decontaminated rapidly (9). Decontamination should be started as soon as possible even before transport to medical centers (50, 51).

Contaminated eyes should be decontaminated within minutes of the exposure to the liquid form of nerve agents to limit eye injury (50). Contaminated eyes should be flushed immediately with water for at least 10 minutes by tilting the head to the side, pulling eyelids apart with fingers, and pouring water slowly into the eyes. There is no need to flush the eyes following the exposure to the vapor form of nerve agents. Covering eyes with bandages is not recommended.

Contaminated clothes should be removed and sealed in non-permeable double bags (50). Contaminated skin should be irrigated with copious water (44). If shower areas are available, a thorough shower with soap and water may be used. If unavailable, washing can be performed aggressively with soap and water or 0.5% sodium hypochlorite solutions, since nerve agents are hydrolyzed by alkaline solutions.

Table 4. Simple Triage and Rapid Treatment (START) for nerve agent casualties*

Category (Priority)	Tag color	Respiratory status	Perfusion status	Mental status
Immediate (1)	Red tag	Respiratory rate>30/min	Decreased or cyanotic	Altered mental status or seizure
Delayed (2)	Tellow tag	Normal	No disturbance	Alert
Minimal (3)	Green tag	Normal	No disturbance	Walking and talking
Expectant (4)	Black tag	No respiratory effort	Prolonged cardiac arrest	Unresponsive

* Based on an Alternative Health Care Facility: Concept of Operations for the Off-Site Triage, Treatment, and Transportation Center (OST^3C) Mass Casualty Care Strategy for a Chemicala Terrorism Incident. Edgewood Chemical Biological Center. 2003.

All exposed persons may be decontaminated before transport to medical facilities (45). Although skin decontamination is not necessary after exposure only to vapor form, their clothes should be removed to eliminate trapped vapor. It is recommended to avoid hot water, strong detergents, and vigorous scrubbing, since they may enhance dermal absorption of nerve agents (50). Lastly, in cases of ingestion, induced emesis should be avoided because of the risk of pulmonary aspiration of gastric contents. If the victim is alert and able to swallow, immediate administration of activated charcoal may be better. Secondary exposure may occur during gastric lavage from victims who have ingested the liquid form of nerve agents (52).

6. Antidotes

Antidotes for nerve agent poisoning include atropine, pralidoxime chloride (2-PAM), diazepam, and tropicamide (9, 49). Both atropine and 2-PAM may be given by intramuscular injection, although intravenous administration is preferred. If auto-injector kits are available, they provide a better way to administer the antidotes in a prehospital stage (9). One type of auto-injector automatically delivers 2 mg of atropine, while another type automatically delivers 600 mg of 2-PAM. Recommendations for antidote dosages for nerve agents are provided in Table 4.

Atropine rapidly reverses cholinergic overload at muscarinic synapses but has no effects at nicotinic synapses. For a field-loading dose, atropine can be given at 2, 4, or 6 mg, with re-treatment every 5 to 10 minutes until breathing and secretions of patients improve. There is no upper limit for a dose of atropine, but a total average dose for a severely afflicted adult patient would usually be 20 to 30 mg.

2-PAM is an oxime that acts as an acetylcholinesterase reactivator by binding to nerve agents and removing them from the enzyme (53). 2-PAM can remove nerve agents from acetylcholinesterase if administered before the 'aging', which indicates that a side chain on nerve agents falls off the complex. If aged, the complexes are negatively charged, which 2-PAM cannot reactivate anymore (54). Among nerve agents, sarin ages in 3 to 5 hours. Initial field-loading doses for 2-PAM are 600, 1200, or 1800 mg. Since blood pressure elevation may occur after administration of 45 mg/kg in adults, field use of intramuscular 2-PAM may be restricted to 1800 mg per hour. During the time when more oxime cannot be given, atropine alone is recommended. In hospital settings, 2.5 to 25 mg/kg of 2-PAM intravenously has been found to reactivate 50% of inhibited acetylcholinesterase. The usual recommendation is 1000 mg by slow intravenous drip over 20 to 30 min, with no more than 2500 mg over a period of 1 to 1.5 h (2).

Diazepam is indicated for treatment of seizures related to nerve agents (55). Prolonged seizures may lead to permanent brain injury and thus should be treated aggressively. For treatment of nerve agent-induced status epilepticus, adult patients may require 30 to 40 mg diazepam intramuscularly (56). Patients with flaccid paralysis should have electroencephalogram monitoring because external seizure activity may not be recognized in such patients. To reverse miosis and relieve ocular pain, topical tropicamide may be used (24).

One recent study suggested that galantamine, a reversible and centrally acting acetylcholinesterase inhibitor used for treatment of mild to moderate Alzheimer's disease, protects animals from the acute toxicity of lethal doses of the nerve agents such as soman and sarin (57). Further investigations are needed for galantamine as an alternative antidote against nerve agent poisoning.

Table 5. Recommendations for antidote dose for nerve agent*

Patient Age	Mild/Moderate symptoms†	Severe symtoms‡
Infant (0 - 2 yrs)	Atropine: 0.05 mg/kg IM PAM: 15 mg/kg IM	Atropine: 0.1 mg/kg IM PAM: 25 mg/kg IM
Child (2 - 10 yrs)	Atropine: 1 mg IM PAM: 15 mg/kg IM	Atropine: 2 mg IM PAM: 25 mg/kg IM
Adolescent (>10 yrs)	Atropine: 2 mg IM PAM: 15 mg/kg IM	Atropine: 4 mg IM PAM: 25 mg/kg IM
Adult	Atropine: 2 to 4 mg IM PAM: 600 mg IM	Atropine: 6 mg IM PAM: 1800 mg IM
Elderly, frail	Atropine: 1 mg IM PAM: 10 mg/kg IM	Atropine: 2 to 4 mg IM PAM: 25 mg/kg IM

PAM=pradoxime chloride; IM=intramuscular injection
* Based on Agency for Toxic Substances and Disease Registry.
Medical management guidelines for nerve agents;
tabun (GA); sarin (GB); soman (GD); and VX.
Centers for Disease Control and Prevention. 2007.
† Mild/Moderate symptoms include localized sweating, muscle fasciculations, nausea, vomiting, mild weakness, and dyspnea.
‡ Severe symptoms include unconsciousness, convulsions apnea, and flaccid paralysis.

7. Transportation to Medical Facility

As described in the toxicology section, nerve agents are highly toxic and can cause a coma and seizure within several seconds and deaths from respiratory failure within minutes (4). Thus, prehospital management should begin with rapid assessment of vital signs and timely management of the airway, breathing, and circulation (39, 41). Since respiratory failure is the principal cause of mortality in nerve gas poisoning, early airway protection and ventilatory support are crucial for treating cases with severe toxicity (2).

If patients are comatose, hypotensive, convulsive or have cardiac dysrhythmia, they should be treated according to advanced cardiac life support protocols (priority 1), or otherwise tagged as expectant (priority 4). Diazepam should be used to control convulsions (56). Other benzodiazepines may be used, although barbiturates and phenytoin are not effective in convulsions related to nerve agent poisoning. If trauma is suspected, cervical immobilization should be maintained manually and a de-contaminable cervical collar and a backboard may be applied when feasible. Intravenous access and continuous monitoring of cardiac rhythm should also be established in seriously ill-patients (2).

Patients who are seriously symptomatic and patients who have a history or evidence of significant exposure should be transported to a medical facility for further evaluation (39, 41, 45). Others may be discharged at the scene after their contact addresses are recorded. Those discharged should be advised to seek medical care promptly if symptoms develop. If contaminated patients are expected to arrive at a hospital emergency department, they must be decontaminated before being allowed to enter the facility.

No laboratory tests are available to directly measure nerve agent levels in serum or urine. Thus, the acute effects of nerve agents can be estimated by measuring the percent reduction in the activity of blood erythrocyte cholinesterase in patients. Erythrocyte cholinesterase and plasma cholinesterase (pseudocholinesterase) have a physiologic role as buffers for the tissue acetylcholinesterase found in the nervous system. These 2 enzymes are clinically important, because their activities can be assayed directly in blood, whereas the tissue acetylcholinesterase cannot. Activity of erythrocyte cholinesterase is a more sensitive indicator of nerve agent toxicity than that of plasma cholinesterase. However, activity of erythrocyte cholinesterase is subject to some individual variation. Therefore, without knowing the baseline value of erythrocyte cholinesterase in individuals, estimating the percent reduction in enzyme activity is difficult. In addition, there is a poor correlation between effects of nerve agents and the percent reduction of erythrocyte cholinesterase activity at low-dose exposures, although severe clinical effects may be related to a 20-25% reduction in erythrocyte cholinesterase activity. A rising level of erythrocyte cholinesterase indicates that no further nerve agent absorption is occurring and that the enzyme is regenerating. RBC cholinesterase is replaced fully every 120 days at the natural regeneration rate (about 1% per day) of erythrocytes. It is important to draw blood for erythrocyte cholinesterase activity level prior to administering oxime antidotes such as 2-PAM.

8. Disposition

All patients who have had the exposure to nerve agents should be observed carefully, since there are potential delayed effects from nerve gas agents (2, 45). Patients who have inhalation exposure and who complain of any chest symptoms should be closely observed and examined periodically for at least 12 hours to identify delayed-onset symptoms and signs. Effects from skin exposure to liquid form may not develop for up to 18 hours following exposure. Thus, patients who may have been exposed to the liquid form must be kept under observation for at least 18 hours. Patients exposed only to the vapor form, who have no symptoms when they reach the medical facility, may not need to be admitted (9).

Patients with severe exposure should be followed and evaluated for chronic central nervous system complications (17). Sequential blood erythrocyte cholinesterase activity may be measured at weekly to monthly intervals to be stabilized in the normal range. This normalization process may take 3 to 4 months after severe poisoning.

Prevention of Mass Casualty from Nerve Agent Poisoning

Nerve agent exposure may occur as a result of an industrial accident involving nerve agent production, accidental release from a military stockpile, chemical warfare, and chemical terrorism. Nerve gas chemical terrorism can cause not only lethal consequences fpr exposed individuals but also chaos for local emergency medical services (4). Local states caused by a nerve gas attack may be as chaotic as that of a natural disaster. To minimize the impact on public health from nerve gas chemical terrorism, responsible organizations have to establish a comprehensive mass casualty management program. We may propose the following concepts for responsible organizations, based on the lessons learned through the two sarin attacks in Japan.

All rescuers and emergency department staff should become accustomed to general relief operations of a massive disaster setting by repeated drills (41). They should be required to know the basic characteristics of a nerve gas attack (16). Moreover, some of them should be trained as experts for task forces that are required to conduct anti- nerve gas attack strategy including immediate hazard identification, decontamination, triage, appropriate therapy, and secondary exposure prevention (58). All hospitals with active emergency departments need to have frequently updated and posted disaster plans, manuals and yearly drills. Ideally, disaster drills should involve an entire city if the city size is small or an entire ward or county if the city size is large, by conducting these community-wide drills possibly every 2 to 3 years.

Prehospital triage should be executed properly to organize the transport of victims to hospitals. A single hospital could be easily overwhelmed (7). Good Samaritans transferred some casualties by car in the Tokyo sarin attack; however, transport should have been undertaken by rescuers in the personal protective equipment. Secondary exposure of the Good Samaritans could lead to additional casualties.

An information center should be set up as soon as a nerve gas attack is suspected (8). Even a brief delay in the initial response may yield a tremendous number of additional casualties. The functions of healthcare providers in emergency departments to provide rapid and effective treatment can be enhanced by timely and accurate information. Substantial information can be shared among the related institutions to achieve an optimal resource allocation at the Hot Zone as well as in emergency departments. Information is also important for families as well as local communities and a whole country. The information center should undertake effective information distribution to the public on behalf of related institutions. Otherwise, each hospital would need to be interacting with crowded individuals and mass media, which could lead to chaos.

Although training healthcare providers to treat nerve gas intoxication in a mass casualty scenario is a complicated task, one group recently has developed a simulation-based training program (59). Such a scenario is an unfamiliar medical situation involved with decontaminating patients before definitive medical treatment and providing physical protection to medical teams before decontamination. Simulation training may be superior to traditional training menus to train healthcare providers to manage nerve gas casualties and to learn about the limitations of providing conventional medical care in this setting.

Lastly, and most importantly, production and stockpiling of chemical warfare agents are prohibited by the Chemical Weapons Convention in the international community. However, scientists have contributed to the production of weapons of mass destruction. Scientists, including the members of Aum Shinrikyo, seemed to have also had an important role in production of chemical weapons. Consequently, they have violated the basic bioethical principle, "primum non nocere". Thus, ethics education for current and future generations of scientists could be one of the important tools for a primary prevention measure against chemical weapons (60).

This chapter was written with the intent to give assistance to rescuers, emergency medical technicians, and healthcare providers in dealing with critical mass casualty management of chemical weapons, especially sarin and nerve gas attacks. Responsible professionals around the world may need to consider the recommendations for the potentially catastrophic threat of a nerve gas attack.

Acknowledgments

No conflict of interests.

References

[1]   Hu H, Cook-Deegan R, Shukri A. The use of chemical weapons. Conducting an investigation using survey epidemiology. *JAMA* 1989;262(5):640-643.

[2]   Medical Management of Chemical Casualties Handbook. 3rd ed: Aberdeen Proving Ground, Md: USAMRICO; 2000.

[3]   Weinbroum AA, Rudick V, Paret G, Kluger Y, Ben Abraham R. Anaesthesia and critical care considerations in nerve agent warfare trauma casualties. *Resuscitation* 2000;47(2):113-23.

[4]   Tokuda Y, Kikuchi M, Takahashi O, Stein GH. Prehospital management of sarin nerve gas terrorism in urban settings: 10 years of progress after the Tokyo subway sarin attack. *Resuscitation* 2006;68(2):193-202.

[5]   Okumura T, Takasu N, Ishimatsu S, Miyanoki S, Mitsuhashi A, Kumada K, et al. Report on 640 victims of the Tokyo subway sarin attack. *Ann Emerg Med* 1996;28(2):129-35.

[6]   Okumura T, Suzuki K, Fukuda A, Kohama A, Takasu N, Ishimatsu S, et al. The Tokyo subway sarin attack: disaster management, Part 1: Community emergency response. *Acad Emerg Med* 1998;5(6):613-7.

[7]   Okumura T, Suzuki K, Fukuda A, Kohama A, Takasu N, Ishimatsu S, et al. The Tokyo subway sarin attack: disaster management, Part 2: Hospital response. *Acad Emerg Med* 1998;5(6):618-24.

[8]   Okumura T, Suzuki K, Fukuda A, Kohama A, Takasu N, Ishimatsu S, et al. The Tokyo subway sarin attack: disaster management, Part 3: National and international responses. *Acad Emerg Med* 1998;5(6):625-8.

[9]   Agency for Toxic Substances and Disease Registry. Medical management guidelines for nerve agents tabun (GA); sarin (GB); soman (GD); and VX. In: *Centers for Disease Control and Prevention;* 2003.

[10]   Kamiura M. Difference between Sarin and VX. In; 2004.

[11]   Hartmann HM. Evaluation of risk assessment guideline levels for the chemical warfare agents mustard, GB, and VX. *Regul Toxicol Pharmacol* 2002;35(3):347-56.

[12]   Acute Exposure Guideline Levels (AEGLs) for Nerve Agents GA, GB, GD and GF (CAS Reg. Nos. 77-81-6, 107-44-8, 96-64-0, and 329-99-7), Draft 1. National Advisory Committee on Acute Exposure Guideline Levels for Hazardous Substances. . In: *US EPA;* 2000.

[13]   Acute Exposure Guideline Levels (AEGLs) for Nerve Agent VX (CAS Reg. No. 50782-69-9), Draft 1. National Advisory Committee on Acute Exposure Guideline Levels for Hazardous Substances. In: *US EPA;* 2000.

[14]   Standing Operating Procedures, Version 08-02. National Advisory Committee on Acute Exposure Guideline Levels for Hazardous Substances. In: *US EPA*; 2000.

[15]   Sulfur Mustard (Agent HD) CAS Reg. No. 505-60-2: Interim Acute Exposure Guideline Levels (AEGLs), for NAS/COT Subcommittee for AEGLs, Interim 1. National Advisory Committee on Acute Exposure Guideline Levels for Hazardous Substances. In: *US EPA;* 2000.

[16]   Sidell FR, Borak J. Chemical warfare agents: II. Nerve agents. *Ann Emerg Med* 1992;21(7):865-71.

[17]   Lee EC. Clinical manifestations of sarin nerve gas exposure. *JAMA* 2003;290(5):659-62.

[18]   Rickett DL, Glenn JF, Beers ET. Central respiratory effects versus neuromuscular actions of nerve agents. *Neurotoxicology* 1986;7(1):225-36.

[19]   Murata K, Araki S, Yokoyama K, Okumura T, Ishimatsu S, Takasu N, et al. Asymptomatic sequelae to acute sarin poisoning in the central and autonomic nervous system 6 months after the Tokyo subway attack. *J Neurol* 1997;244(10):601-6.

[20]   Hurst CG NJ, Romano JA. Part 7. Bioterrorism and Clinical Medicine. Chapter 206. Chemical Bioterrorism. In: *Harrison's Online. New York,* NY: McGraw-Hills ACCESS Medicine; 2004.

[21]   Broomfield CA, Kirby SD. Progress on the road to new nerve agent treatments. *J Appl Toxicol* 2001;21 Suppl 1:S43-6.

[22]   Johns R. The Effect of Low Concentrations of GB on the Human Eye, Medical Laboratories Research Report No. 100, Publication Control No. 5030-100 (CMLRE-ML-52). : *Army Chemical Center,* Aberdeen Proving Ground, MD.; 1952.

[23]   Nozaki H, Hori S, Shinozawa Y, Fujishima S, Takuma K, Kimura H, et al. Relationship between pupil size and acetylcholinesterase activity in patients exposed to sarin vapor. *Intensive Care Med 1*997;23(9):1005-7.

[24]   Kato T, Hamanaka T. Ocular signs and symptoms caused by exposure to sarin gas. *Am J Ophthalmol* 1996;121(2):209-10.

[25]   Nakajima T, Ohta S, Fukushima Y, Yanagisawa N. Sequelae of sarin toxicity at one and three years after exposure in Matsumoto, Japan. *J Epidemiol* 1999;9(5):337-43.

[26]   Sekijima Y, Morita H, Yanagisawa N. Follow-up of sarin poisoning in Matsumoto. *Ann Intern Med* 1997;127(11):1042.

[27]   Yokoyama K, Araki S, Murata K, Nishikitani M, Okumura T, Ishimatsu S, et al. A preliminary study on delayed vestibulo-cerebellar effects of Tokyo Subway Sarin Poisoning in relation to gender difference: frequency analysis of postural sway. *J Occup Environ Med* 1998;40(1):17-21.

[28]   Yokoyama K, Araki S, Murata K, Nishikitani M, Okumura T, Ishimatsu S, et al. Chronic neurobehavioral effects of Tokyo subway sarin poisoning in relation to posttraumatic stress disorder. *Arch Environ Health* 1998;53(4):249-56.

[29]   Harigel GG, Carnegie Endowment for International P. *Chemical and Biological Weapons: Use in Warfare, Impact on Society and Environment: Carnegie Endowment for International Peace;* 2001.

[30]   Morita H, Yanagisawa N, Nakajima T, Shimizu M, Hirabayashi H, Okudera H, et al. Sarin poisoning in Matsumoto, Japan. *Lancet* 1995;346(8970):290-3.

[31]   Nagao M, Takatori T, Matsuda Y, Nakajima M, Iwase H, Iwadate K. Definitive evidence for the acute sarin poisoning diagnosis in the Tokyo subway. *Toxicol Appl Pharmacol* 1997;144(1):198-203.

[32]   Okudera H, Morita H, Iwashita T, Shibata T, Otagiri T, Kobayashi S, et al. Unexpected nerve gas exposure in the city of Matsumoto: report of rescue activity in the first sarin gas terrorism. *Am J Emerg Med* 1997;15(5):527-8.

[33]   Nakajima T, Sato S, Morita H, Yanagisawa N. Sarin poisoning of a rescue team in the Matsumoto sarin incident in Japan. *Occup Environ Med* 1997;54(10):697-701.

[34]   Ohbu S, Yamashina A, Takasu N, Yamaguchi T, Murai T, Nakano K, et al. Sarin poisoning on Tokyo subway. *South Med* J 1997;90(6):587-93.

[35]   Woodall J. *Tokyo subway gas attack. Lancet* 1997;350(9073):296.

[36]   Ohyoku T, Iwanami A, Shimizu E, Kato S. Long term follow-up study for victims of Toko subway sarin attack. Seishin igaku (*Clinical psychiatry*) 2003;45(1):21-30.

[37]   Miyaki K, Nishiwaki Y, Maekawa K, Ogawa Y, Asukai N, Yoshimura K, et al. Effects of sarin on the nervous system of subway workers seven years after the Tokyo subway sarin attack. *J Occup Health* 2005;47(4):299-304.

[38]   Mueller M, Borland C. Delayed cyanide poisoning following acetonitrile ingestion. *Postgrad Med J* 1997;73(859):299-300.

[39]   Guidelines for Responding to a Chemical Weapons Incident. In: *Edgewood Chemical Biological Center;* 2003.

[40]   Minamizawa M, Miura K. Lessons learned from hospital decontamination drill against sarin disaster. *Japanese Journal of Disaster Medicine* 2003;8(1):58-62.

[41]   Chemical Weapons Improved Response Program (CW IRP) 2000 Summary Report. In: *Edgewood Chemical Biological Center;* 2001.

[42]   Army Medical NBC Battlebook. Department of Defense. Mount Laurel, NJ: *Progressive Management;* 2001.

[43]   Guidance on the use of hoods with chemical protective respirators and chemical protective suits. In: *Edgewood Chemical Biological Center;* 2002.

[44]   Domestic Preparedness Report (August, 2003). Guidelines for Incident Commander's Use of Firefighter Protective Ensemble (FFPE) with Self-Contained Breathing Apparatus (SCBA) for Rescue Operations during a Terrorist Chemical Agent Incident. In: *Edgewood Chemical Biological Center;* 2003.

[45]   An Alternative Health Care Facility: Concept of Operations for the Off-Site Triage, Treatment, and Transportation Center (OST³C) Mass Casualty Care Strategy for a Chemical Terrorism Incident. In: *Edgewood Chemical Biological Center;* 2003.

[46]   Guidelines for mass fatality management during terrorist incidents involving chemical agents. In: *Edgewood Chemical Biological Center;* 2003.

[47]   Medical Examiner/Coroner Guide for Mass Fatality Management of Chemically Contaminated Remains. In: *Edgewood Chemical Biological Center;* 2000.

[48]   Ben Abraham R, Weinbroum AA. Resuscitative challenges in nerve agent poisoning. *Eur J Emerg Med* 2003;10(3):169-75.

[49]   Yamamoto J, Fujishima S. Diagnosis and management of sarin and VX chemical terrorism. *Kokyuu* 2002;21(11):1020-3.

[50]   Guidelines for Mass Casualty Decontamination during a Terrorist Chemical Agent Incident. . In: *Edgewood Chemical Biological Center;* 2003.

[51]   Guidelines for Cold Weather Mass Decontamination During a Terrorist Chemical Agent Incident. In: *Edgewood Chemical Biological Center;* 2003.

[52]   Okumura S, Okumura T, Ishimatsu S, Miura K, Maekawa H, Naito T. Clinical review: Tokyo - protecting the health care worker during a chemical mass casualty event: an important issue of continuing relevance. *Crit Care* 2005;9(4):397-400.

[53]   Arnold J. CBRNE-Nerve Agents, G-series: Tabun, Sarin, Soman. In: eMedicine eMedicine.com, Inc.; 2004.

[54]   Holstege CP, Kirk M, Sidell FR. Chemical warfare. Nerve agent poisoning. *Crit Care Clin* 1997;13(4):923-42.

[55]   Newmark J. Therapy for nerve agent poisoning. *Arch Neurol* 2004;61(5):649-52.

[56]   Murphy MR, Blick DW, Dunn MA, Fanton JW, Hartgraves SL. Diazepam as a treatment for nerve agent poisoning in primates. *Aviat Space Environ Med* 1993;64(2):110-5.

[57]   Albuquerque EX, Pereira EFR, Aracava Y, Fawcett WP, Oliveira M, Randall WR, et al. Effective countermeasure against poisoning by organophosphorus insecticides and nerve agents. *Proc Natl Acad Sci USA* 2006;103(35):13220-13225.

[58]   Improved Response Program for the Department of Justice, Office of Justice Programs. Law Enforcement Officers Guide for Responding to Chemical Terrorist Incidents. . In: *Edgewood Chemical Biological Center;* 2003.

[59]   Berkenstadt H, Ziv A, Barsuk D, Levine I, Cohen A, Vardi A. The Use of Advanced Simulation in the Training of Anesthesiologists to Treat Chemical Warfare Casualties. *Anesth Analg* 2003;96(6):1739-1742.

[60]   Tokuda Y. Teaching ethics in Japan. *Lancet* 1995;345(8964):1574.

In: Global Terrorism Issues and Developments
Editor: Rene A. Larche, pp. 233-245

ISBN: 978-1-60021-930-6

Chapter 10

ANALYSING THE EFFECTS OF MORTALITY SALIENCE ON PREJUDICE AND DECISION-TAKING

Agustin Echebarria- Echabe and Francisco J. Valencia Gárate*

Department of Social Psychology. Psychology faculty. The University of the Basque
Country. Tolosa avenue, 70. San Sebastian 20009. Spain

Abstract

Recently (Echebarria & Fernandez, 2006) we carried out a quasi-experimental study on the
effects of the terrorist attacks against the railways in Madrid and found that these attacks
provoked a generalized prejudice directed not only against groups regarded as the responsible
of the attacks but also against other non-related group (Jews). A generalized displacement
toward more conservative values and political options was also found. Here we present two
follow-up experimental studies designed to analyse the socio-psychological processes that
might underlie these changes. The first study manipulated, through pictures, the salience of
death- related thoughts without involving any personal or group based threat. The generalized
increment of prejudices and group bias are reproduced but only at an implicit level. The
second study proved that mortality salience affects how social dilemmas are approached.
Participants assigned to the mortality salient condition approached a health related dilemma in
terms of losses, independently of how it was experimentally framed. In contrast, control
participants shifted their choices in function of the experimental manipulation. We discuss the
implications of these results in terms of understanding the effects of terrorism from the Terror
Management Theory.

The Terror Management Theory (TMT) (Greenberg, Pyszczynski, & Solomon, 1986;
Landau, Johns, Greenberg, Pyszczynski, Martens, Goldenberg, & Solomon, 2004) is based on
the work of Ernest Becker (1973) and suggests that the awareness of mortality facilitates the
social construction of, and continuing investment in, a cultural worldview that protects people
from death-related fears by presenting a meaningful and orderly world and standard of value
by which one´s own life is perceived as significant and enduring.

---

[*] E-mail: pspeteta@ss.ehu.es

The TMT proposes that one distinctive human characteristic is that the phylogenetic development of the brain, together with the development of symbolic communication systems and culture, has made possible the emergence of self-consciousness. Perhaps the human being is the only animal that is conscious of the finite duration of life. Thus, two conflicting forces are in permanent struggle: the survival instinct, present in all animals, and the consciousness of the finite nature of life. This consciousness raises feelings of existential anxiety that can be coped with by means of two resources: self-esteem and adherence to the group's cultural values and world-views.

There is ample evidence that the salience of mortality awareness has a variety of effects: increasing desire to have children (Wisman & Goldenberg, 2005); derogation of deviant ingroup members (See & Petty, 2006); increment of pro-social behaviours but only on behalf of ingroup members (Jonas, Schimel, Greenberg, & Pyszczynski, 2002; van den Bos, Poortvliet, Maas, Miedema, & van den Ham, 2005); strong attachment to ingroups and derogation of outgroups (Arndt, Schimel, Greenberg, Pyzczynski, & Solomon, 2002; Dechesne, Janssen, & van Knippenberg, 2000); negative evaluation of wilderness (Koole & Van den Berg, 2005); intensification of beliefs in supernatural agents (angels, demons, etc.) (Norenzayan & Hansen, 2006); attachment to ingroup values and worldviews (Cozzolino, Staples, Meyers, & Samboceti, 2004) and derogation of alternative worldviews (Schmeichel & Martens, 2005); promotion of affiliation (Wisman & Koole, 2003); increment of prejudice against older people (Martens, Greenberg, Schimel, & Landau, 2004); preference for information that supports one's own choices and decisions (Jonas, Greenberg, & Frey, 2003); or preference for simple knowledge structures (for example adherence to explanations presenting the world as fair) (Landau, Johns, Greenberg, Pyzczynski, Martens, Goldenberg, & Solomon, 2004).

More interesting for our interests, TMT has been used as a theoretical approach to understand the effects of terrorism. For example, Landau and colleagues (2004) proposed that the 9/11 terrorist attacks increased the accessibility of death-related thoughts leading to positive attitudes toward Bush and his counter-terrorism policies. In the same way, Pyszczynski and colleagues (2006) proved that making mortality salient increased Iranian students support of martyrdom attacks against US forces and conservative American students' support for massive attacks in Iraq. It is hypothesized that terrorism directly arouses existential anxiety by reminding us of the frail nature of our lives.

Recently we (Echebarria & Fernandez, 2006) published a study of the effects that Islamic terrorist attacks in Madrid (11 March, 2004) had on general attitudes of the Spanish population. It must be remembered that these attacks (there were three coordinated attacks) targeted the railways system, causing two hundred deaths and hundreds of injuries. In a quasi-experimental design we were able to collect data about conservatism, liberalism, authoritarianism, political orientation, and prejudice just before and after the attacks. We found a generalized tendency to increase the adherence to conservative values, a displacement towards more conservative ideological positions, a stronger authoritarianism, as well as an increment of prejudice not only directed against Arabs, but also extended against another group, Jews. However, the nature of the study left open a number of questions about the underlying psychosocial processes involved in these changes. It is be possible that the processes described by the TMT were not responsible for these changes and another more parsimonious explanation could shed light on the situation. Hewstone, Rubin, & Willis (2002) stated that one of the common criticisms of TMT is that the effects of mortality salience (death-related thoughts) can be reinterpreted as the effects of self-relevant threats in general. Namely, it could be hypothesized that the attacks roused feelings of threat against the ingroup. It is well known in the literature that attacks against ingroup members enhance a number of changes within and between groups (Sherif, 1966; Sherif, Harvey, White, Hood, & Sherif, 1961;Tajfel, 1978, 1981). Groups that feel they are under threat increase the attachment to previous group values and beliefs, increase cohesion, and develop prejudices against outgroups. And all these changes can occur without the participation of death-related thoughts. In fact, Hart, Shaver, & Goldenberg (2005) proved that the same effects of mortality salience could be found as a result of attachment threats (imagine a romantic break-up) or threats against ingroup worldviews without directly involving mortality questions.

Given the impossibility of researching into the role played by death- related thoughts we decided to designed two laboratory studies to look into these issues.

The first study aimed to determine whether the increasing prejudice found in our study can be explained by the death-related thoughts alone without involving any reference to one's own death or group threat. The second study was oriented towards establishing whether the conservative changes induced by mortality awareness are part of a more general change in the way social dilemmas are approached.

Study 1

Sample and Procedure

A hundred and fifteen undergraduate students enrolled in an introductory course of social psychology participated in this study. As happens in this kind of sample most of them were women (100). They were informed that the study was designed to collect data about a number of topics studied by social psychology in order to use the data in the practical sessions of the course. The experiment was carried out in three phases.

The first phase manipulated the salience of death- related thoughts. Students were randomly assigned to two groups: mortality versus control group. The mortality salience was manipulated through an aesthetic task. Two pictures were printed in a booklet. In the mortality condition the two pictures were taken from the tenebrist pictorical movement (see annex). This was a counter-reform picture school developed in the 17th century with numerous references to themes related to death and strong contrasts between light and shadow. Participants assigned to the control condition were exposed to two bright abstract pictures from the 20th century (see annex). Participants were asked to concentrate on the pictures and list in a free format all the thoughts that came into their minds while observing the pictures. This thought- listing variable was introduced to check the effectiveness of the experimental manipulation and analyse the role played by death- related thoughts.

In the second phase participants communicated the extent to which they felt joy, fear, anxiety, anguish, and anger (1 = not at all and 5 = a lot). Moreover, they completed several tasks that evaluated visual accuracy and mathematical thinking. These were introduced as filler tasks.

Anti-Arab prejudice was measured in the third phase. Firstly, participants responded to the paper-and-pencil version of the IAT (Implicit Association Task) created by Lowery,

Hardin and Sinclair (2001). In the centre of the page 36 word-pairs are presented in each condition. Each pair shows a name in capital letters and just below a word. The task is presented as a categorization task. Subjects have to decide if each name is a Spanish or an Arab name and if the word printed below has positive or negative connotations. Categorization conditions are printed on the top of each page. For instance on the right appear the heading "ARAB- positive" and on the left "SPANISH- negative". Participants have to make a mark on the left of a "NAME- word" each time an "Arab-name/ positive-word" is found. Each time a "Basque- name/ negative-word" is found participants have to make a mark on the right. Pairs that do not correspond to any of the two categorization conditions should be left unmarked. Participants were instructed to work quickly for 20 seconds in each trial. Four trials (36 pairs and 20 seconds for each one) were completed. The first was a training task. Women's and men's names were paired with 36 words with positive (18) and negative (18) connotations. The instruction was to find Women's-name and positive words and men's-names and negative words pairs. The second was also a trial reversing the instruction: Man name- positive words and Women- name and negative word. The third and forth were critical trials. Here, Spanish and Arab names were paired with positive and negative words. The instruction of the third task was to find out "Arab-name/positive word" and "Spanish-name/negative word" pairs. The instruction was reversed in the fourth trial (Arab-name/negative word/ Spanish-name- positive word" pairs). Average trial response latencies were calculated by dividing the number of correct answers within each trial by 20 (seconds). The final IAT score was assessed by the difference in the average number of correct responses on the critical prejudice-congruent (Arab-negative/ Spanish-positive) trial versus average number of correct responses on the critical prejudice incongruent (Arab-positive/ Spanish-negative) trial.

The IAT was followed by two explicit measures of Anti-Arab prejudice. The first was an adaptation of McConahay's (1986) Modern Racism scale (the alpha reliability coefficient in our study was = 0.79) and the second was the Echebarria and Fernandez (in press) Anti-Arab prejudice scale (alpha = 0.91).

Results

The effect of the mortality manipulation was checked. Participants assigned to the death-thoughts inducing condition reported more death-related thoughts ($X = 1.46$, $SD = .97$) than participants placed in the control condition ($X = 0.13$, $SD = 0.34$) ($F (1,113) = 90.69$, $p \leq .001$). The correlation between the experimental manipulation and the number of death-related thoughts was very strong ($r = .67$).

Also preliminarily to the main analysis, correlations between the explicit and implicit measures of prejudice were computed. The correlation between the two explicit measures was high ($r = 0.99$, $p \leq .001$). By contrast, the correlations between the Modern racism ($r = 0.11$, p = .223) and the Anti-Arab ($r = 0.16$, $p = .10$) scales and the IAT were not significant. This goes in the well-established direction of independence between explicit and implicit prejudices.

Differences were analysed between implicit and explicit anti-Arab prejudice of participants assigned to the mortality versus control conditions. There were no differences in the Modern Racism (F (1,113) = 0.43, p = .523) and the Anti- Arab (F (1,113) = 0.15, p = .696) scales. In contrast, the mortality manipulation had a significant effect on the implicit measure of prejudice (IAT) (F (1,113) = 40.61, $p \leq$ .001). IAT scores were higher in the mortality (X = 0.11, SD = .14) than the control (F (1, 113) = -0.05, SD = .12) condition. We must remember than higher scores means more efficient performance on the prejudice-congruent than on the prejudice-incongruent trials.

The feelings aroused by the mortality manipulation were also analysed. Emotions were not affected by the experimental manipulation. Thus, it seems that it was death thoughts induced by the manipulation, and not feelings of fear, that were responsible for the increasing implicit anti-Arab prejudice.

In our previous study (Echebarria & Fernandez, 2006) we found that the terrorist attacks provoked a generalized prejudice extended to groups no directly involved in the attacks. We tried to analyse whether our manipulation also affected gender bias. Taking the training trials, an IAT score was computed based on prejudices against men. The reason for this choice was that 100 out of the 115 participants were women. The IAT resulted from subtracting the number of correct answers in the incongruent condition (women-name- negative word/ men-name –positive word) from the number of correct answers in the congruent condition (women-name/positive word/ men-name/negative word) and dividing the total by 20. The manipulation had also a significant effect in this index (F (1, 108) = 4.26, p = .04). Women in the mortality condition had higher scores than those assigned to the control condition (X = .05, SD = .008 versus X = .01, SD = .008). In other words, although lower than in the Arab case, the mortality condition also led an increment of group bias amongst our female participants.

Discussion

The attacks against the railway in Madrid provoked a generalized increment of explicit prejudices against Arabs and Jews. But we could not explore the psycho- social factors underlying these changes. At least three factors could be responsible for them: death-related thoughts induced by the exposition to the images broadcast by the mass media, feelings of fear, or a perception of threat against the ingroup. Our laboratory study provides some tentative answers to this question. Here, we used a completely new method to induce death-related thoughts without involving any direct threat either against personal or social identities. The dominant method to induce mortality salience involves thinking of one's own death. Thus, the effects of death-related thoughts and threats against personal identity are confounded. In other words, the traditional findings of studies based on the TMT could be explained as the results of responses against personal or group threats, without recurring to death-related thoughts or consciousness of mortality. In this line, Hart, Shaver and Goldenberg (2005) show that the same effects caused by the dominant manipulation of TMT (thinking of one's own immediate death) could be induced by other threats against personal identity (thinking about divorce or separation from a romantic partner), without making any reference to death. In our study about the effect of terrorist attacks and in the classical manipulation of the TMT there are explicit threats against individual or social identities. One effect of these threats is the increment of explicit prejudice and group bias. In this study we avoided any explicit personal threats and tried to induce only death-related thoughts. The result was that the manipulation increased implicit but not explicit anti- Arab prejudice. Moreover, these attitude changes were also extended to attitudes towards gender groups.

These results point out the complexity of the socio-psychological processes that underlie at least the changes found in the manipulations of TMT. We speculate that there are two independent processes working in this setting: one is related to the induction of death-related thoughts, and the other is related to threats against some component of the global self (either the personal and/ or the social identity). In the extent to which these two processes are independent, each one could have different effects on group bias and prejudice. Personal or group threats can explain overt and explicit changes while death- related thoughts could explain implicit changes. More research is necessary to disentangle the diversity of processes involved.

Mortality Salience and Decision-taking

As mentioned above, the second aim of this paper was to enquire into the socio-psychological processes responsible for the effects of mortality salience on general ideological positions, namely the tendency to endorse more conservative values and positions after exposure to factors that enhance the salience of mortality. We hypothesised that the ideological changes observed in our previous study (Echebarria & Fernández, 2006) might be a specific example of a more general tendency to adopt preventive and conservative decisions in all kinds of social dilemmas including issues not directly related to politics. We combined the TMT theory and the studies of Kahneman and Tversky (1979; Tversky & Kahneman, 1981) on the use of heuristic rules in decision-taking contexts.

We must remember that these authors formalised decision strategies known long ago as common sense or folk psychology. There are longstanding proverbs in Spanish and English folk knowledge that make recommendations about how to behave in decision-making situations. The first one ("de perdidos al río" or "when there is nothing to lose, throw caution to the wind") explains how to take decisions in loss-framed contexts. It recommends that when all is lost it is time to take risky and uncertain decisions. In loss situations the risky and uncertain decisions may help to reduce and/ or avoid losses. Kahneman and Tversky (1979) formalised this rule. They stated that social dilemmas framed in term of losses push us to assume risky and uncertain decisions (here presented in probabilistic terms). Coming back to common-sense knowledge, the second proverb says that it is better to secure what has been won than to risk it by trying to win more ("más vale pájaro en mano que cientos volando" or "a bird in the hand is worth two in the bush"). This means that when a social dilemma is framed is terms of gains or benefits, people adopt a conservative decision strategy, holding what has been won and not risking losing it all by trying to win more. According to the authors, although people like to win, they fear losing more. There is an asymmetry between the impact that wins and losses have, the impact of losses is stronger than that of wins. The biggest intuition of these authors was to prove that the use of these heuristic rules was not exclusive to ordinary people but was present in the professional decisions taken by economists (Fennema & Wakker, 1997), physicians (Levin & Chapman, 1990, 1993), or public health designers (Quattrone & Tversky, 1988).

How can mortality salience affect decisions in dilemma situations? We think that mortality salience and death-related thoughts put people in a pessimistic, negative, or loss-framed state of mind. Social dilemmas in general are regarded in terms of risk of losing. This means that if a social dilemma is framed in term of losses, both subjects exposed to a mortality salience manipulation and control subjects will adopt the same strategy (risky or uncertain alternatives). In contrast, if a social dilemma is framed in terms of gains, both groups will choose different alternatives. Control subjects would be sensitive to the change in the way the social dilemma is framed (win) and shift their strategies, opting for certainty and security. In contrast, people submitted to the salience mortality manipulation, to the extent that it induces a negative or loss- focused state of mind, should be relatively insensitive to the shift in the way the dilemma is framed and should continue to adopt strategies typical of loss-framed social dilemmas.

Study 2

Procedure

A 2 (salient mortality versus control) by 2 (losses versus wins framed dilemmas) experimental study was designed to test the above-mentioned hypothesis. The dependent variable was the preference for either (a) a health programme that specifies the exact number (certain alternative) of people that will survive or die (depending on how the dilemma is framed), r (b) a health programme that presents the expected efficiency in probabilistic terms (probabilistic or uncertain alternative).

Sixty-seven university undergraduate students participated in this study.

The study was carried out in three apparently unrelated phases.

The first was presented as a study about personality evaluation. Here, the mortality salience manipulation was introduced. The classical mortality salience manipulation was used in this study. Participants in the mortality salience conditions were asked to think about their own death and (a) write down all they would think and feel in the process of dying and (a) what would happen to their body after death. Subjects assigned to the control condition were asked to imagine they had a ad toothache and explain what their thoughts and feelings would be.

All the participants filled the Positive and Negative Affect Schedule (PANAS) (Watson, Clark, & Tellegen, 1988). This served as a filler task typically introduced after the mortality salience manipulation and before measuring its effects on the dependent variables.

The Social dilemmas were introduced in the third phase. This was an adaptation of the Tversky and Kahneman (1981) study f the Asian bird flu (aviar fever). This phase was presented as a study on strategies used in decision-making situations. Participants were asked to imagine that "a mortal variant of the Asian bird flu (aviar fever) that affects humans will reach our country. Epidemiologists calculate that 600 people will be infected. The public health minister has summoned the most prestigious specialists in this type of disease. Two alternative programs have been proposed". In the *loss-framed condition,* participants were informed that if the first program (program a) is implemented 400 of the infected patients will die (certainty option); while if the second program (program b) is implemented the 66.6 % of infected patients will die (probabilistic or uncertain option). In the *benefit-framed condition*, participants were informed that if the first program (program a) is implemented 200 infected-patients will survive (certainty option) whereas if the second program (program b) is implemented 33.3 % of infected persons will survive (probabilistic option). Participants were asked to choose between option "a" or "b". This was the dependent variable measured at a categorial level. It is important to note that in both the experimental conditions the effect of implementing the programs was the same: 400 patients will die and 200 patients will survive.

Results

Given the nature of our dependent variable the correlation between the two options is perfect ($r = -1.00$). Thus, we decided to transform this variable into a dummy variable with option-b (probabilistic or uncertain) as "1" and option-a (secure or certain) as "0". The reason for taking that decision was that option-b reflects decisions taken under a "loss-framed" or negative state of mind. It must be remembered that we speculated that the mortality salience was expected to create a similar state of mind.

An ANOVA was performed with the dummy-variable as the dependent variable and mortality salience (one's own death versus toothache) and the framing (loss versus benefit) manipulations as independent variables. The framing main effect (F (1,63) = 18.51, $p \le .001$) and the framing by mortality salience interaction effect (F (1,63) = 3.70, p = .05) were significant (mortality main effect, F (1,63) = 0.33, $p = .571$). Means and standard deviation are printed in table 1.

It is important to remember that the means represent the percentage of participants in each condition that chose the probabilistic or uncertain option (1- means represents the percentage of participants that chose the other option).

The framing main effect reproduced the heuristic decision rules predicted by Kahneman and Tversky (1979). When the dilemma is framed in terms of loss, the large majority of participants decided to adopt the uncertain, probabilistic, or risky option ($M = 0.75, SD = .43$) whereas when the dilemma is framed in terms of gains or benefit, the majority chose the secure or certain option ($M = 0.71, SD = .46$).

Post-hoc contrasts were carried out in order to analyse in depth the effects of the mortality by the framing interaction. Firstly, a comparison between participants assigned to the mortality salience condition indicates that they were not affected by the framing manipulation (F (1,34) = 2.56, $p = .12$). They seemed to have been quite insensitive to the framing manipulation. Even in the win or benefit framing condition almost half of them chose the uncertain or probabilistic option. In contrast, control participants (toothache) were deeply influenced by the framing manipulation (F (1,29) = 24.11, $p \le .001$). The majority of control-subjects assigned to the benefit condition chose the secure or certain option ($1 - 0.17 = 0.83$) while the large majority of those assigned to the loss condition opted for the probabilistic or uncertain option.

Table 1. ANOVA. Means and standard deviations

Variables	M	SD
Mortality Condition		
Loss-Framing	0.70	.47
Benefit-Framing	0.44	.51
Toothache Condition		
Loss-Framing	0.85	.37
Benefit-Framing	0.17	.38

Discussion

This second study was designed to address the question of whether the conservative value and political changes observed as a consequence of making mortality salient was a particular example of a more general change in the way that social dilemmas are approached. Taking the Kahneman and Tversky (1979; Tversky & Kahneman, 1981) heuristic rules as indices of a more general way to approach social problems we found that mortality salience predisposed subjects to the adoption of alternatives that reflect a negative or pessimistic approach to social problems (loss- framed situations). Participants submitted to a salient mortality manipulation were insensitive to the way the health dilemma was framed. They chose in a higher percentage strategies usually used in loss- conditions. This was not the case for control-participants, who shifted their preferences depending on how the problems were framed.

Conclussion

We have presented two follow-up studies designed to respond to some questions that remained open after our previous study about the effects of the terrorist attacks against the railways in Madrid. One of the more influential current theories used to understand the effect of terrorism is the Terror Management Theory (TMT) (Greenberg, Pyszczynski, & Solomon, 1986; Landau, Johns, Greenberg, Pyszczynski, Martens, Goldenberg, & Solomon, 2004). In short, it has been proposed that terrorism raises feelings of existential anxiety because it reminds people of the limited nature of their own existence. However, there are some unanswered questions due in part to the way in which mortality salience is manipulated. We think that there are several socio-psychological processes underlying the effects observed by the method used almost exclusively in the laboratories: asking participants to imagine their own death. We think that at least three different processes are involved in this: real threat against our personal identity; the cognitive process of thinking about death-related issues; and the fear aroused by the manipulation. There is some experimental evidence that indicates that some of these processes may explain the typical results found by the TMT. Hart, Shaver, & Goldenberg (2005) found that threats against personal self-regard not involving death-related thoughts (romantic break-ups) produce similar effects. Hewstone, Rubin, and Willis (2002) stated that the effects of TMT could be due to threats against personal and social identities. It is important to clarify the role played by these factors, because each one may affect different variables.

Our first study analysed the effects on prejudice of inducing death-related thoughts without involving a direct personal threat (observing pictures displaying death-related topics). We found that these death-related thoughts increased prejudice against Arabs and enhanced gender group bias but only at an implicit level. These changes were not reflected at an overt or explicit level. This induces us to speculate that some kind of personal or group threat should be added to death-related thoughts to translate inner changes into an overt rejection of outgroups.

The second study showed that the conservative value and political changes induced by the salience of mortality ay be a particular example of a more general change in the way people address social dilemmas. Mortality salience seems to induce a negative or pessimistic state of mind. We found that subjects under a mortality salience manipulation adopted decision-making rules that reflect an approach to social dilemmas framed in term of losses.

We think that TMT will continue to represent one of the more fruitful theoretical approaches to the understanding of the effects of terrorism in the population. Nevertheless some data indicates that the underlying processes may be more numerous that previously supposed. This is why we think that more experimental and correlational studies are needed to disentangle the complexity of processes involved in this experience.

Annex

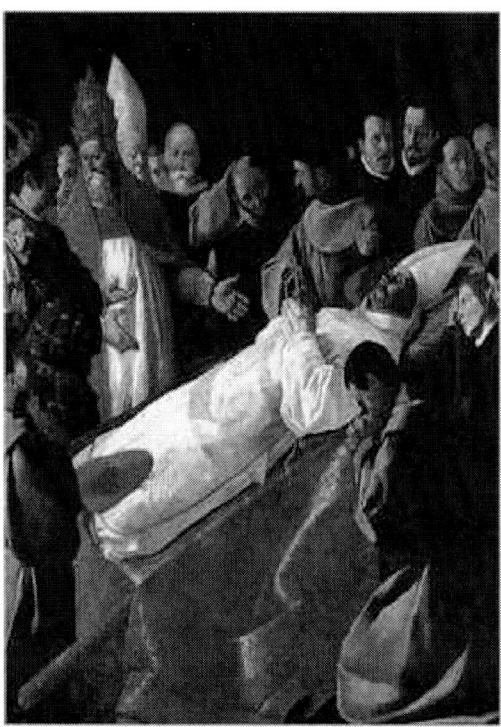

Mortality condition.

Control condition.

References

Arndt, J., Greenberg , J., Schimel J., Pyzczynski, T., & Solomon, S. (2002). To belong or not to belong that is the question: Terror management and identification with ender and ethnicity. *Journal of Personality and Social psychology 3*, 26-43.

Becker, E. (1973). *The denial of death*. New York: Academic Press.

Cozzolino P. J., Staples, A. D., Meyers L. S., & Samboceti, J. (2004). Greed, death, and values: From error management to transcendence management theory. *Personality and Social Psychology Bulletin, 30*, 278-292.

Dechesne, M., Janssen, J., & van Knipenberg, A. (2000). Derogation and distancing as terror management strategies: The moderating role of need for closure and permeability of group boundaries. *Journal of Personality and Social Psychology, 79*, 923-932.

Echebarria, A. & Fernandez, E. (2006). Effects of terrorism on attitudes and ideological orientation. *European Journal of Social psychology, 36*, 259- 265.

Echebarria, A. & Fernández, E. (in press). A new scale of Anti-Arab prejudice: Reliability and validity evidence. *Journal of Applied Social Psychology.*

Fennema, H. & Wakker, D. (1997). Original and cumulative prospect theory: A discussion of empirical differences. *Journal of behavioural Decision Making, 10*, 53-64.

Friedman, R. & Arndt, J. (2005). Reexploring the connection between terror management theory and dissonance theory. *Personality and Social Psychology Bulletin, 31*, 1217-1225.

Greenberg, J., Pyzczynski, T., & Solomon, S. (1986). The causes and consequences of a need for self-esteem: A terror management theory. In R. F. Baumeister (Ed.), *Public self and private self* (pp. 189-212). New York: Springer-Verlag.

Hart, J., Shaver, P. R., & Goldenberg, J. L. (2005). Attachment, self-esteem, worldviews, and terror management: Evidence for a tripartite security system. *Journal of Personality and Social Psychology, 88*, 999-1013.

Hewstone, M., Rubin, M., & Willis, H. (2002). Intergroup bias. *Annual Review of Psychology, 53*, 575-604.

Jonas, E., Greenberg, J., & Frey, D. (2003). Connecting terror management and dissonance theory: Evidence that mortality salience increases the preference for supporting information after decisions. *Personality and Social Psychology Bulletin, 29*, 1181-1189.

Jonas, E., Schimel, J., Greenberg, J., & Pyzczynski, T. (2002). The scrooge effect: Evidence that mortality salience increases prosocial attitudes and behavior. *Personality and Social Psychology Bulletin, 8*, 42-1335.

Kahneman, D. & Tversky, A. (1979). Prospect theory: An analysis of decisions under risk. *Economatrica, 47*, 313-327.

Koole S. L. & Van en Berg, A. (2005). Lost in wilderness: Terror management , action orientation and nature evaluation. *Journal of Personality and Social Psychology, 8*, 1014-1028.

Landau, M. J., Solomon, S., Greenberg, J., Cohen, F., Pyzczynski, T., Arndt, J., Miller, C. H., Ogilvie, D., & Cook, A. (2004). Deliver Us from evil: The effects of mortality salience and reminders of 9/11 on support for president George W. Bush. *Personality and Social Psychology Bulletin, 30*, 1136-1150.

Landau, M. J., Johns, M., Greenberg, J., Pyzczynski, T., Martens, A., Goldenberg, J. L., & Solomon, S. (2004). A function of form: Terror management and structuring the social world. *Journal of Personality and Social Psychology, 87*, 190-210.

Levin, J.P. & Chapman, P. P. (1990). Risk taking, frame of reference, and characterization of victims groups in AIDS treatment decisions. *Journal of experimental Social Psychology, 26*, 421-434.

Levin, J. P. & Chapman, P. P. (1993). Risky decision making and allocation of resources for leukemis and AIDS programs. *Health Psychology, 12*, 110-117.

Lowery, B. S., Hardin, C. D., & Sinclair, S. (2001). Social influence effect on automatic racial prejudice. *Journal of Personality and Social Psychology, 81*, 842-855.

McConahay, J. (1986). Modern racism, ambivalence, and the modern racism scale. In J. F. Dovidio & S. L. Gaertner (Eds.), *Prejudice, discrimination, and racism* (pp. 91-126). San Diego: Academic Press.

Martens, A., Greenberg, J., Schimel, J., & Landau, M. J. (2004). Ageism and death: Effects of mortality salience and perceived similarity to elders on reaction to elderly people. *Personality and Social Psychology Bulletin, 30*, 1524-1536.

Noreayan, A. & Hansen, I. G. (2006). Belief in supernatural agents in he face of death. *Personality and Social Psychology Bulletin 32*, 174187.

Pyzczynski, T., Abdollahi, A., Solomon, S., Greenberg, J., Cohen, F., & Weise, D. (2006). Mortality salience, martyrdom, and military might: The great Satan versus the axis of evil. *Personality and Social Psychology Bulletin, 32*, 525-537.

Qattrone, G. A. & Tversky, A. (1988). Contrasting rational and psychological analyses of political choice. *American Political Science Review, 82*, 719-736.

Schmeichel, B. J. & Martens, A. (2005). Self-affirmation and mortality salience: Affirming values reduces worldview defense and death-thought accessibility. *Personality and Social Psychology Bulletin, 31*, 658-667.

See, Y., M. & Petty, R. E. (2006). Effects of mortality salience on evaluation of ingroup and outgroup sources: The impact of pro- versus counterattitudinal positions. *Personality and Social Psychology Bulletin, 32*, 405-416.

Sherif, M. (1966). *Group conflict and cooperation.* London: Routledge and Kegan Paul Ltd.

Sherif, M., Harvey, O. J., White, B. J., Hood, W. R., & Sherif, C. W. (1961). *Intergroup conflict and cooperation. The Robber's cave experiment.* Norman, Okñahome: University Book Exchange.

Tajfel, H. (1978). *Differentiation between social groups.* London: Academic Press.

Tajfel, H. (1981). *Human groups & social categories.* Cambridge: Cambridge University Press.

Tversky, A. & Kahneman, D. (1981). The framing of decisions and the psychology of choice. *Science, 211*, 453-458.

Van Des Bos, K, Pootvliet, P. M., Maas, M., Miedema, J., & van den Ham, E. J. (2005). An enquiry concerning the principles of cultural norms nd values: The impact of uncertainty and mortality salience on reactions to violations and bolstering of cultural worldviews. *Journal of Experimental Social Psychology, 41*, 91-113.

Watson, D., Clark, L. A., & Tellegen, A. (1988). Development and validation of brief measures of positive and negative affect: The PANAS scale. *Journal of Personality and Social Psychology, 54*, 1063-1070.

Wisman, A. & Koole S. L. (2003). Hiding in the crowd: Can mortality salience promote affiliation with others who oppose one's woldviews? *Journal of Personality and Social Psychology, 84*, 11-526.

Wisman, A. & Goldenberg, J. L. (2005). From the rave o the cradle: Evidence hat mortality salience engenders a desire of offspring. *Journal of Personality and Social Psychology 9*, 46-61.

INDEX

C

E

F

J

K

L

N

S

T

U